SCHOOL-LIVE!

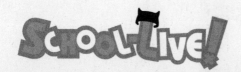

SCHOOL-LIVE! ❾

SADORU CHIBA
NORIMITSU KAIHOU
(Nitroplus)

Translation: Leighann Harvey

Lettering: Alexis Eckerman

GAKKOU GURASHI! Vol. 9
©Nitroplus / Norimitsu Kaihou, Sadoru Chiba, Houbunsha. All rights reserved. First published in Japan in 2017 by HOUBUNSHA CO., LTD., Tokyo. English translation rights in United States, Canada, and United Kingdom arranged with HOUBUNSHA CO., LTD through Tuttle-Mori Agency, Inc., Tokyo.

English translation © 2017 by Yen Press, LLC

Yen Press
1290 Avenue of the Americas
New York, NY 10104

Visit us at yenpress.com
facebook.com/yenpress
twitter.com/yenpress
yenpress.tumblr.com
instagram.com/yenpress

First Yen Press Edition: December 2017

Yen Press is an imprint of Yen Press, LLC.
The Yen Press name and logo are trademarks of Yen Press, LLC.

The publisher is not responsible for websites (or their content) that are not owned by the publisher.

Library of Congress Control Number: 2015952613

ISBNs: 978-0-316-41408-1 (paperback)
       978-0-316-44834-5 (ebook)

10 9 8 7 6 5 4 3 2 1

BVG

Printed in the United States of America

Chapter 49　Choice

THE

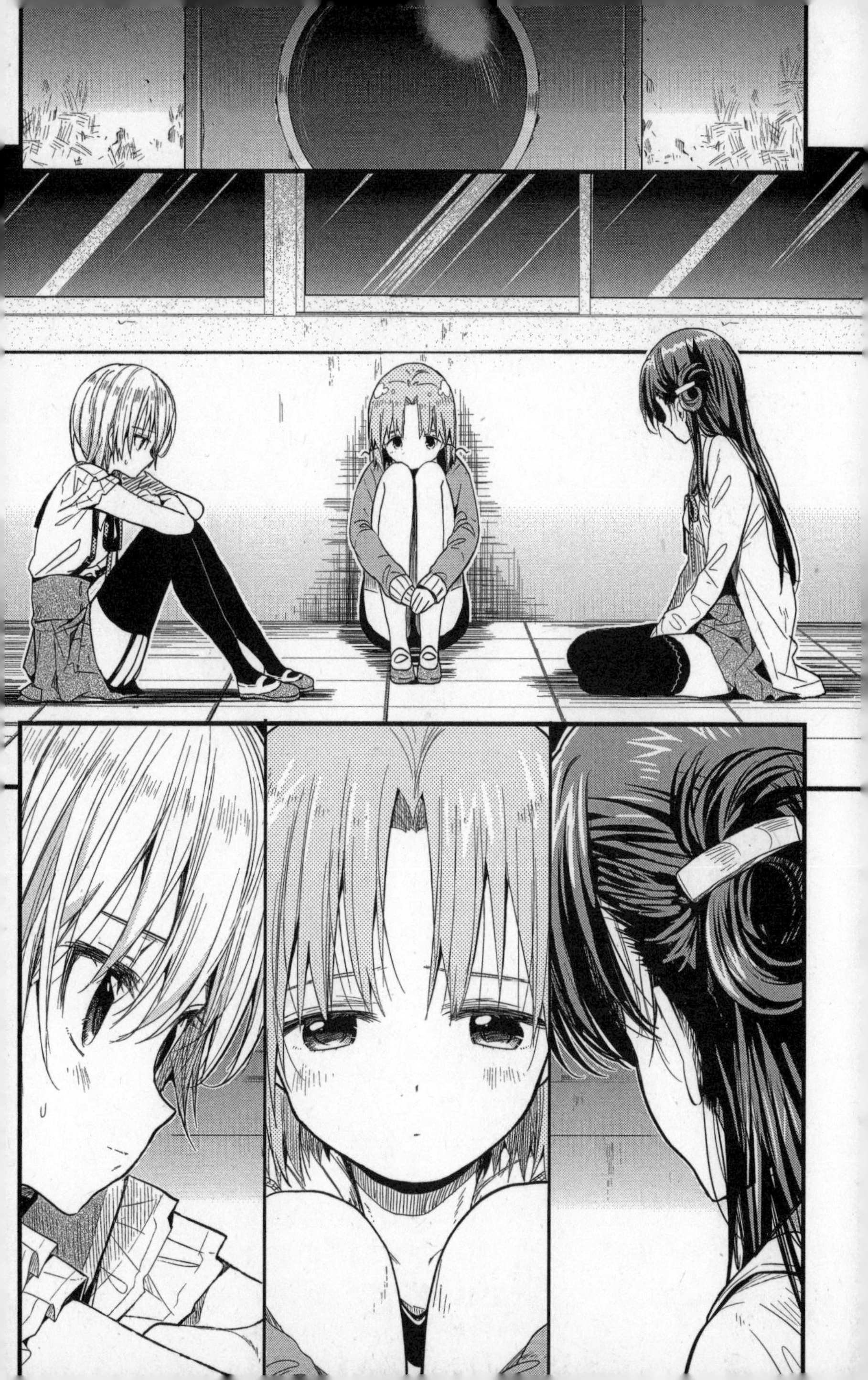

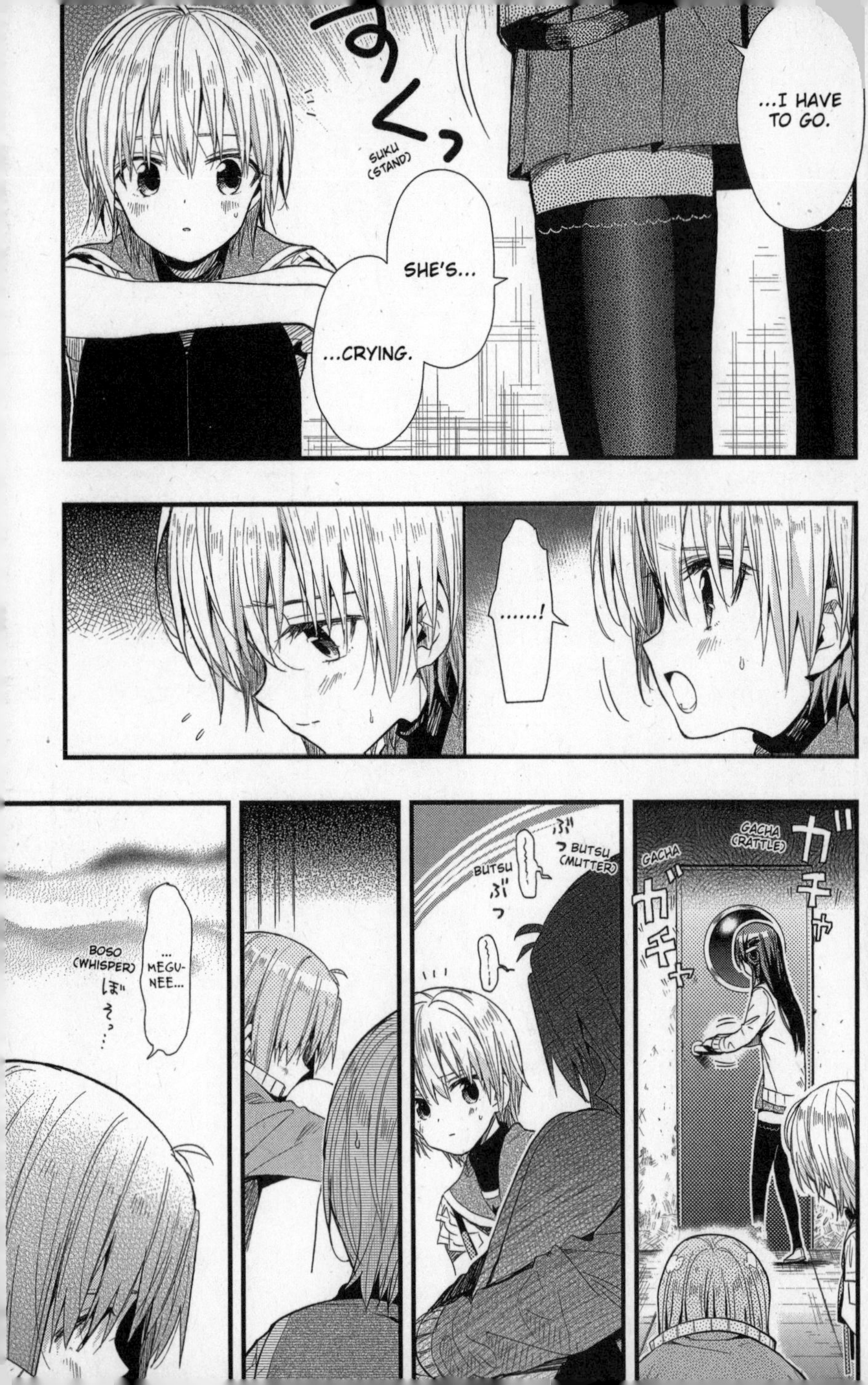
...I HAVE TO GO.
すくっ
SUKU (STAND)
SHE'S...
...CRYING.
......!
ガチャ
GACHA (RATTLE)
ガチャ
GACHA
ぶつ
BUTSU (MUTTER)
ぶつ
BUTSU
...MEGU-NEE...
BOSO (WHISPER)
ぼそっ...

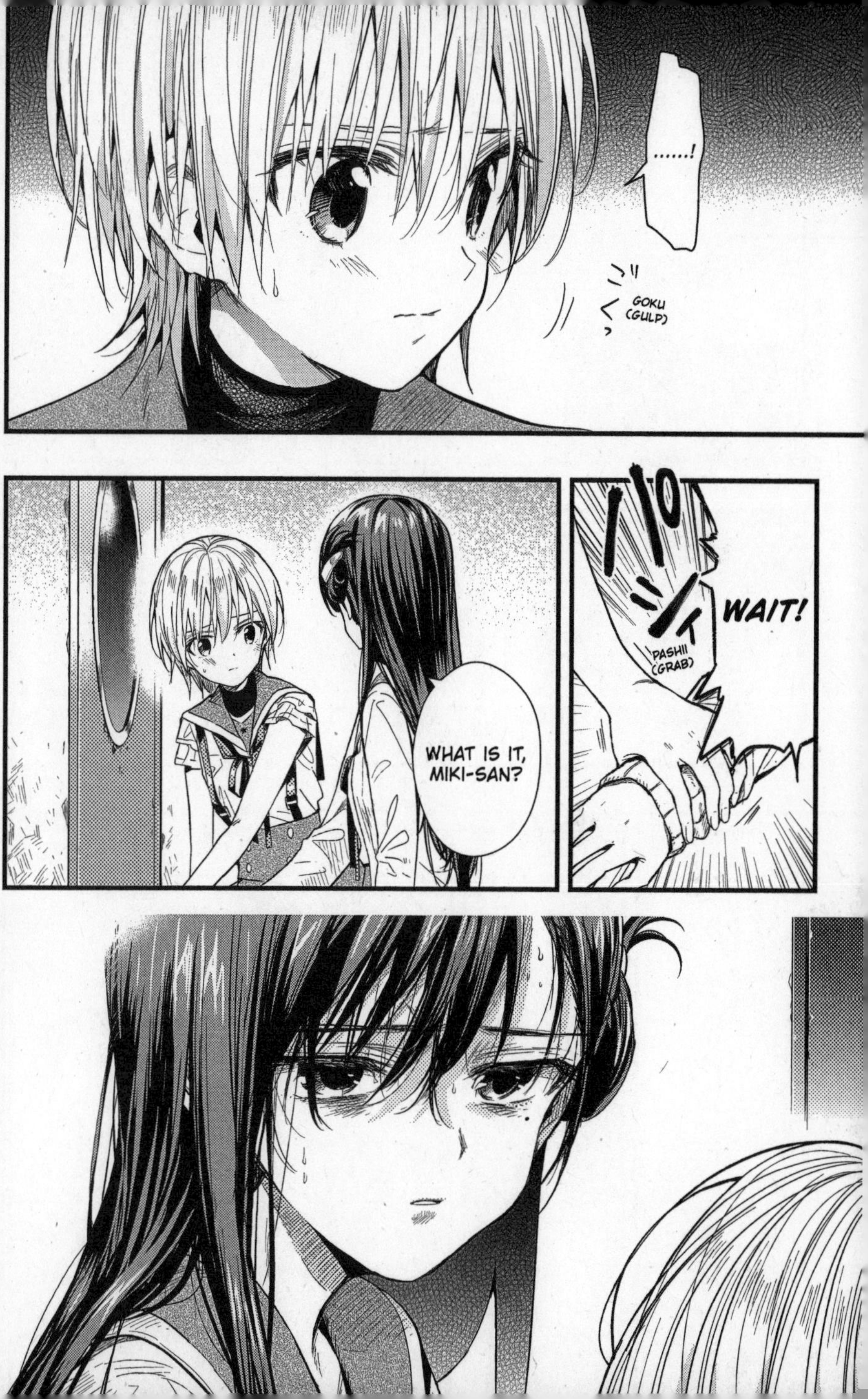
......!
GOKU (GULP)
WAIT!
PASHII (GRAB)
WHAT IS IT, MIKI-SAN?

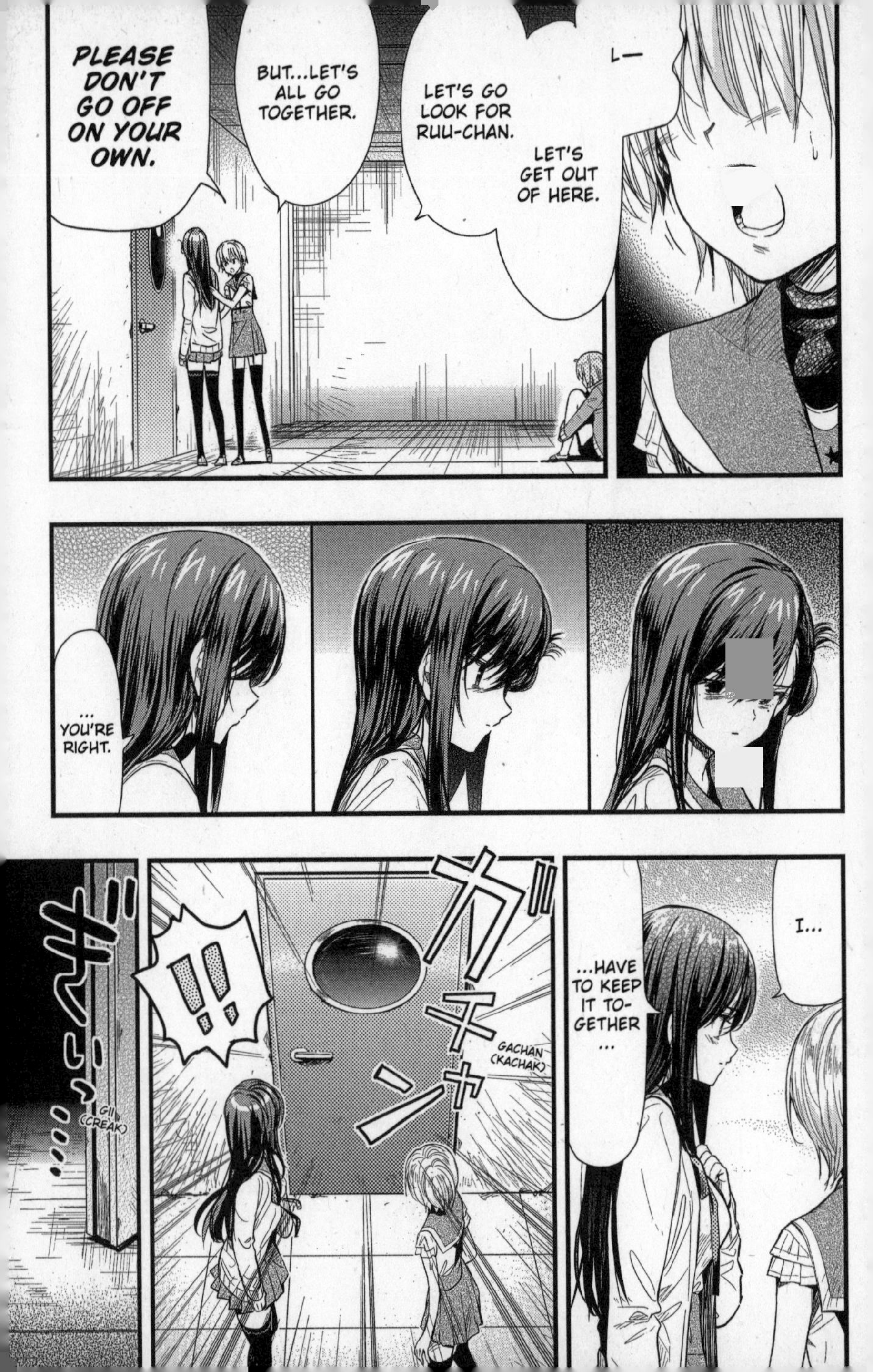
L—
LET'S GO LOOK FOR RUU-CHAN.
LET'S GET OUT OF HERE.
BUT...LET'S ALL GO TOGETHER.
PLEASE DON'T GO OFF ON YOUR OWN.
... YOU'RE RIGHT.
I...
...HAVE TO KEEP IT TO-GETHER ...
GACHAN (KACHAK)
!!
GII (CREAK)

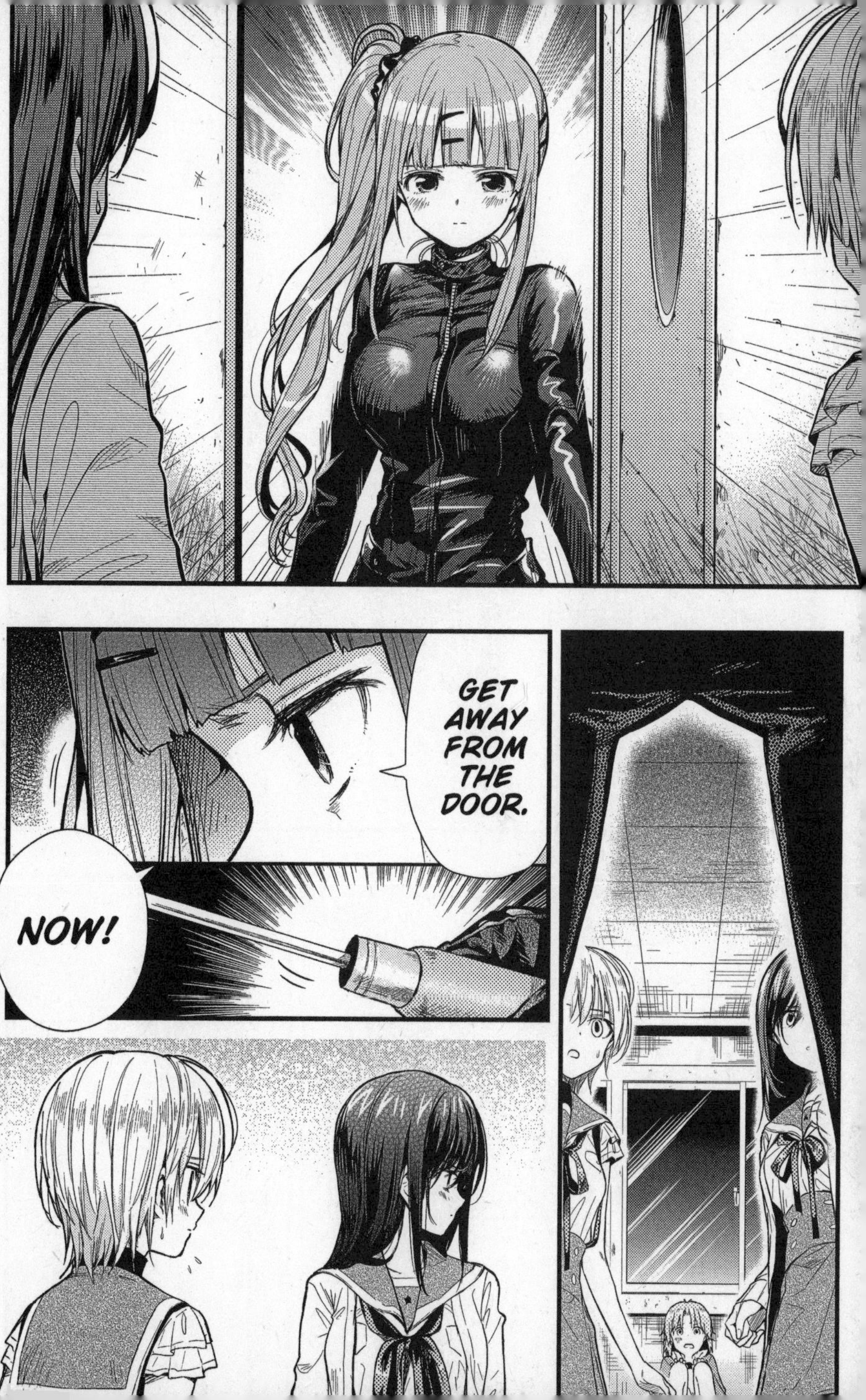
GET AWAY FROM THE DOOR.
NOW!

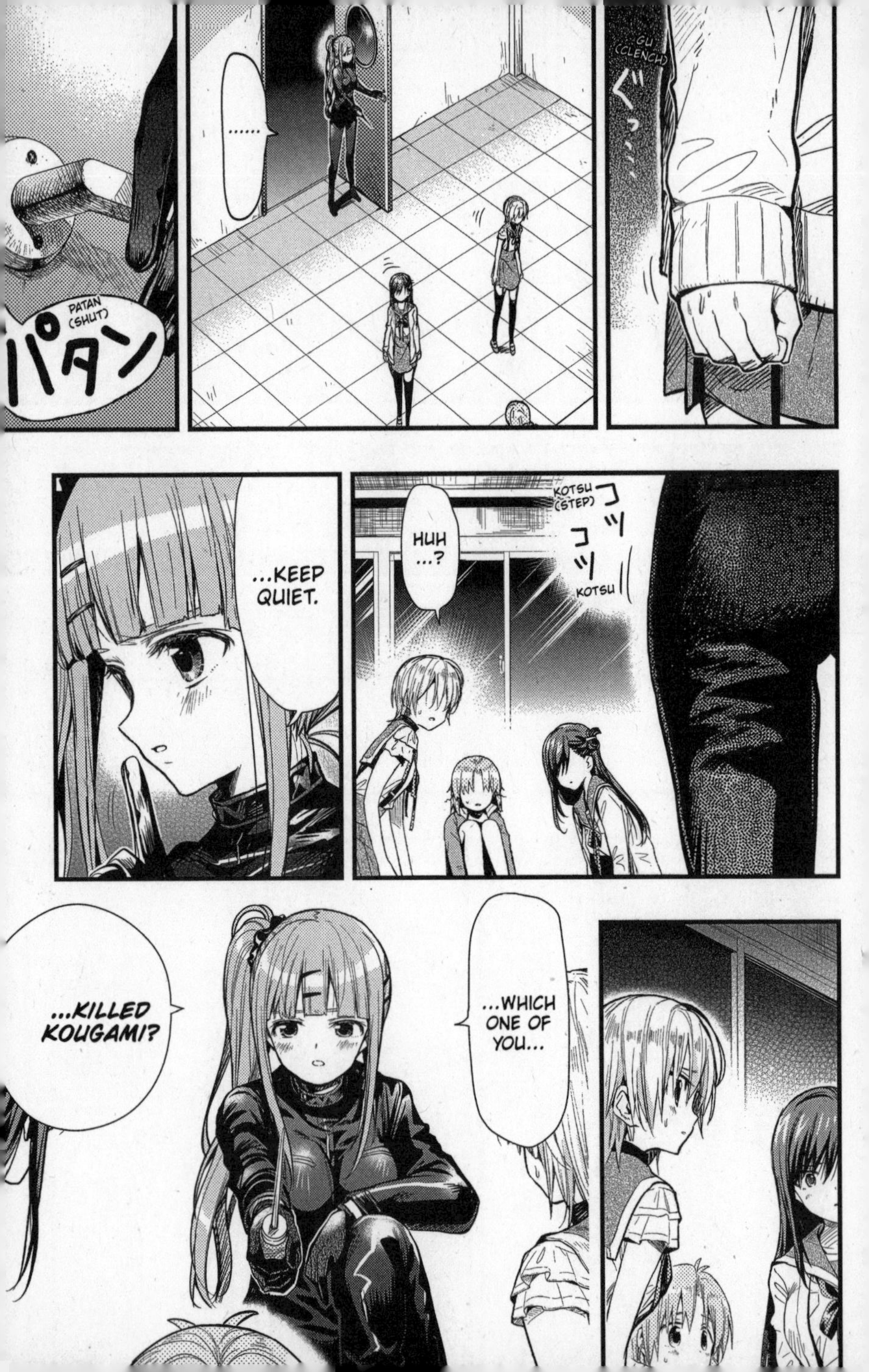
GU (CLENCH)
ぐっ……
……
PATAN (SHUT)
パタン
KOTSU (STEP)
コツ
コツ
KOTSU
HUH ...?
...KEEP QUIET.
...WHICH ONE OF YOU...
...KILLED KOUGAMI?

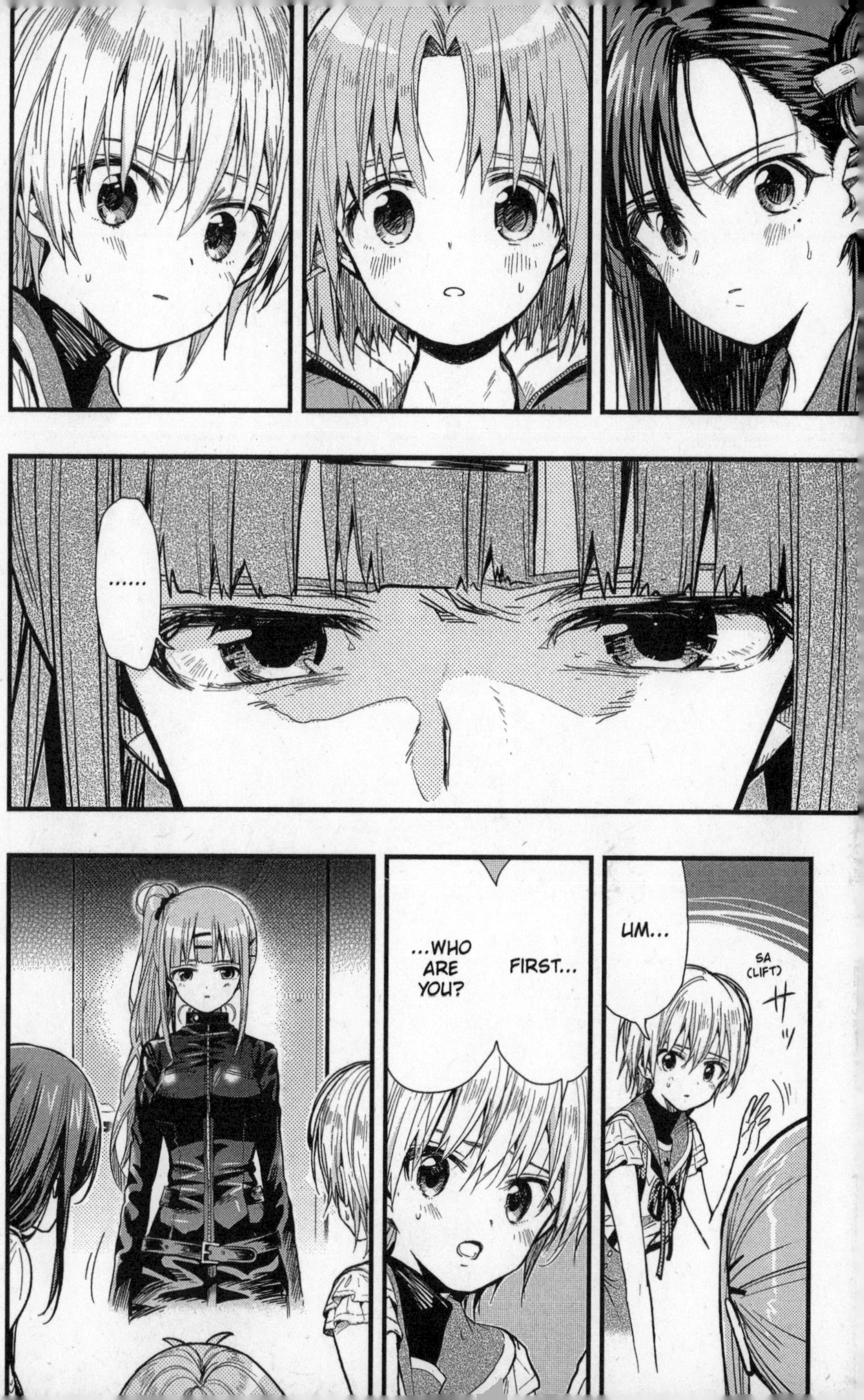
……
UM…
SA
(LIFT)
FIRST…
…WHO ARE YOU?

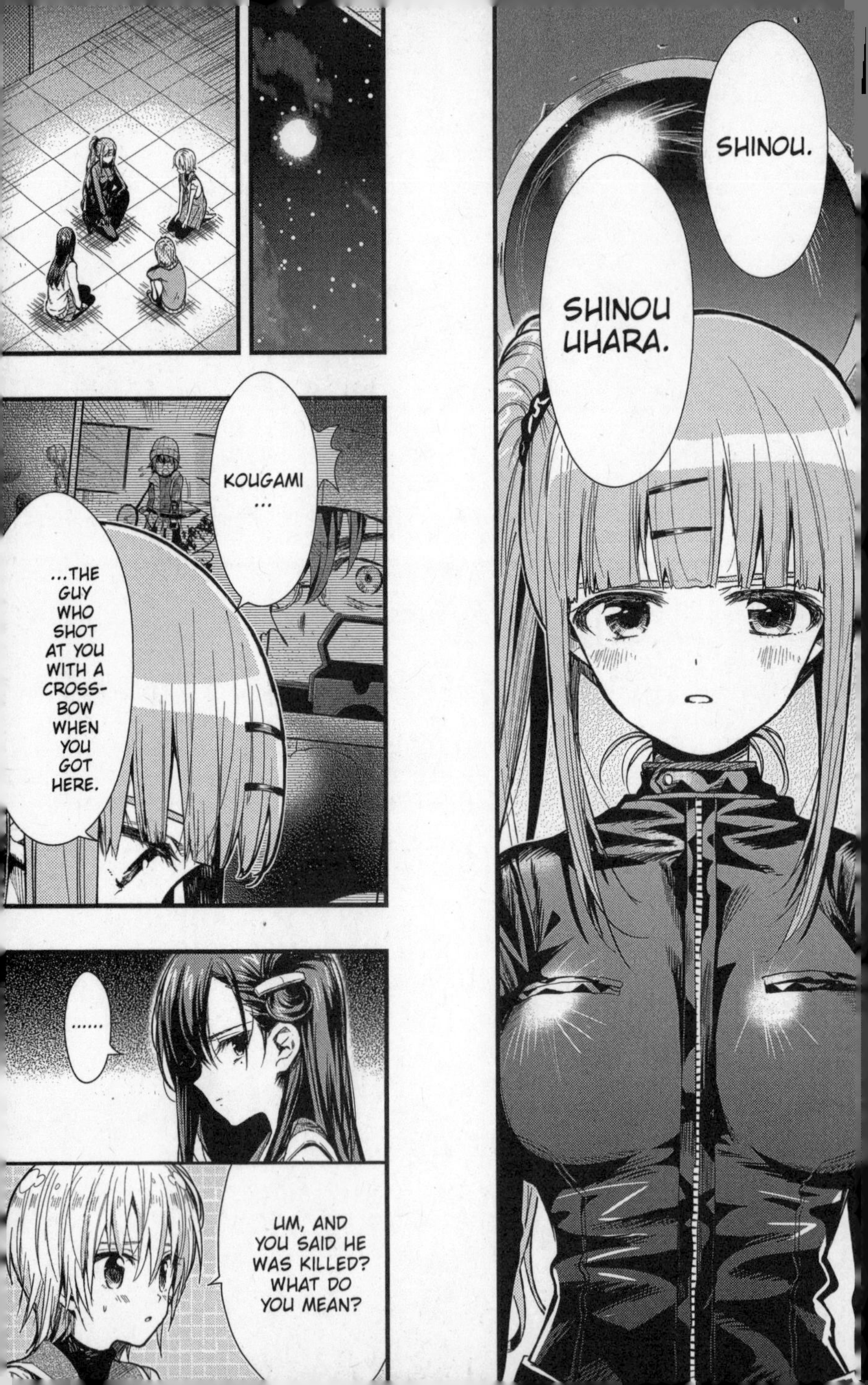
SHINOU.
SHINOU UHARA.
KOUGAMI ...
...THE GUY WHO SHOT AT YOU WITH A CROSS-BOW WHEN YOU GOT HERE.
......
UM, AND YOU SAID HE WAS KILLED? WHAT DO YOU MEAN?

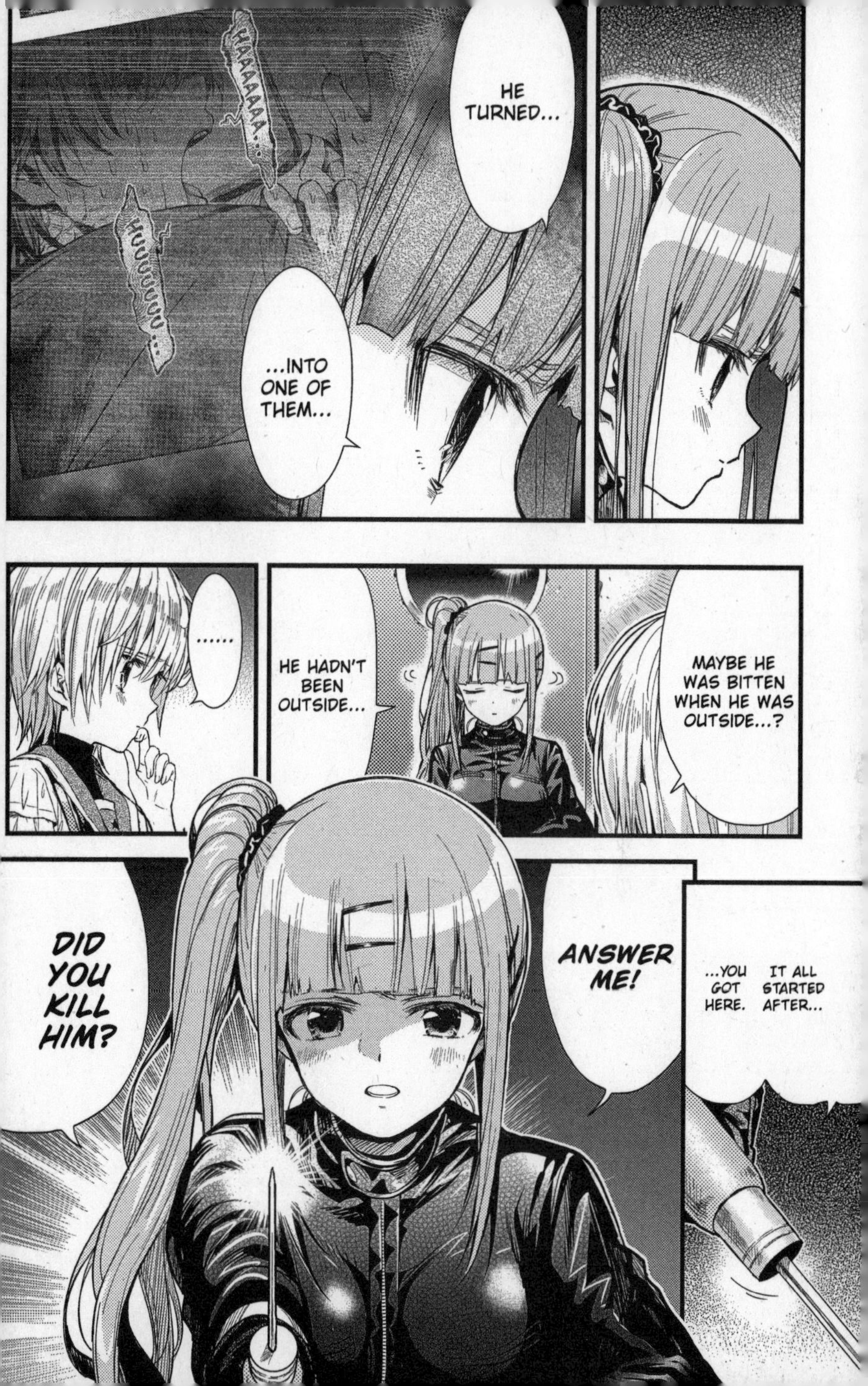
HE TURNED...
HAAAAAAA...
...INTO ONE OF THEM...
HUUUUUUUU...
MAYBE HE WAS BITTEN WHEN HE WAS OUTSIDE...?
HE HADN'T BEEN OUTSIDE...
......
IT ALL STARTED AFTER...
...YOU GOT HERE.
ANSWER ME!
DID YOU KILL HIM?

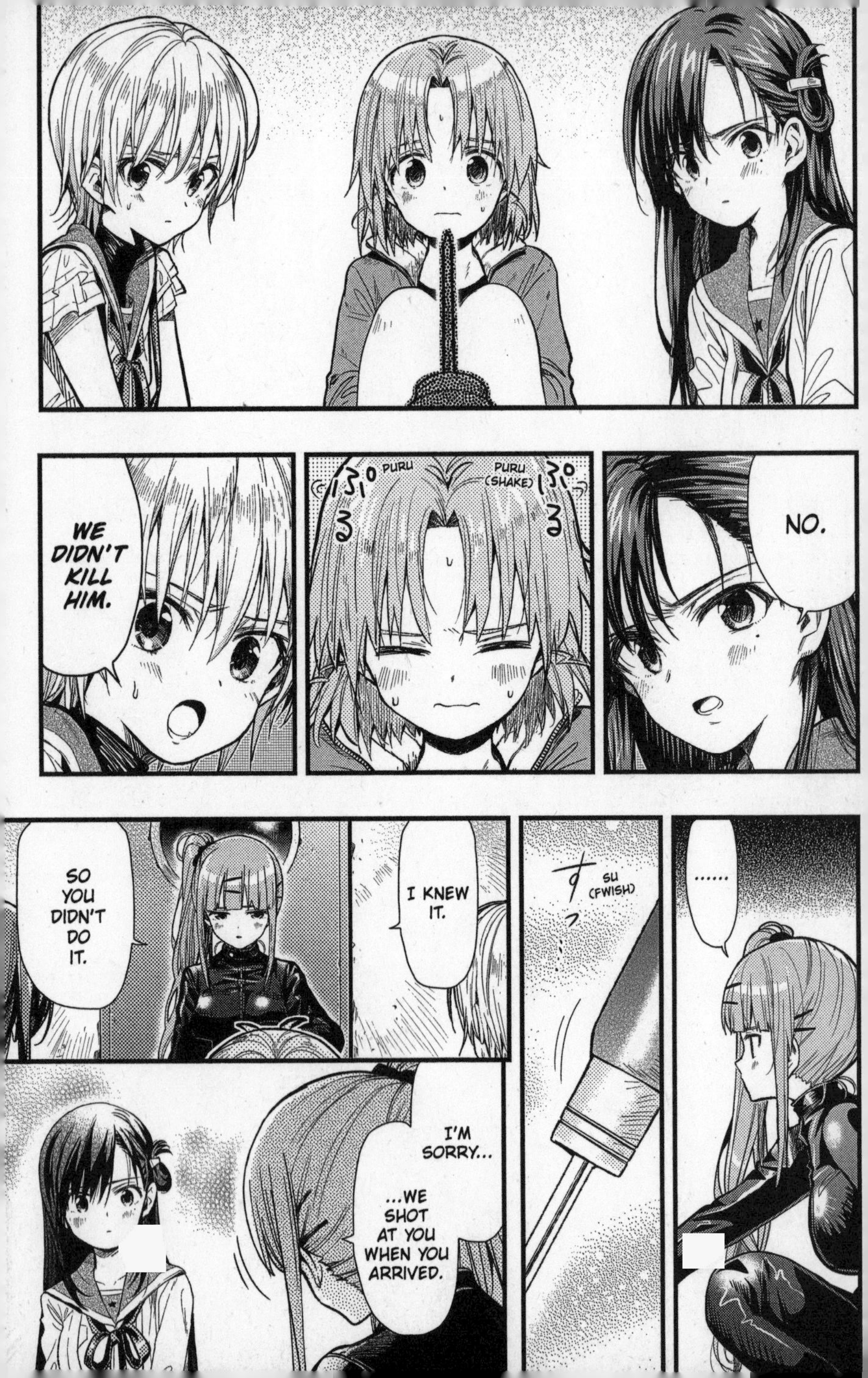
NO.
PURU
PURU (SHAKE)
WE DIDN'T KILL HIM.
......
SU (FWISH)
I KNEW IT.
SO YOU DIDN'T DO IT.
I'M SORRY...
...WE SHOT AT YOU WHEN YOU ARRIVED.

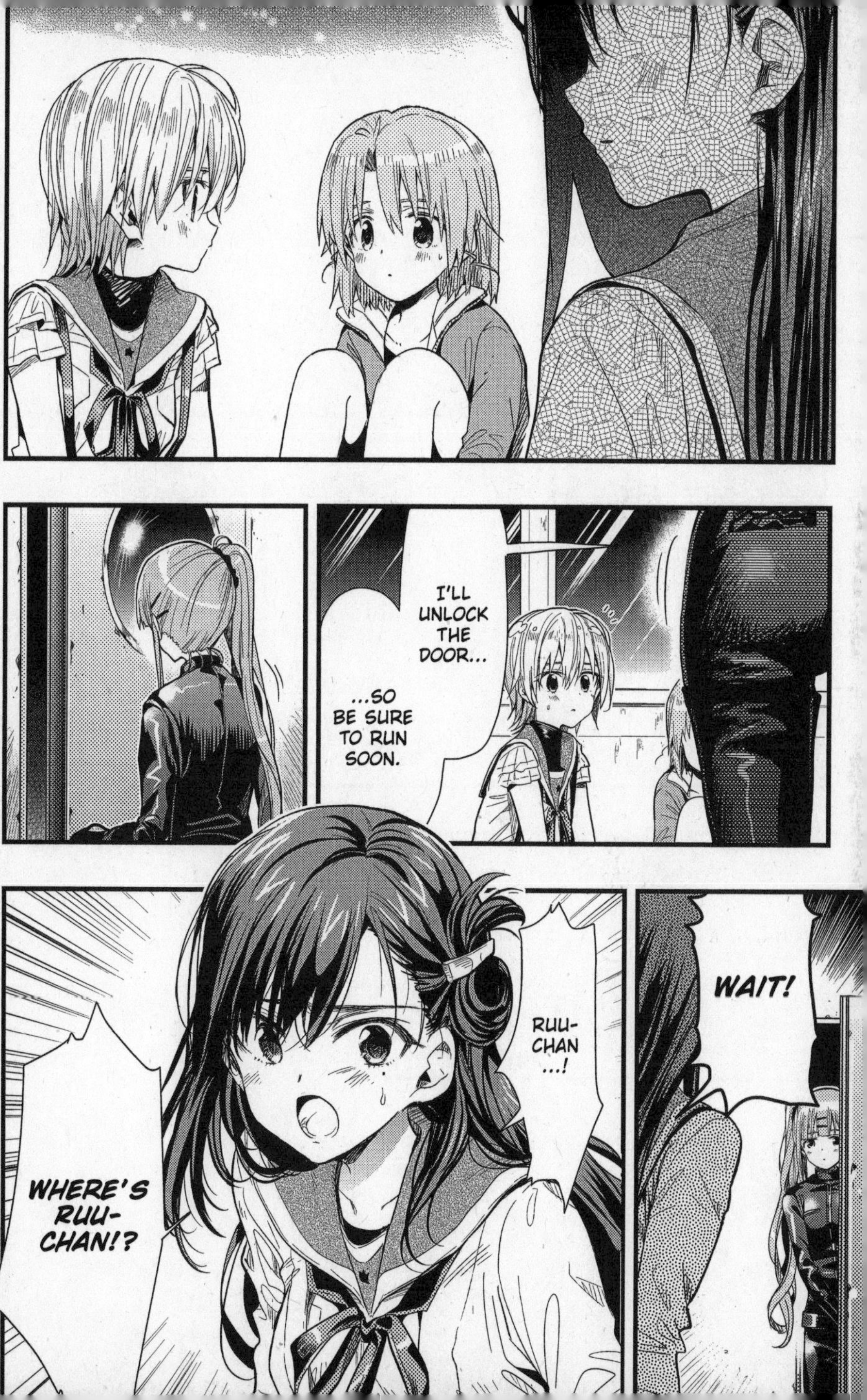
I'LL UNLOCK THE DOOR...
...SO BE SURE TO RUN SOON.
WAIT!
RUU-CHAN ...!
WHERE'S RUU-CHAN!?

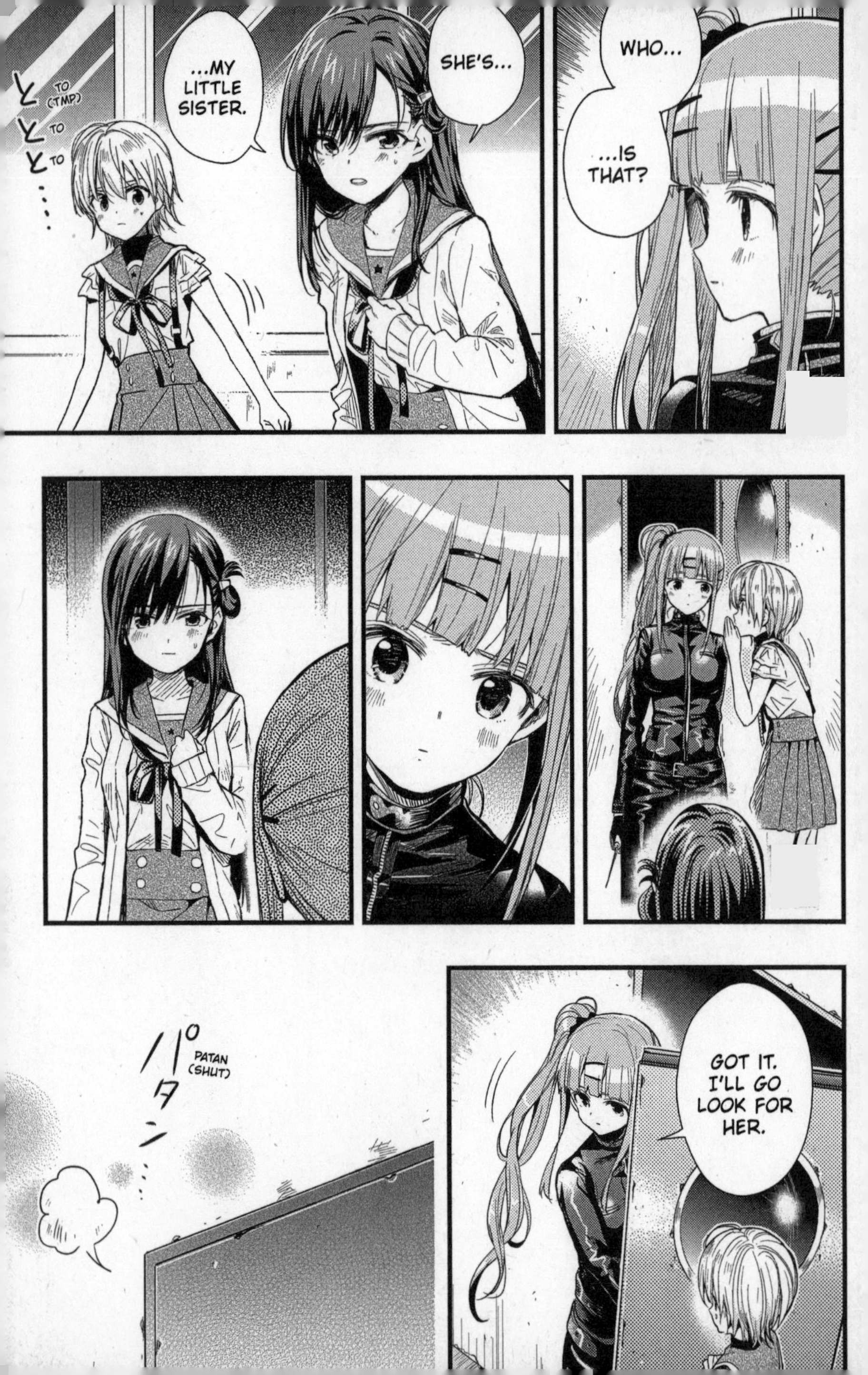
WHO...
...IS THAT?
SHE'S...
...MY LITTLE SISTER.
と TO (TMP)
と TO
と TO
GOT IT. I'LL GO LOOK FOR HER.
パタン
PATAN (SHUT)

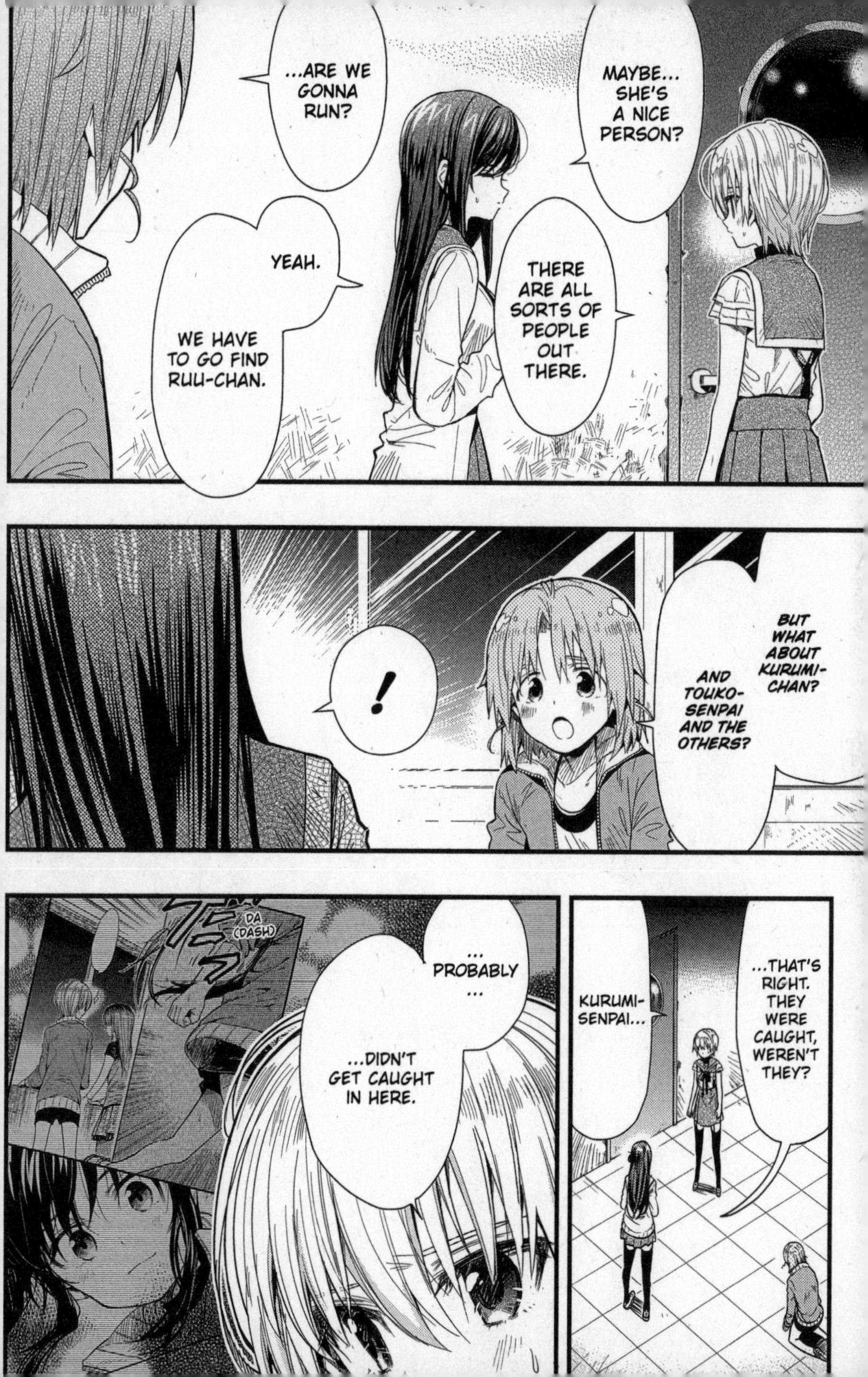
MAYBE... SHE'S A NICE PERSON?
THERE ARE ALL SORTS OF PEOPLE OUT THERE.
...ARE WE GONNA RUN?
YEAH.
WE HAVE TO GO FIND RUU-CHAN.
BUT WHAT ABOUT KURUMI-CHAN?
AND TOUKO-SENPAI AND THE OTHERS?
!
...THAT'S RIGHT. THEY WERE CAUGHT, WEREN'T THEY?
KURUMI-SENPAI...
... PROBABLY ...
...DIDN'T GET CAUGHT IN HERE.
DA (DASH)

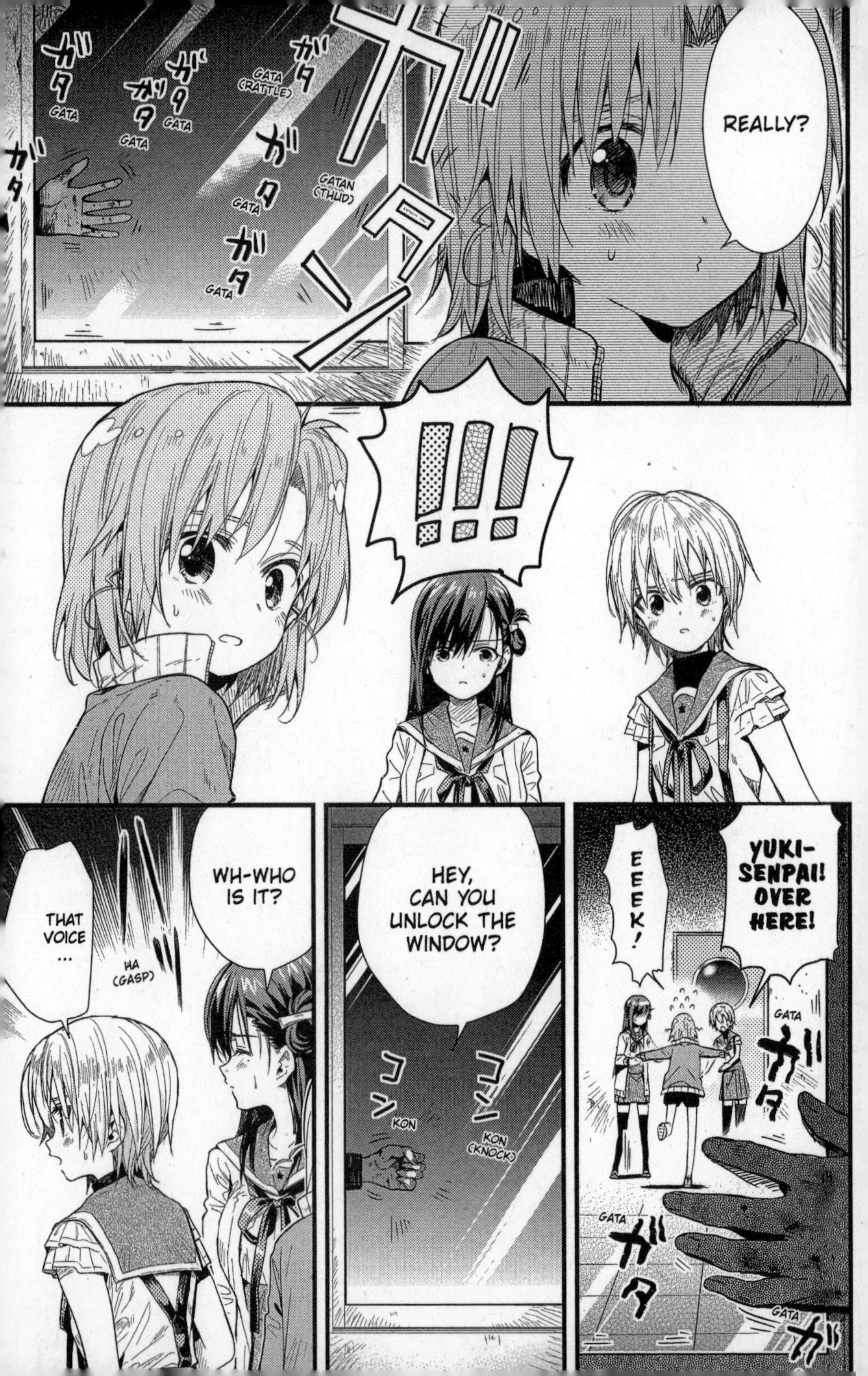
REALLY?
ガタン
GATAN (THUD)
GATA (RATTLE)
GATA
GATA
GATA
GATA
GATA
!!!
YUKI-SENPAI! OVER HERE!
EEEK!
GATA
GATA
GATA
HEY, CAN YOU UNLOCK THE WINDOW?
KON (KNOCK)
KON
WH-WHO IS IT?
HA (GASP)
THAT VOICE ...

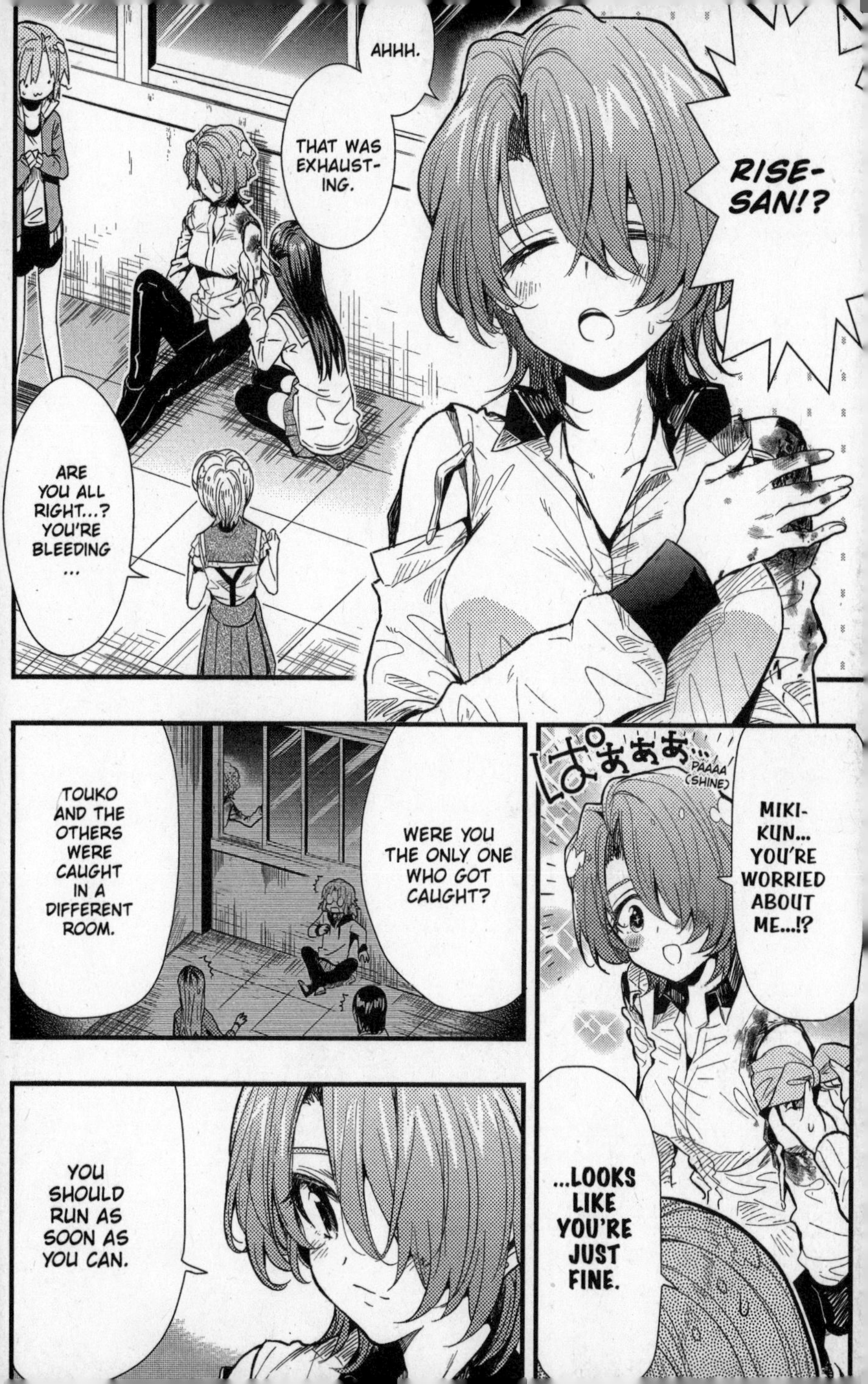
RISE-SAN!?
AHHH.
THAT WAS EXHAUST-ING.
ARE YOU ALL RIGHT...? YOU'RE BLEEDING...
ぱぁぁぁ…
PAAAA (SHINE)
MIKI-KUN... YOU'RE WORRIED ABOUT ME...!?
...LOOKS LIKE YOU'RE JUST FINE.
WERE YOU THE ONLY ONE WHO GOT CAUGHT?
TOUKO AND THE OTHERS WERE CAUGHT IN A DIFFERENT ROOM.
YOU SHOULD RUN AS SOON AS YOU CAN.

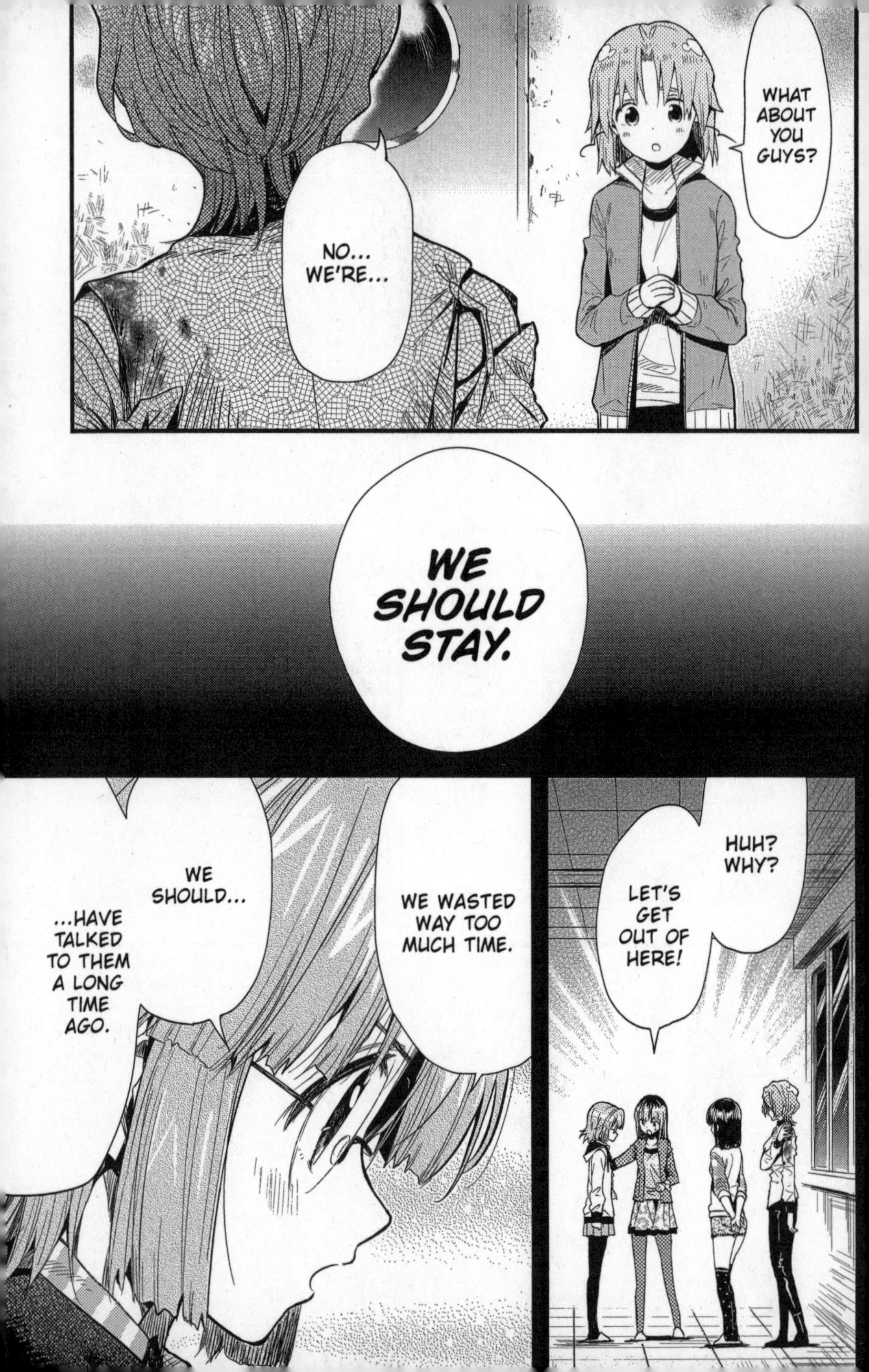
WHAT ABOUT YOU GUYS?
NO... WE'RE...
WE SHOULD STAY.
HUH? WHY?
LET'S GET OUT OF HERE!
WE WASTED WAY TOO MUCH TIME.
WE SHOULD...
...HAVE TALKED TO THEM A LONG TIME AGO.

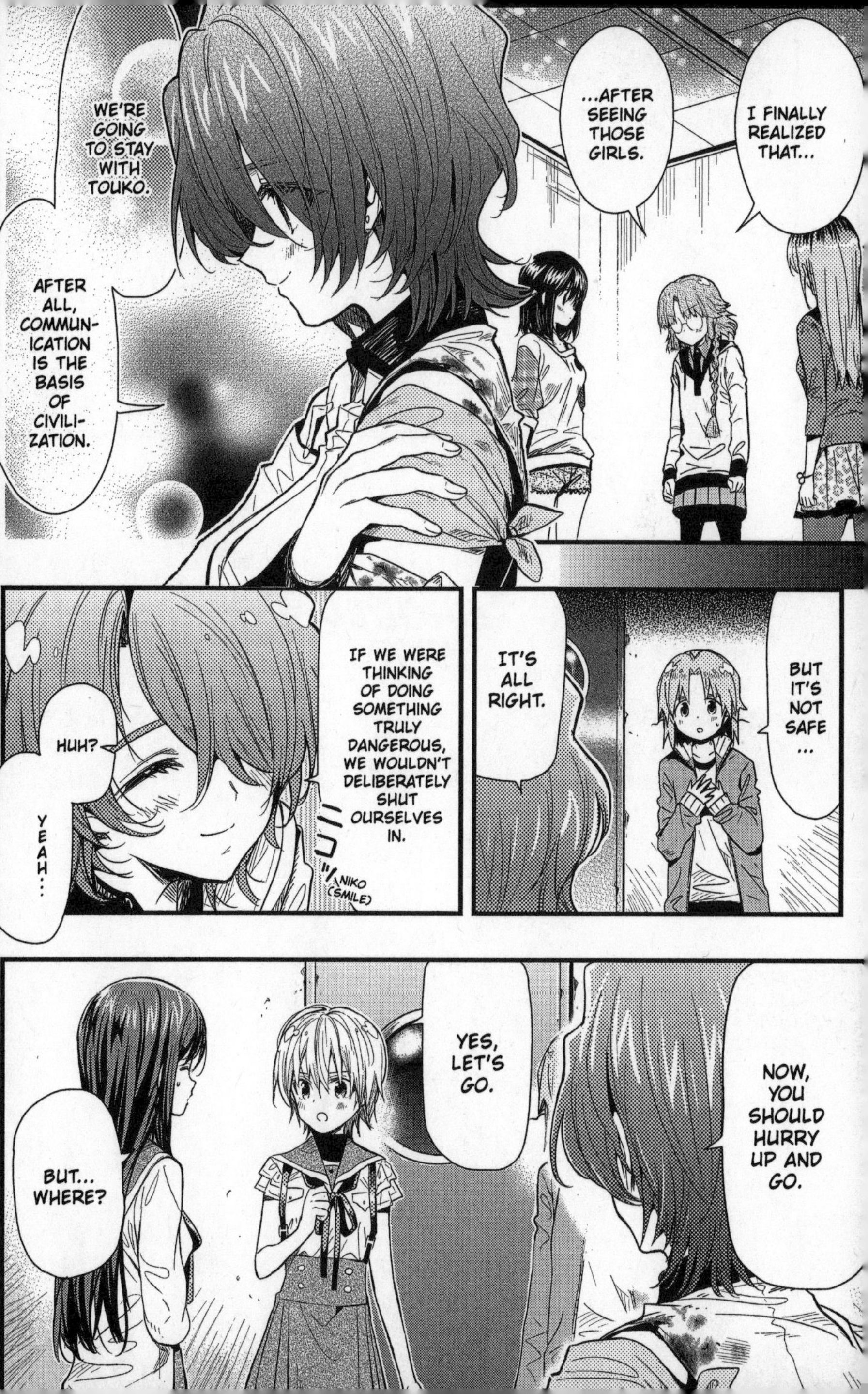
I FINALLY REALIZED THAT...
...AFTER SEEING THOSE GIRLS.
WE'RE GOING TO STAY WITH TOUKO.
AFTER ALL, COMMUNICATION IS THE BASIS OF CIVILIZATION.
BUT IT'S NOT SAFE...
IT'S ALL RIGHT.
IF WE WERE THINKING OF DOING SOMETHING TRULY DANGEROUS, WE WOULDN'T DELIBERATELY SHUT OURSELVES IN.
HUH?
NIKO (SMILE)
YEAH...
NOW, YOU SHOULD HURRY UP AND GO.
YES, LET'S GO.
BUT... WHERE?

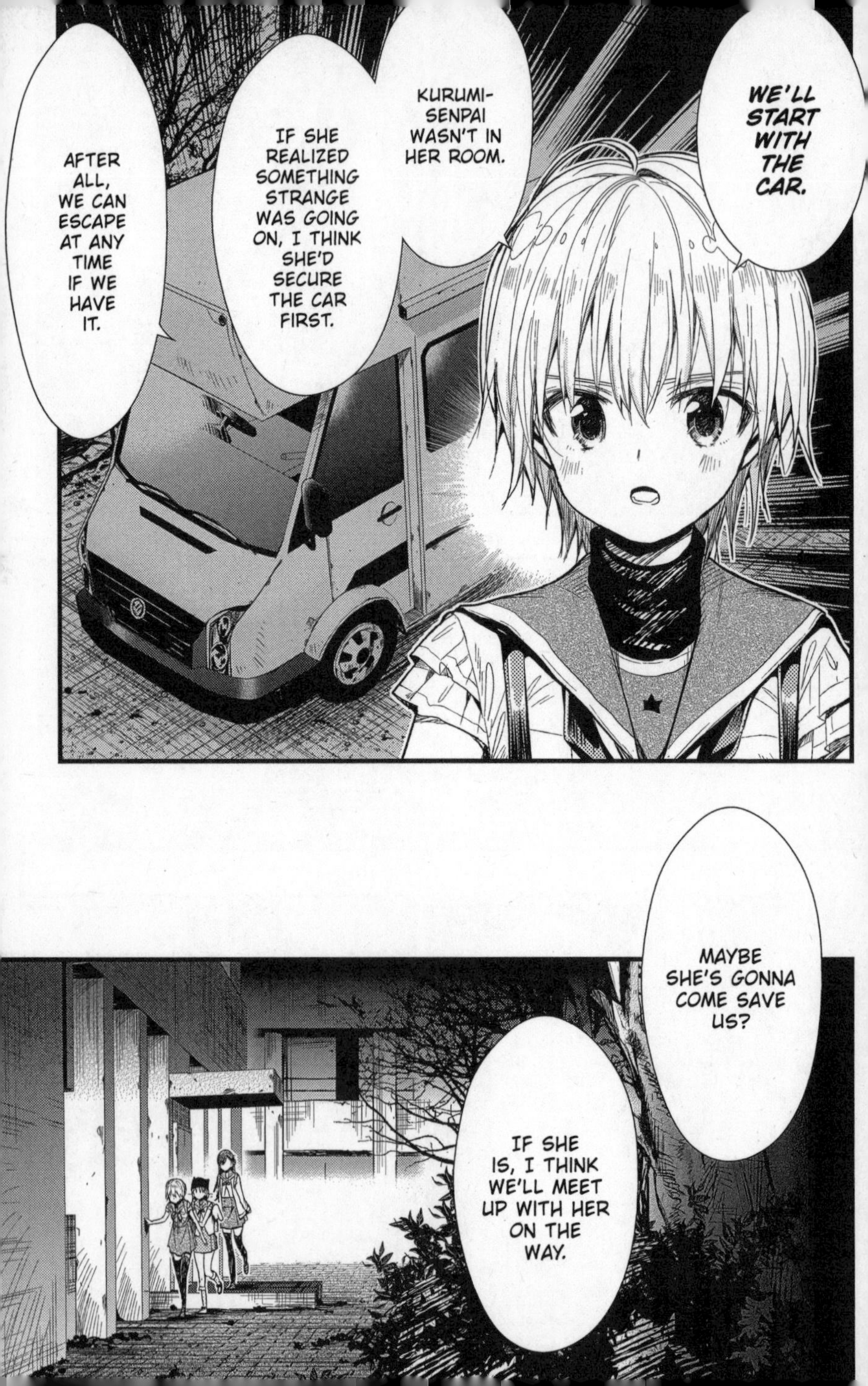
WE'LL START WITH THE CAR.
KURUMI-SENPAI WASN'T IN HER ROOM.
IF SHE REALIZED SOMETHING STRANGE WAS GOING ON, I THINK SHE'D SECURE THE CAR FIRST.
AFTER ALL, WE CAN ESCAPE AT ANY TIME IF WE HAVE IT.
MAYBE SHE'S GONNA COME SAVE US?
IF SHE IS, I THINK WE'LL MEET UP WITH HER ON THE WAY.

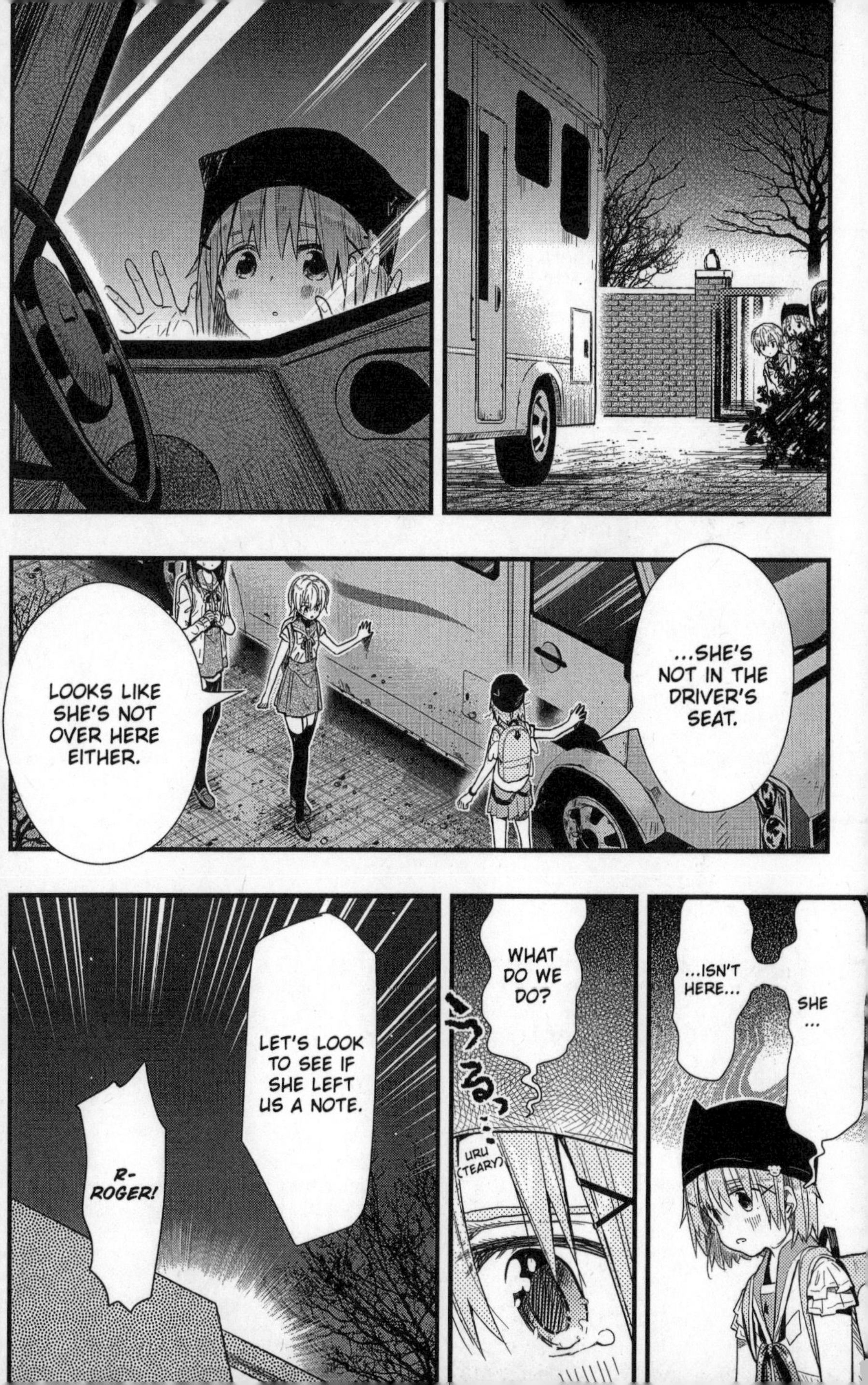
...SHE'S NOT IN THE DRIVER'S SEAT.
LOOKS LIKE SHE'S NOT OVER HERE EITHER.
SHE ...
...ISN'T HERE...
WHAT DO WE DO?
URU (TEARY)
LET'S LOOK TO SEE IF SHE LEFT US A NOTE.
R-ROGER!

PERA
(LIFT)

I WONDER...IF KURUMI-CHAN WAS SLEEPING IN HERE.

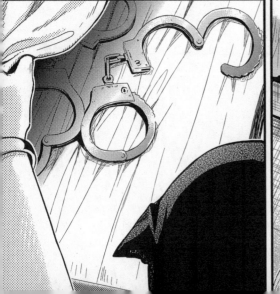

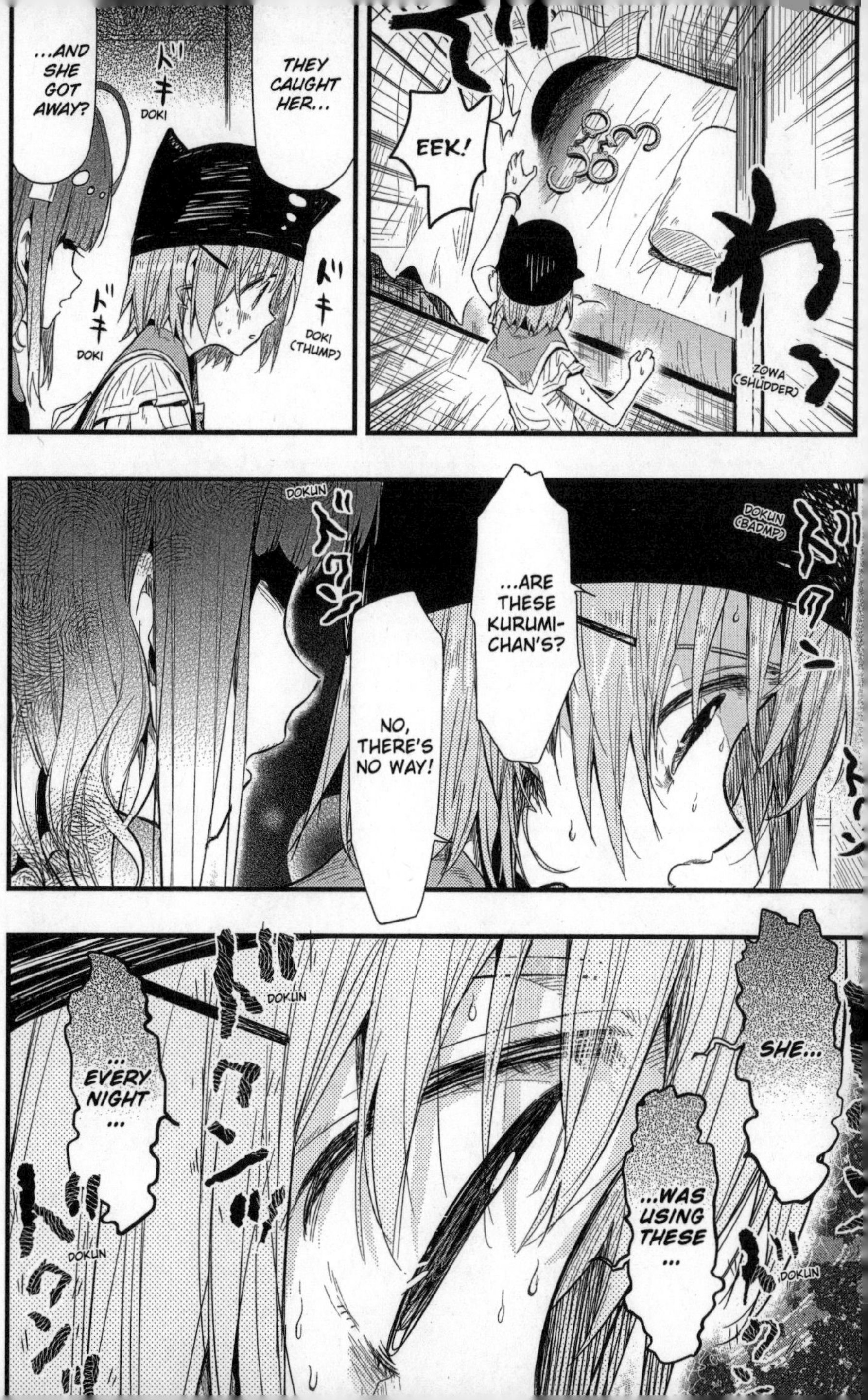
EEK!
ZOWA (SHUDDER)
THEY CAUGHT HER...
...AND SHE GOT AWAY?
ドキ
DOKI (THUMP)
ドキ
DOKI
ドキ
DOKI
DOKUN (BADMP)
...ARE THESE KURUMI-CHAN'S?
NO, THERE'S NO WAY!
DOKUN
SHE...
...WAS USING THESE ...
DOKUN
DOKUN
... EVERY NIGHT ...
DOKUN

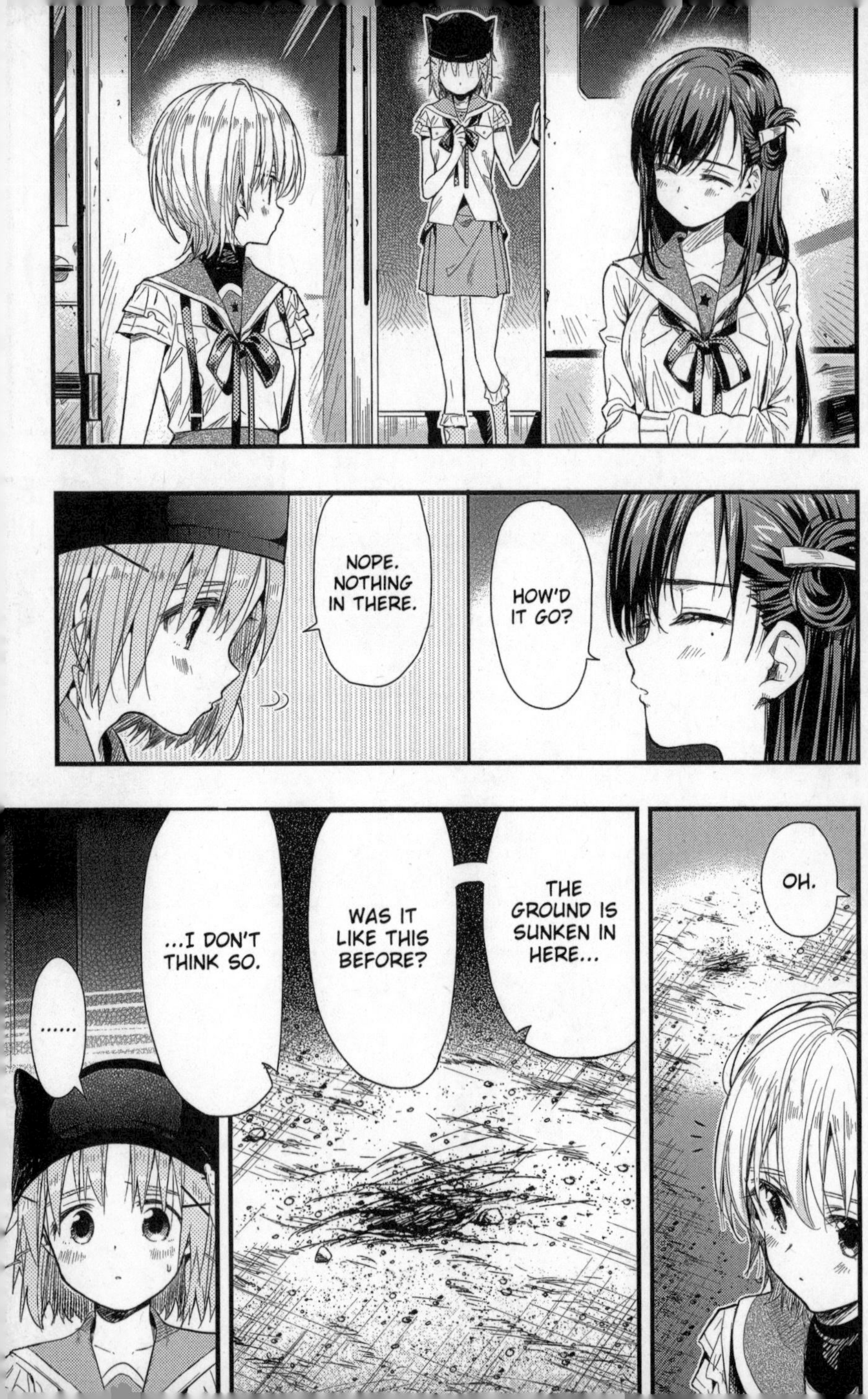
HOW'D IT GO?
NOPE. NOTHING IN THERE.
OH.
THE GROUND IS SUNKEN IN HERE...
WAS IT LIKE THIS BEFORE?
...I DON'T THINK SO.
......

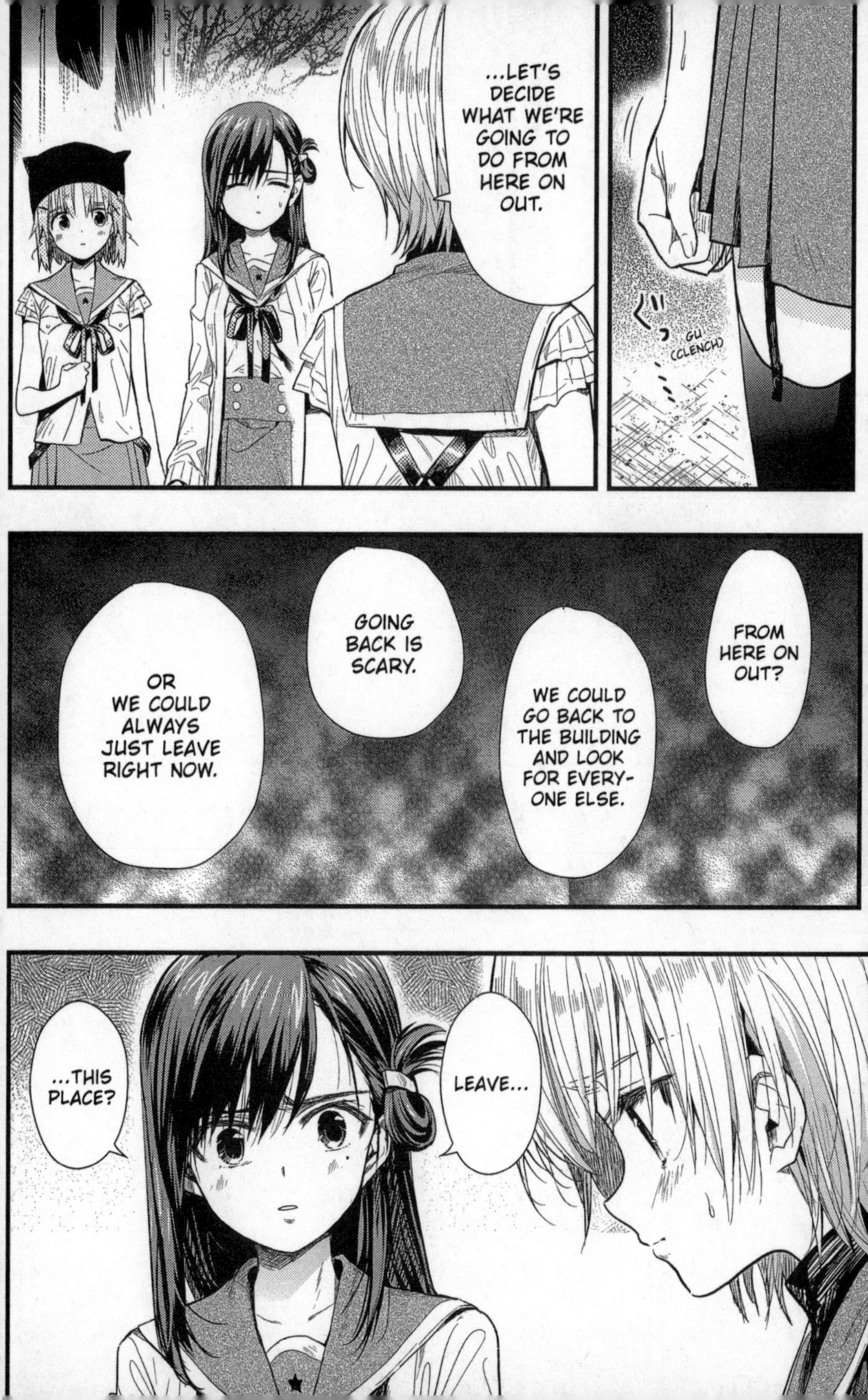
ぐっ
GU (CLENCH)
...LET'S DECIDE WHAT WE'RE GOING TO DO FROM HERE ON OUT.
FROM HERE ON OUT?
WE COULD GO BACK TO THE BUILDING AND LOOK FOR EVERY-ONE ELSE.
GOING BACK IS SCARY.
OR WE COULD ALWAYS JUST LEAVE RIGHT NOW.
LEAVE...
...THIS PLACE?

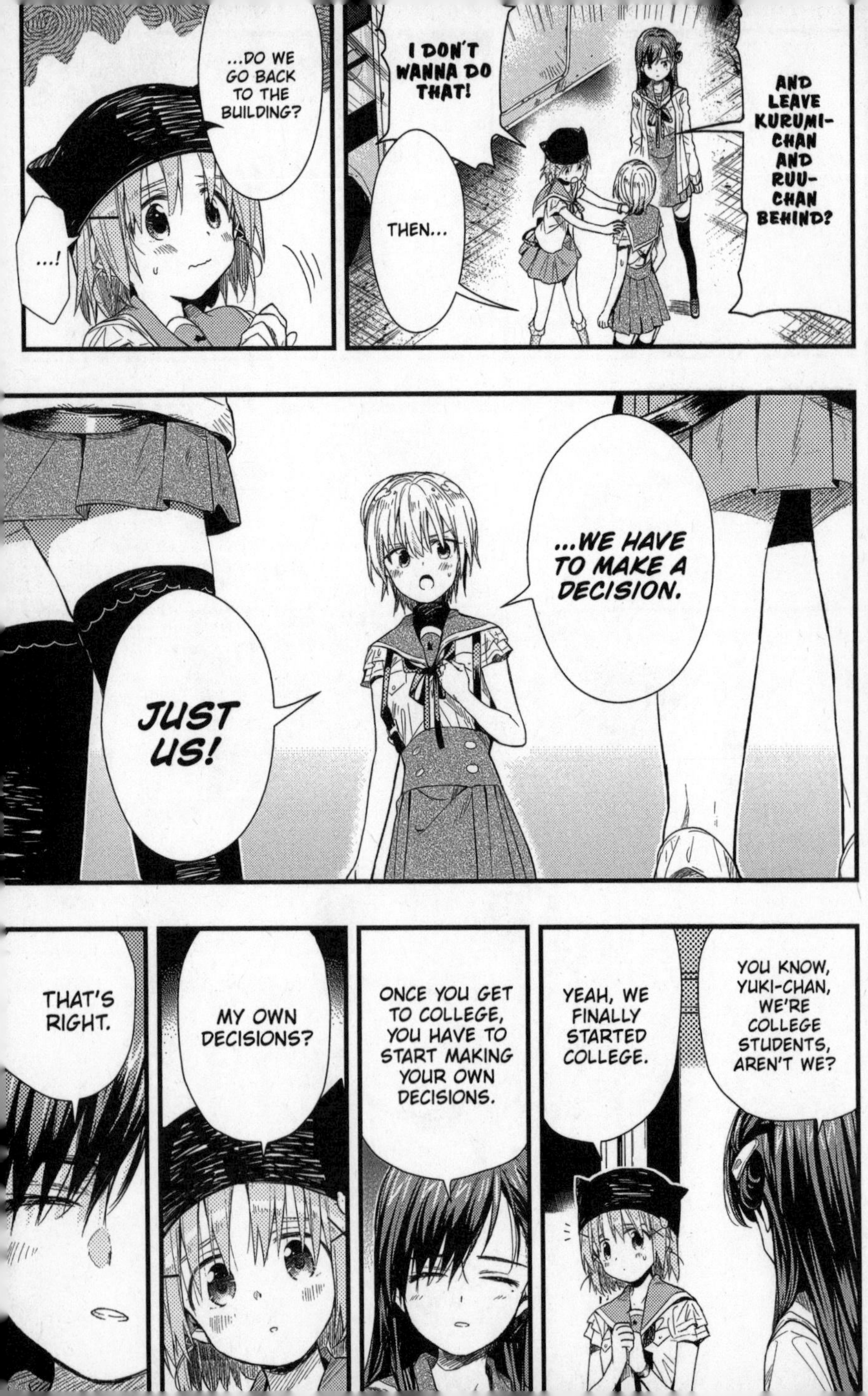
AND LEAVE KURUMI-CHAN AND RUU-CHAN BEHIND?
I DON'T WANNA DO THAT!
THEN...
...DO WE GO BACK TO THE BUILDING?
...!
...WE HAVE TO MAKE A DECISION.
JUST US!
YOU KNOW, YUKI-CHAN, WE'RE COLLEGE STUDENTS, AREN'T WE?
YEAH, WE FINALLY STARTED COLLEGE.
ONCE YOU GET TO COLLEGE, YOU HAVE TO START MAKING YOUR OWN DECISIONS.
MY OWN DECISIONS?
THAT'S RIGHT.

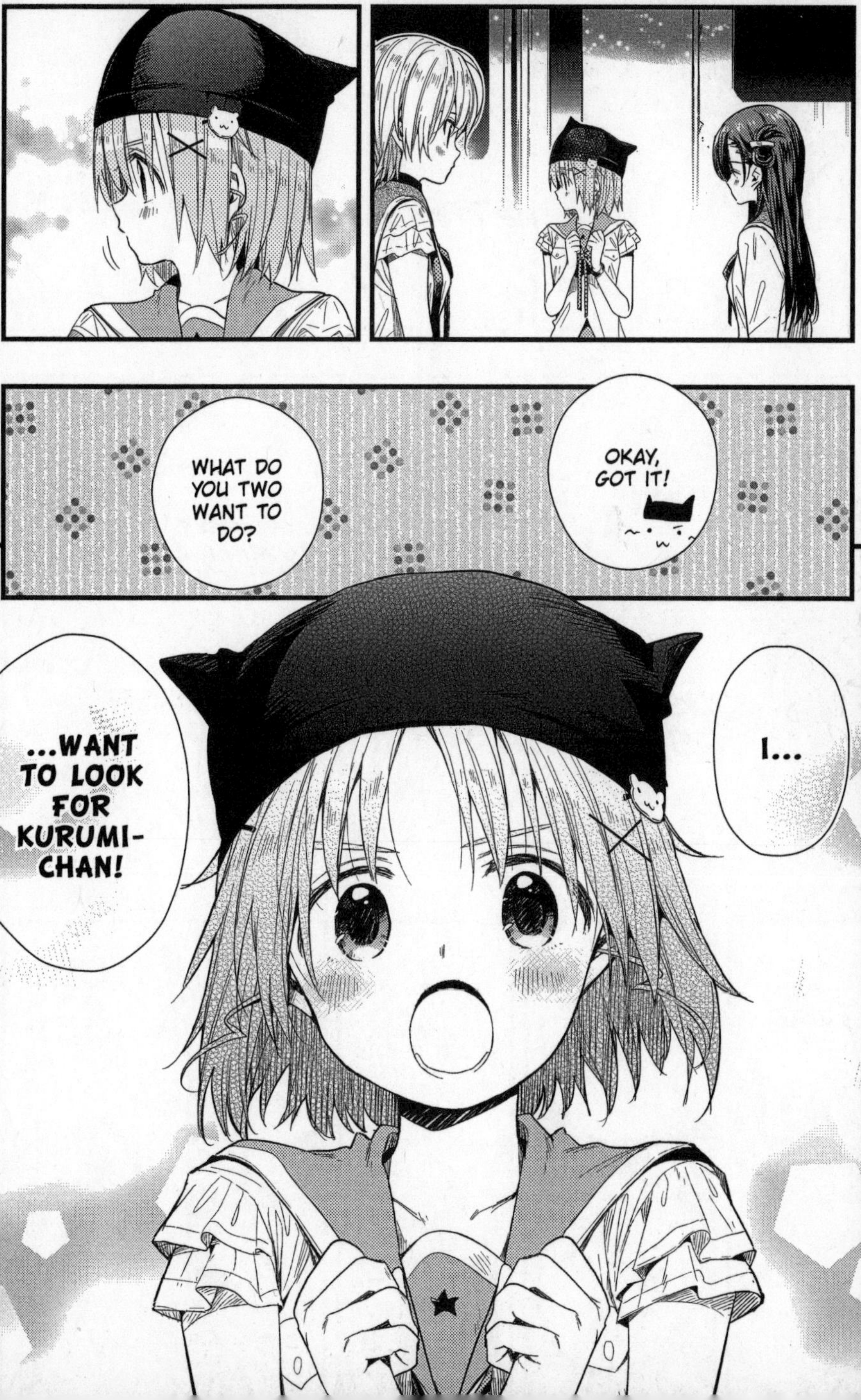
OKAY, GOT IT!
WHAT DO YOU TWO WANT TO DO?
I...
...WANT TO LOOK FOR KURUMI-CHAN!

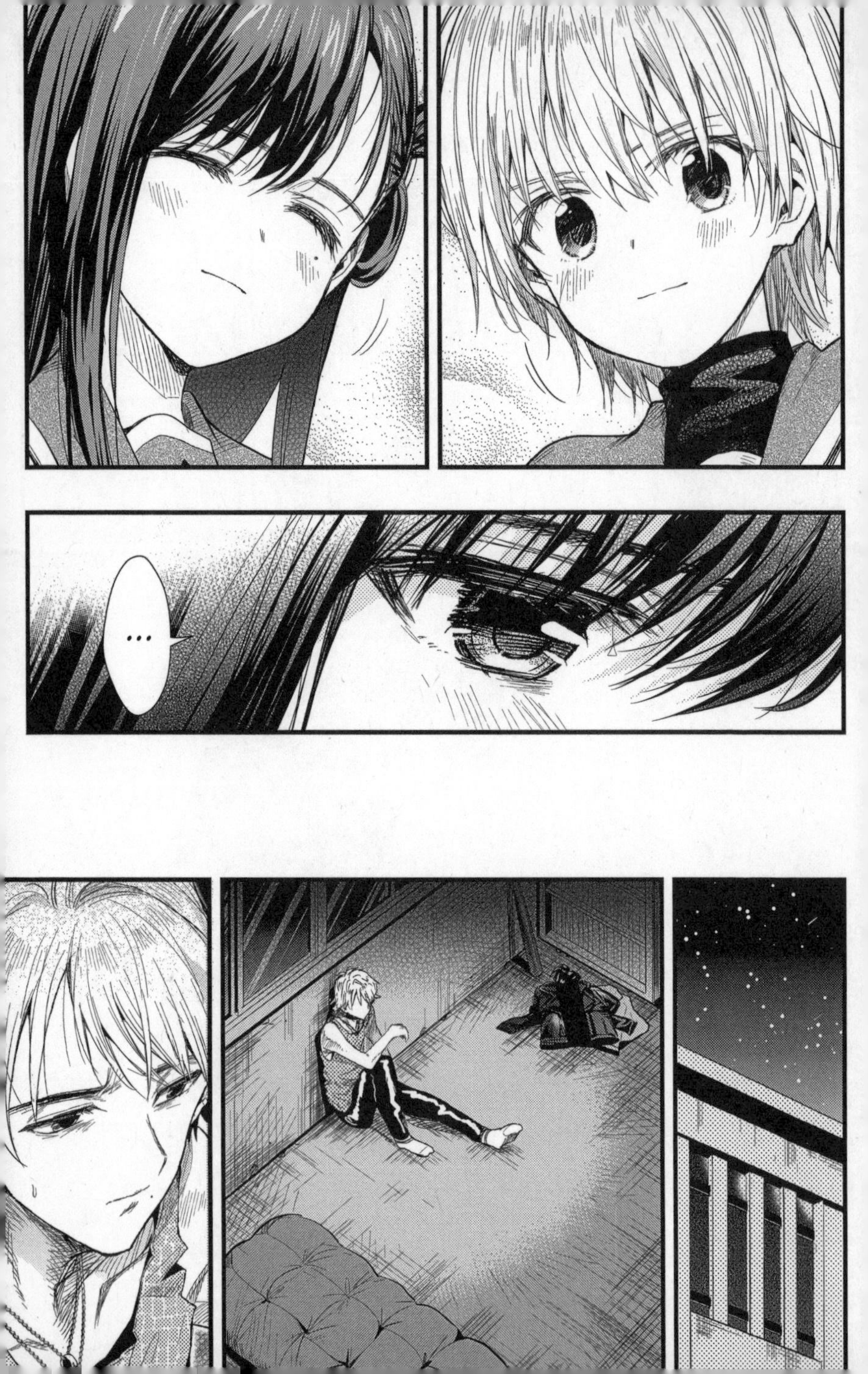
...

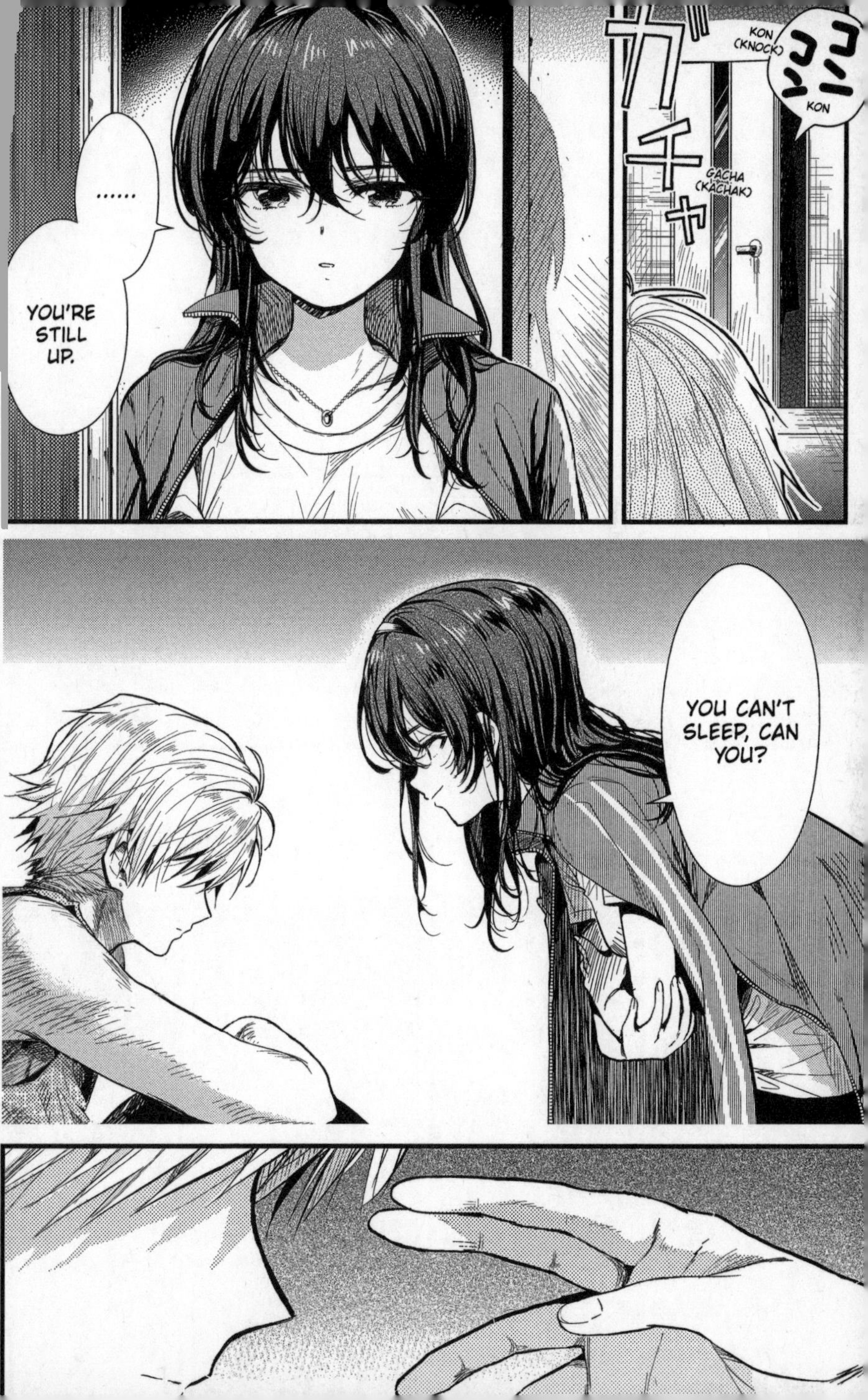コンコン
KON (KNOCK)
KON
ガチャ
GACHA (KACHAK)
......
YOU'RE STILL UP.
YOU CAN'T SLEEP, CAN YOU?

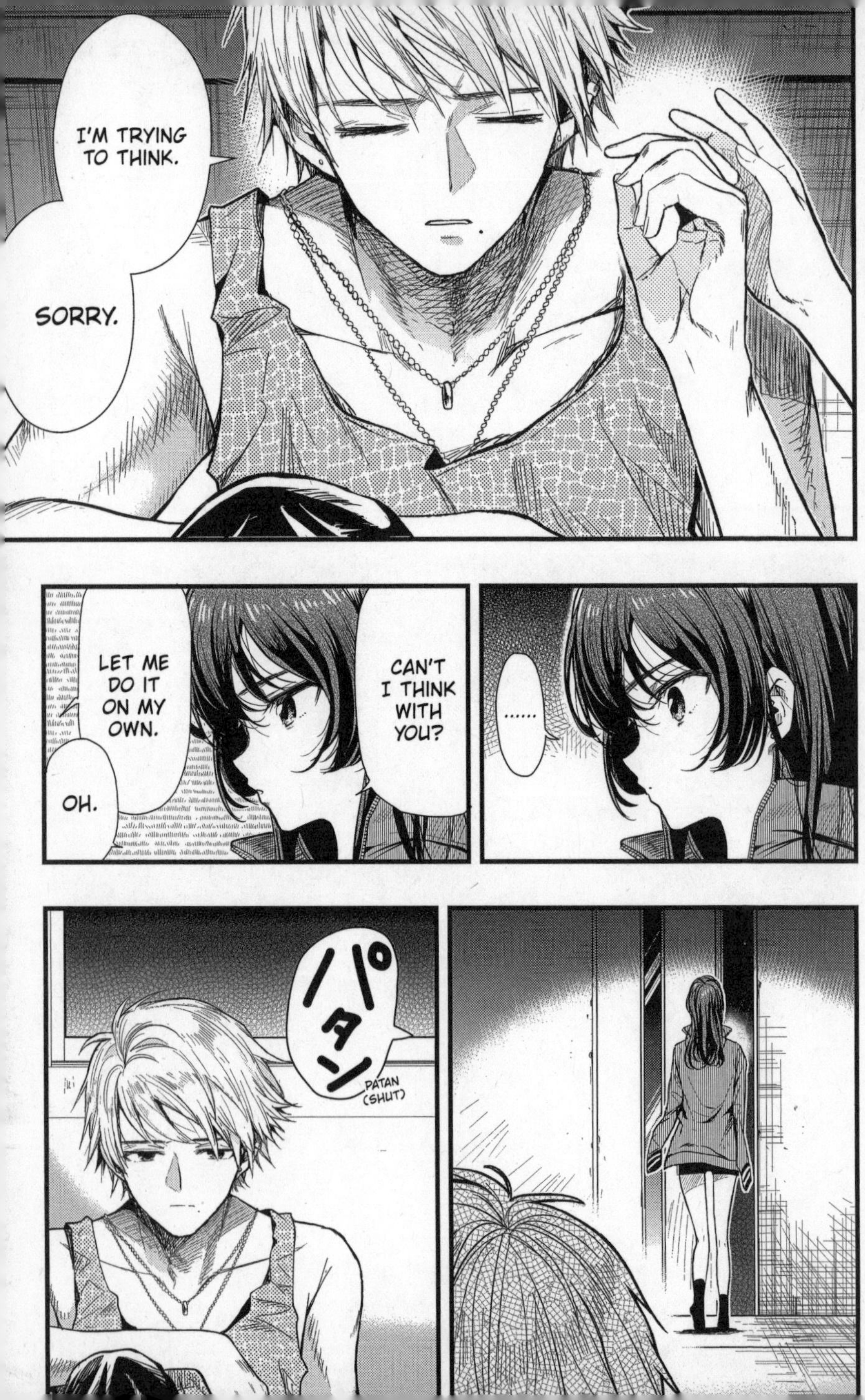
I'M TRYING TO THINK.
SORRY.
......
CAN'T I THINK WITH YOU?
LET ME DO IT ON MY OWN.
OH.
パタン
PATAN (SHUT)

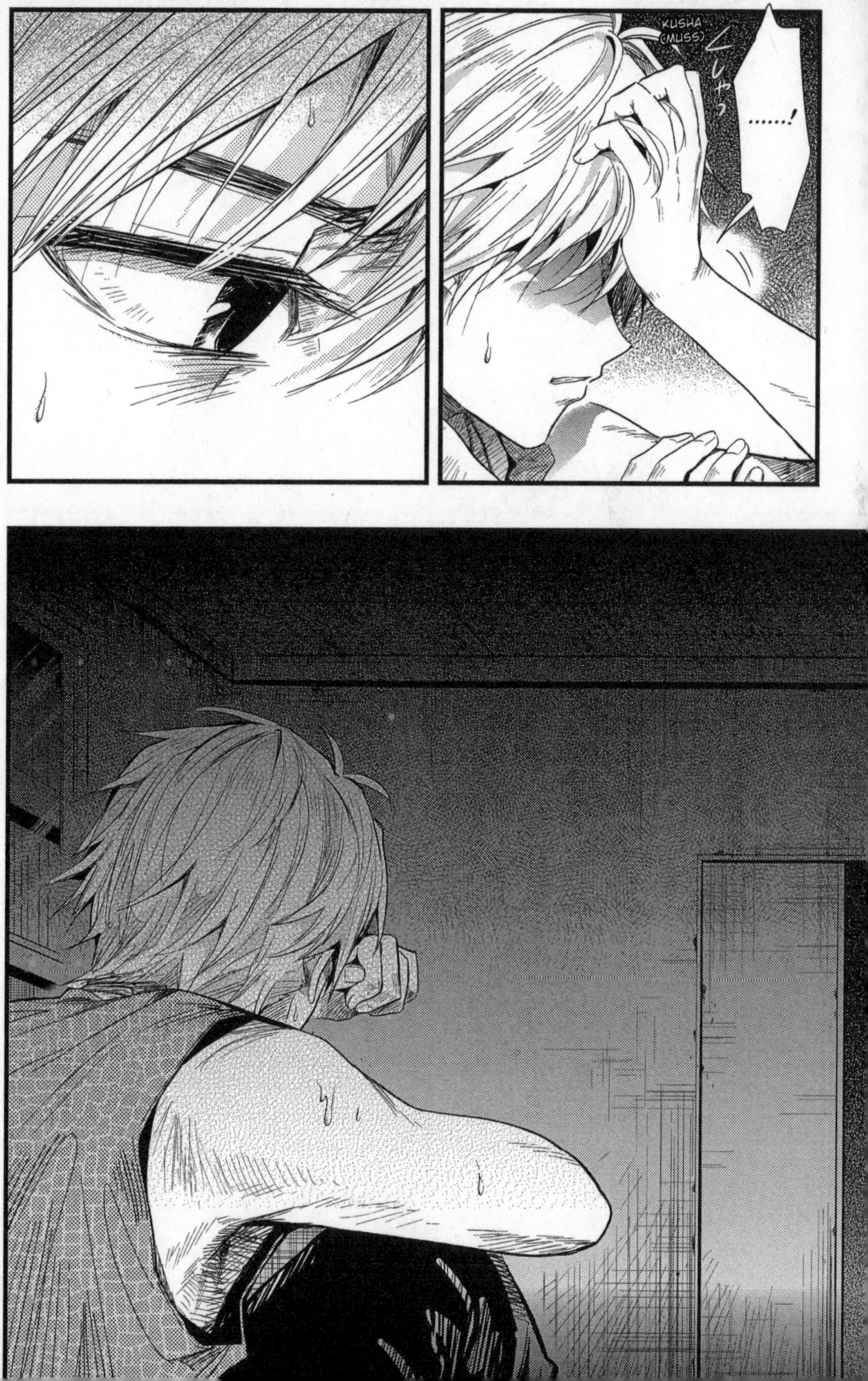
KUSHA (MUSS)
くしゃっ
......!

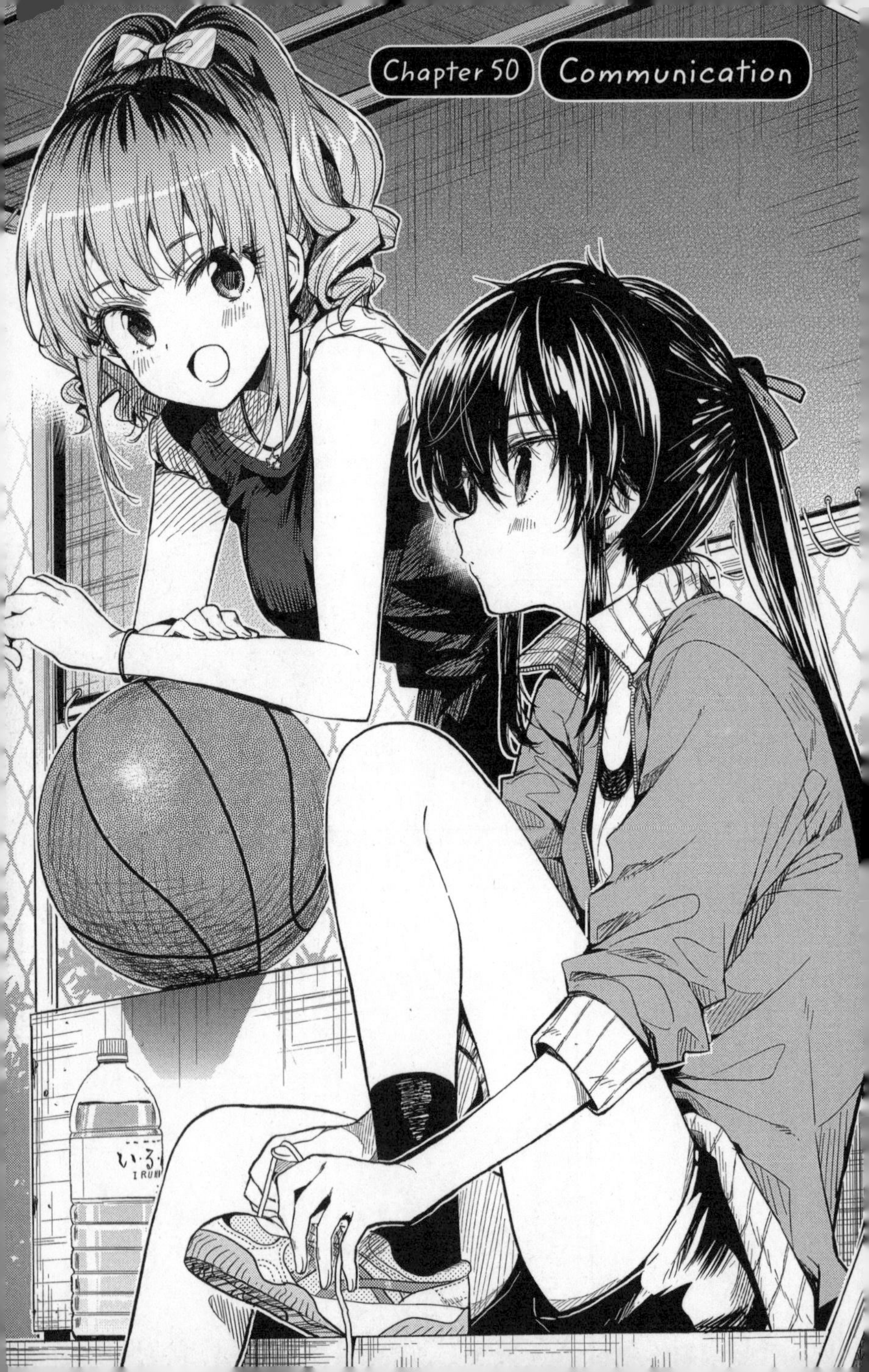
Chapter 50
Communication

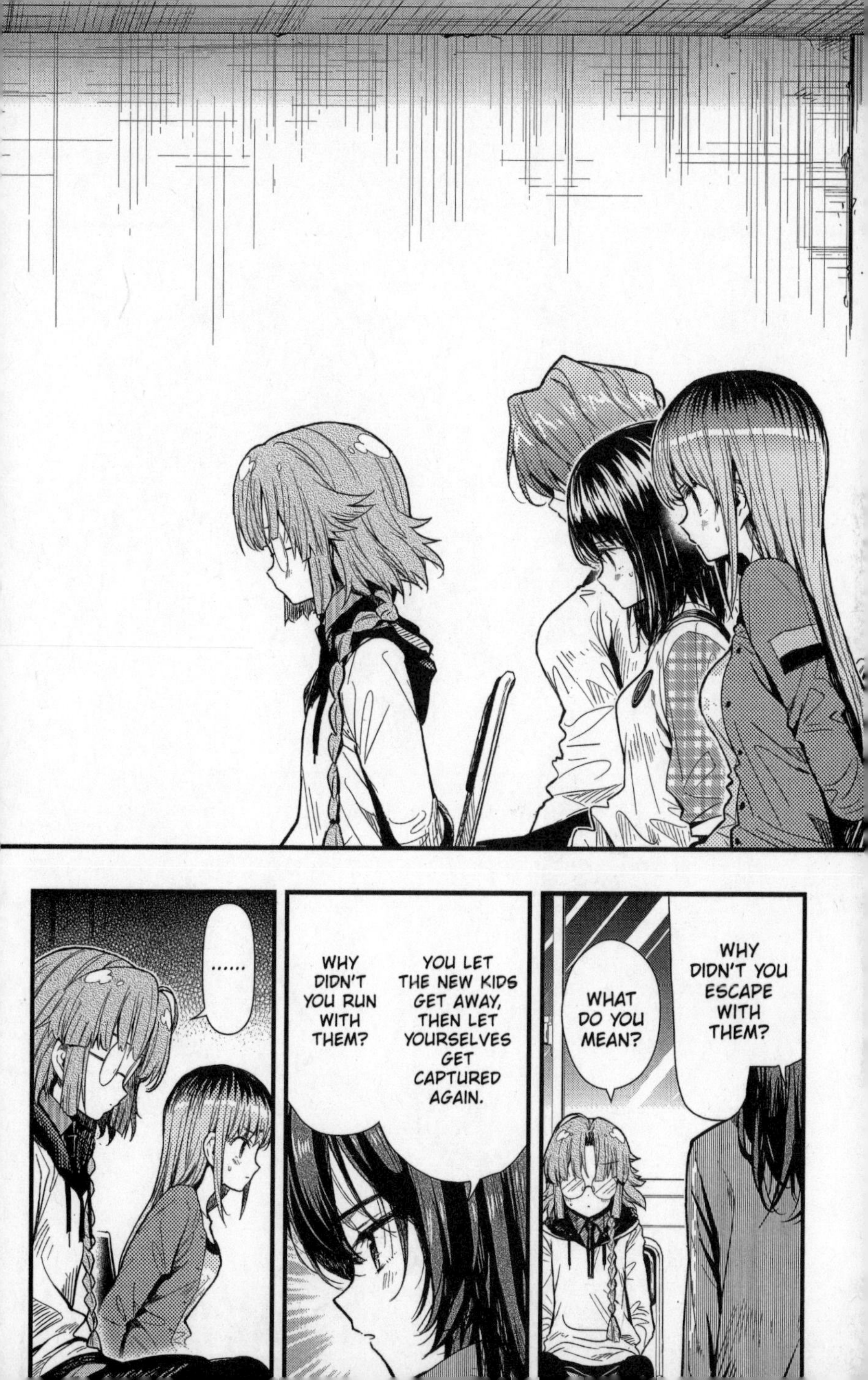
WHY DIDN'T YOU ESCAPE WITH THEM?
WHAT DO YOU MEAN?
YOU LET THE NEW KIDS GET AWAY, THEN LET YOURSELVES GET CAPTURED AGAIN.
WHY DIDN'T YOU RUN WITH THEM?
......

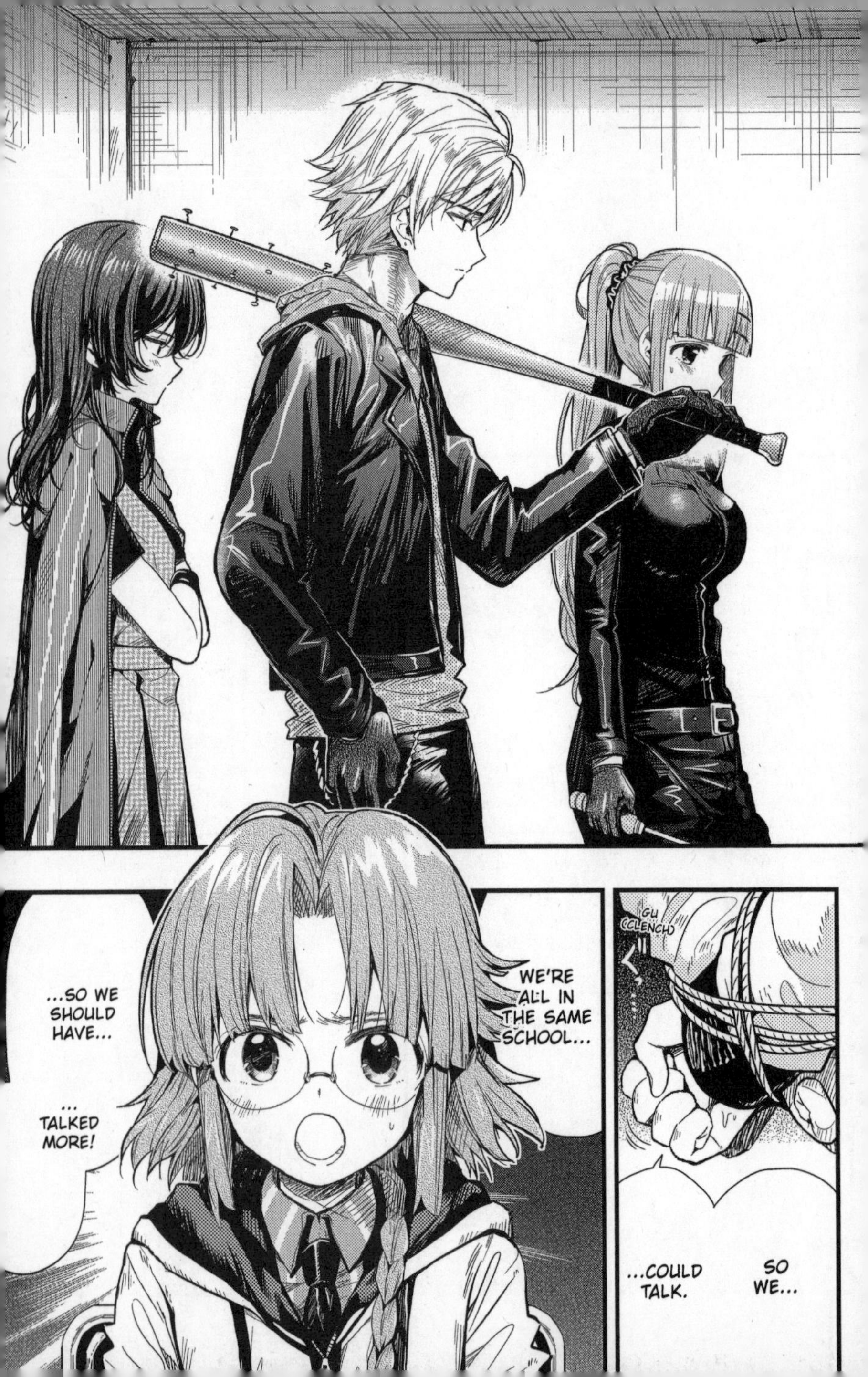
GU (CLENCH)
SO WE...
...COULD TALK.
WE'RE ALL IN THE SAME SCHOOL...
...SO WE SHOULD HAVE...
... TALKED MORE!

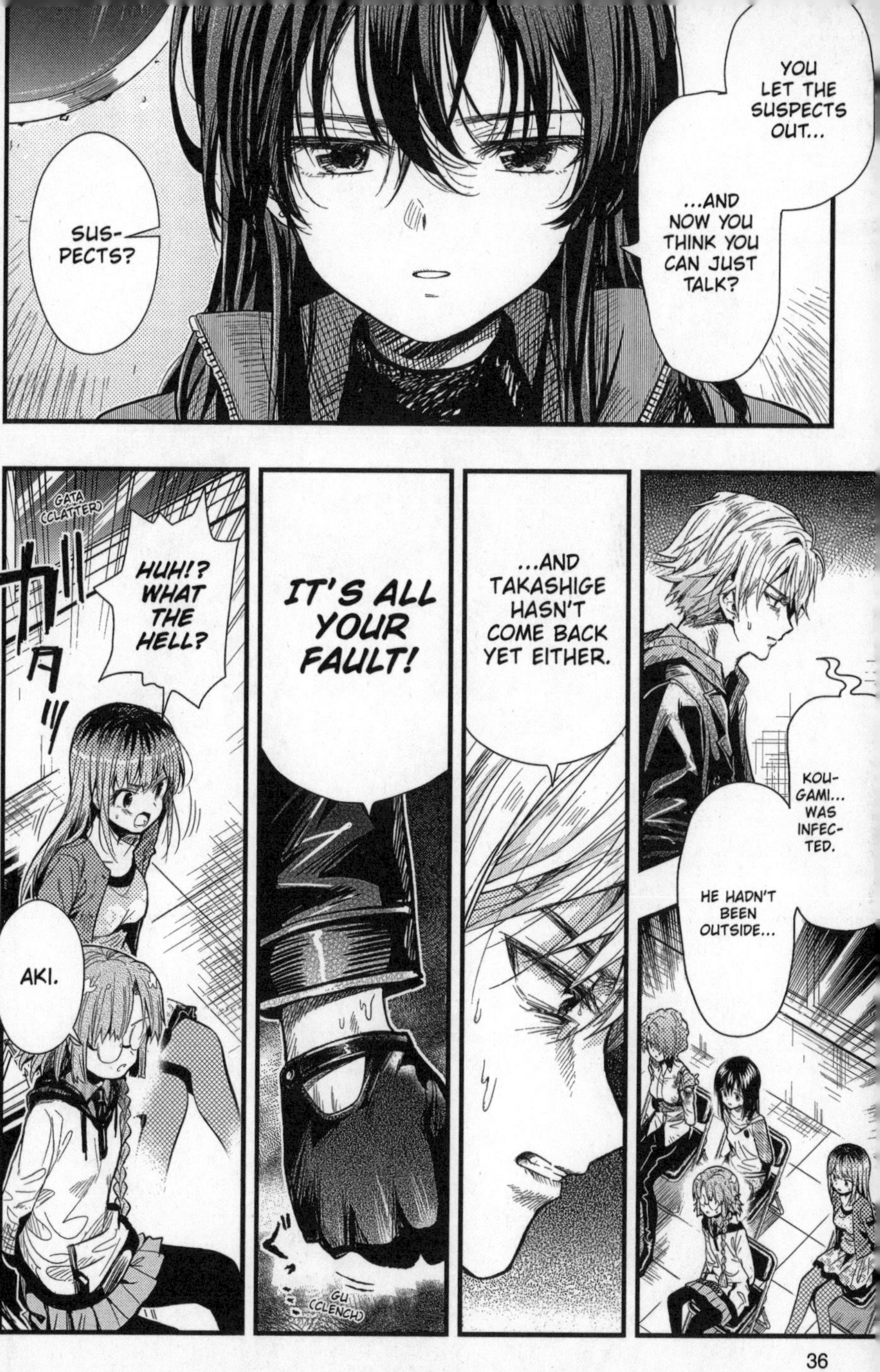
YOU LET THE SUSPECTS OUT...
...AND NOW YOU THINK YOU CAN JUST TALK?
SUS-PECTS?
KOU-GAMI... WAS INFECTED.
HE HADN'T BEEN OUTSIDE...
...AND TAKASHIGE HASN'T COME BACK YET EITHER.
IT'S ALL YOUR FAULT!
GU (CLENCH)
GATA (CLATTER)
HUH!? WHAT THE HELL?
AKI.

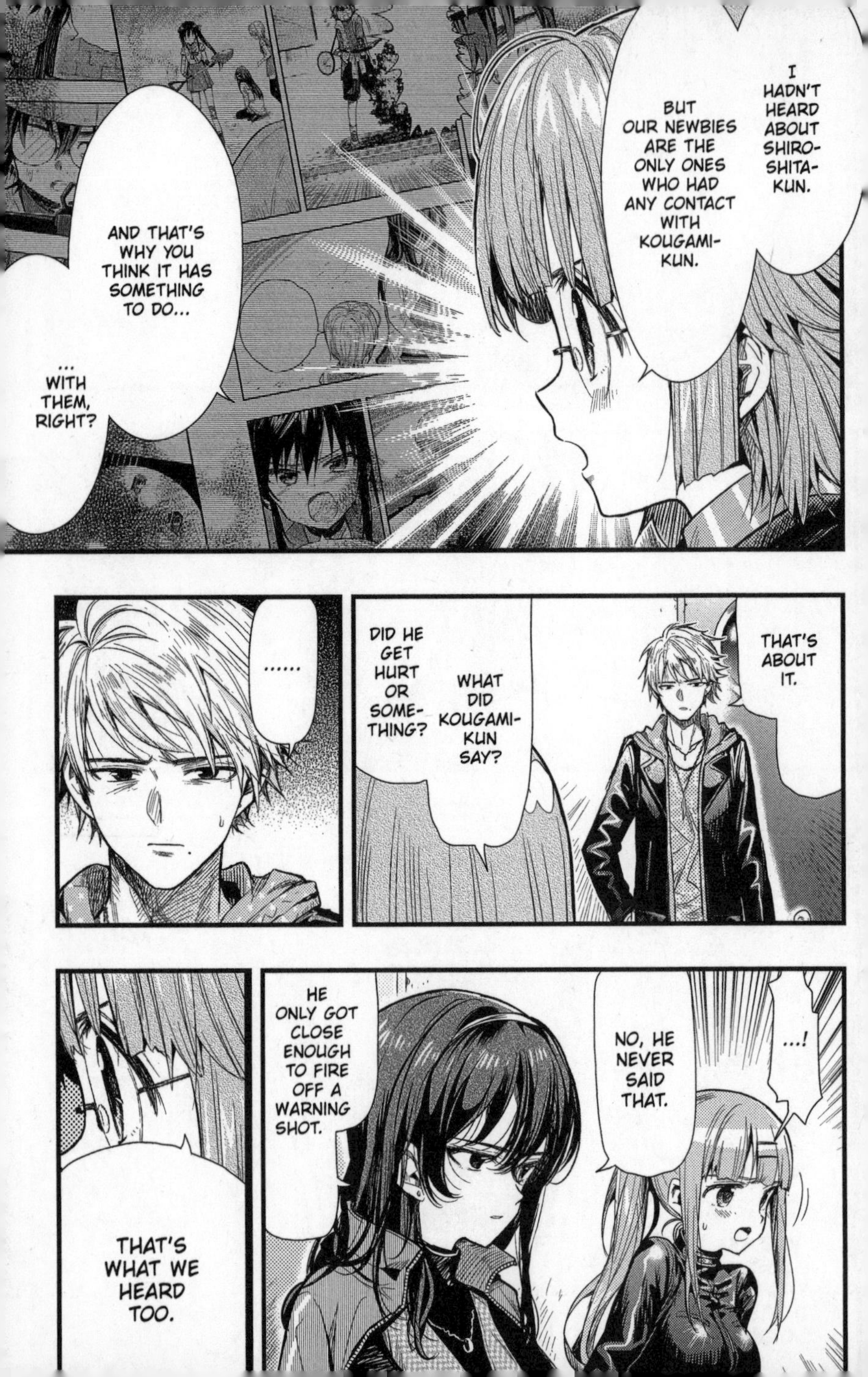
I HADN'T HEARD ABOUT SHIROSHITA-KUN.
BUT OUR NEWBIES ARE THE ONLY ONES WHO HAD ANY CONTACT WITH KOUGAMI-KUN.
AND THAT'S WHY YOU THINK IT HAS SOMETHING TO DO...
...WITH THEM, RIGHT?
THAT'S ABOUT IT.
WHAT DID KOUGAMI-KUN SAY?
DID HE GET HURT OR SOMETHING?
......
...!
NO, HE NEVER SAID THAT.
HE ONLY GOT CLOSE ENOUGH TO FIRE OFF A WARNING SHOT.
THAT'S WHAT WE HEARD TOO.

IN THAT CASE...

...WOULDN'T IT BE KIND OF HARD FOR THEM TO INFECT HIM WITHOUT COMING INTO CONTACT WITH HIM?

IT COULD BE DIFFICULT.

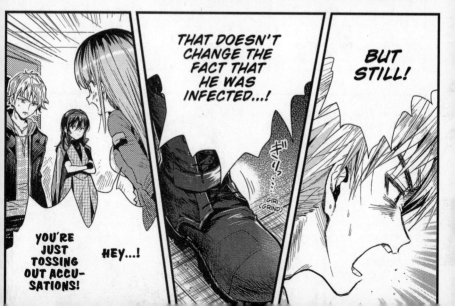

THAT DOESN'T CHANGE THE FACT THAT HE WAS INFECTED...!

BUT STILL!

GIRI (GRIND)

YOU'RE JUST TOSSING OUT ACCUSATIONS!

HEY...!

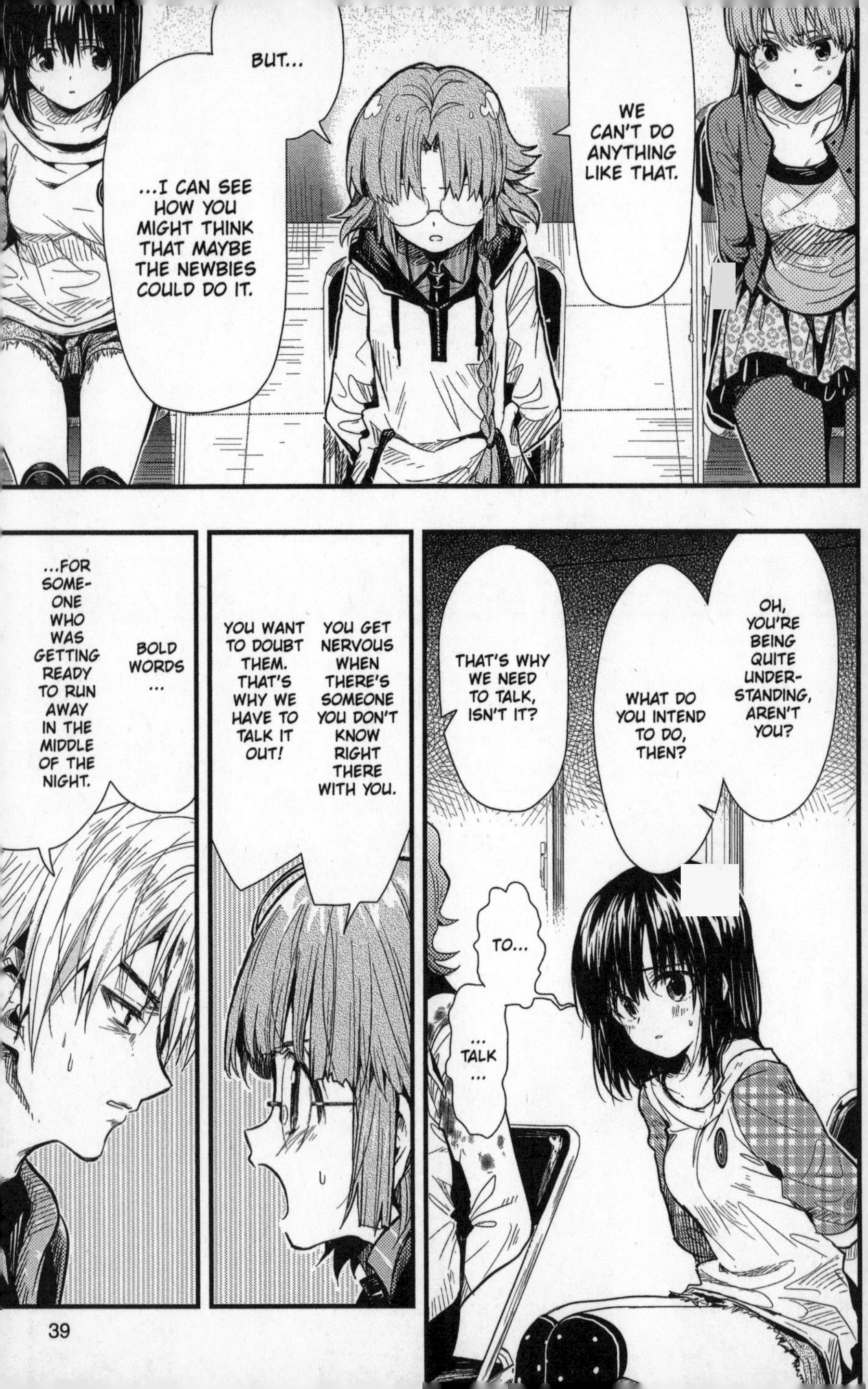
WE CAN'T DO ANYTHING LIKE THAT.
BUT...
...I CAN SEE HOW YOU MIGHT THINK THAT MAYBE THE NEWBIES COULD DO IT.
OH, YOU'RE BEING QUITE UNDER-STANDING, AREN'T YOU?
WHAT DO YOU INTEND TO DO, THEN?
THAT'S WHY WE NEED TO TALK, ISN'T IT?
TO...
...TALK...
YOU GET NERVOUS WHEN THERE'S SOMEONE YOU DON'T KNOW RIGHT THERE WITH YOU.
YOU WANT TO DOUBT THEM. THAT'S WHY WE HAVE TO TALK IT OUT!
BOLD WORDS...
...FOR SOME-ONE WHO WAS GETTING READY TO RUN AWAY IN THE MIDDLE OF THE NIGHT.

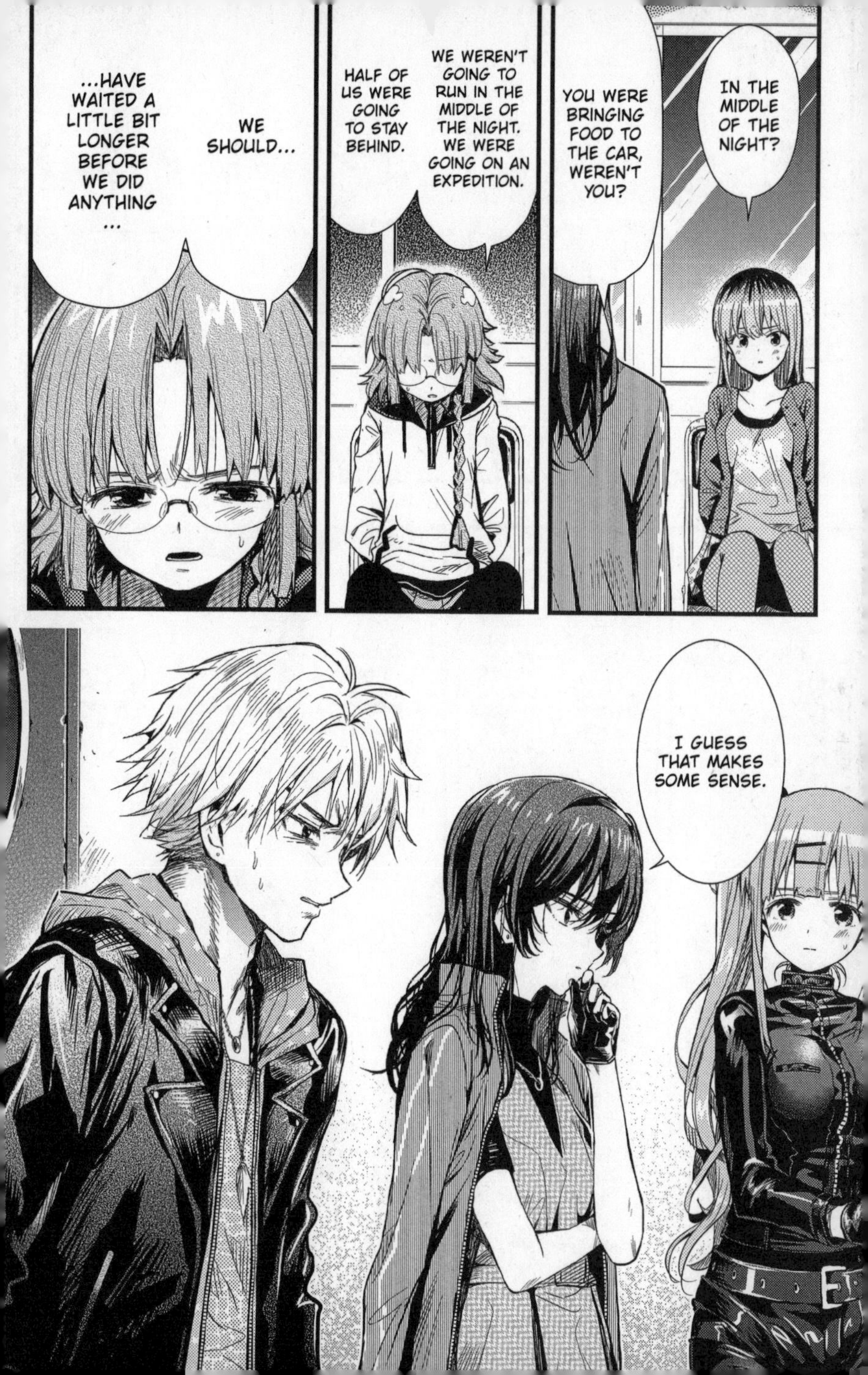
IN THE MIDDLE OF THE NIGHT?
YOU WERE BRINGING FOOD TO THE CAR, WEREN'T YOU?
WE WEREN'T GOING TO RUN IN THE MIDDLE OF THE NIGHT. WE WERE GOING ON AN EXPEDITION.
HALF OF US WERE GOING TO STAY BEHIND.
WE SHOULD...
...HAVE WAITED A LITTLE BIT LONGER BEFORE WE DID ANYTHING...
I GUESS THAT MAKES SOME SENSE.

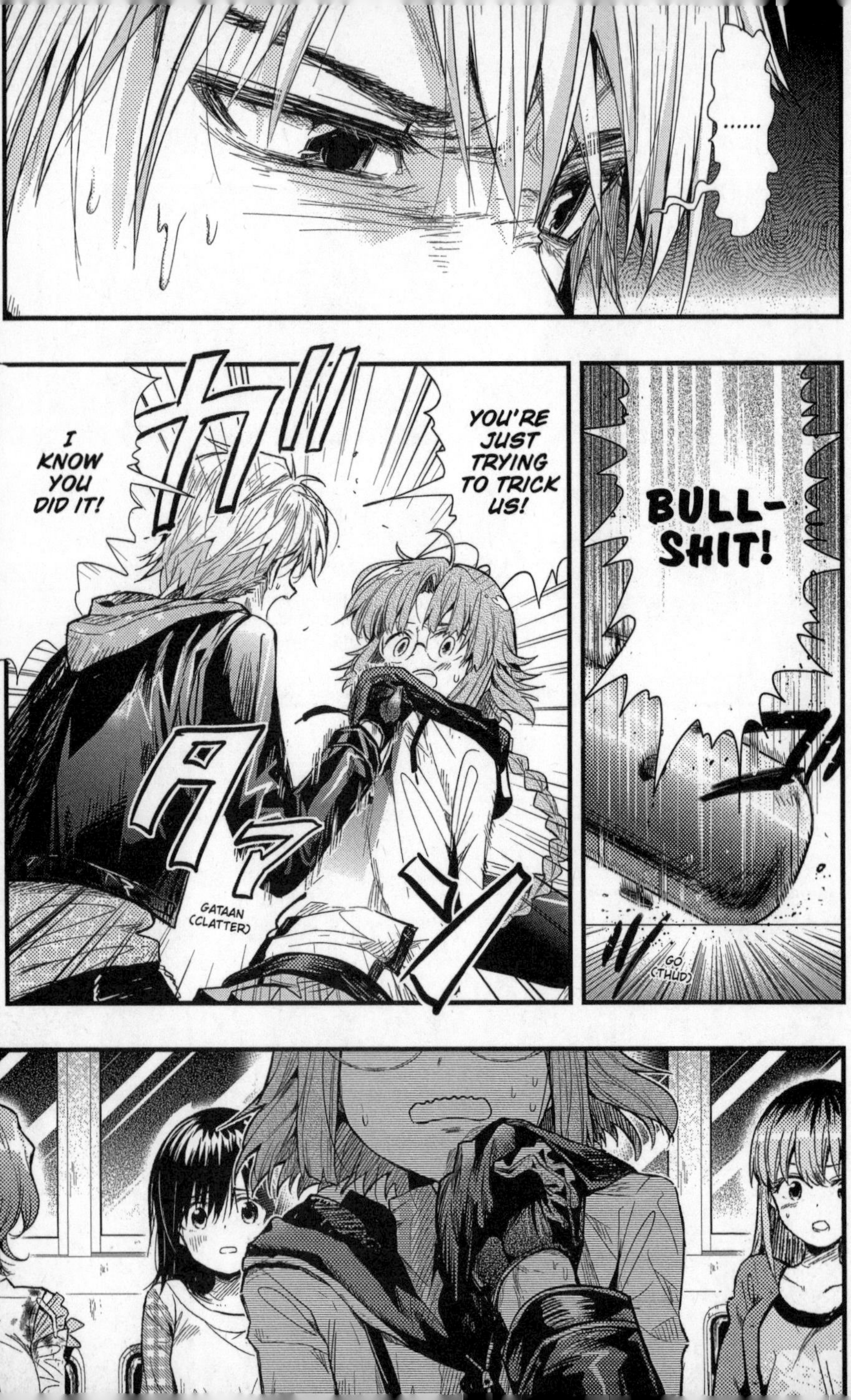
......
BULL-SHIT!
GO (THUD)
YOU'RE JUST TRYING TO TRICK US!
I KNOW YOU DID IT!
GATAAN (CLATTER)

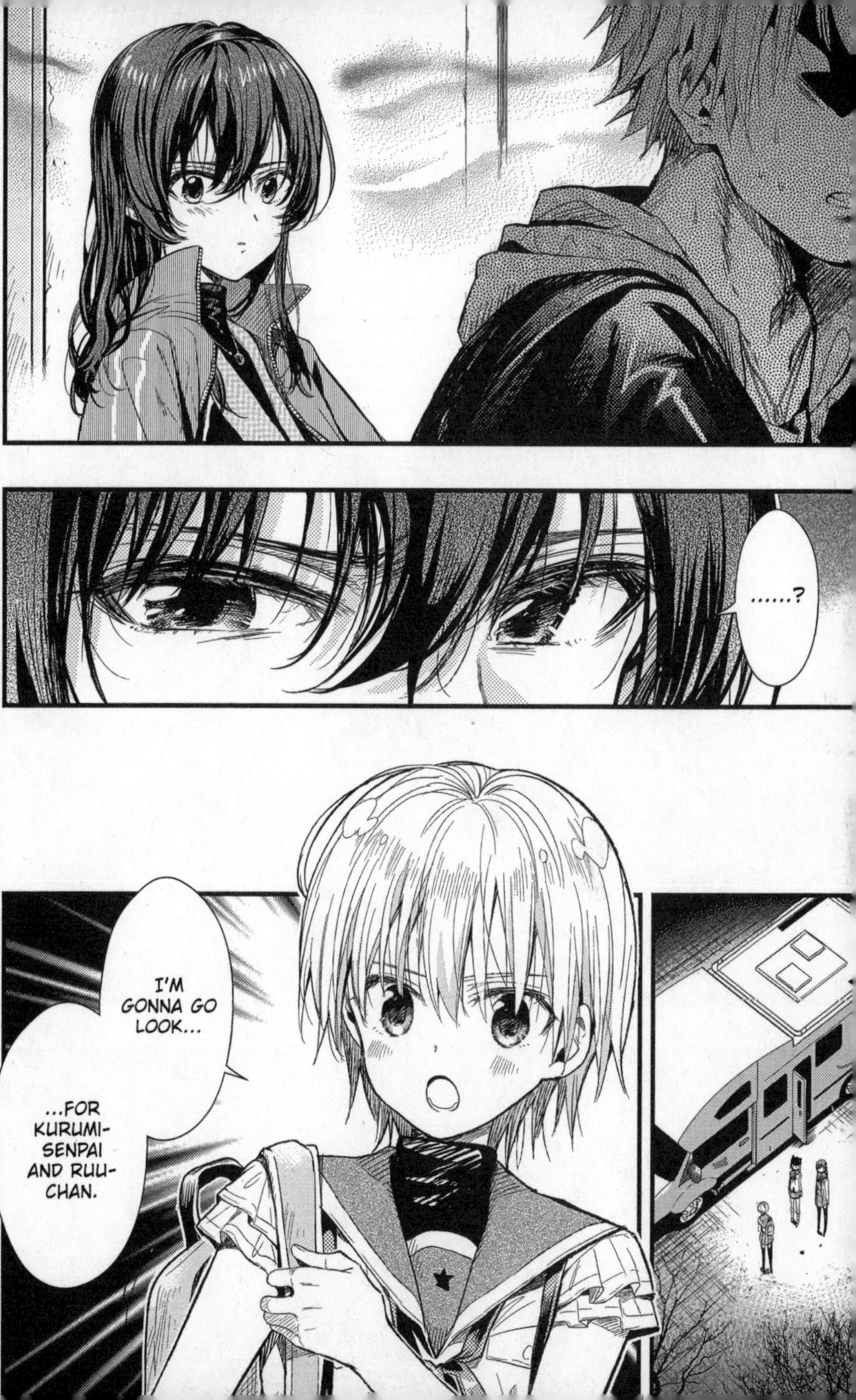
......?
I'M GONNA GO LOOK...
...FOR KURUMI-SENPAI AND RUU-CHAN.

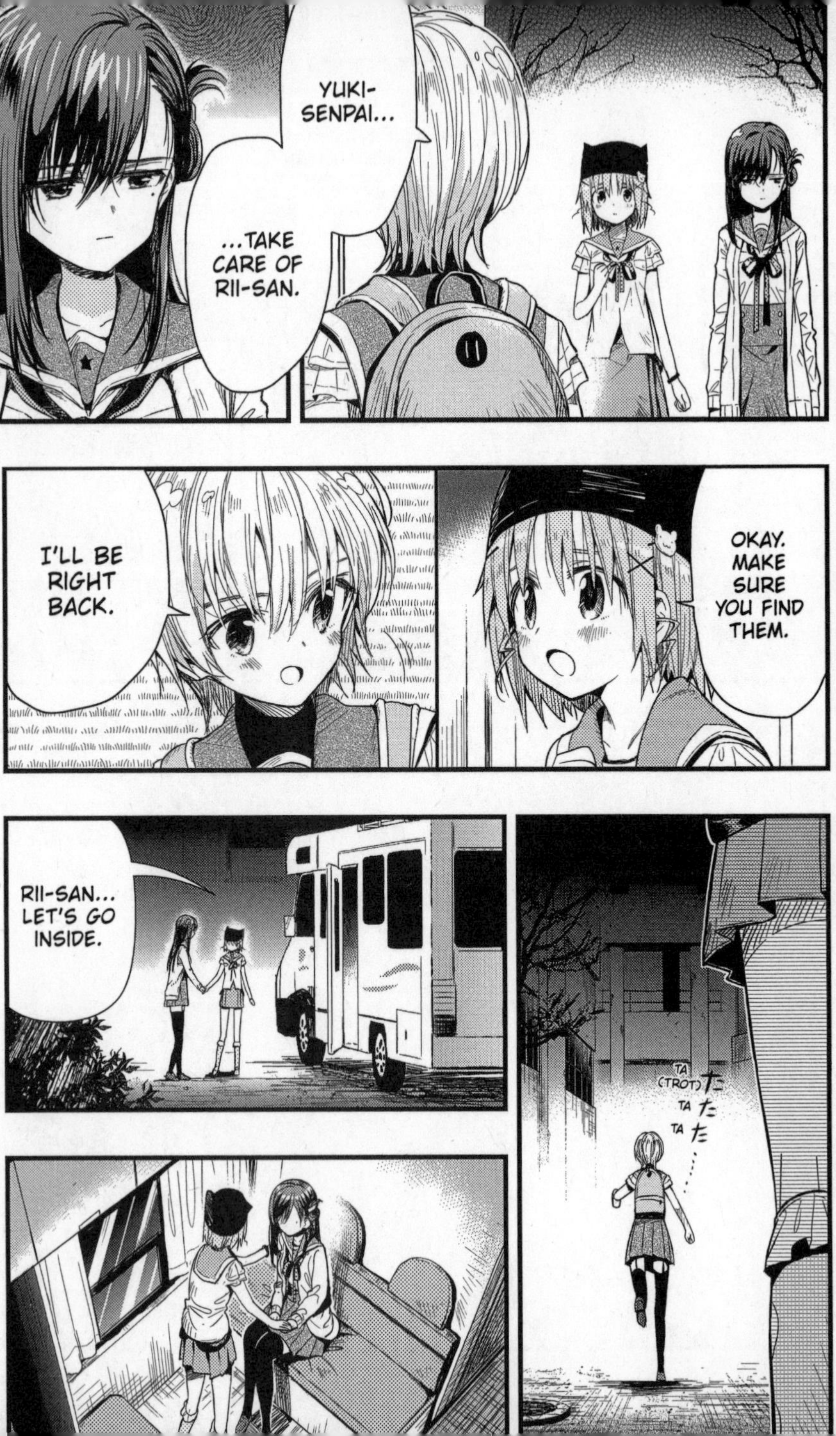
YUKI-SENPAI...
...TAKE CARE OF RII-SAN.
OKAY. MAKE SURE YOU FIND THEM.
I'LL BE RIGHT BACK.
TA (TROT) TA TA
RII-SAN... LET'S GO INSIDE.

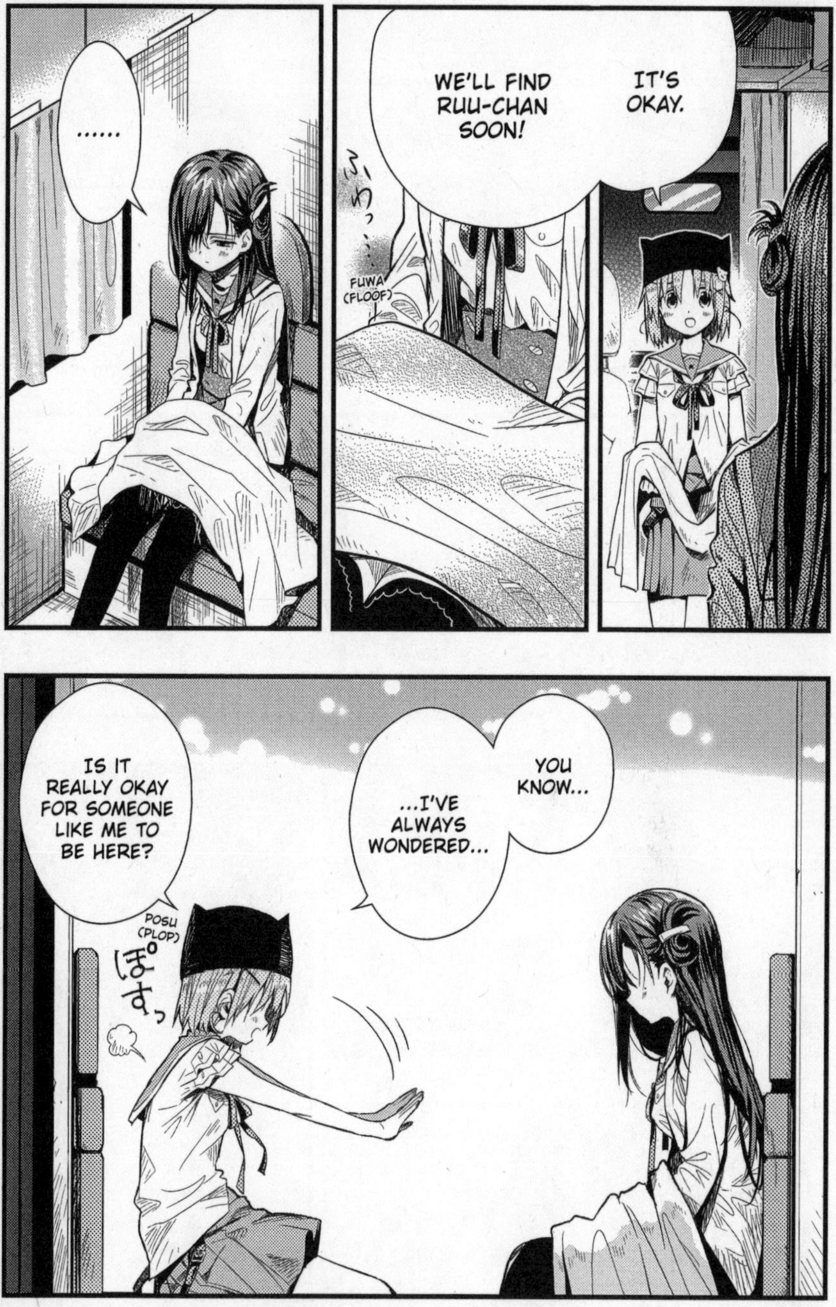
IT'S OKAY.
WE'LL FIND RUU-CHAN SOON!
ふわっ…
FUWA (FLOOF)
......
YOU KNOW...
...I'VE ALWAYS WONDERED...
IS IT REALLY OKAY FOR SOMEONE LIKE ME TO BE HERE?
POSU (PLOP)
ぽすっ

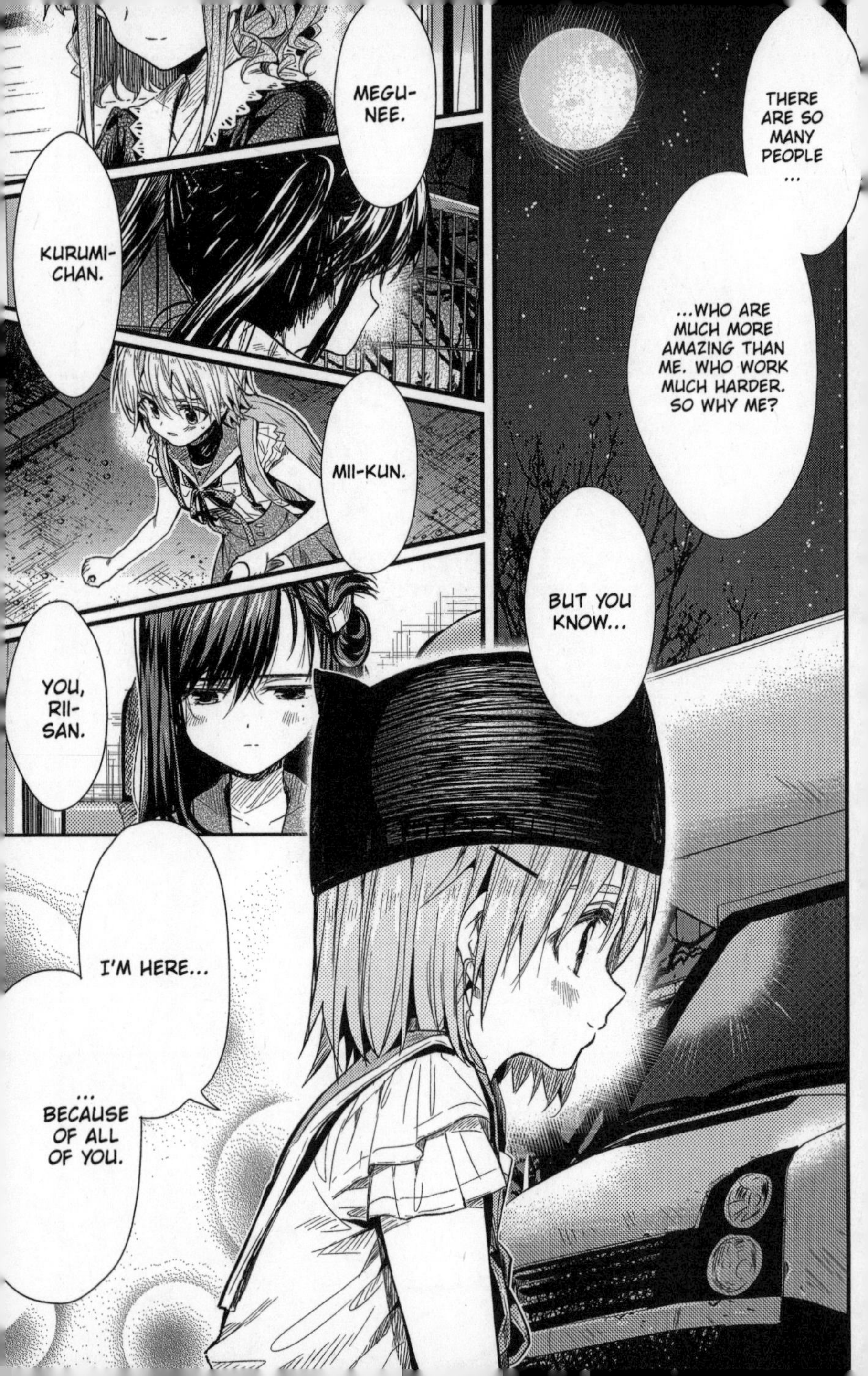
THERE ARE SO MANY PEOPLE...
...WHO ARE MUCH MORE AMAZING THAN ME. WHO WORK MUCH HARDER. SO WHY ME?
BUT YOU KNOW...
MEGU-NEE.
KURUMI-CHAN.
MII-KUN.
YOU, RII-SAN.
I'M HERE...
...BECAUSE OF ALL OF YOU.

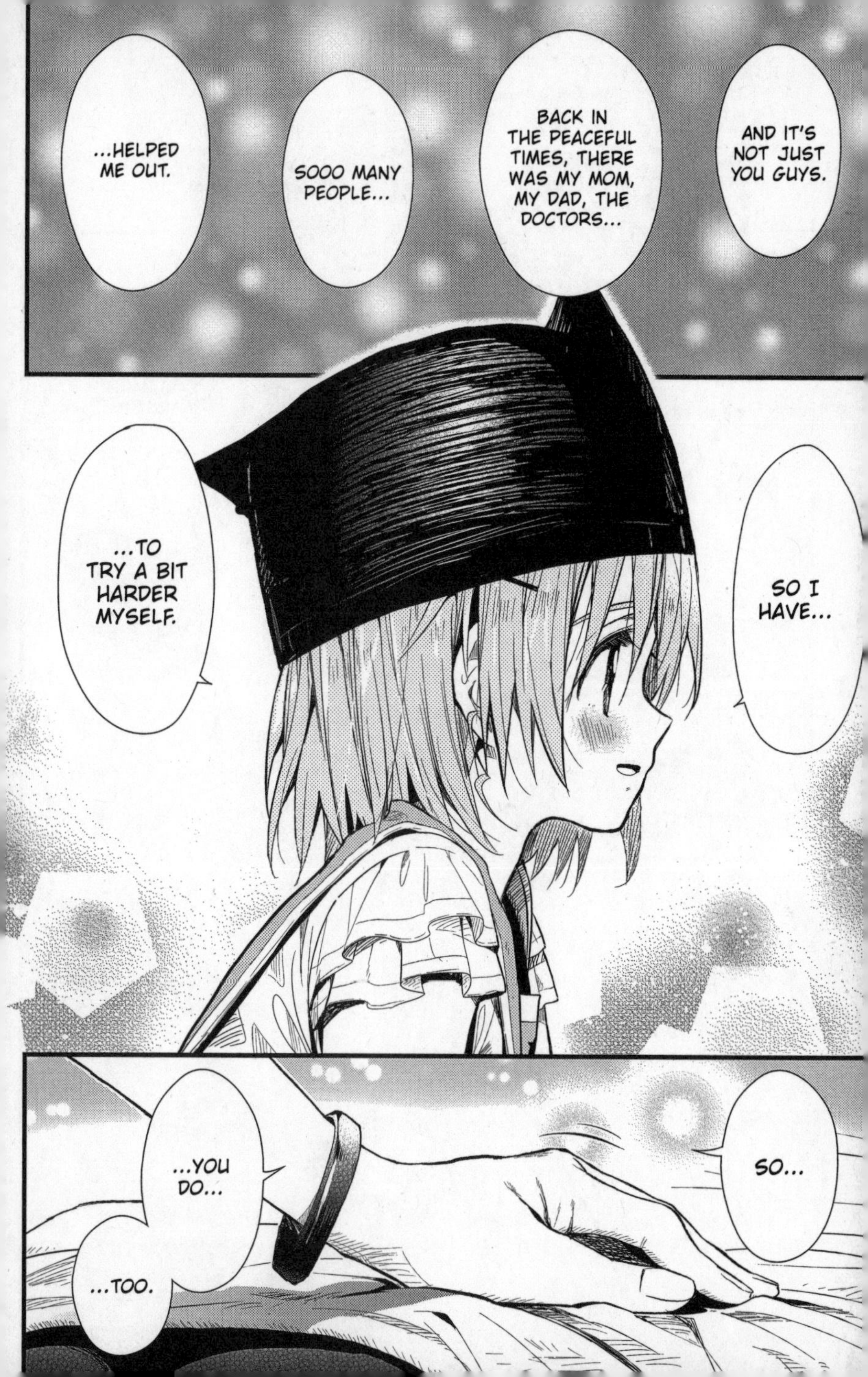
AND IT'S NOT JUST YOU GUYS.
BACK IN THE PEACEFUL TIMES, THERE WAS MY MOM, MY DAD, THE DOCTORS...
SOOO MANY PEOPLE...
...HELPED ME OUT.
SO I HAVE...
...TO TRY A BIT HARDER MYSELF.
SO...
...YOU DO...
...TOO.

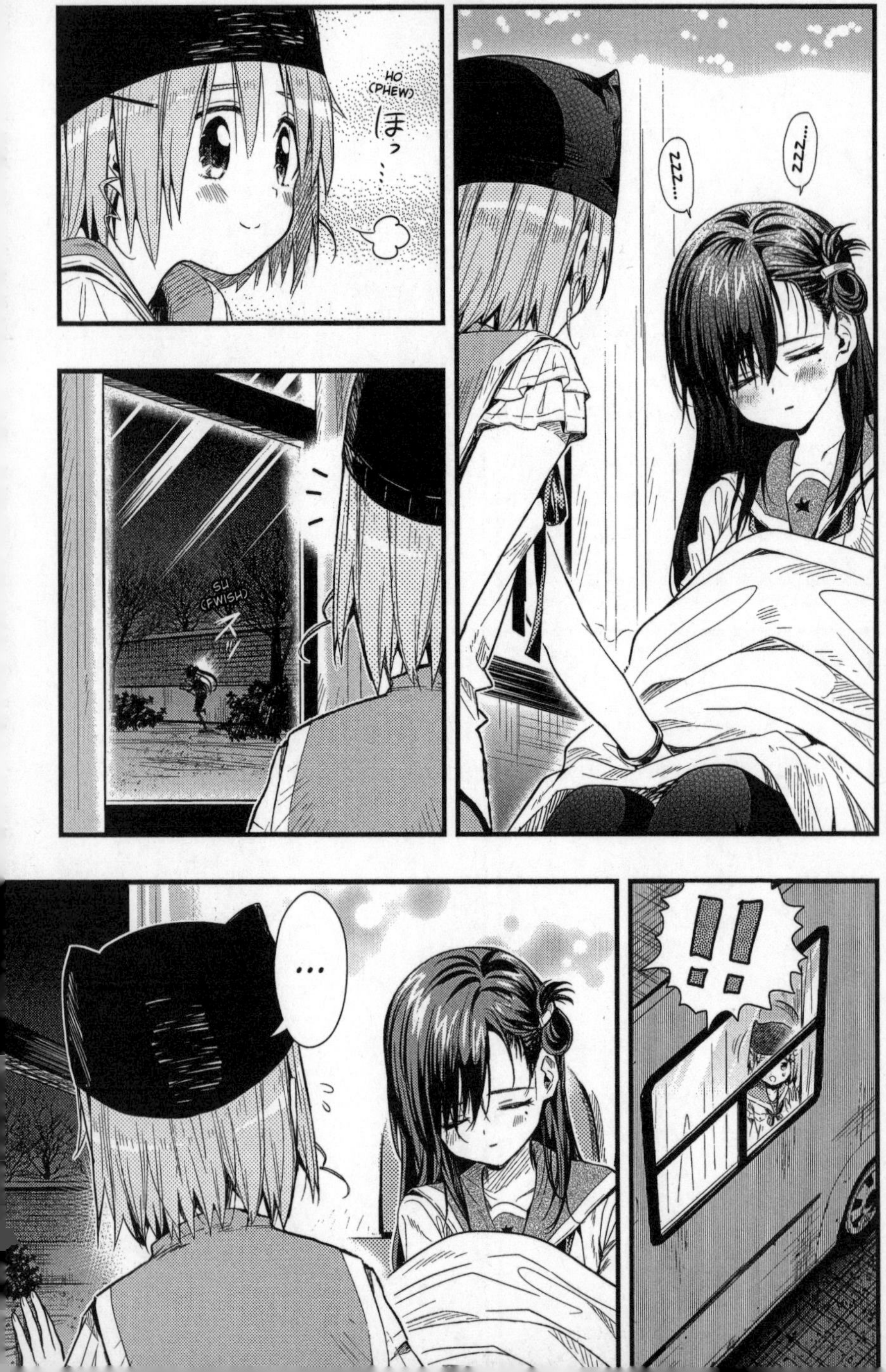
zzz...
zzz...
HO (PHEW)
ほっ…
SU (FWISH)
!!
...

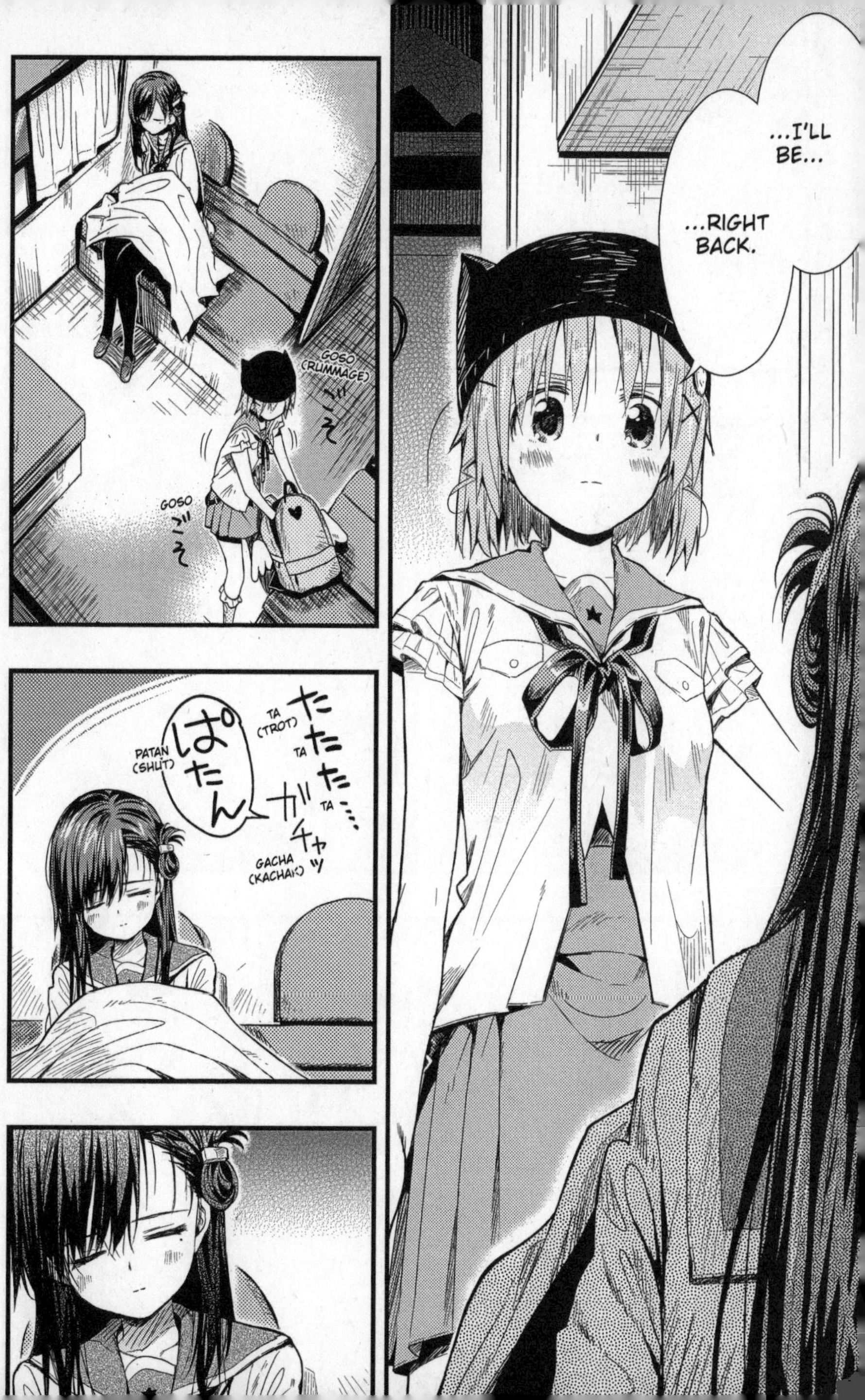
...I'LL BE...
...RIGHT BACK.
GOSO (RUMMAGE) ごそ
GOSO ごそ
TA (TROT) TA TA たたた…
PATAN (SHUT) ぱたん
GACHA (KACHAK) ガチャッ

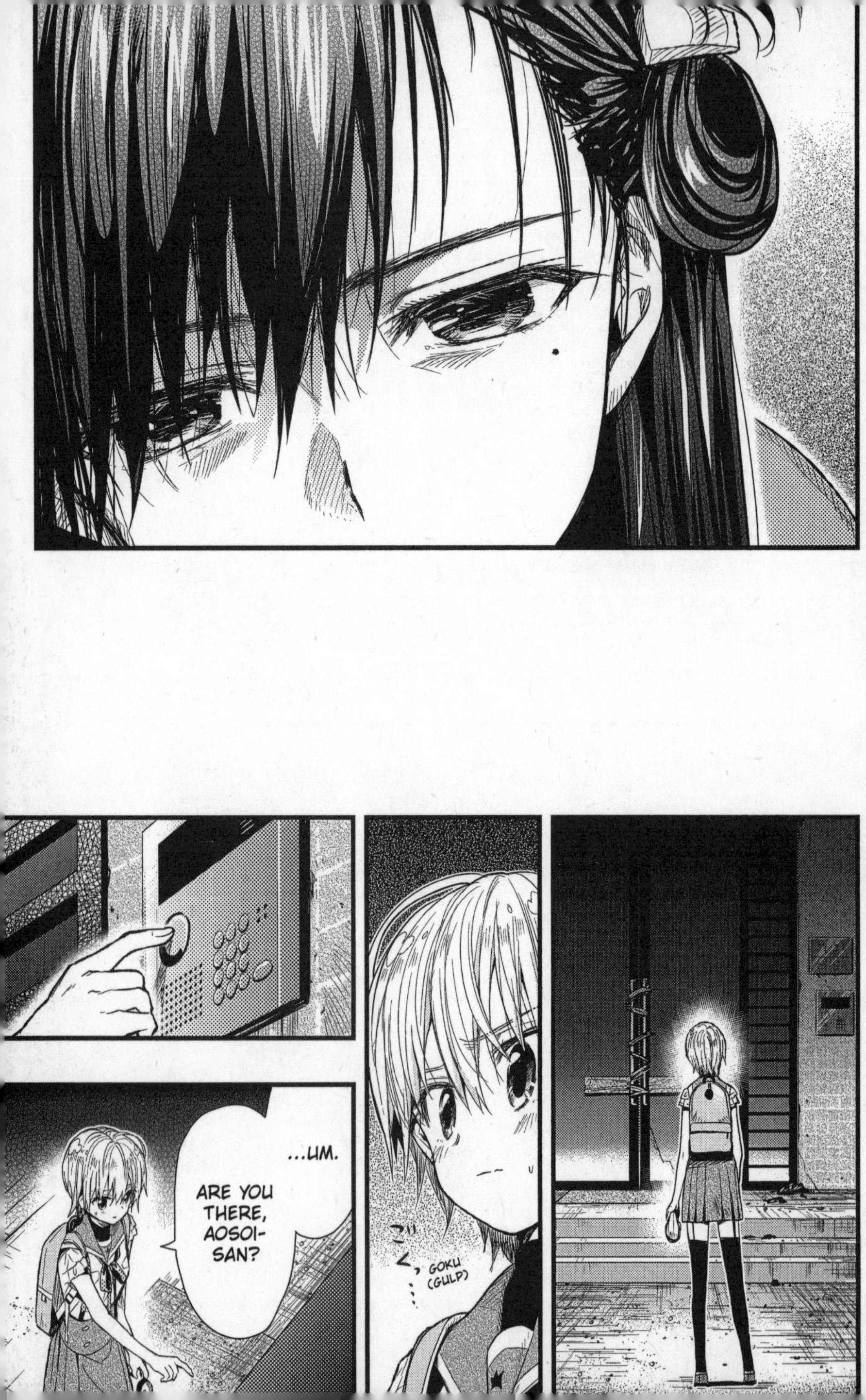
GOKU (GULP)
...UM.
ARE YOU THERE, AOSOI-SAN?

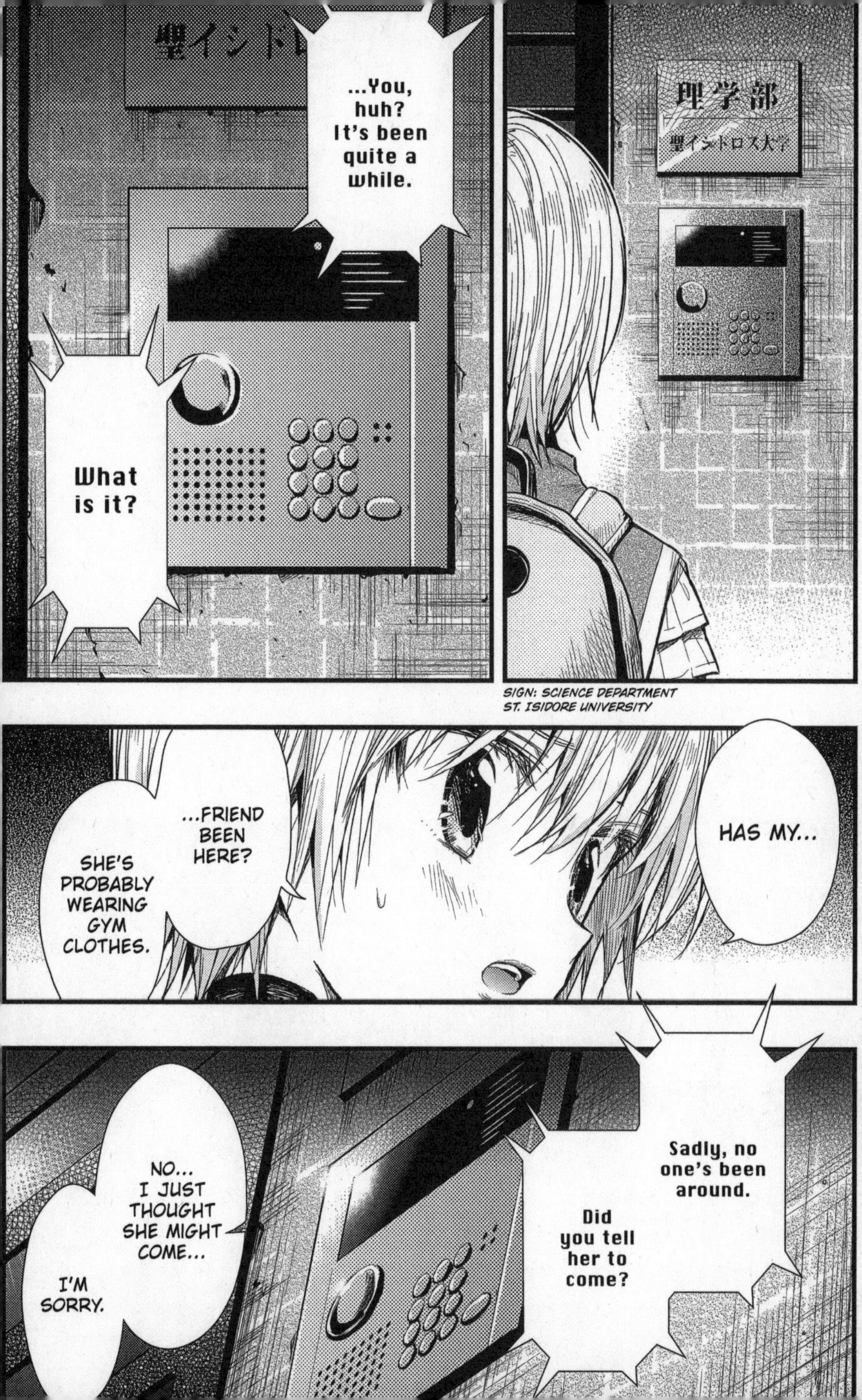
理学部
聖インドロス大学
SIGN: SCIENCE DEPARTMENT
ST. ISIDORE UNIVERSITY
...You, huh? It's been quite a while.
What is it?
HAS MY...
...FRIEND BEEN HERE?
SHE'S PROBABLY WEARING GYM CLOTHES.
Sadly, no one's been around.
Did you tell her to come?
NO... I JUST THOUGHT SHE MIGHT COME...
I'M SORRY.

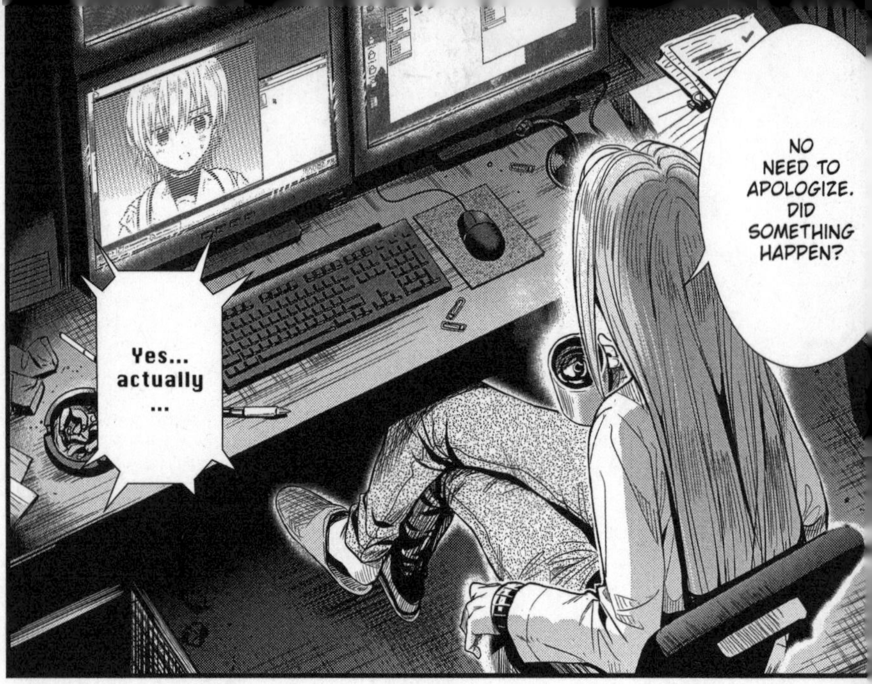
NO NEED TO APOLOGIZE. DID SOMETHING HAPPEN?
Yes... actually ...

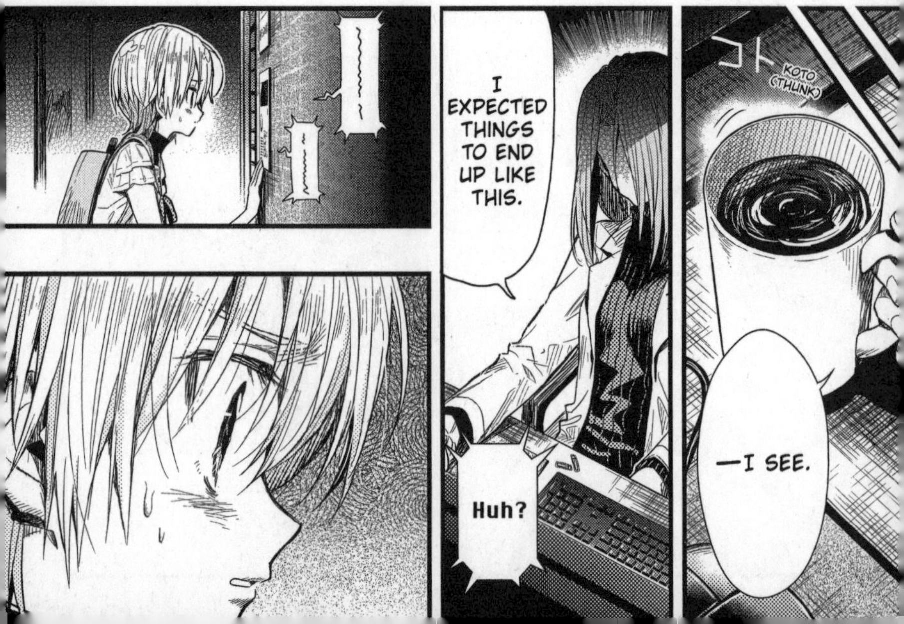
KOTO (THUNK)
—I SEE.
I EXPECTED THINGS TO END UP LIKE THIS.
Huh?

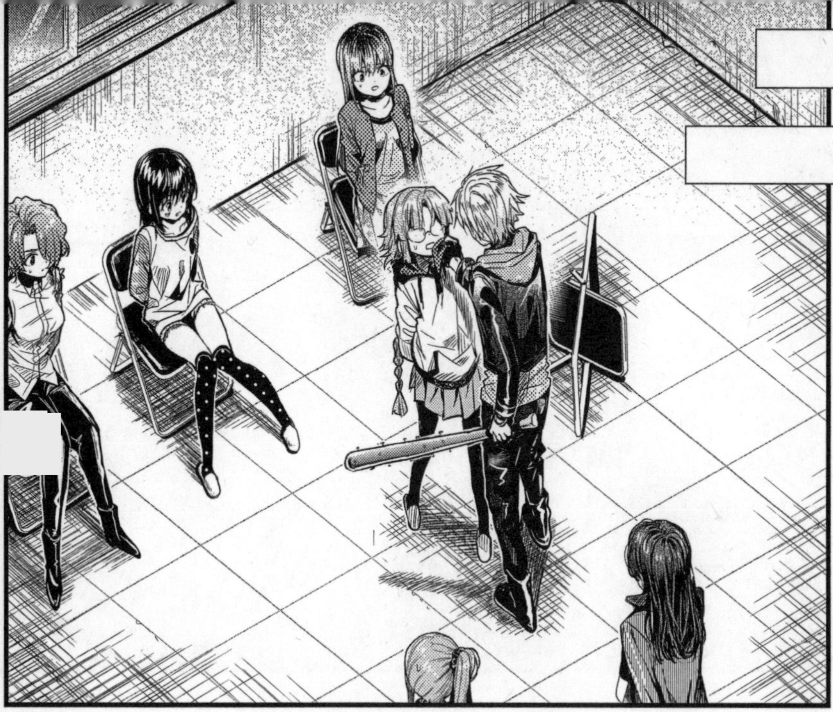

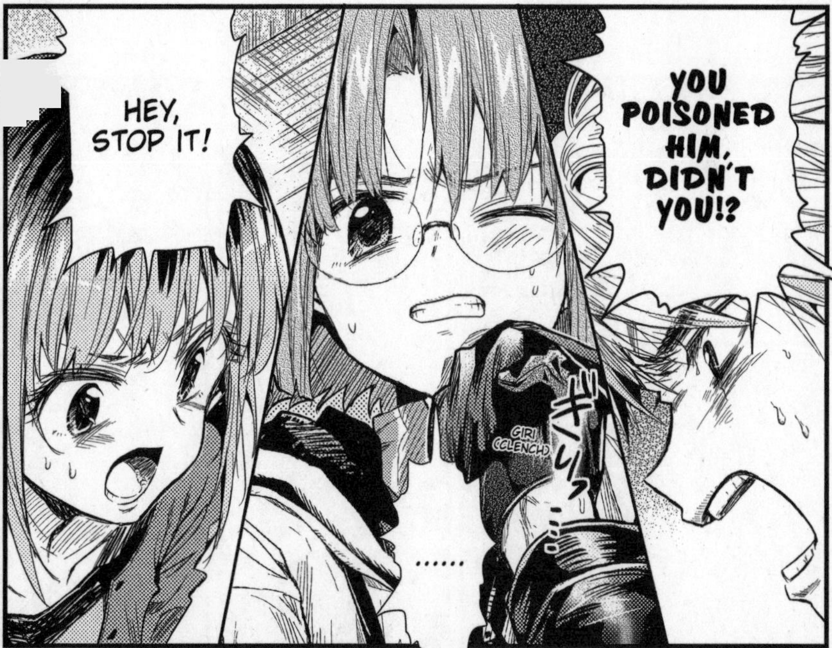
YOU POISONED HIM, DIDN'T YOU!?
HEY, STOP IT!
GIRI (CLENCH)
......

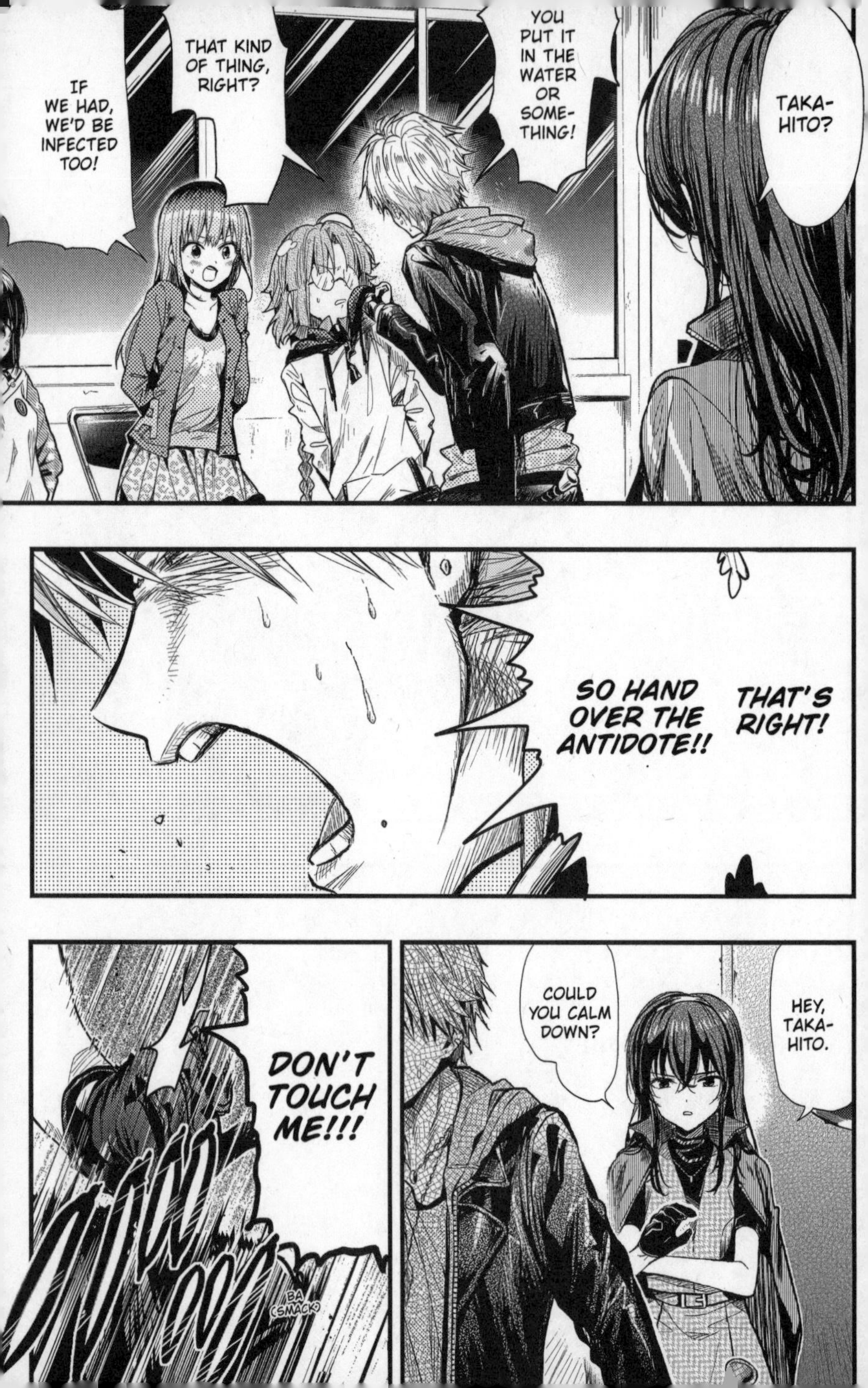
TAKA-HITO?
YOU PUT IT IN THE WATER OR SOME-THING!
THAT KIND OF THING, RIGHT?
IF WE HAD, WE'D BE INFECTED TOO!
THAT'S RIGHT!
SO HAND OVER THE ANTIDOTE!!
HEY, TAKA-HITO.
COULD YOU CALM DOWN?
DON'T TOUCH ME!!!
BA (SMACK)

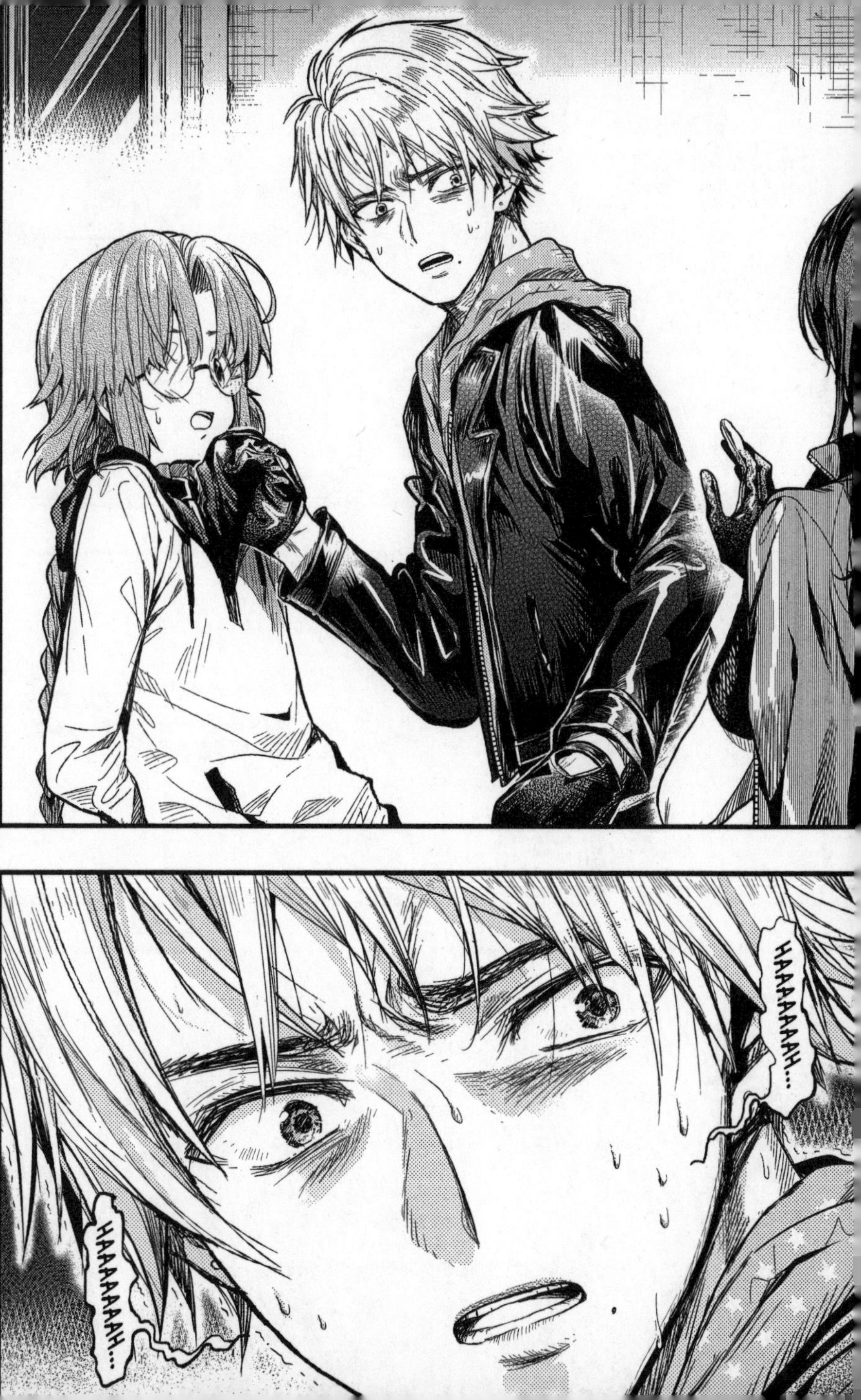
HAAAAAAH...
HAAAAAAH...

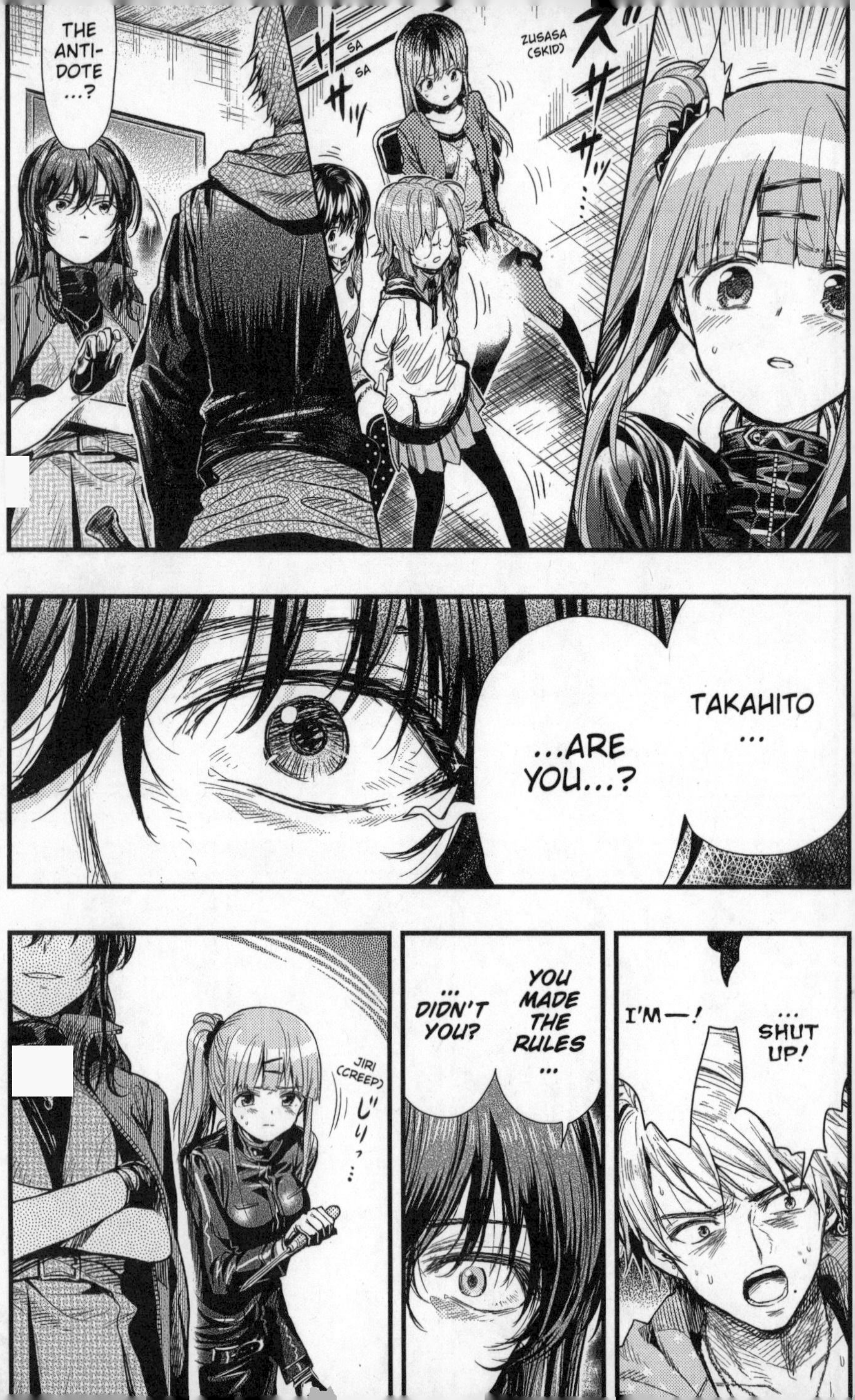
ZUSASA (SKID)
SA
SA
THE ANTI-DOTE ...?
TAKAHITO ...
...ARE YOU...?
... SHUT UP!
I'M—!
YOU MADE THE RULES ...
... DIDN'T YOU?
JIRI (CREEP)

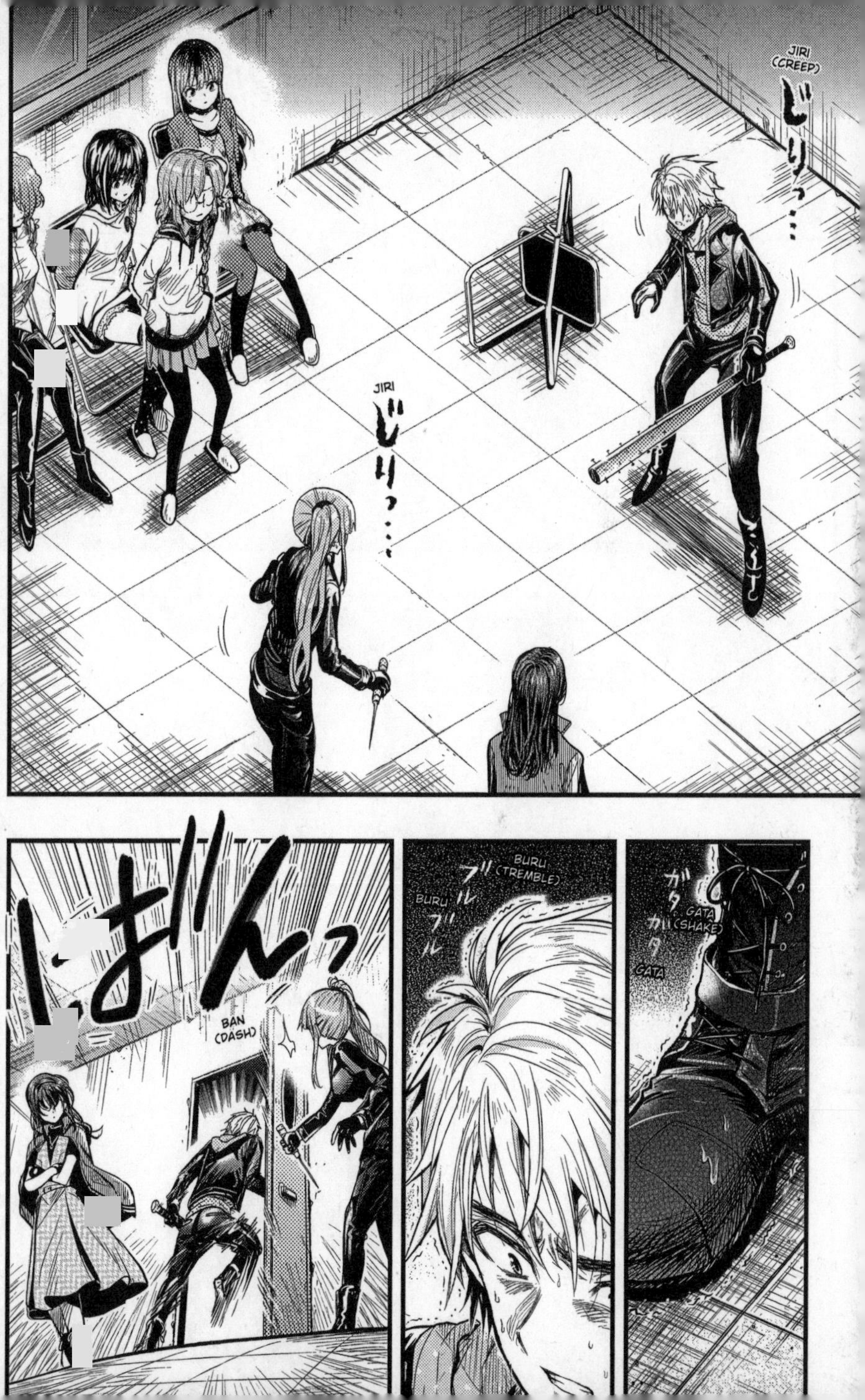
JIRI (CREEP)
JIRI
GATA (SHAKE)
GATA
BURU (TREMBLE)
BURU
BAN (DASH)

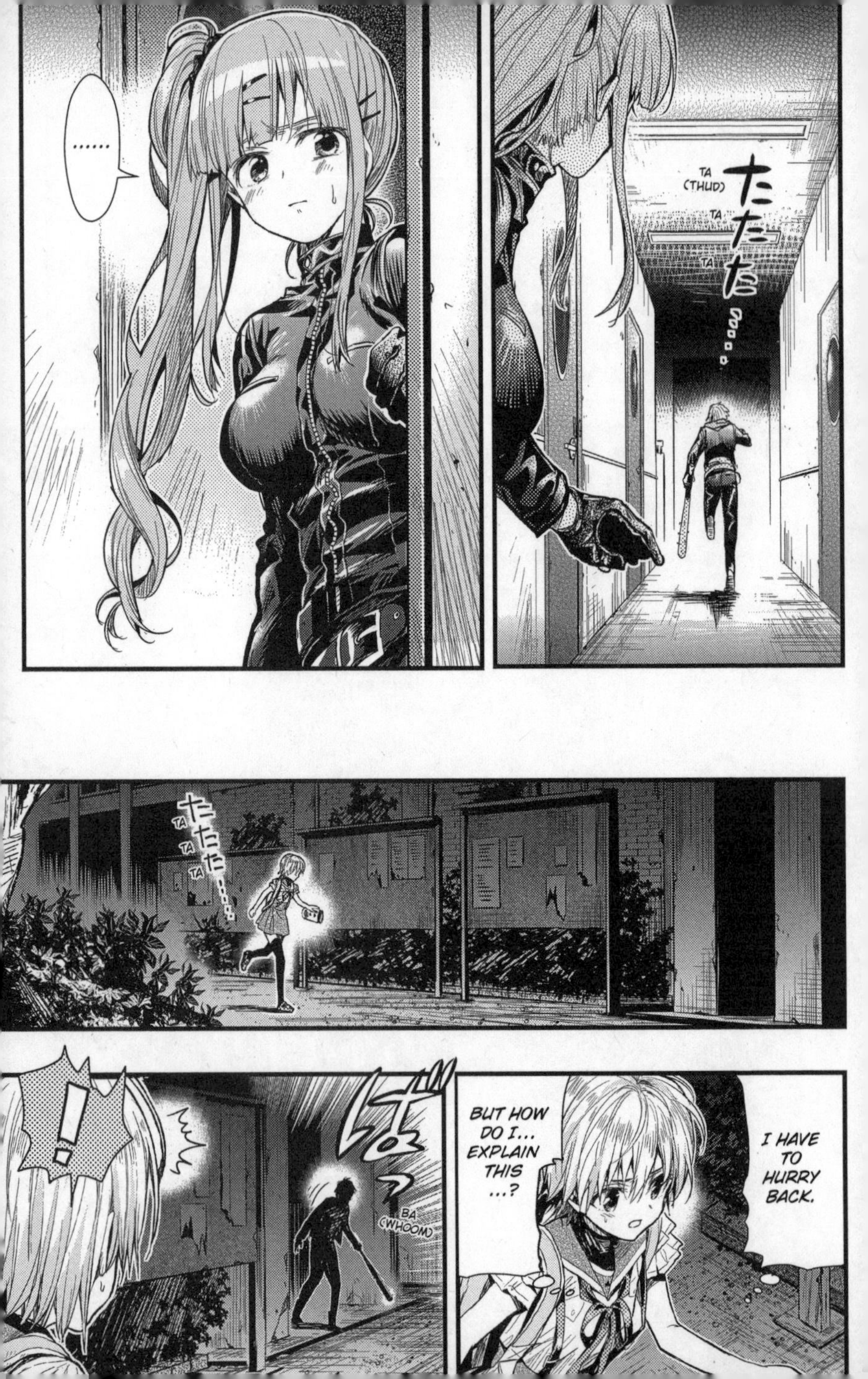
TA (THUD) TA TA
たたた
......
TA TA TA
たたた
I HAVE TO HURRY BACK.
BUT HOW DO I... EXPLAIN THIS ...?
BA (WHOOM)
!

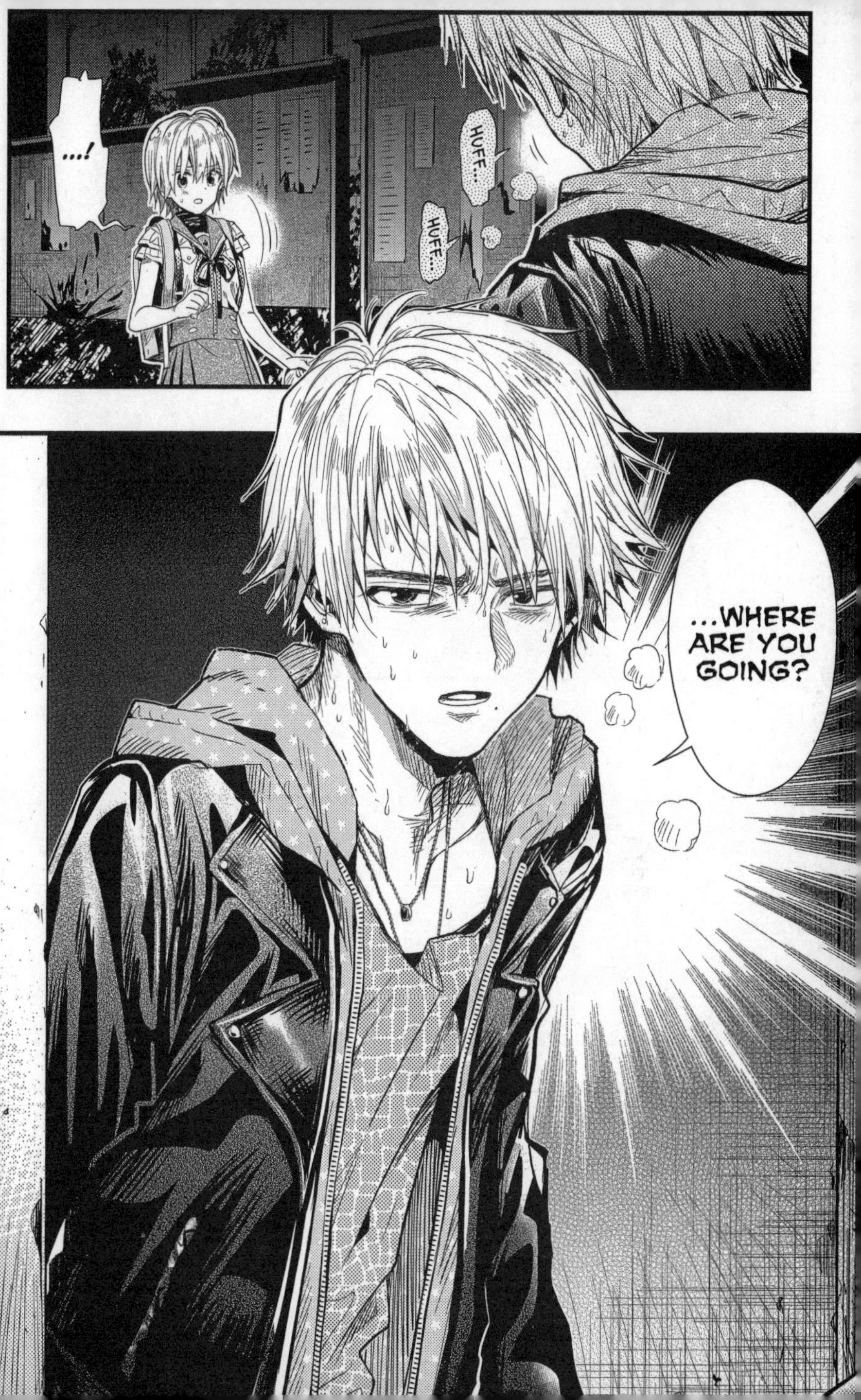
HUFF...
HUFF...
...!
...WHERE ARE YOU GOING?

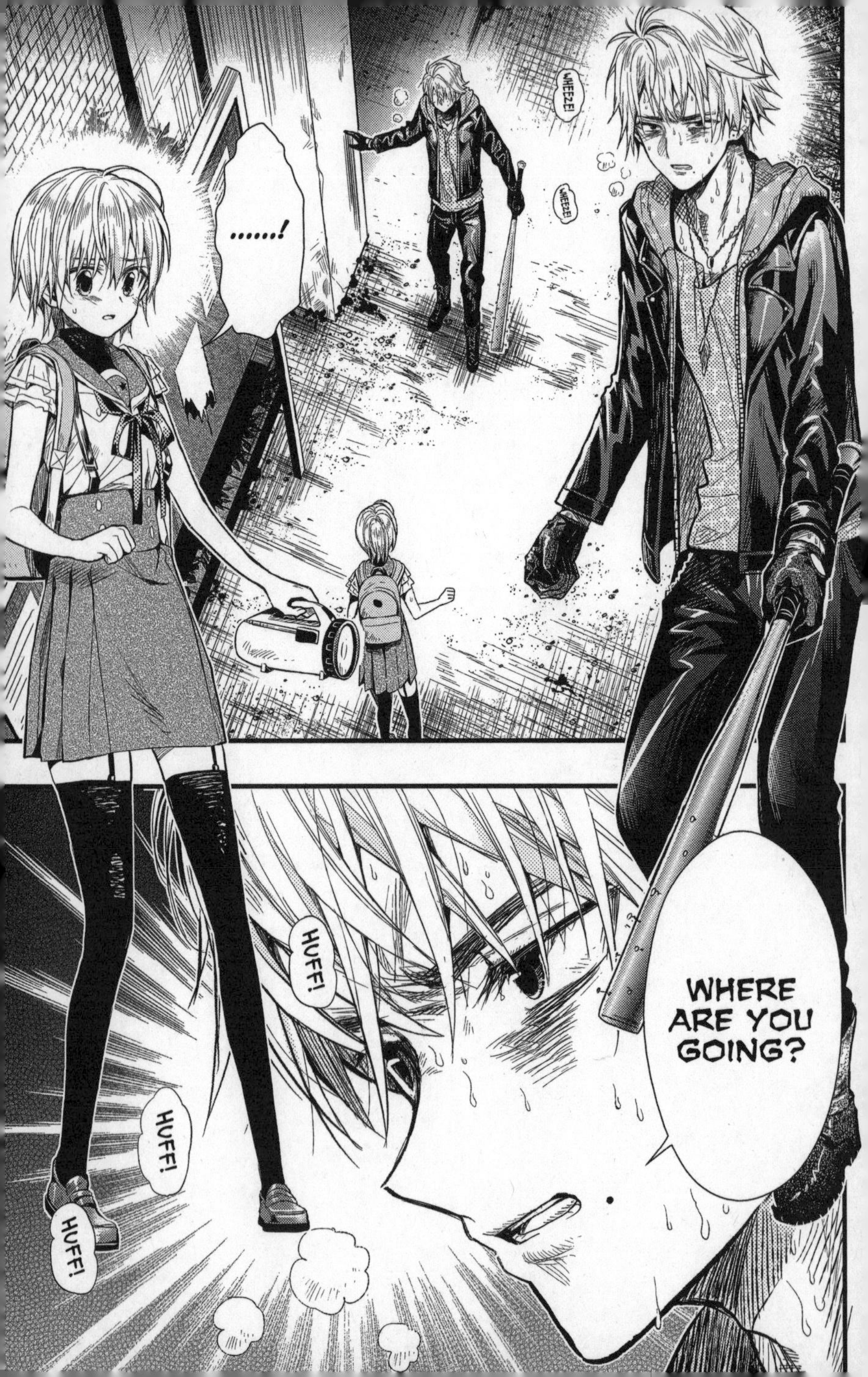
WHEEZE!
WHEEZE!
......!
WHERE ARE YOU GOING?
HUFF!
HUFF!
HUFF!

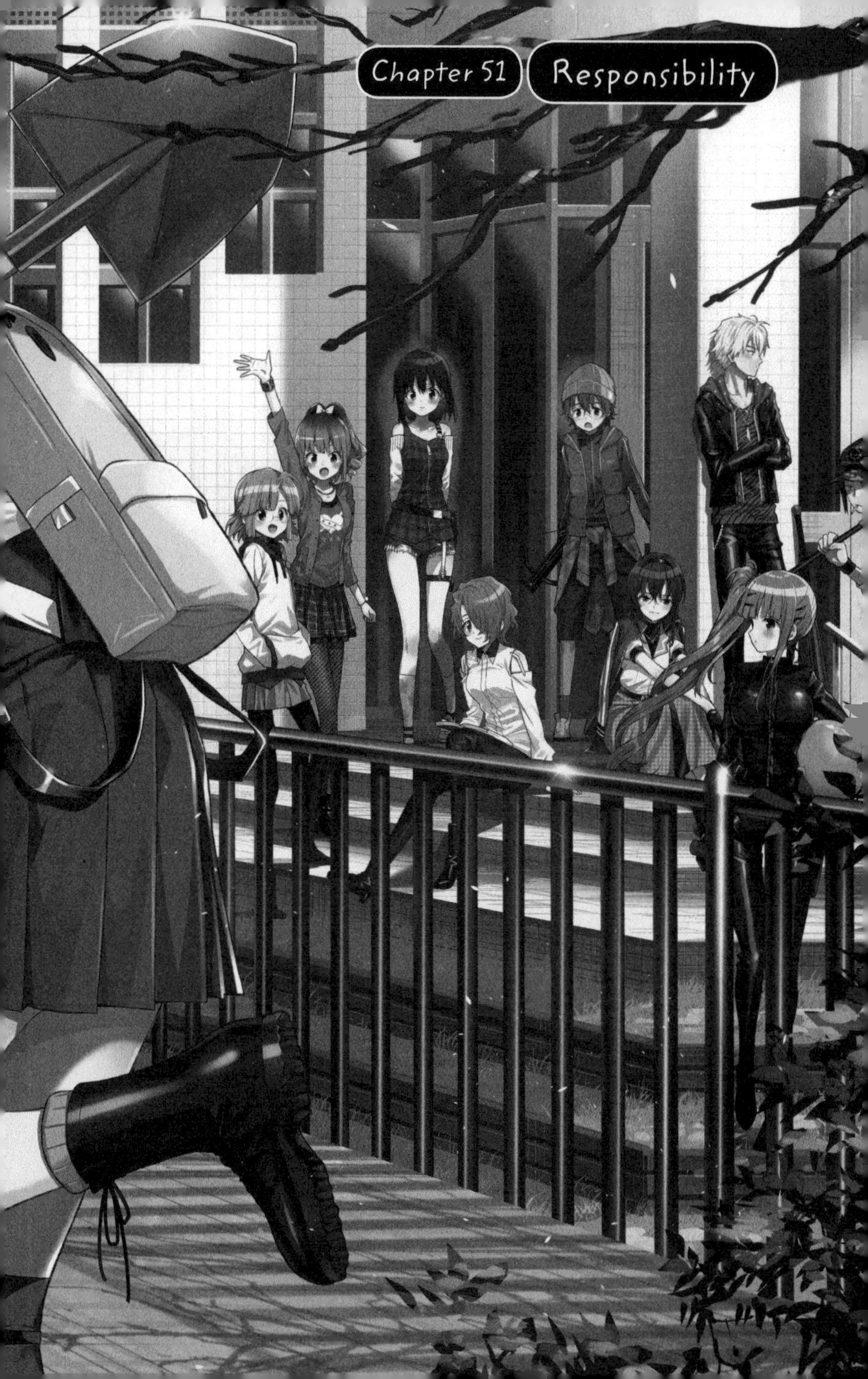
Chapter 51
Responsibility

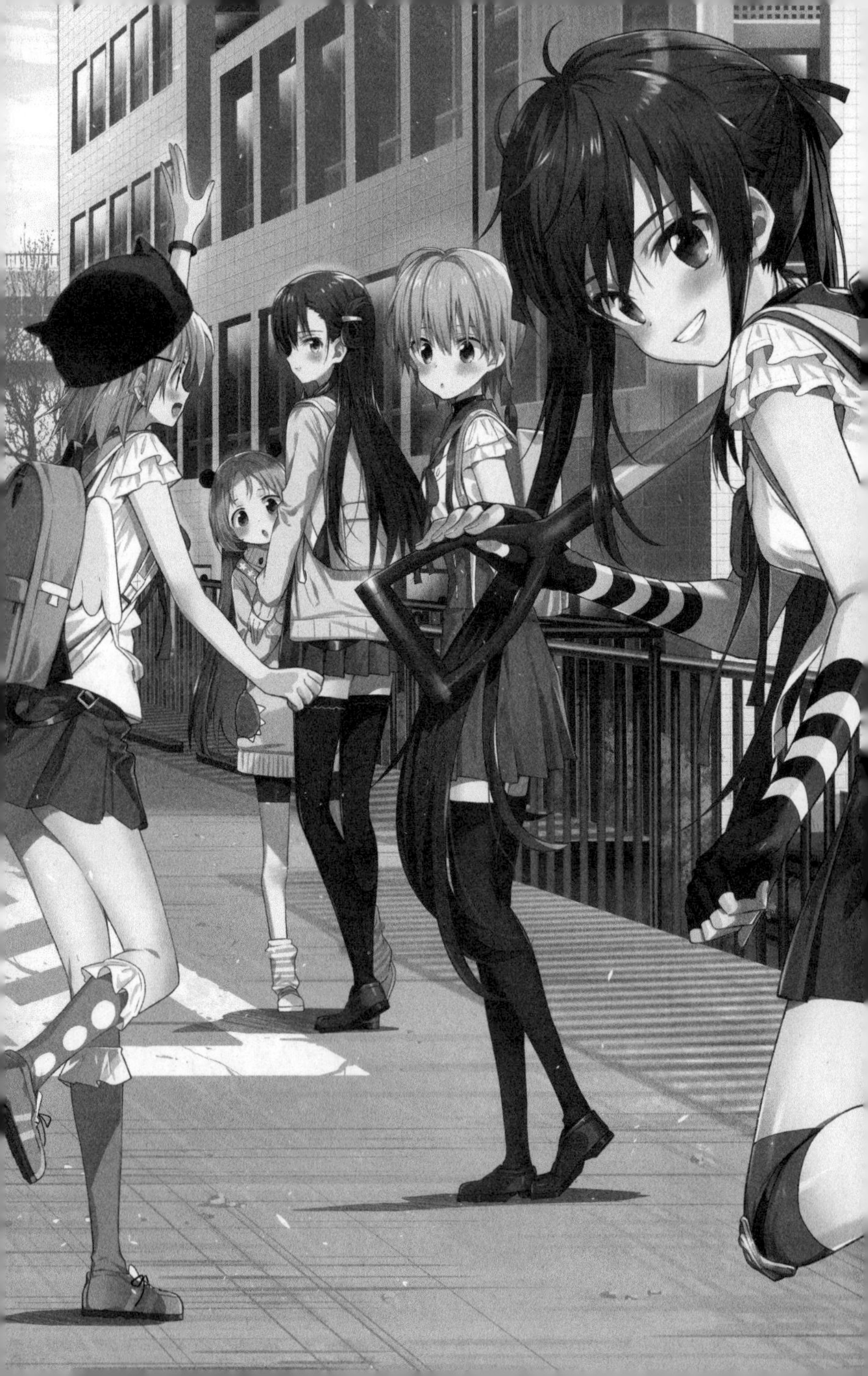

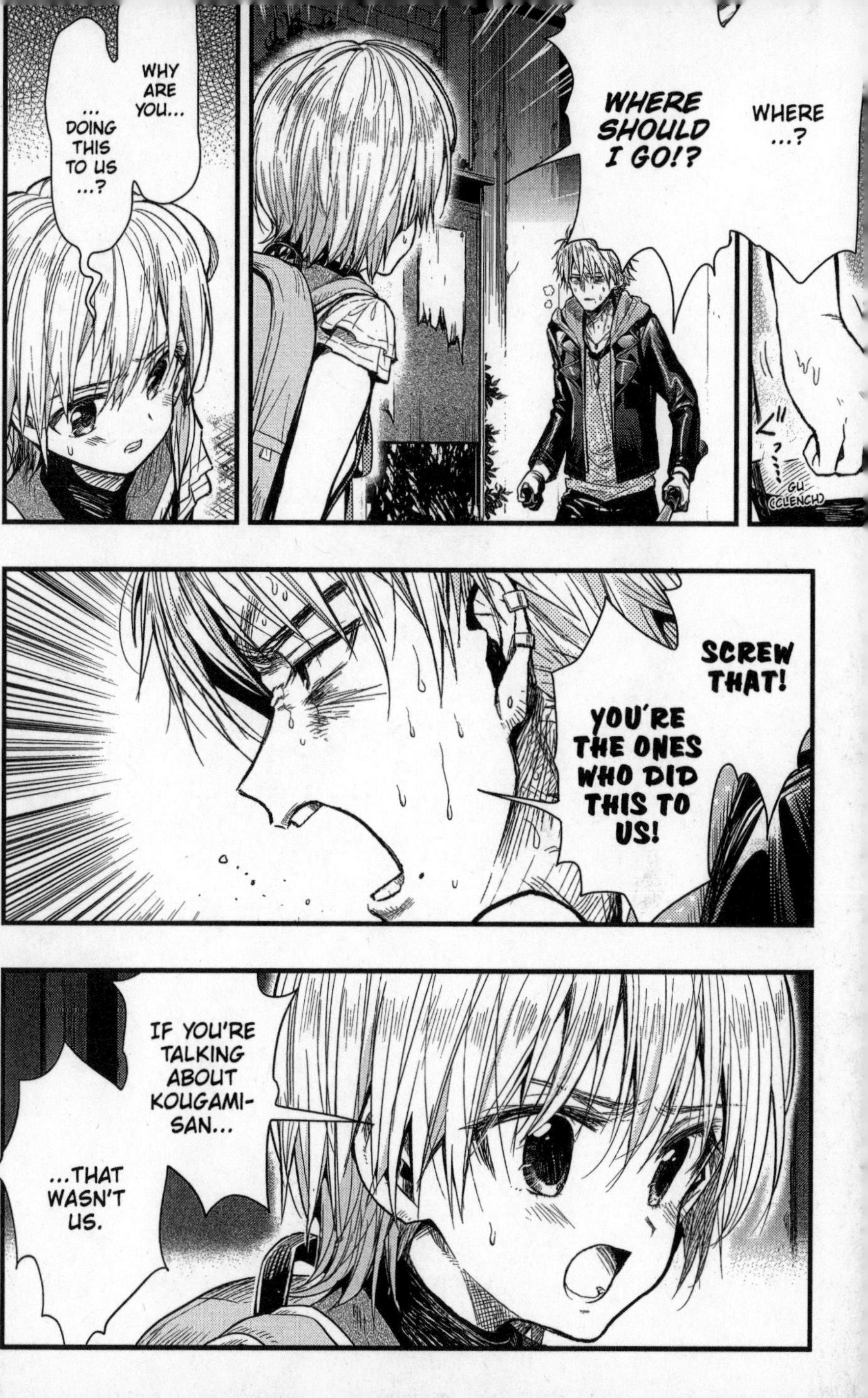
WHERE ...?
WHERE SHOULD I GO!?
GU (CLENCH)
WHY ARE YOU...
... DOING THIS TO US ...?
SCREW THAT!
YOU'RE THE ONES WHO DID THIS TO US!
IF YOU'RE TALKING ABOUT KOUGAMI-SAN...
...THAT WASN'T US.

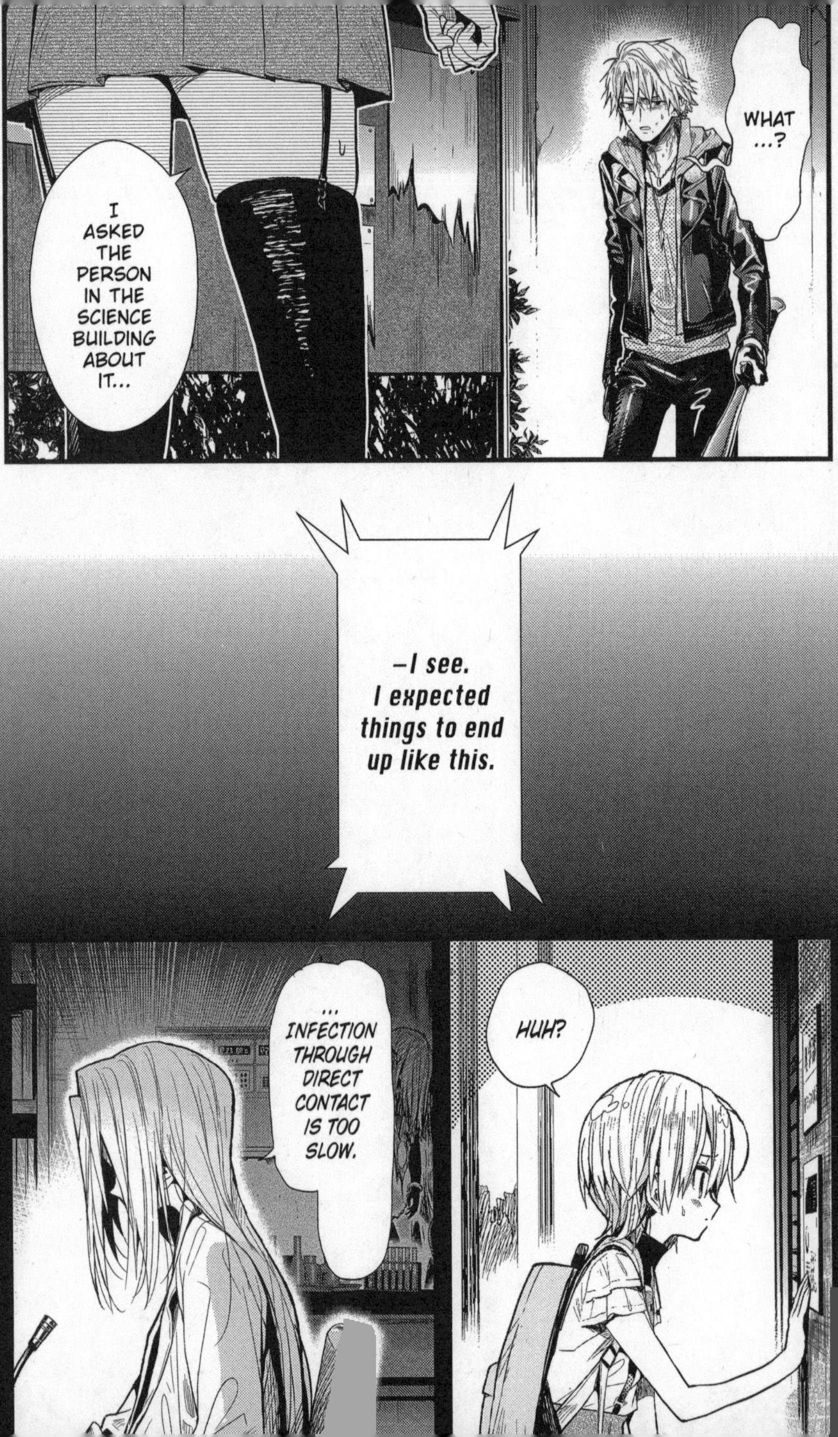
WHAT ...?
I ASKED THE PERSON IN THE SCIENCE BUILDING ABOUT IT...
—I see. I expected things to end up like this.
HUH?
... INFECTION THROUGH DIRECT CONTACT IS TOO SLOW.

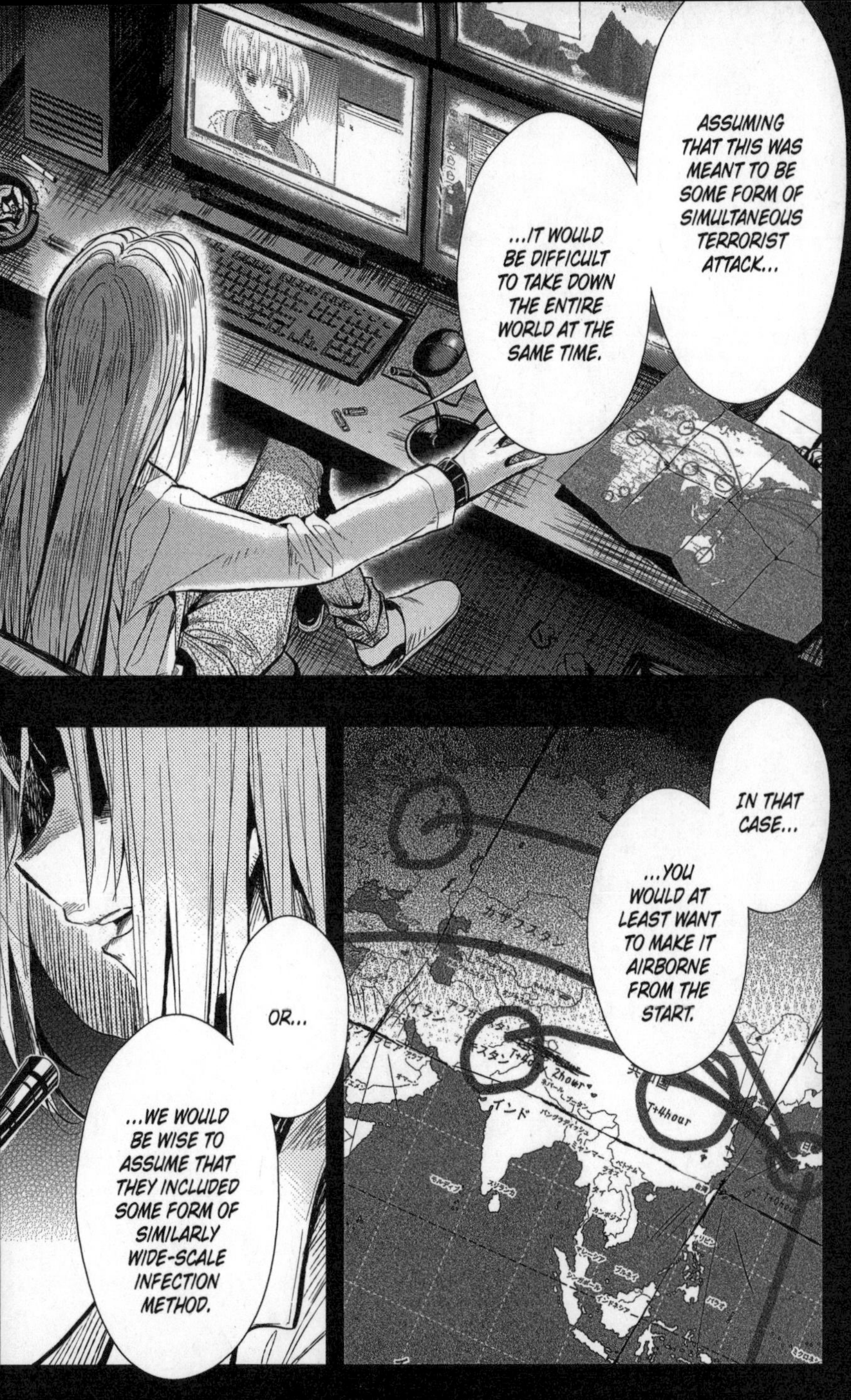
ASSUMING THAT THIS WAS MEANT TO BE SOME FORM OF SIMULTANEOUS TERRORIST ATTACK...
...IT WOULD BE DIFFICULT TO TAKE DOWN THE ENTIRE WORLD AT THE SAME TIME.
IN THAT CASE...
...YOU WOULD AT LEAST WANT TO MAKE IT AIRBORNE FROM THE START.
2hour
T+4hour
インド
OR...
...WE WOULD BE WISE TO ASSUME THAT THEY INCLUDED SOME FORM OF SIMILARLY WIDE-SCALE INFECTION METHOD.

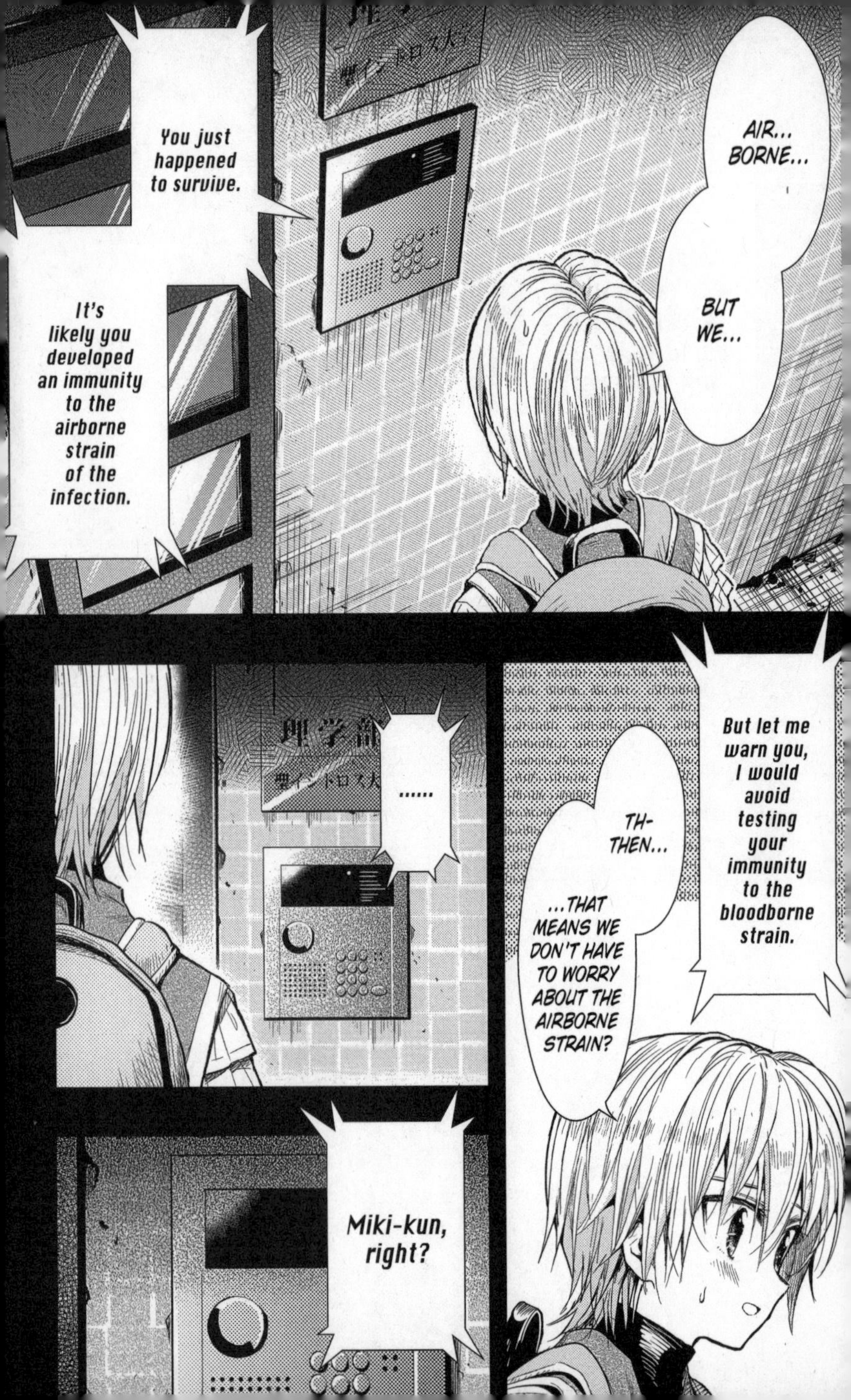
AIR... BORNE... BUT WE...
You just happened to survive.
It's likely you developed an immunity to the airborne strain of the infection.
But let me warn you, I would avoid testing your immunity to the bloodborne strain.
TH- THEN... ...THAT MEANS WE DON'T HAVE TO WORRY ABOUT THE AIRBORNE STRAIN?
......
Miki-kun, right?

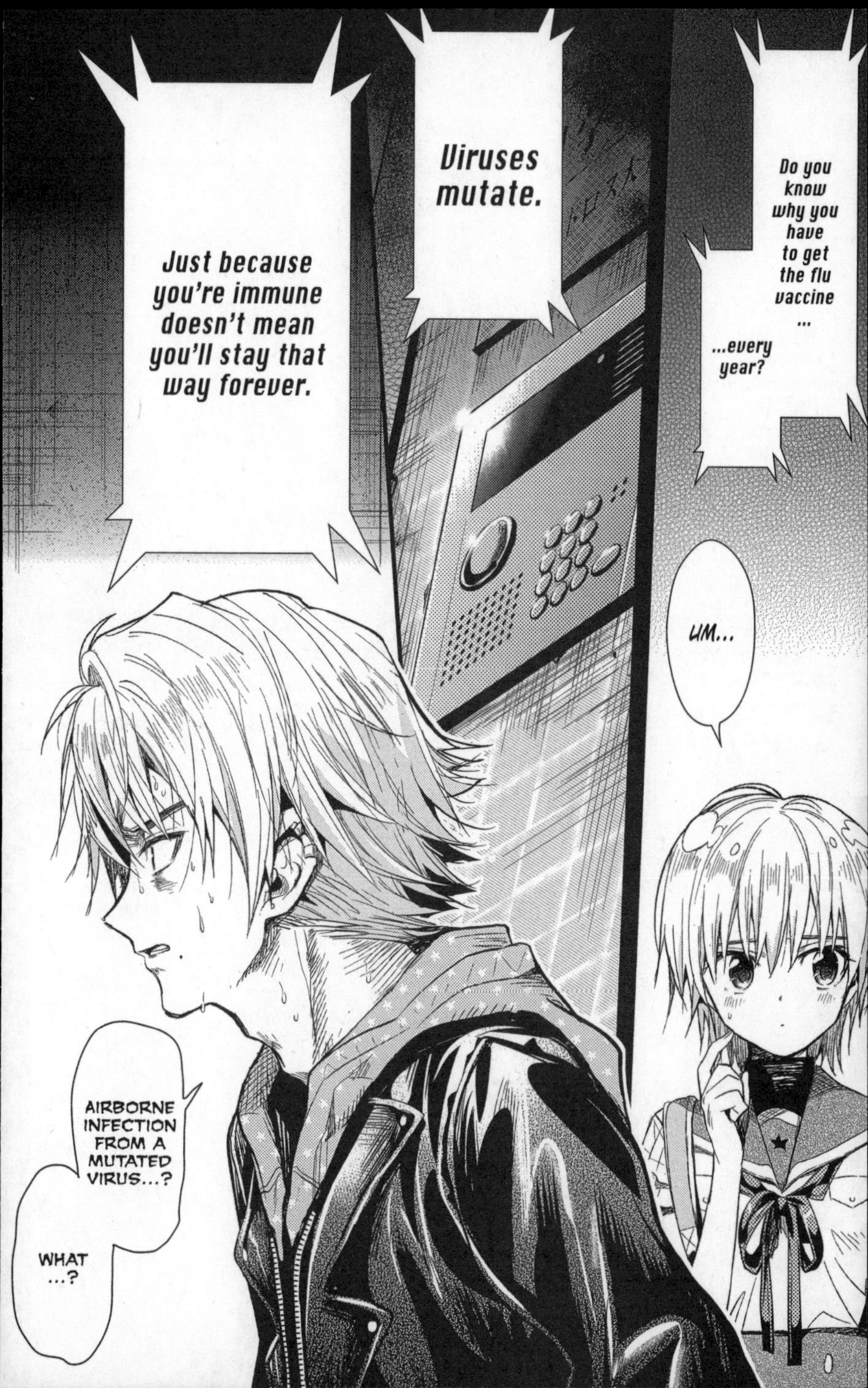
Do you know why you have to get the flu vaccine ...
...every year?
Viruses mutate.
Just because you're immune doesn't mean you'll stay that way forever.
UM...
AIRBORNE INFECTION FROM A MUTATED VIRUS...?
WHAT ...?

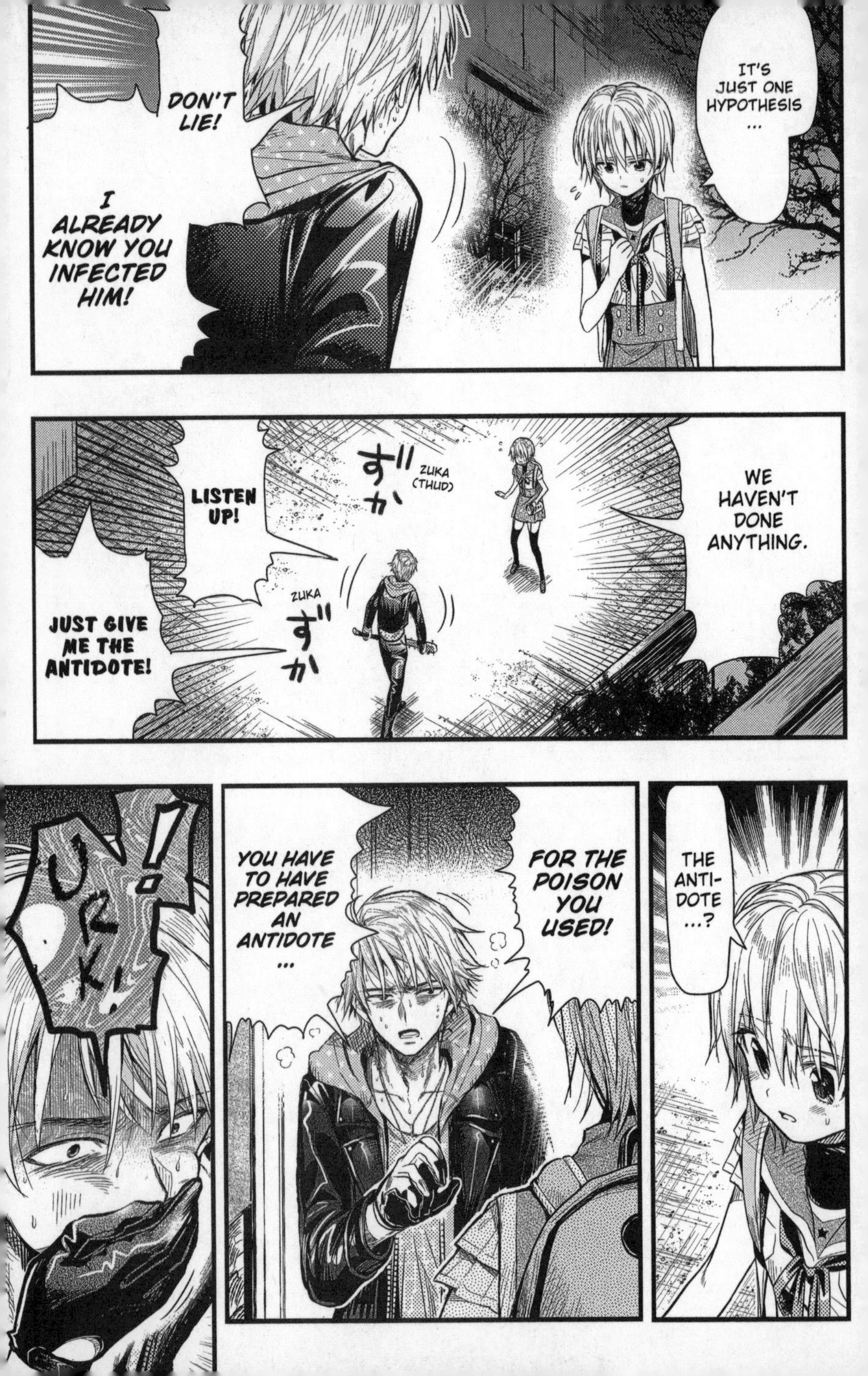
IT'S JUST ONE HYPOTHESIS ...
DON'T LIE!
I ALREADY KNOW YOU INFECTED HIM!
WE HAVEN'T DONE ANYTHING.
ずか
ZUKA (THUD)
LISTEN UP!
ずか
ZUKA
JUST GIVE ME THE ANTIDOTE!
THE ANTI-DOTE ...?
YOU HAVE TO HAVE PREPARED AN ANTIDOTE ...
FOR THE POISON YOU USED!
URK!

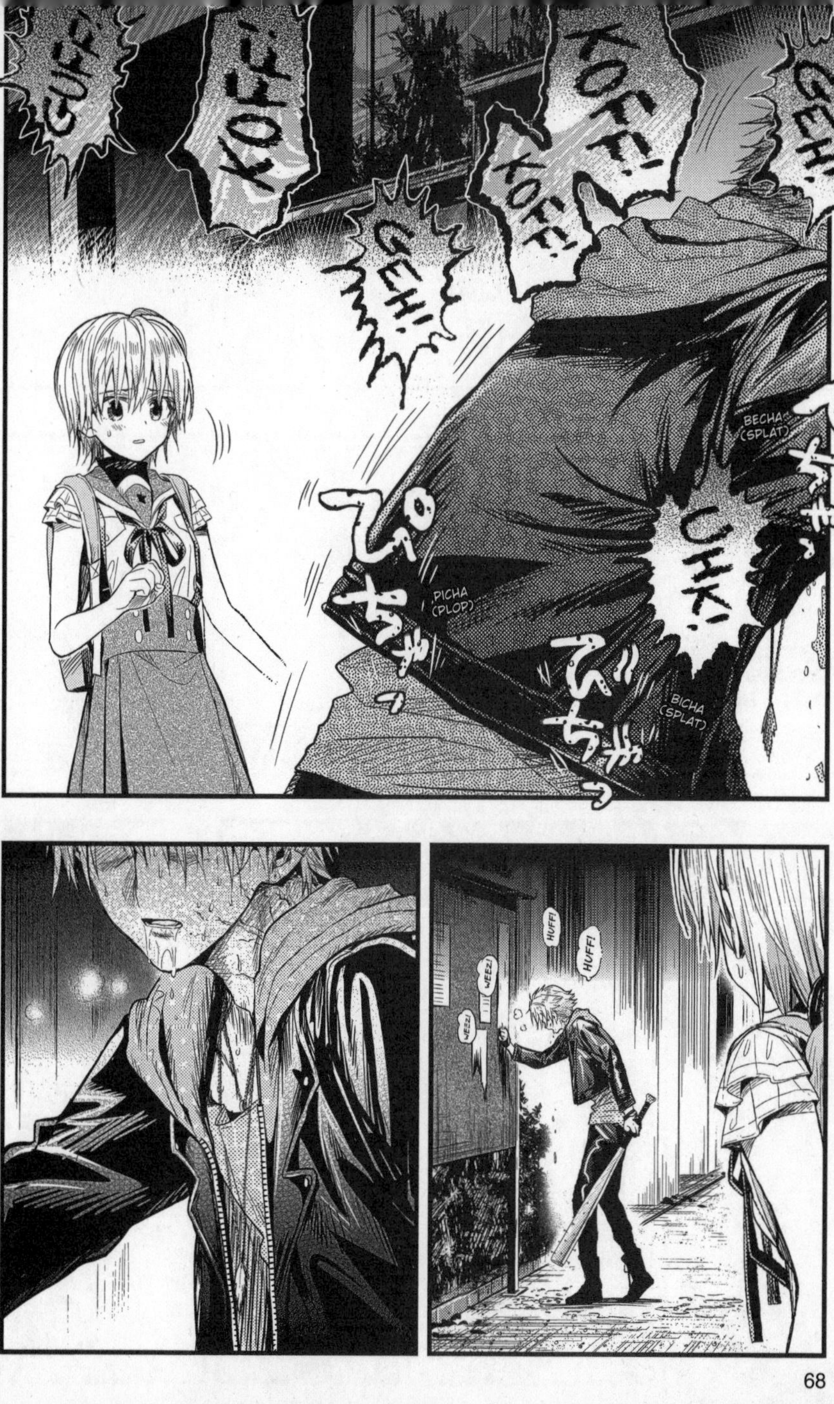
GEH!
KOFF! KOFF!
KOH!
GUH!
GEH!
BECHA (SPLAT)
UHK!
BICHA (SPLAT)
PICHA (PLOP)
HUFF!
HUFF!
WEEZ!
WEEZ!

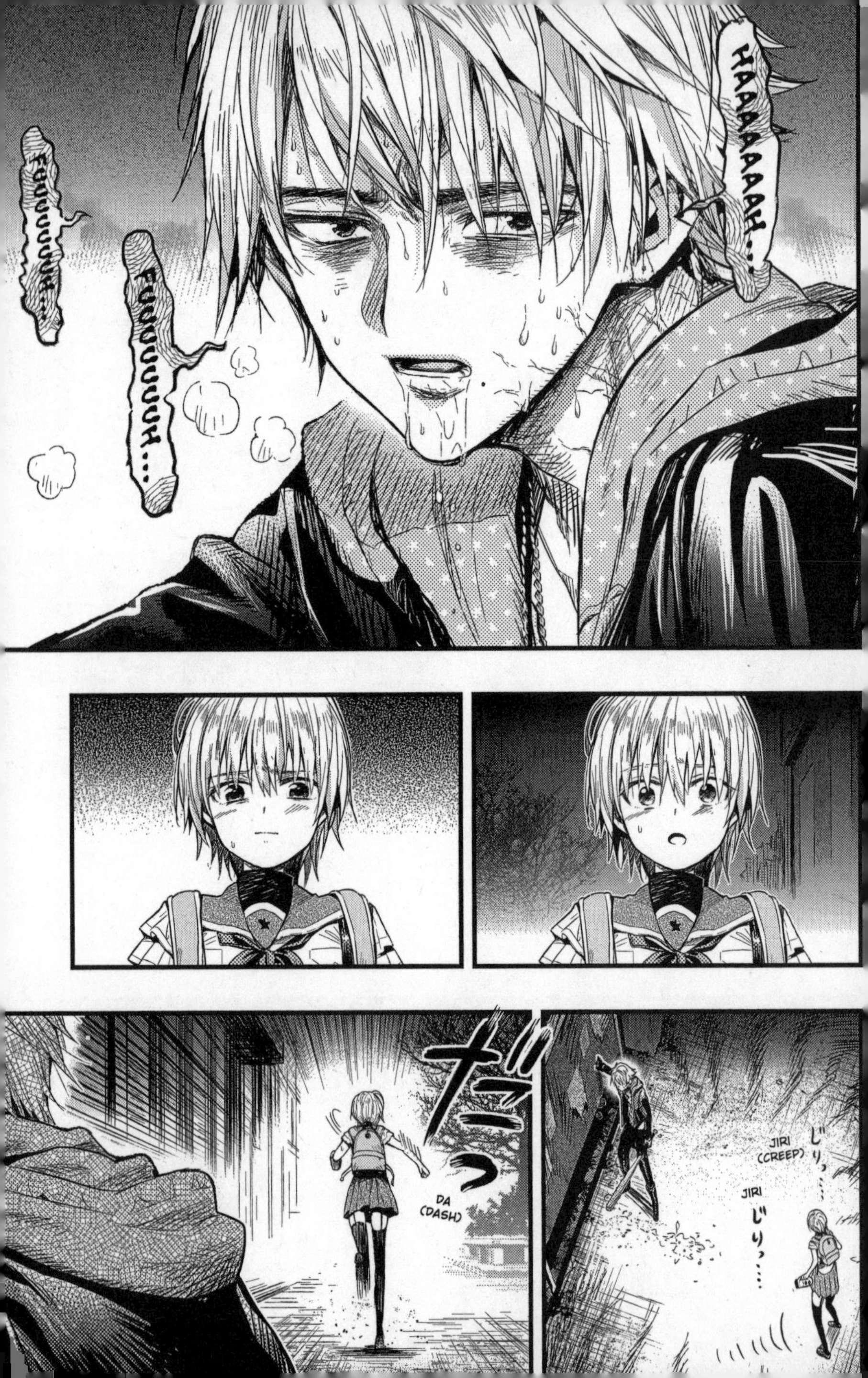
HAAAAAAAAH...
FOOOUUUUUH...
FOOOUUUUUH...
じりっ…
JIRI (CREEP)
じりっ…
JIRI
ダッ
DA (DASH)

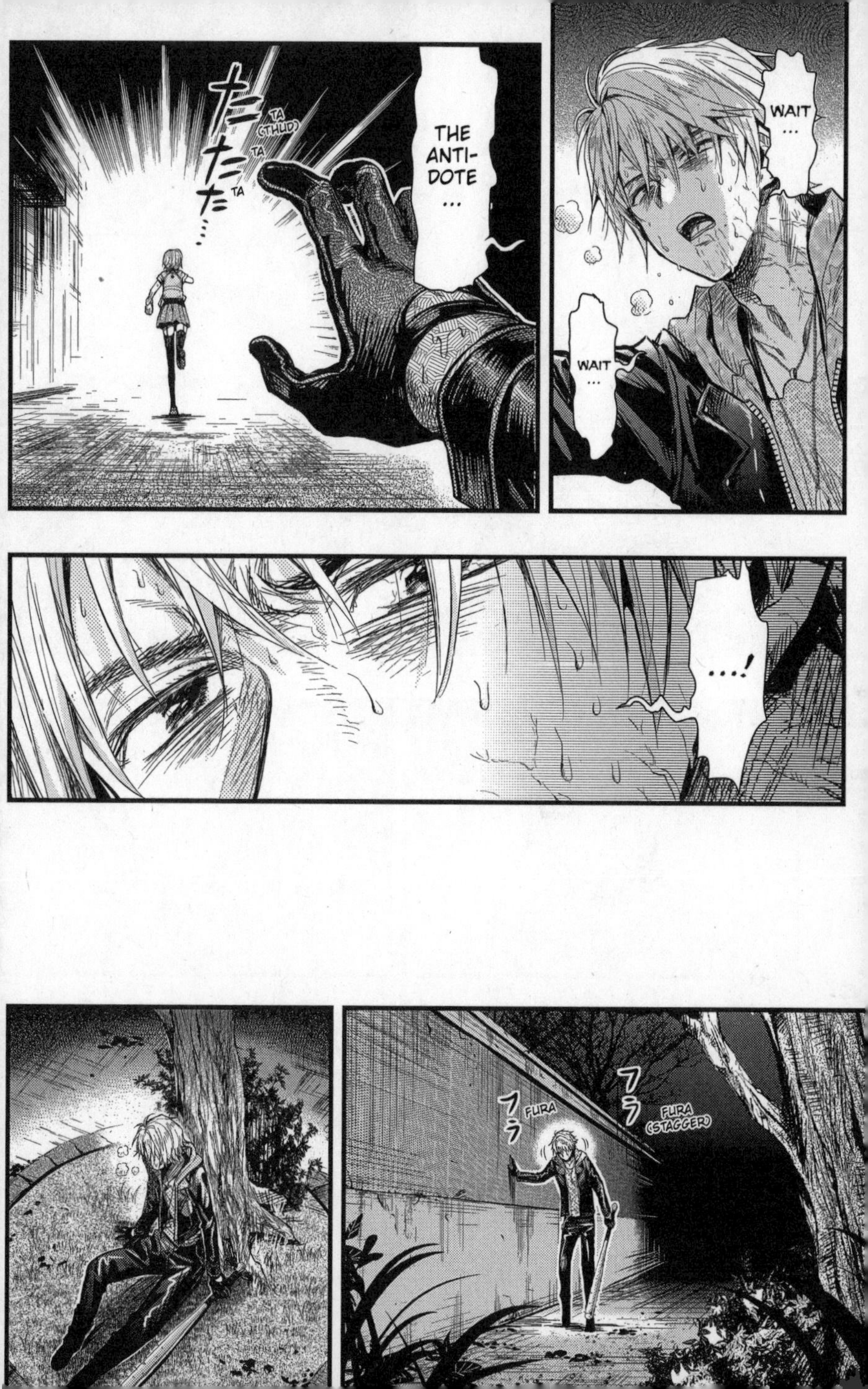
WAIT ...
WAIT ...
THE ANTI-DOTE ...
たーたーた...
TA (THUD) TA TA
...!
フラ
FURA (STAGGER)
フラ
FURA

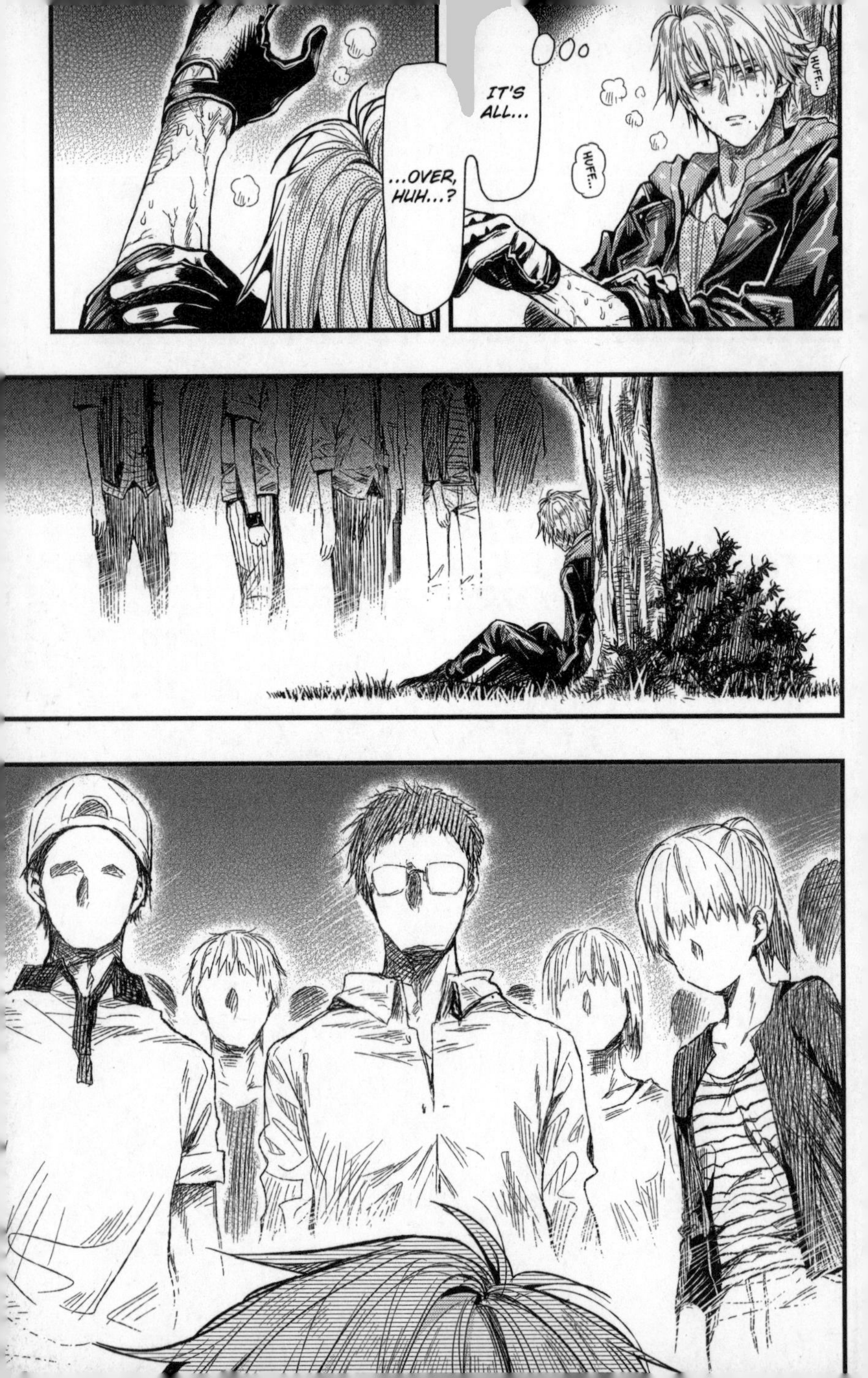
HUFF...
IT'S ALL...
HUFF...
...OVER, HUH...?

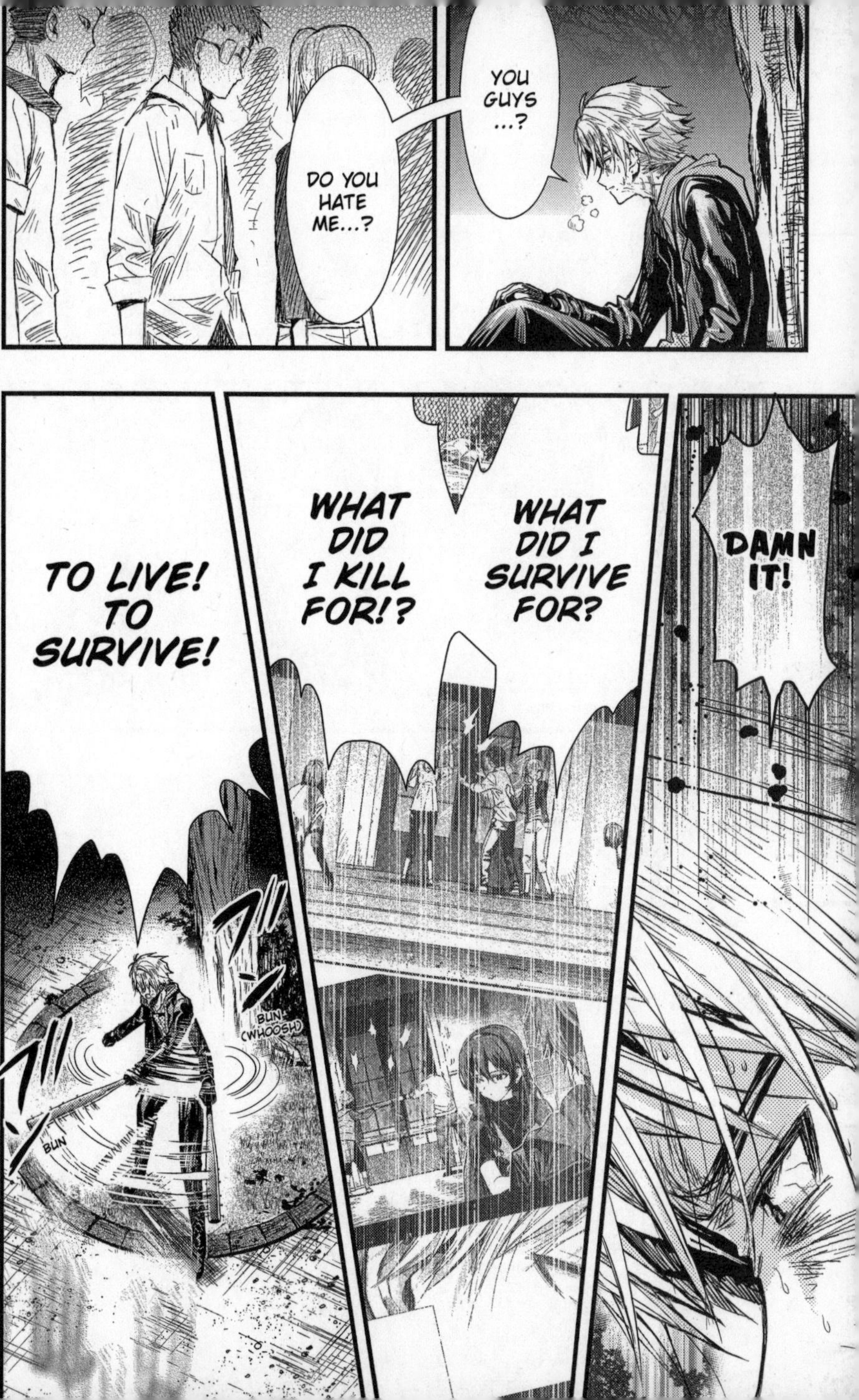
YOU GUYS ...?
DO YOU HATE ME...?
DAMN IT!
WHAT DID I SURVIVE FOR?
WHAT DID I KILL FOR!?
TO LIVE! TO SURVIVE!
BUN (WHOOSH)
BUN

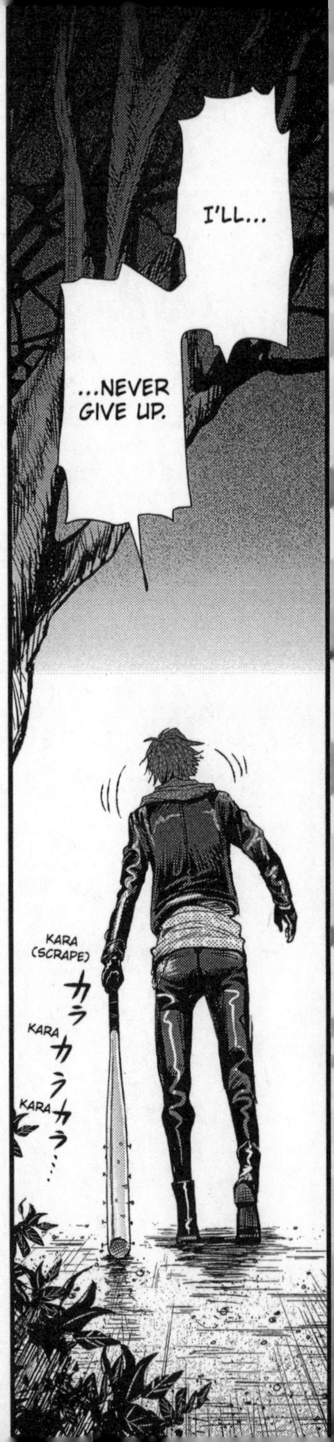
I'LL...
...NEVER GIVE UP.
KARA (SCRAPE)
KARA
KARA
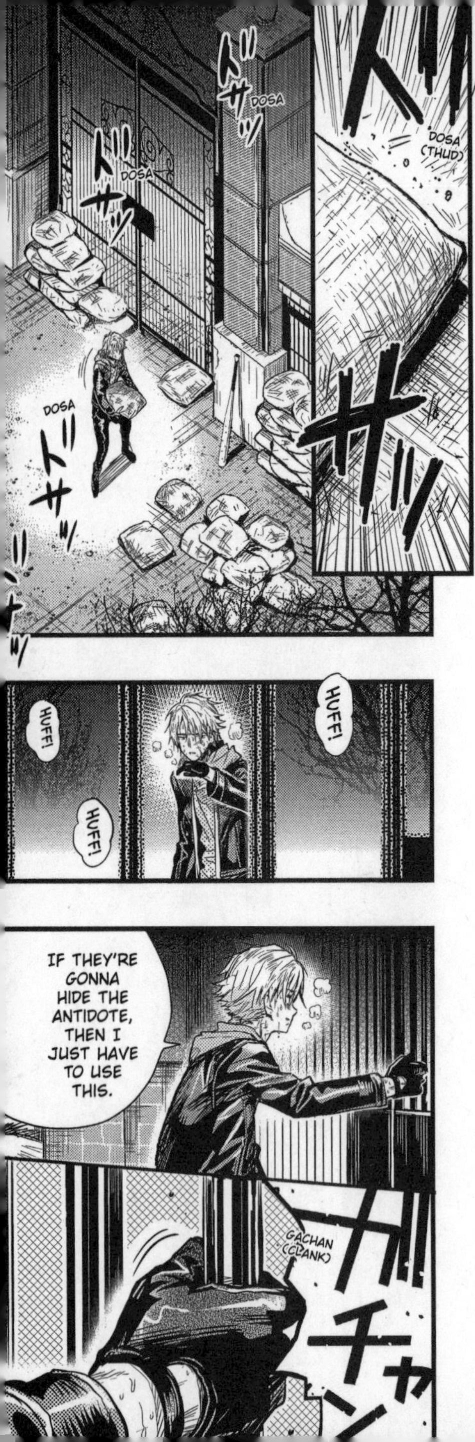
DOSA (THUD)
DOSA
DOSA
DOSA
HUFF!
HUFF!
HUFF!
IF THEY'RE GONNA HIDE THE ANTIDOTE, THEN I JUST HAVE TO USE THIS.
GACHAN (CLANK)

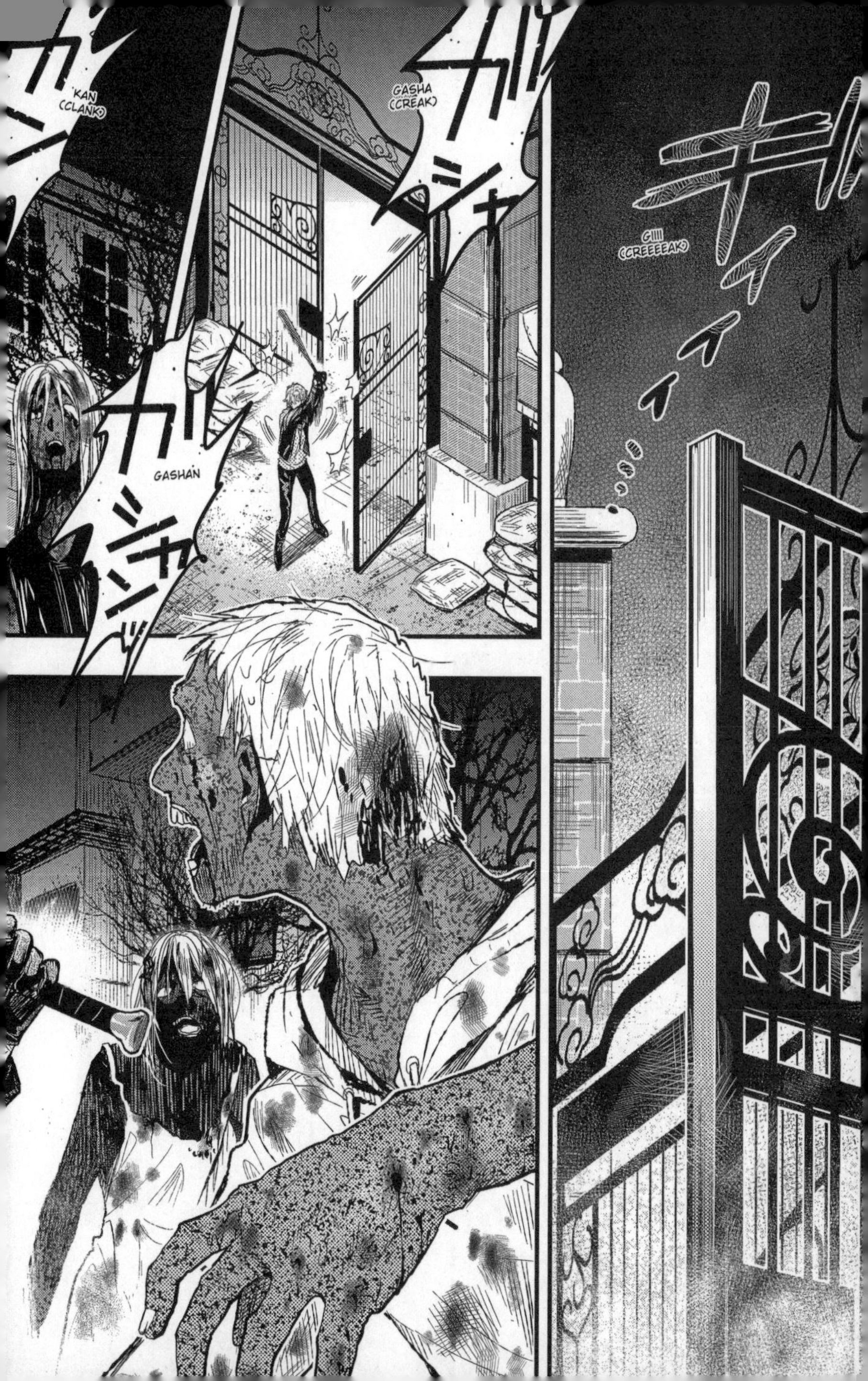
GIIII
(CREEEEEAK)
GASHA
(CREAK)
KAN
(CLANK)
GASHAN

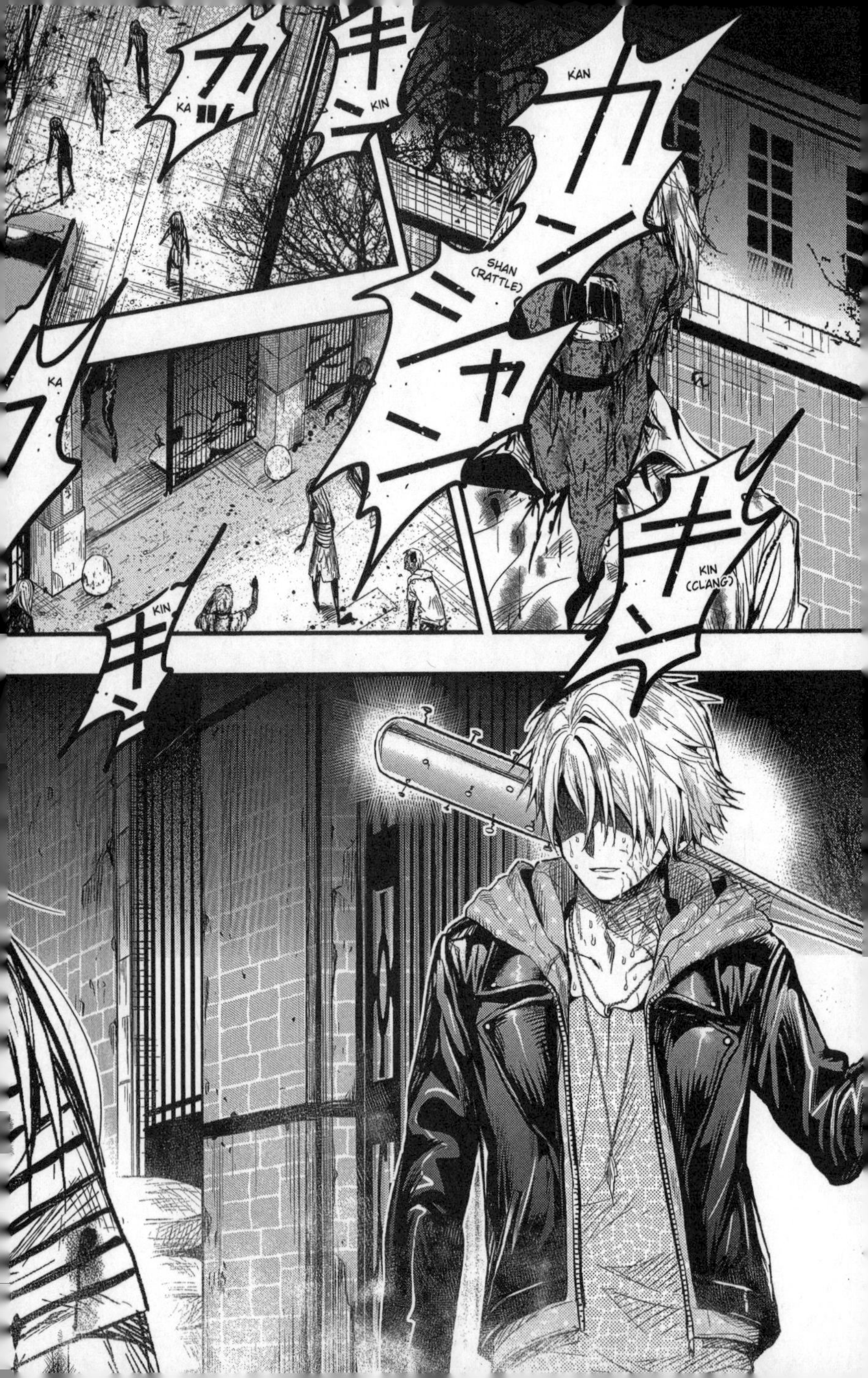
KAN
SHAN (RATTLE)
KIN (CLANG)
KIN
KA
KA
KIN

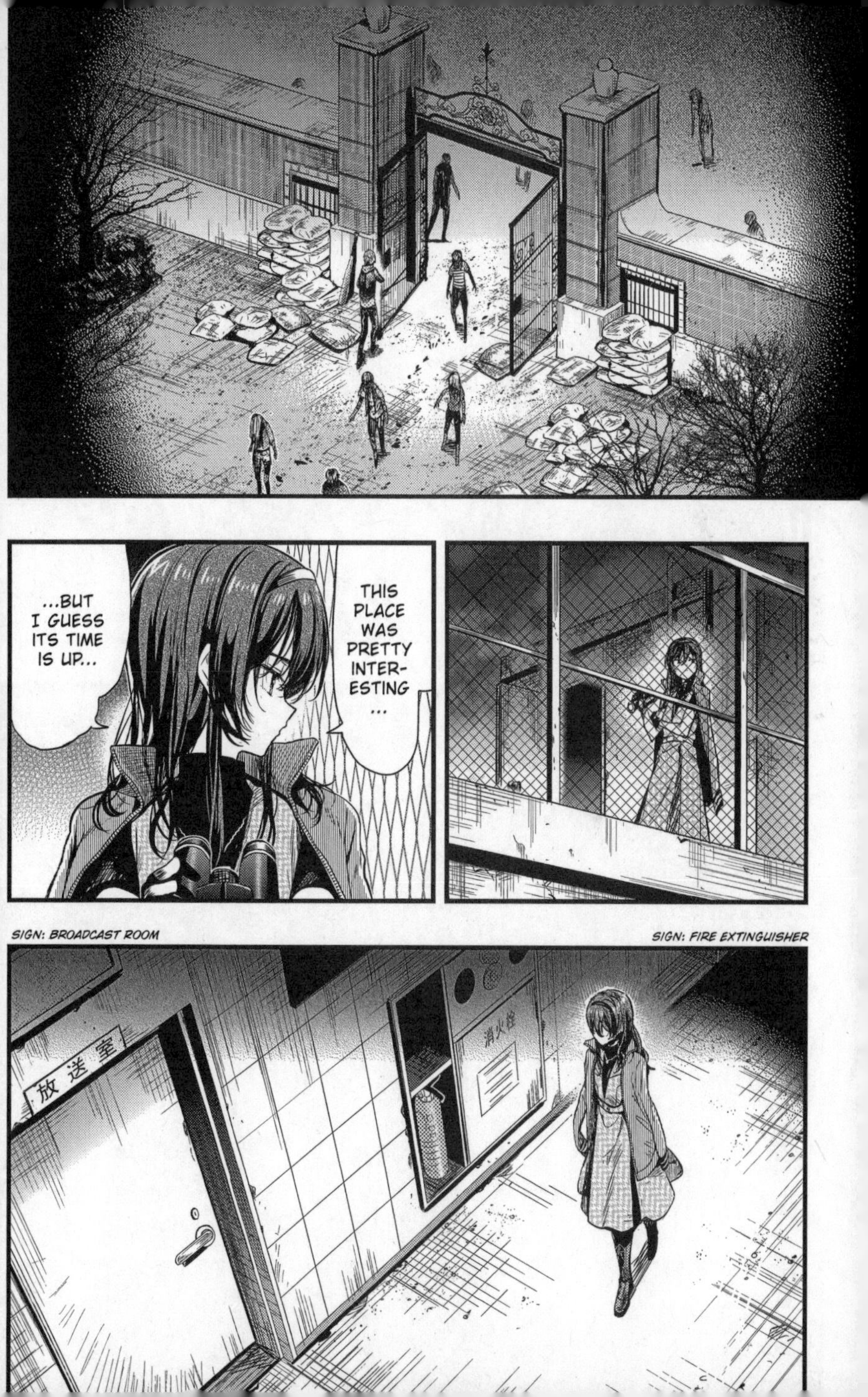
THIS PLACE WAS PRETTY INTERESTING...
...BUT I GUESS ITS TIME IS UP...
SIGN: FIRE EXTINGUISHER
SIGN: BROADCAST ROOM
消火栓
放送室

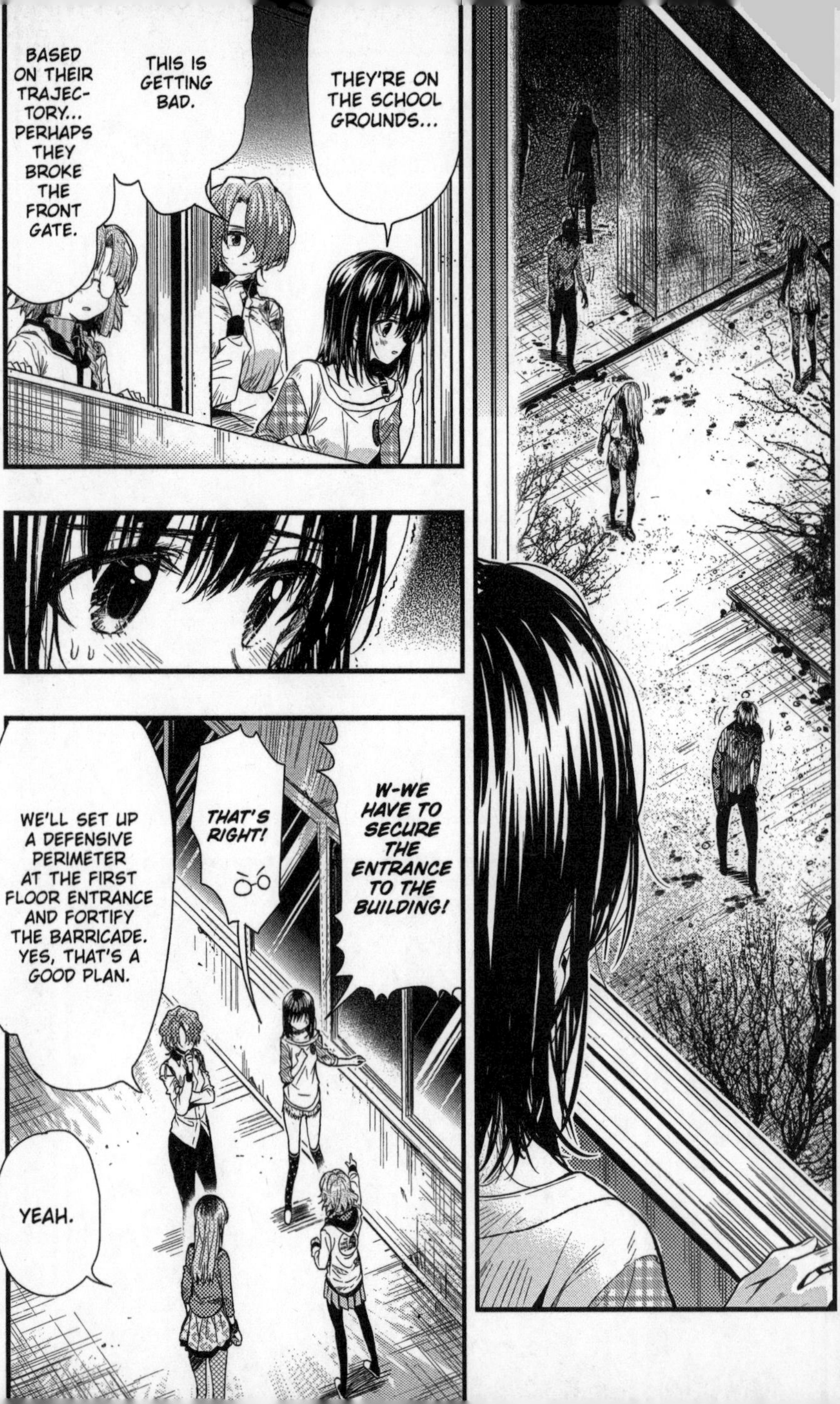
THEY'RE ON THE SCHOOL GROUNDS...
THIS IS GETTING BAD.
BASED ON THEIR TRAJECTORY... PERHAPS THEY BROKE THE FRONT GATE.
W-WE HAVE TO SECURE THE ENTRANCE TO THE BUILDING!
THAT'S RIGHT!
WE'LL SET UP A DEFENSIVE PERIMETER AT THE FIRST FLOOR ENTRANCE AND FORTIFY THE BARRICADE. YES, THAT'S A GOOD PLAN.
YEAH.

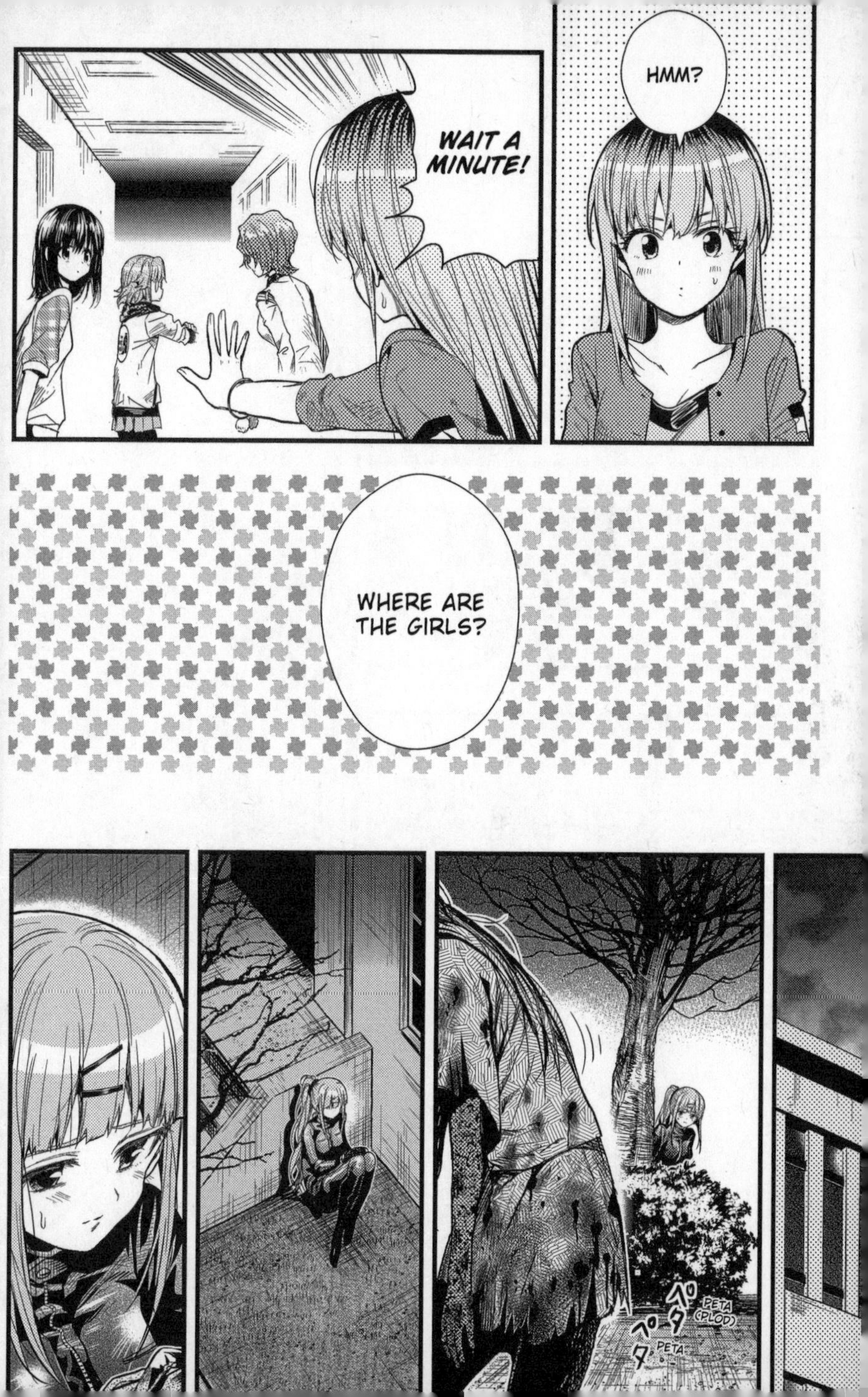
HMM?
WAIT A MINUTE!
WHERE ARE THE GIRLS?
ペタ
PETA (PLOD)
ペタ
PETA

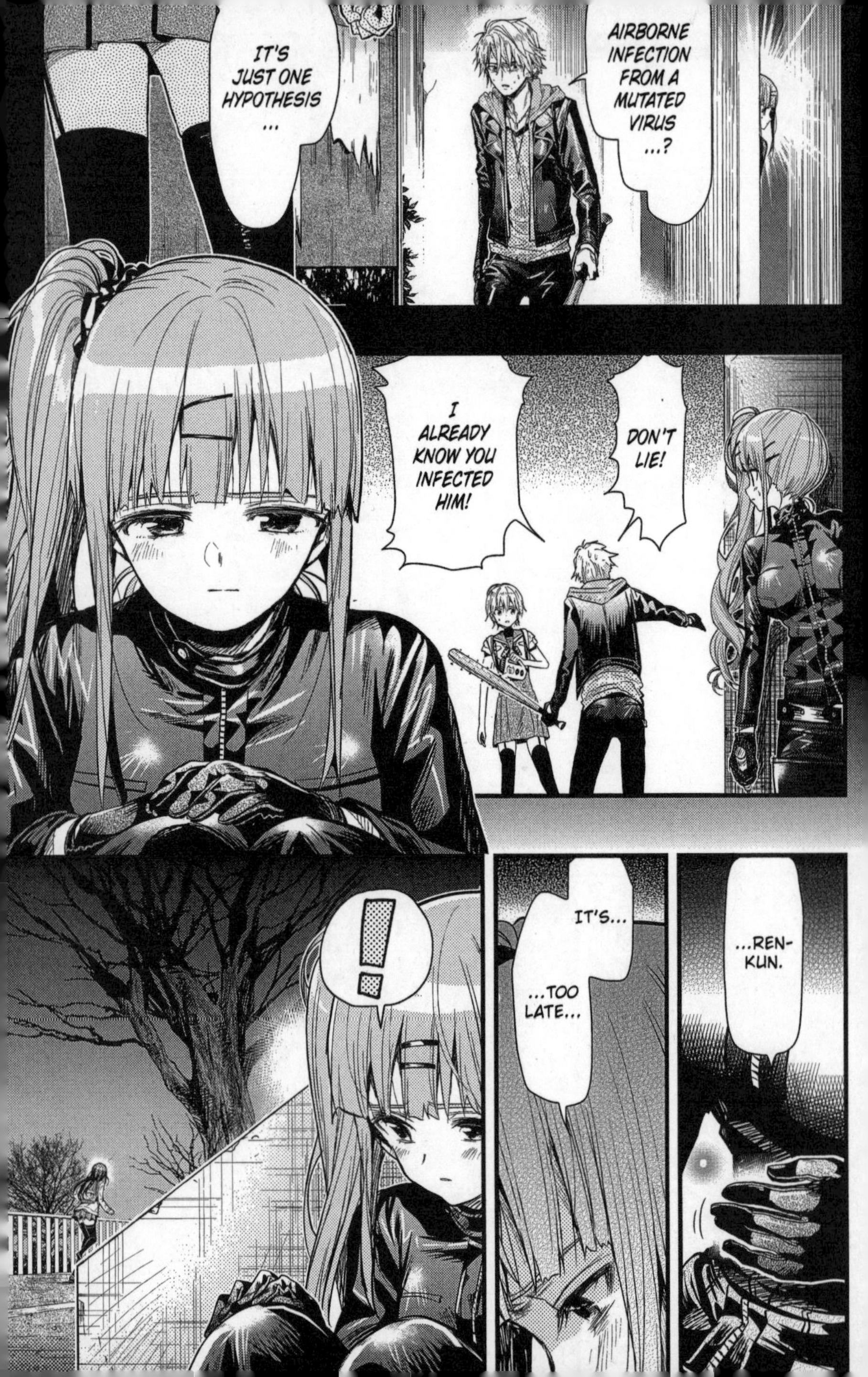
AIRBORNE INFECTION FROM A MUTATED VIRUS ...?
IT'S JUST ONE HYPOTHESIS ...
DON'T LIE!
I ALREADY KNOW YOU INFECTED HIM!
...REN-KUN.
IT'S...
...TOO LATE...
!

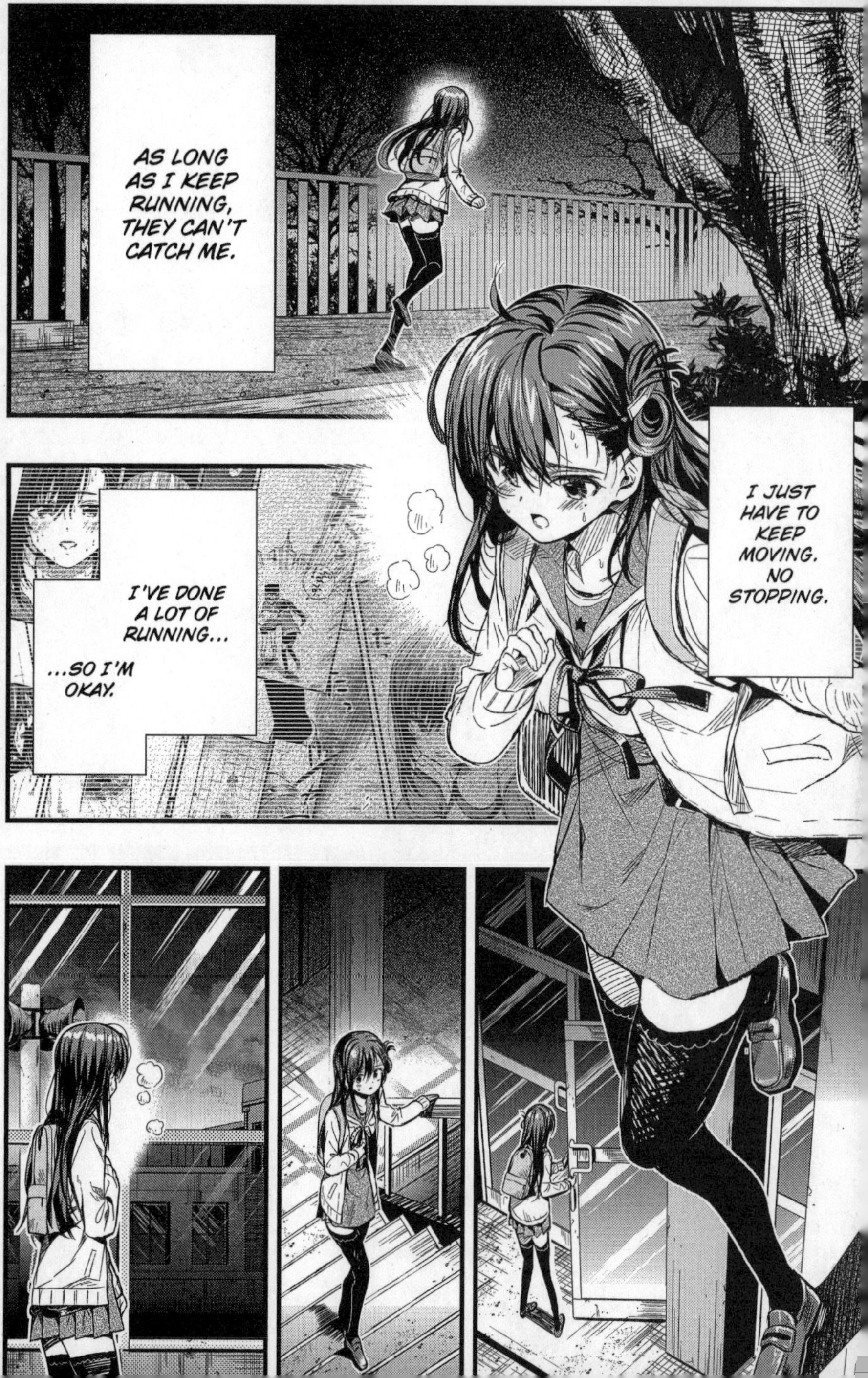
AS LONG AS I KEEP RUNNING, THEY CAN'T CATCH ME.
I JUST HAVE TO KEEP MOVING. NO STOPPING.
I'VE DONE A LOT OF RUNNING...
...SO I'M OKAY.

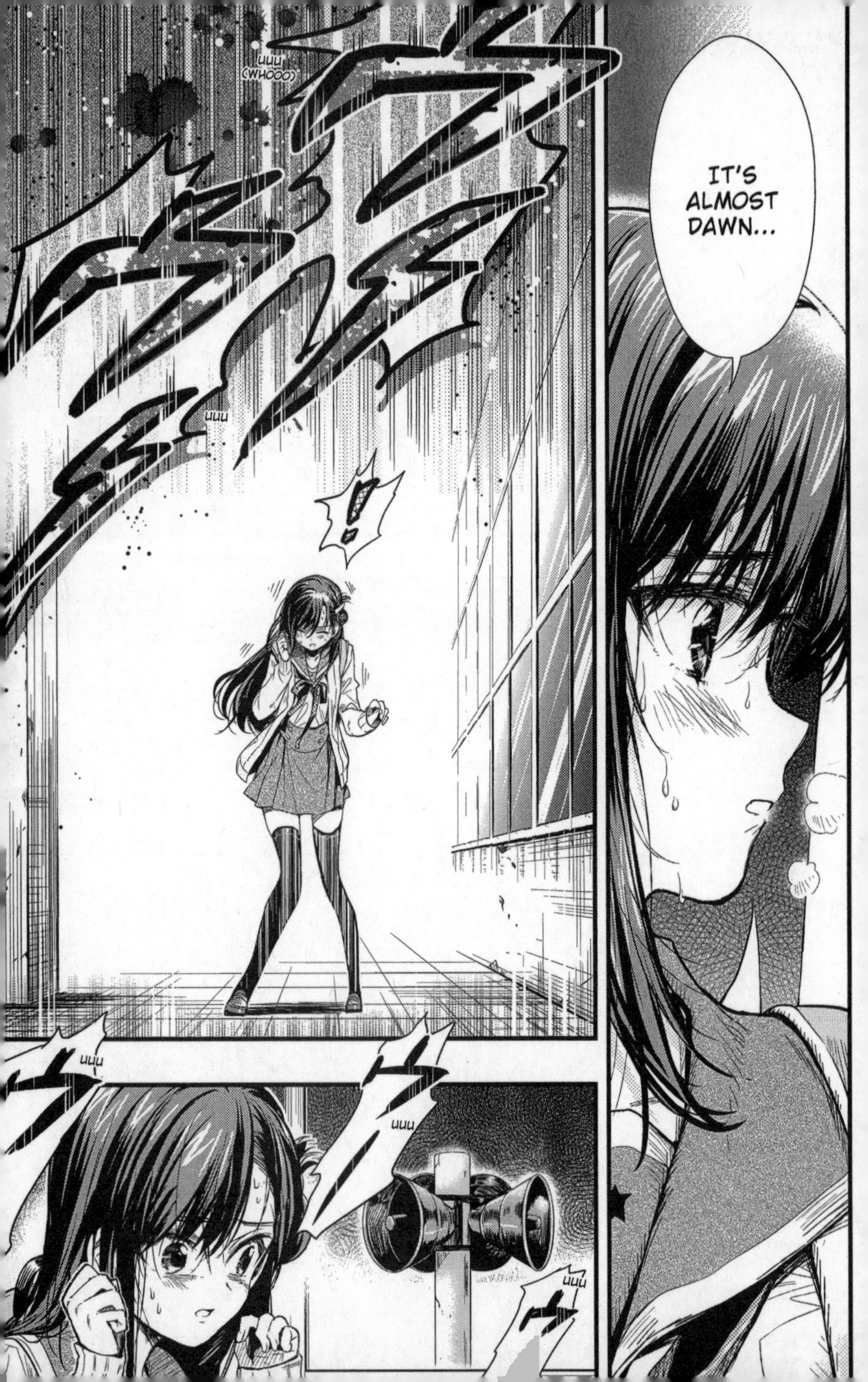
IT'S ALMOST DAWN...
uuu (WHOOO)
uuu
!
uuu
uuu
uuu

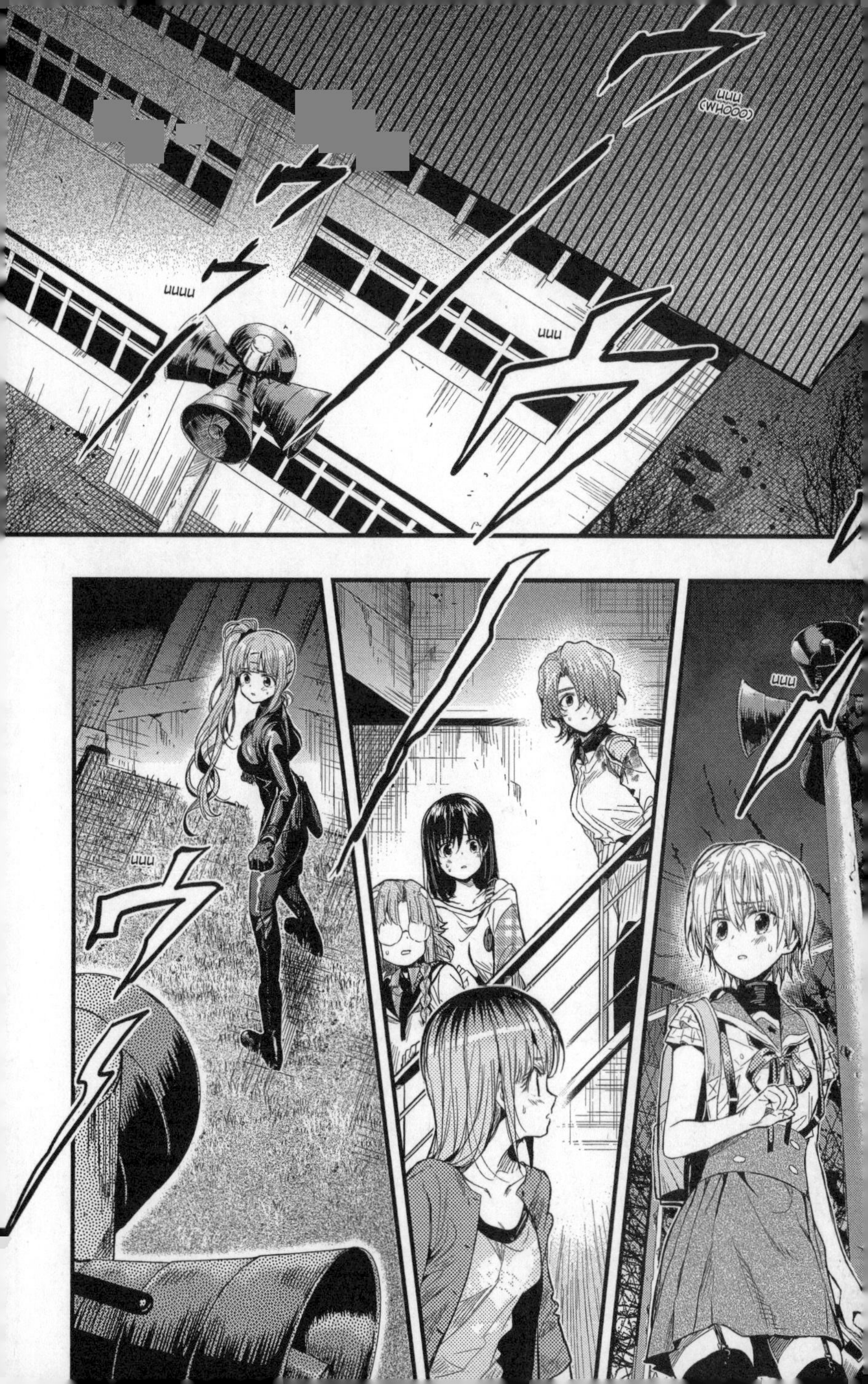
uuu
(WHOOO)
uuu
uuuu
uuu
uuu

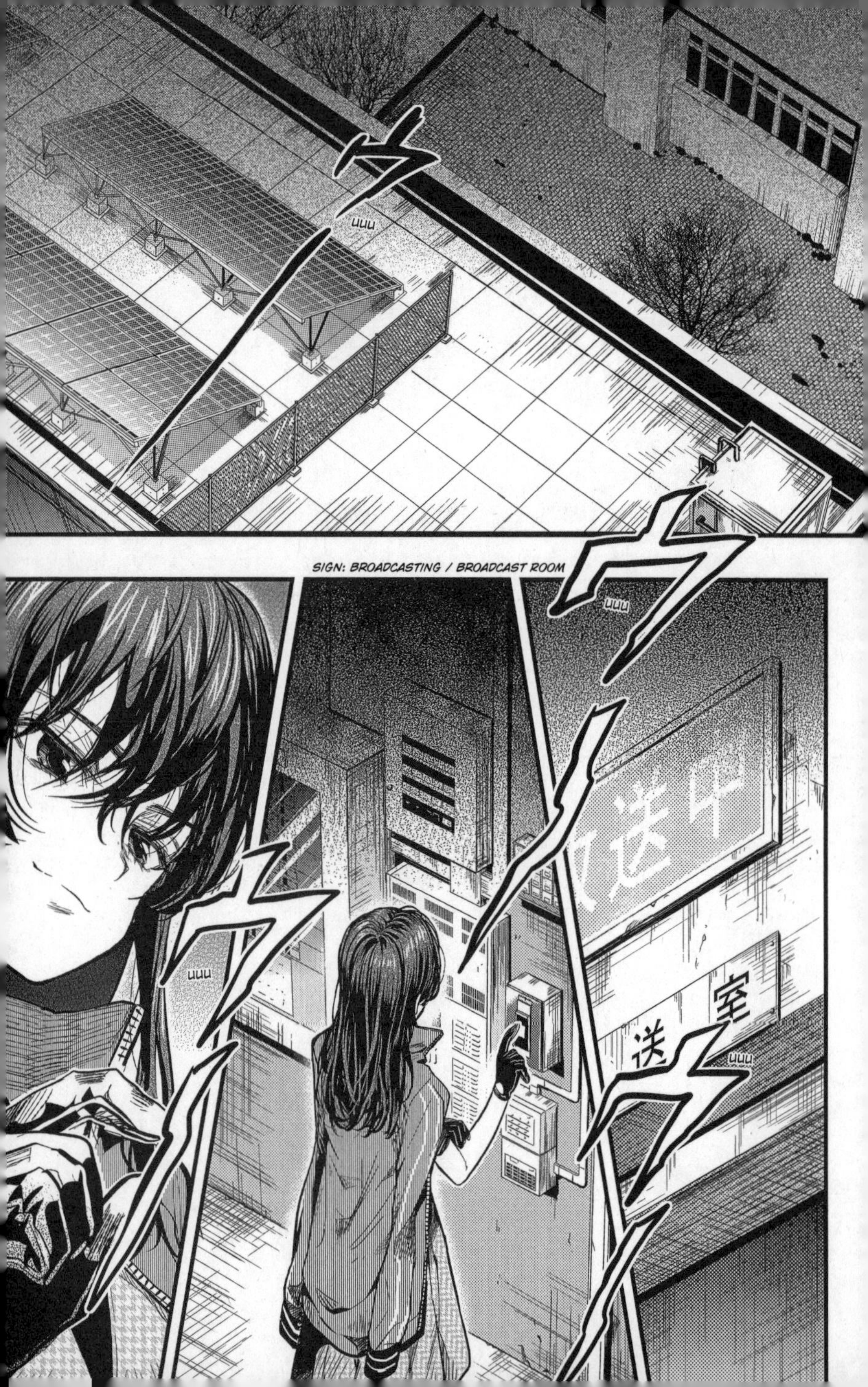
uuu
SIGN: BROADCASTING / BROADCAST ROOM
uuu
uuu
uuu

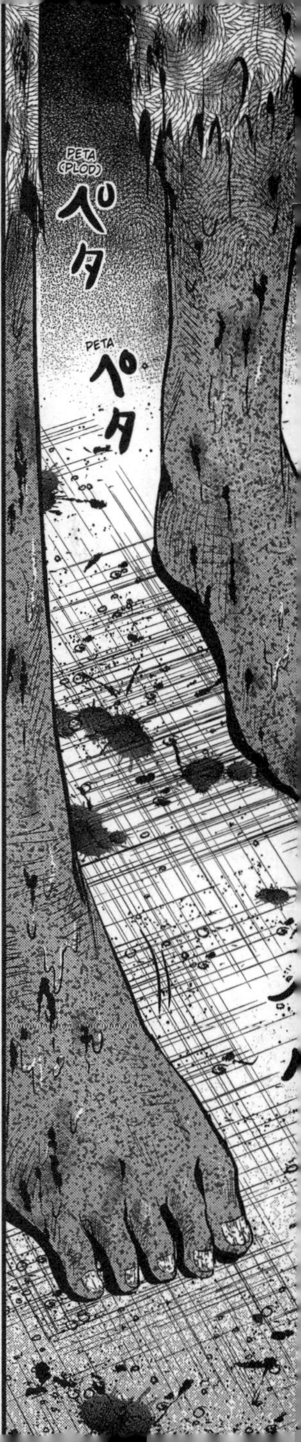
PETA (PLOD)
PETA
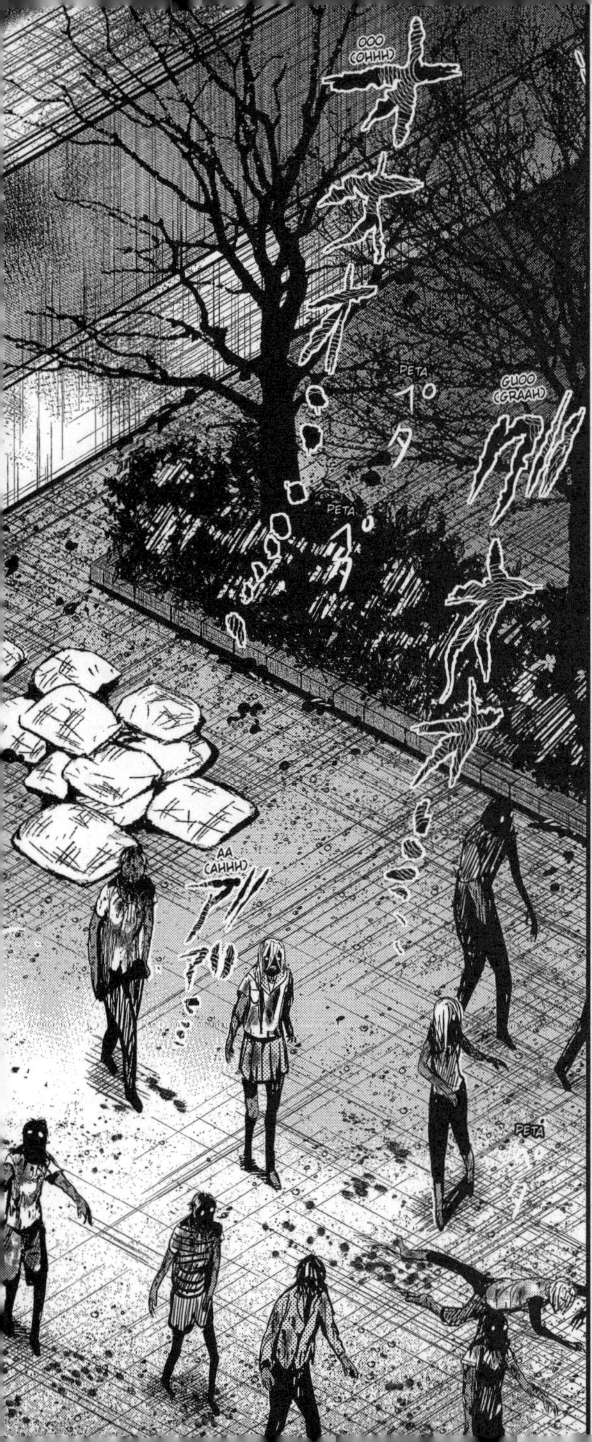
OOO (OHHH)
GUOO (GRAAH)
PETA
PETA
AA (AHHH)
PETA

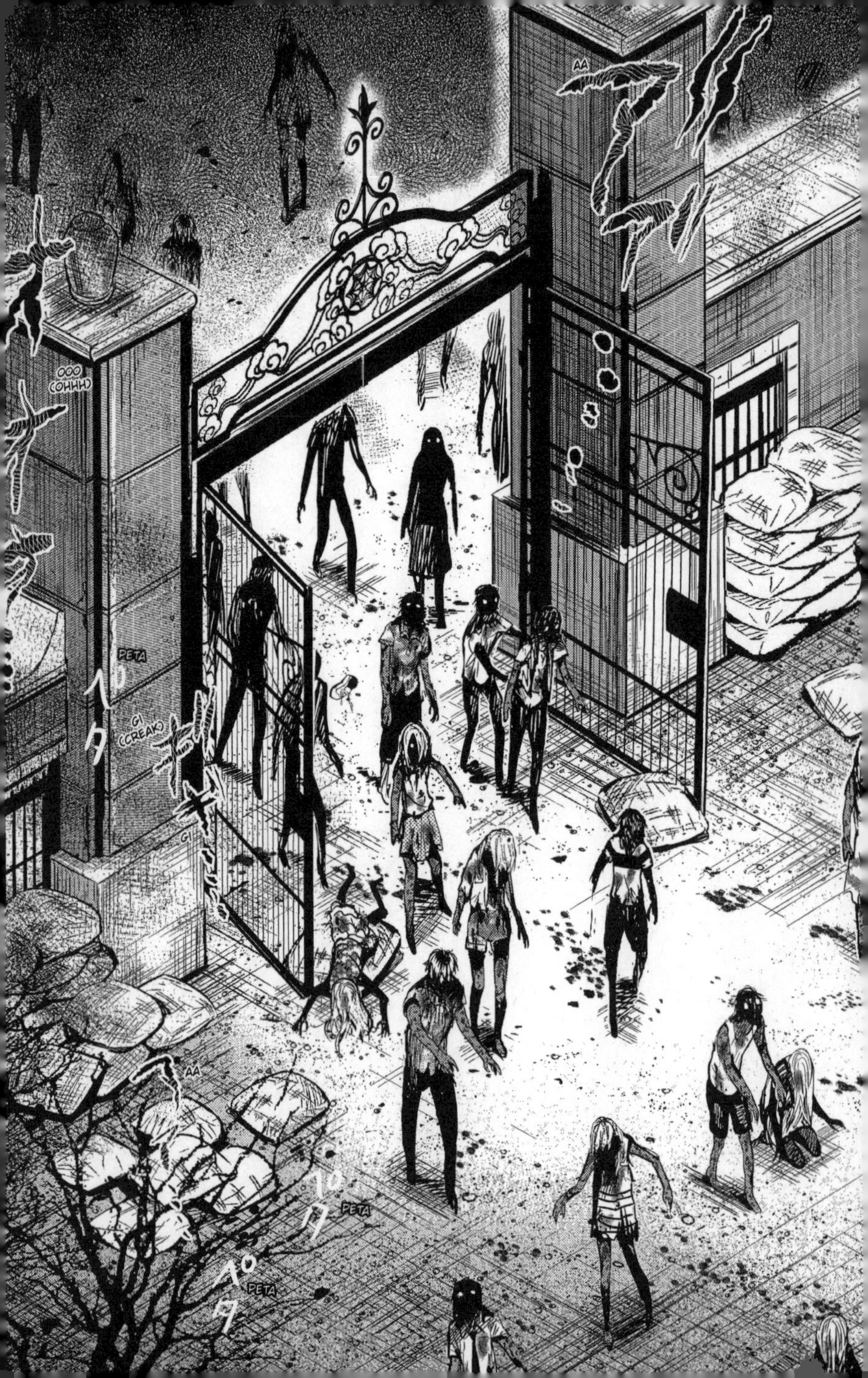
AA
OOO (OHHHH)
PETA
GI (CREAK)
GI
AA
PETA
PETA

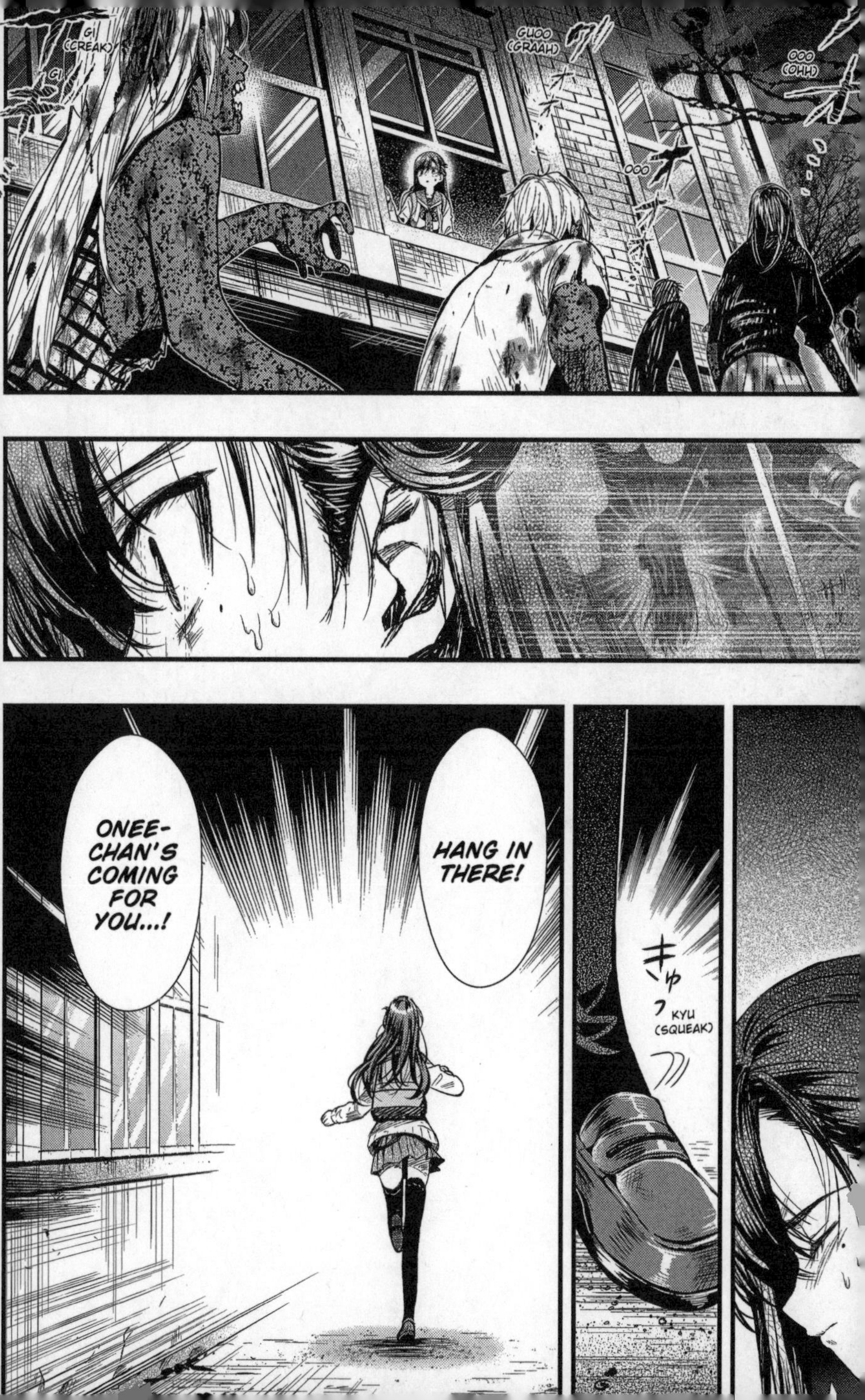
GI (CREAK)
GI
GUOO (GRAAH)
OOO (OHH)
OOO
HANG IN THERE!
ONEE-CHAN'S COMING FOR YOU...!
きゅっ
KYU (SQUEAK)

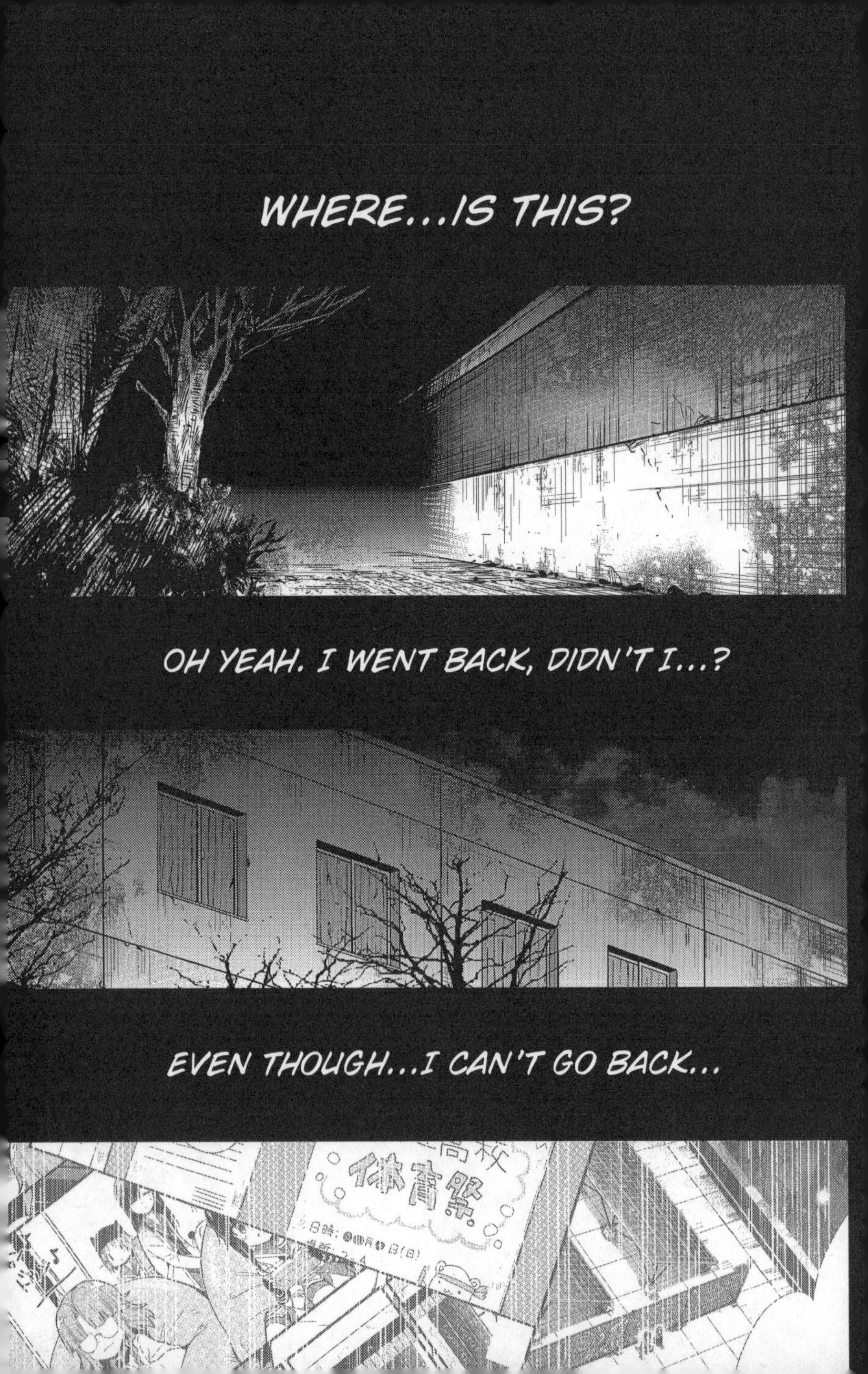
WHERE...IS THIS?
OH YEAH. I WENT BACK, DIDN'T I...?
EVEN THOUGH...I CAN'T GO BACK...
高校
体育祭

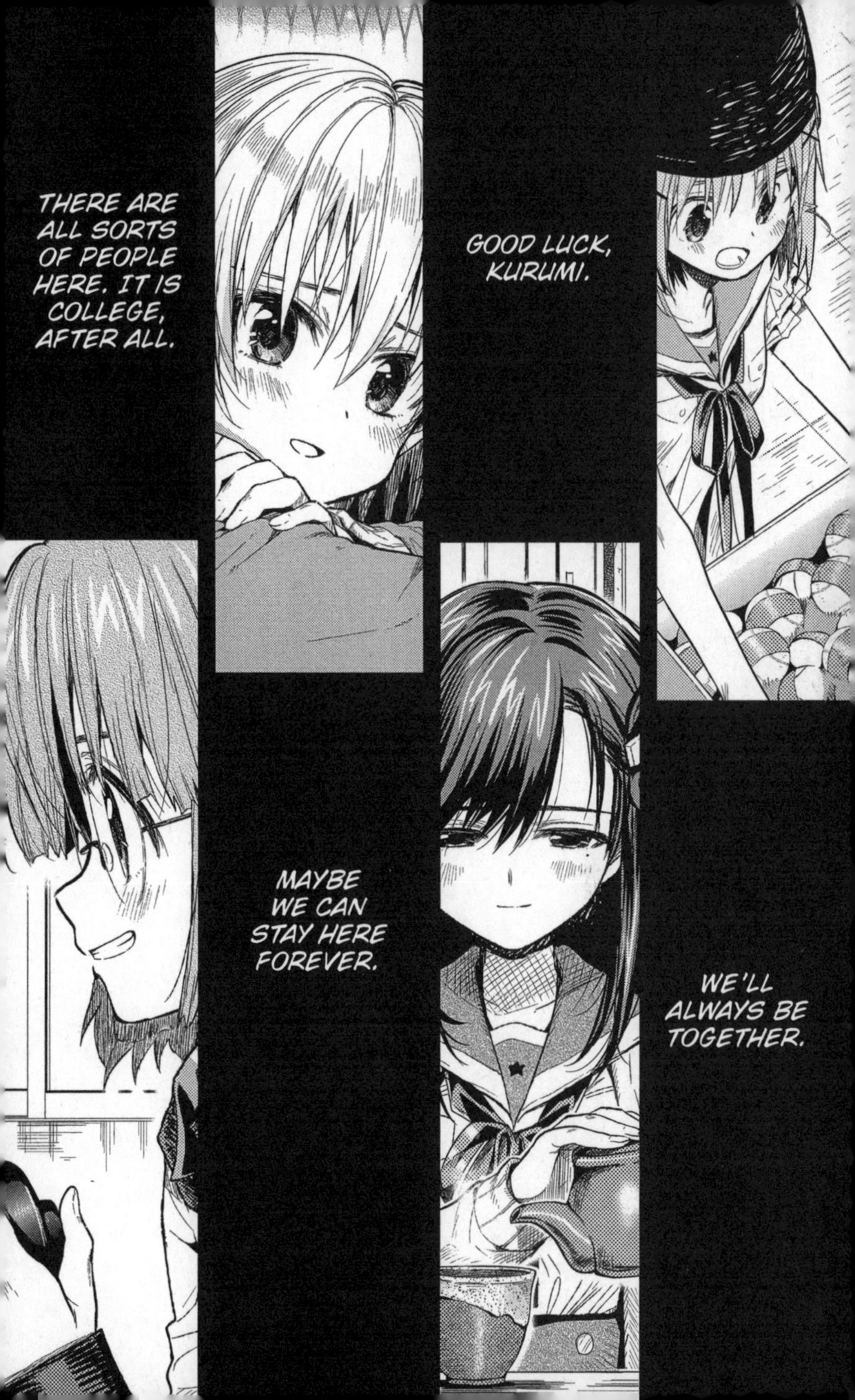
GOOD LUCK, KURUMI.
THERE ARE ALL SORTS OF PEOPLE HERE. IT IS COLLEGE, AFTER ALL.
WE'LL ALWAYS BE TOGETHER.
MAYBE WE CAN STAY HERE FOREVER.

I THOUGHT BEING WITH THEM WOULD RUIN EVERY-THING.

THAT'S...RIGHT...

IT'S...TOO LATE...

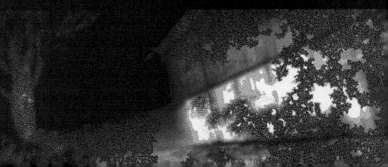

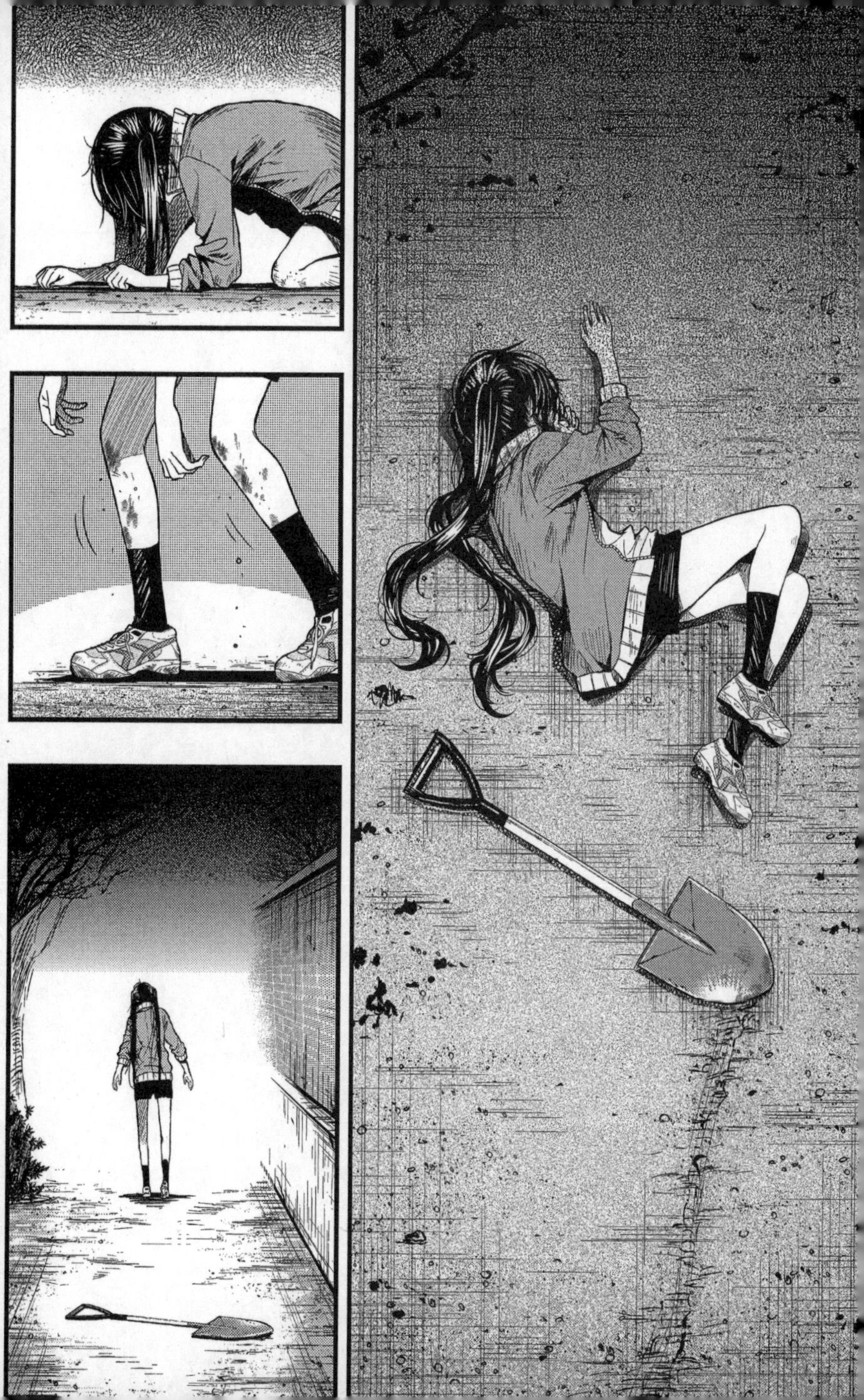

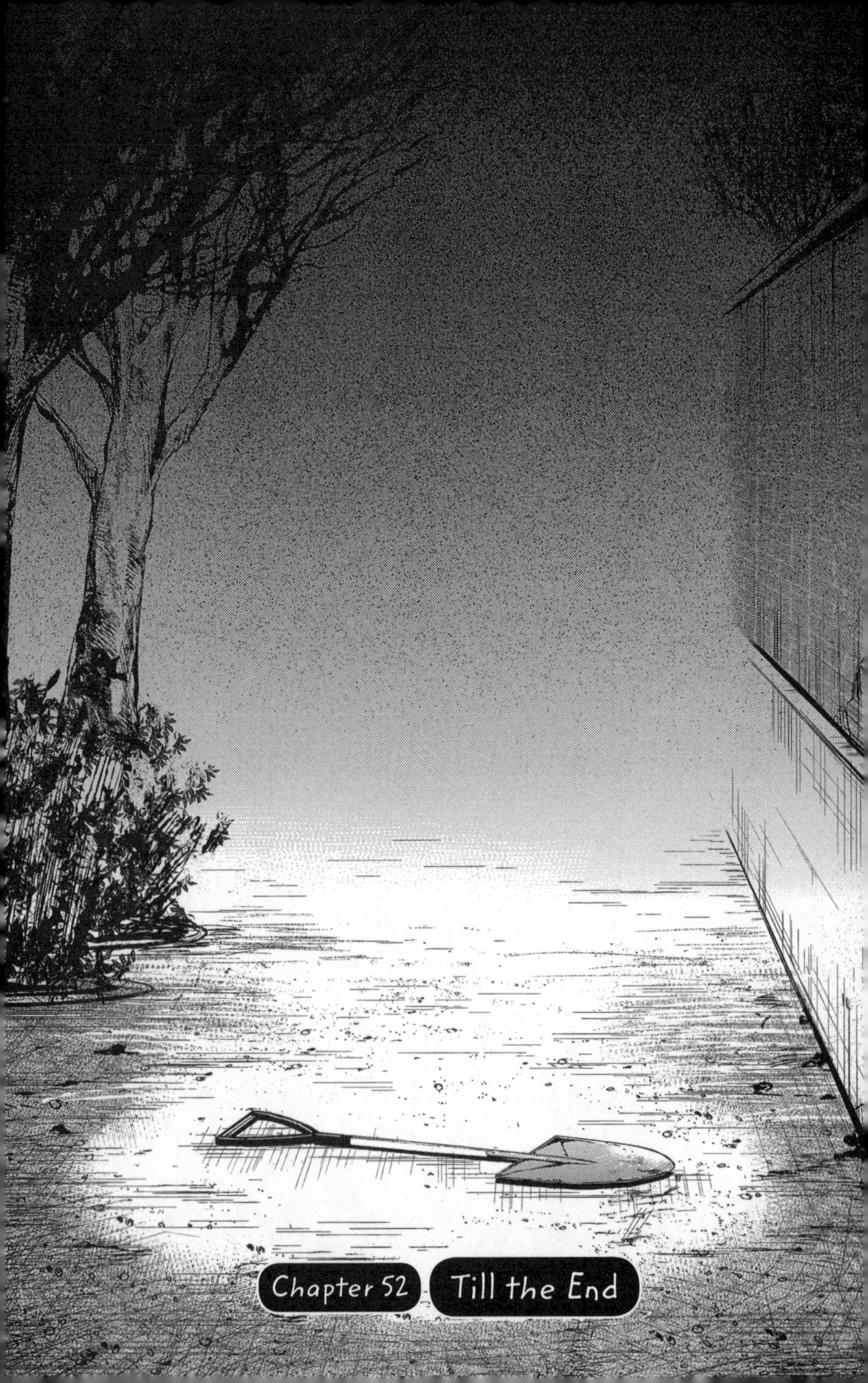
Chapter 52
Till the End

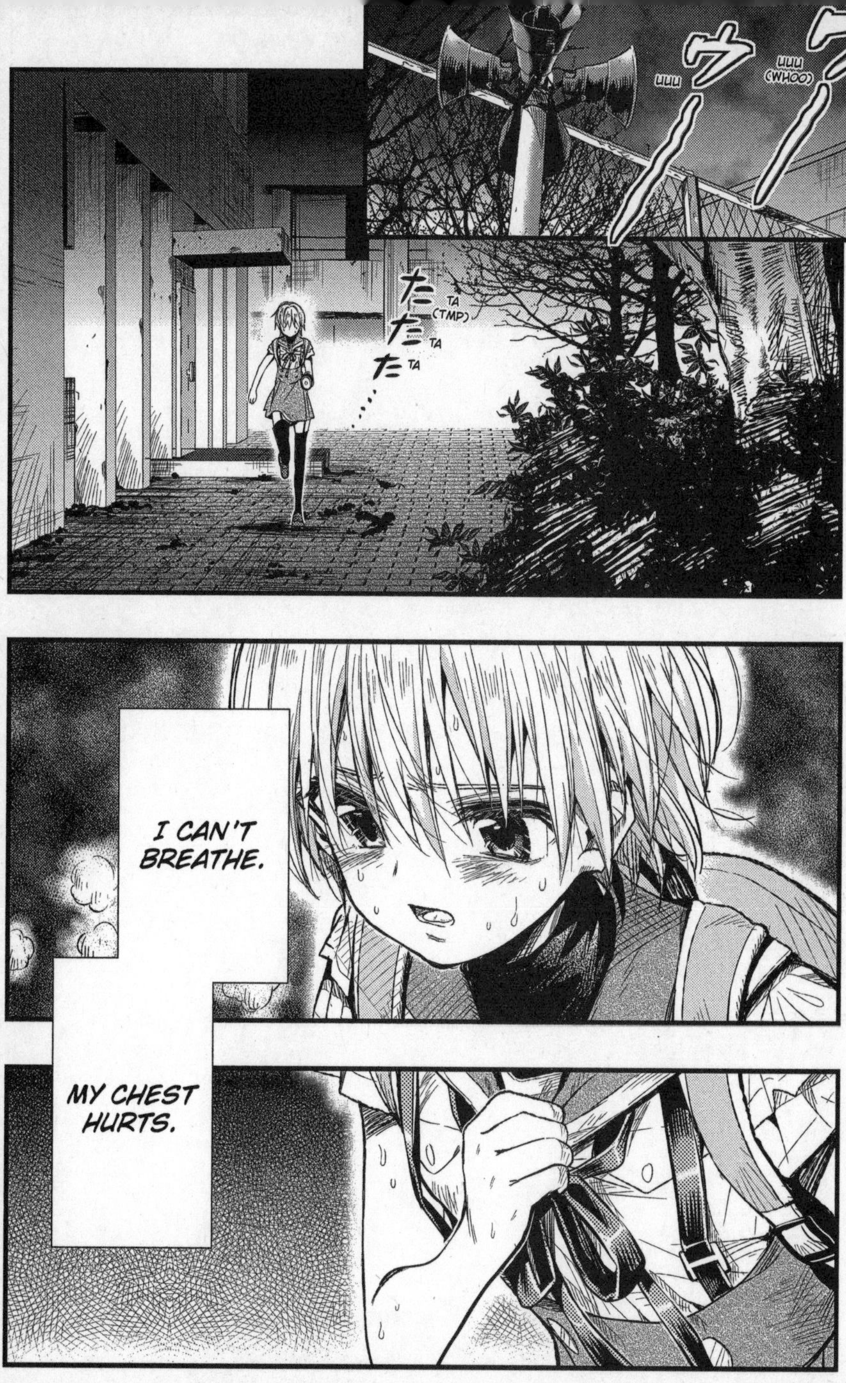

ヴー
UUU (WHOO)
ウー
UUU
た TA (TMP)
た TA
た TA
...
I CAN'T BREATHE.
MY CHEST HURTS.

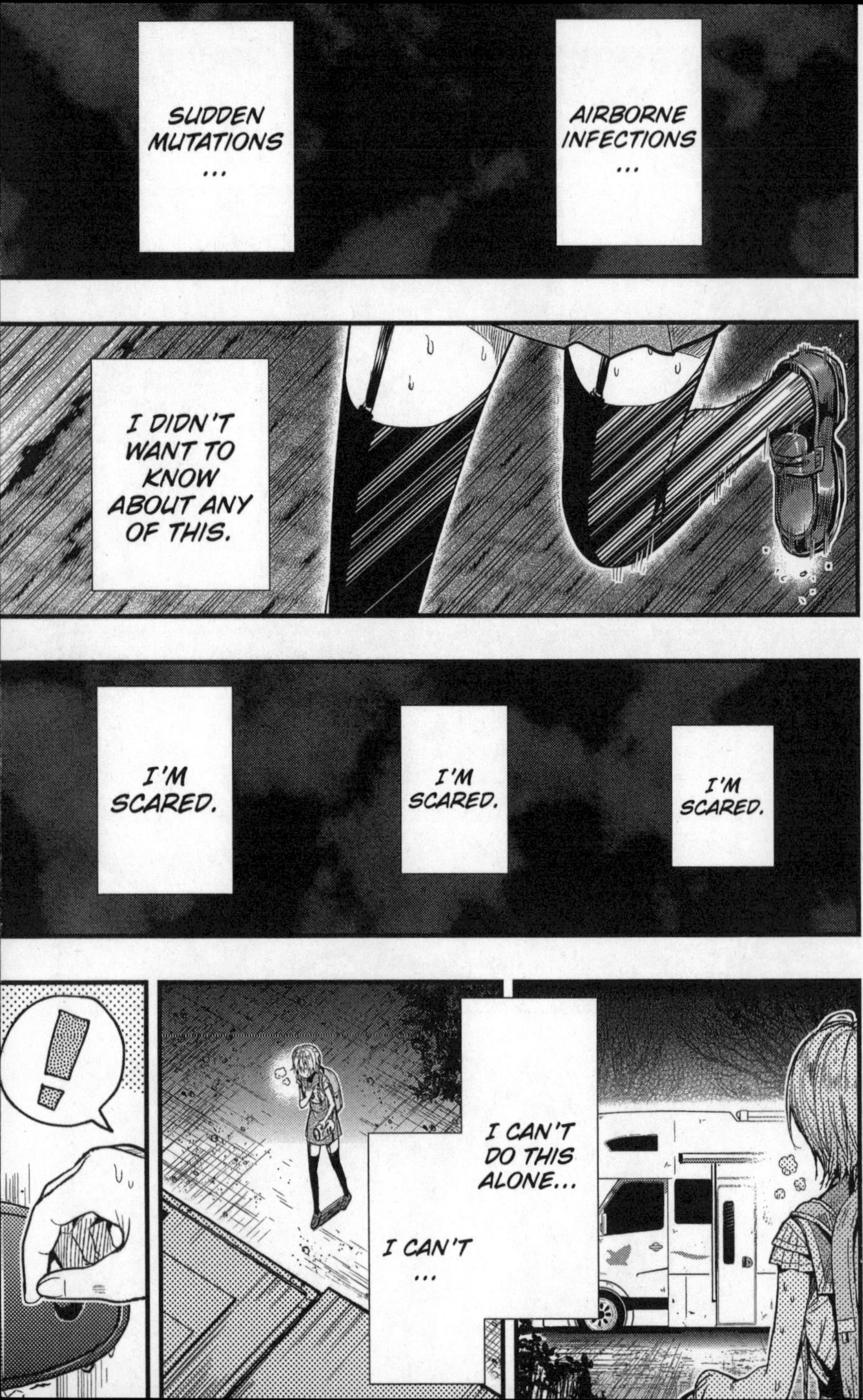
AIRBORNE INFECTIONS ...
SUDDEN MUTATIONS ...
I DIDN'T WANT TO KNOW ABOUT ANY OF THIS.
I'M SCARED.
I'M SCARED.
I'M SCARED.
I CAN'T DO THIS ALONE...
I CAN'T ...
!

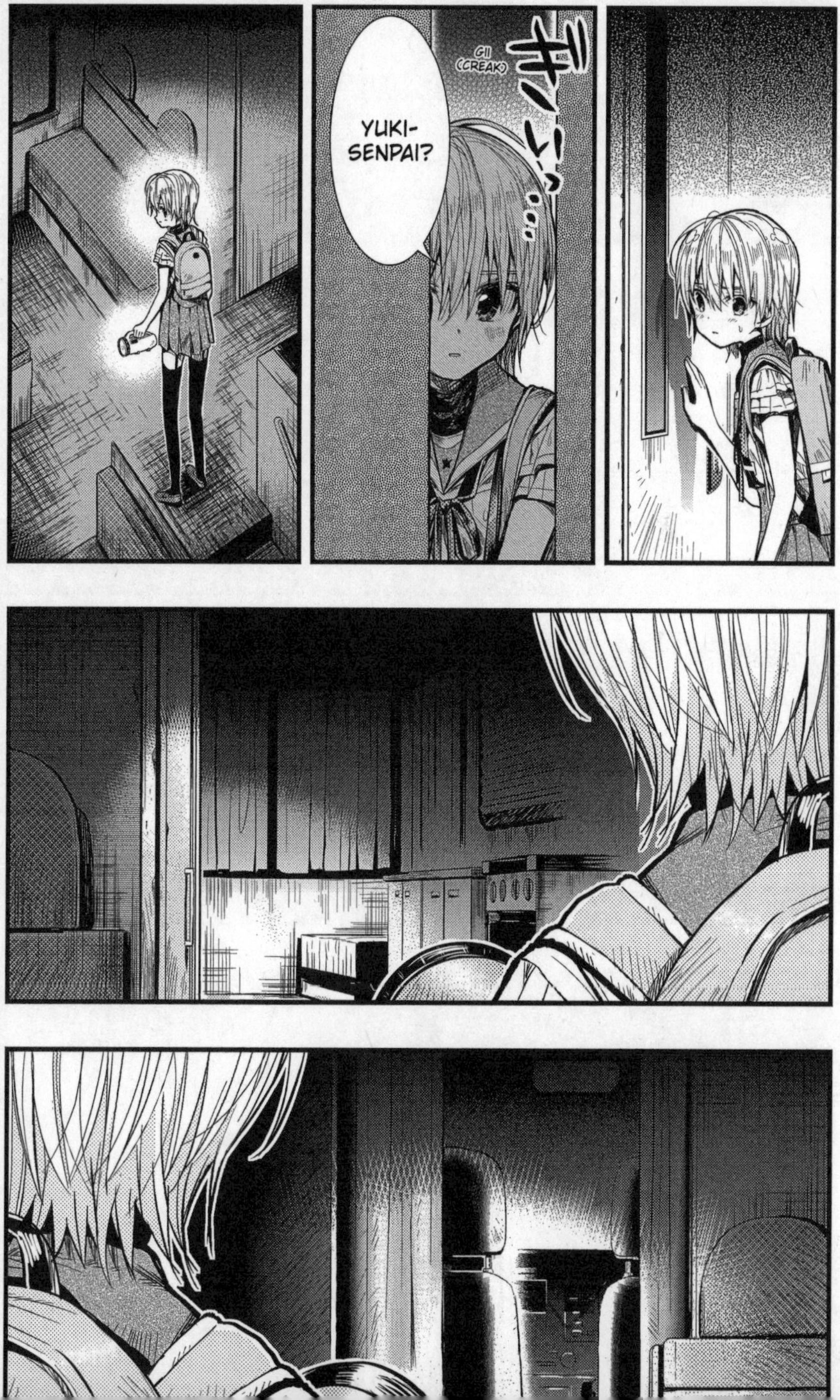
GII (CREAK)
YUKI-SENPAI?

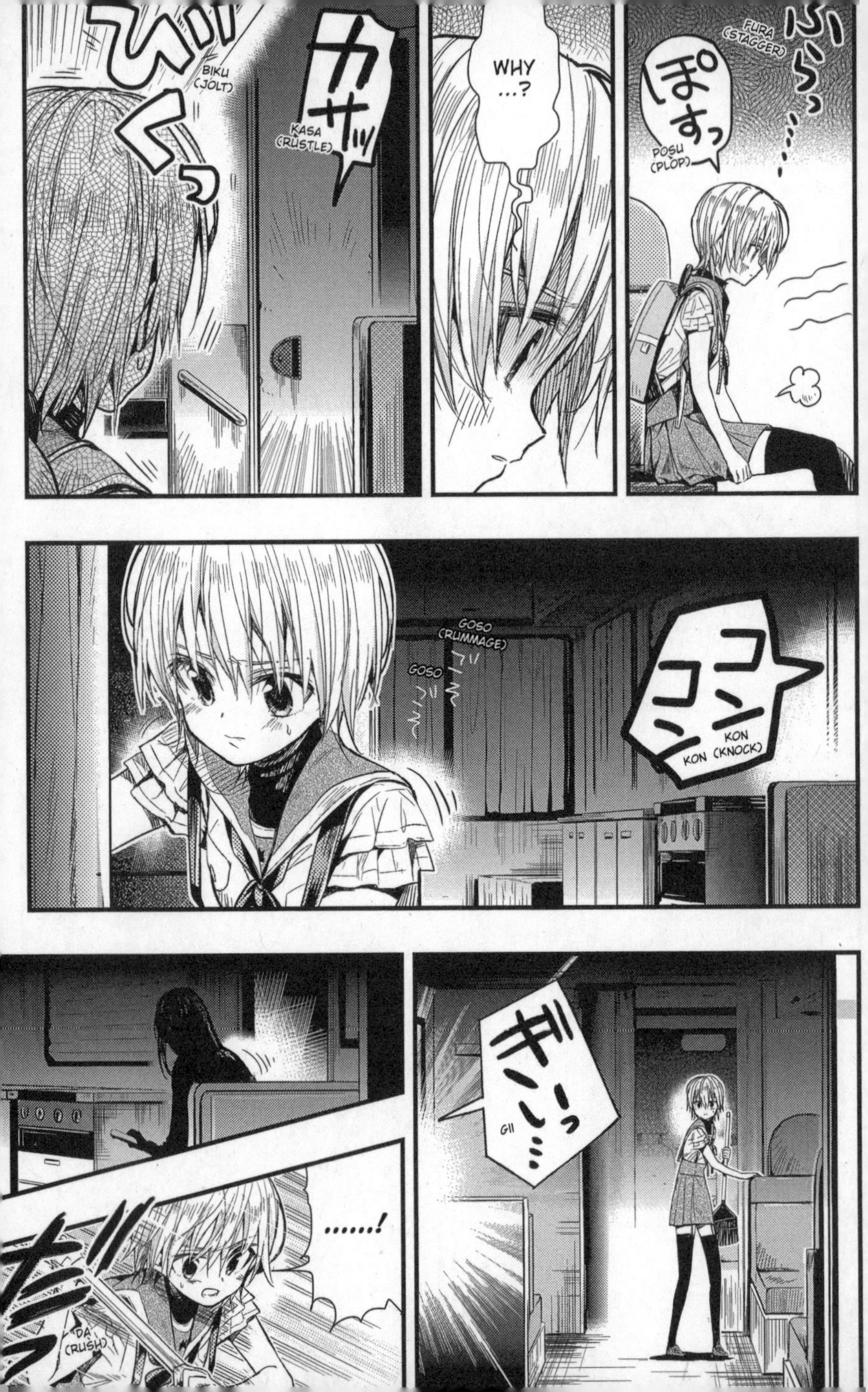
ふらっ…
FURA (STAGGER)
ぽすっ
POSU (PLOP)
WHY …?
カサッ
KASA (RUSTLE)
びくっ
BIKU (JOLT)
コンコン
KON KON (KNOCK)
GOSO (RUMMAGE)
ごそ
GOSO
ごそ
ぎぃっ…
GII
……!
ダッ
DA (RUSH)

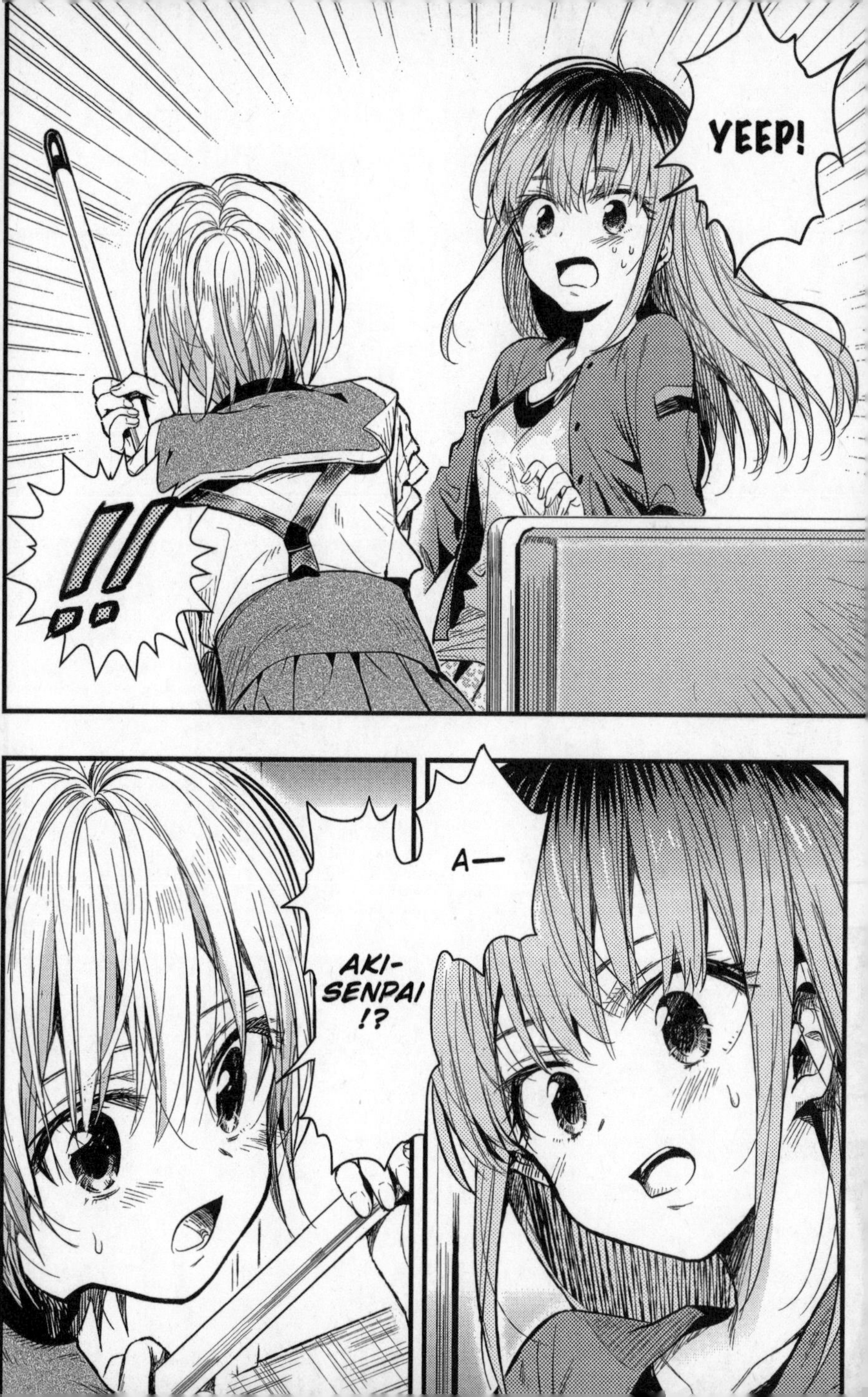
YEEP!
!!
A—
AKI-SENPAI!?

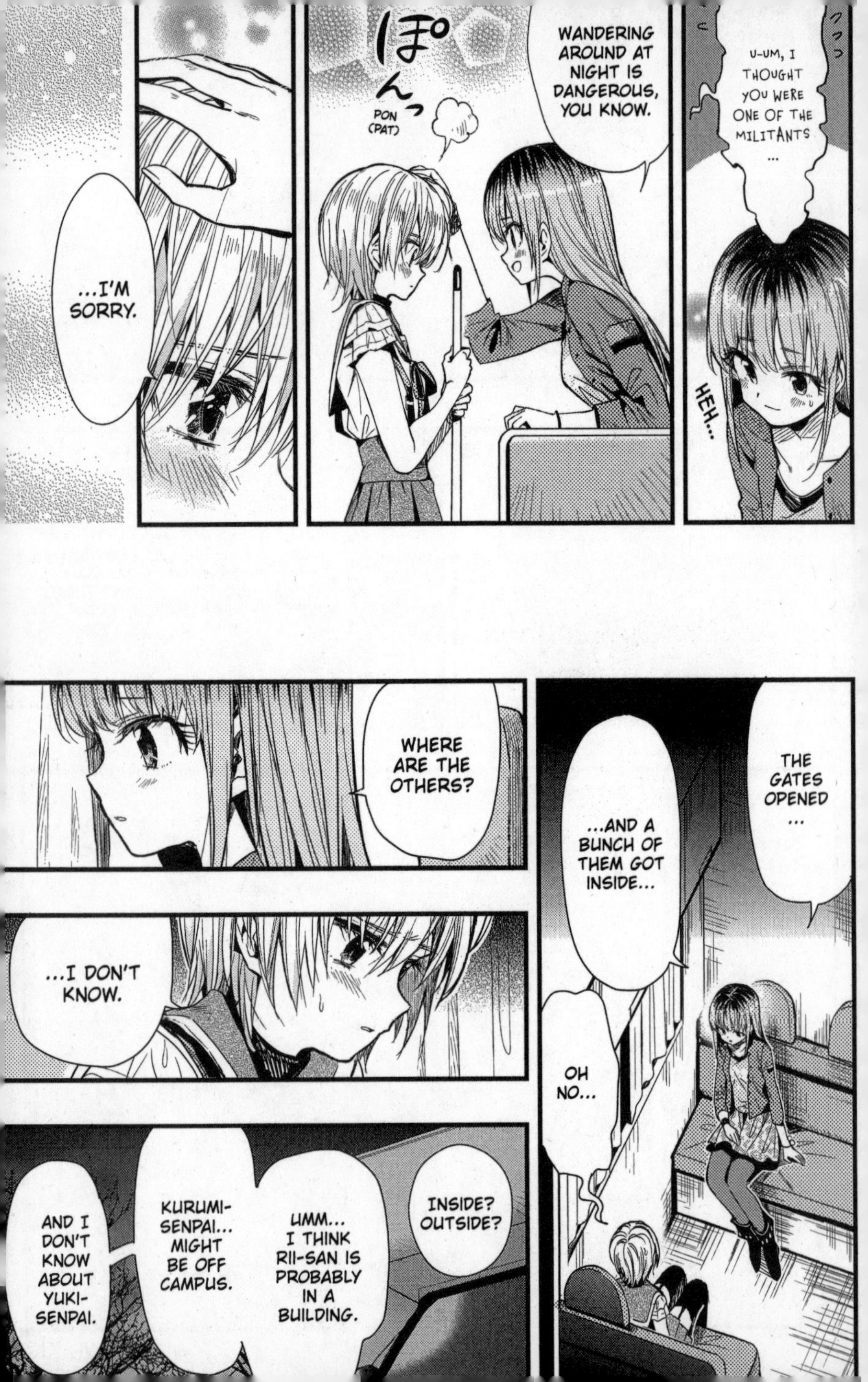
U-UM, I THOUGHT YOU WERE ONE OF THE MILITANTS...
HEH...
WANDERING AROUND AT NIGHT IS DANGEROUS, YOU KNOW.
ぽんっ
PON (PAT)
...I'M SORRY.
THE GATES OPENED...
...AND A BUNCH OF THEM GOT INSIDE...
OH NO...
WHERE ARE THE OTHERS?
...I DON'T KNOW.
INSIDE? OUTSIDE?
UMM... I THINK RII-SAN IS PROBABLY IN A BUILDING.
KURUMI-SENPAI... MIGHT BE OFF CAMPUS.
AND I DON'T KNOW ABOUT YUKI-SENPAI.

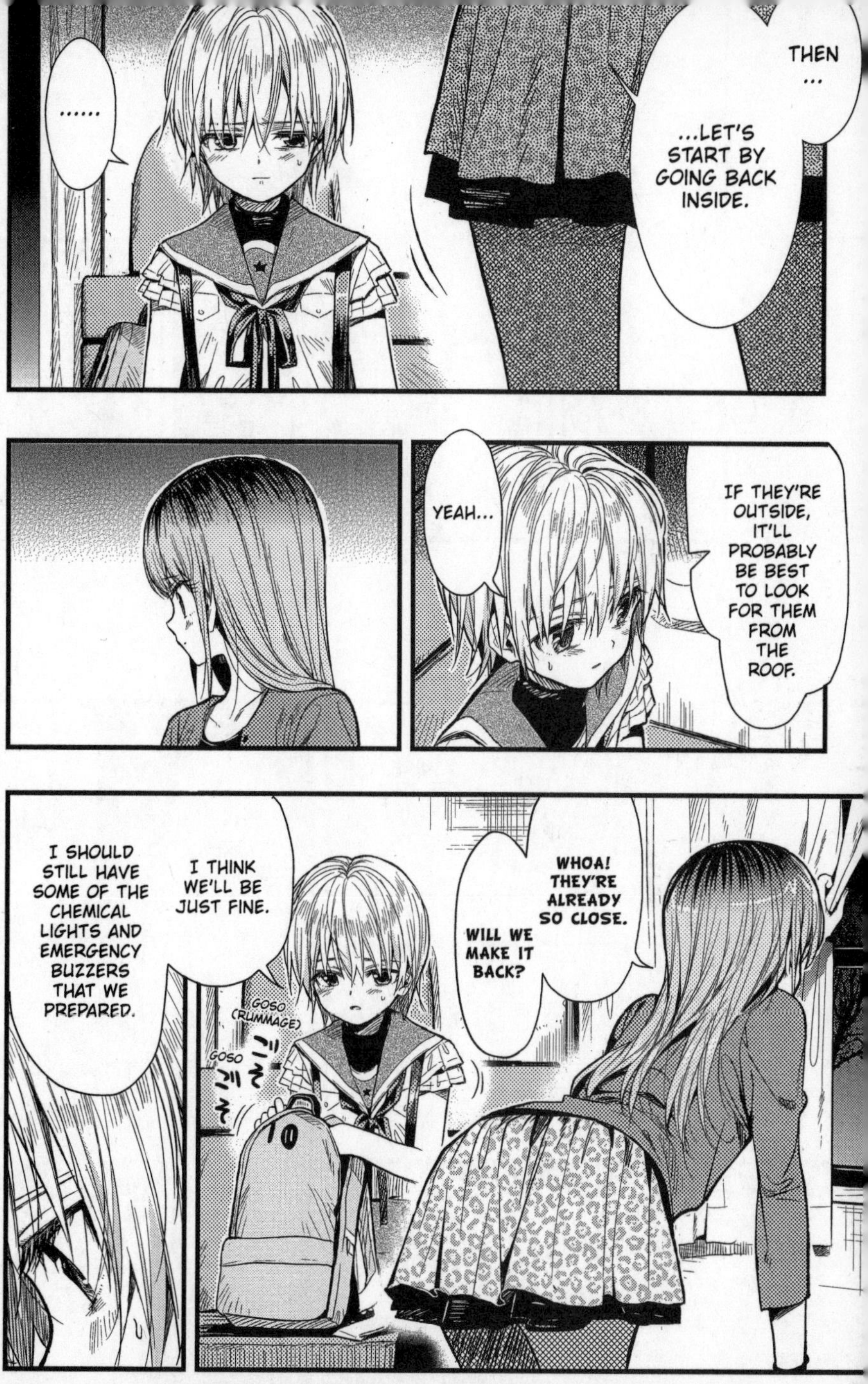
THEN ...
...LET'S START BY GOING BACK INSIDE.
......
IF THEY'RE OUTSIDE, IT'LL PROBABLY BE BEST TO LOOK FOR THEM FROM THE ROOF.
YEAH...
WHOA! THEY'RE ALREADY SO CLOSE.
WILL WE MAKE IT BACK?
GOSO (RUMMAGE) ごそ
GOSO ごそ
I THINK WE'LL BE JUST FINE.
I SHOULD STILL HAVE SOME OF THE CHEMICAL LIGHTS AND EMERGENCY BUZZERS THAT WE PREPARED.

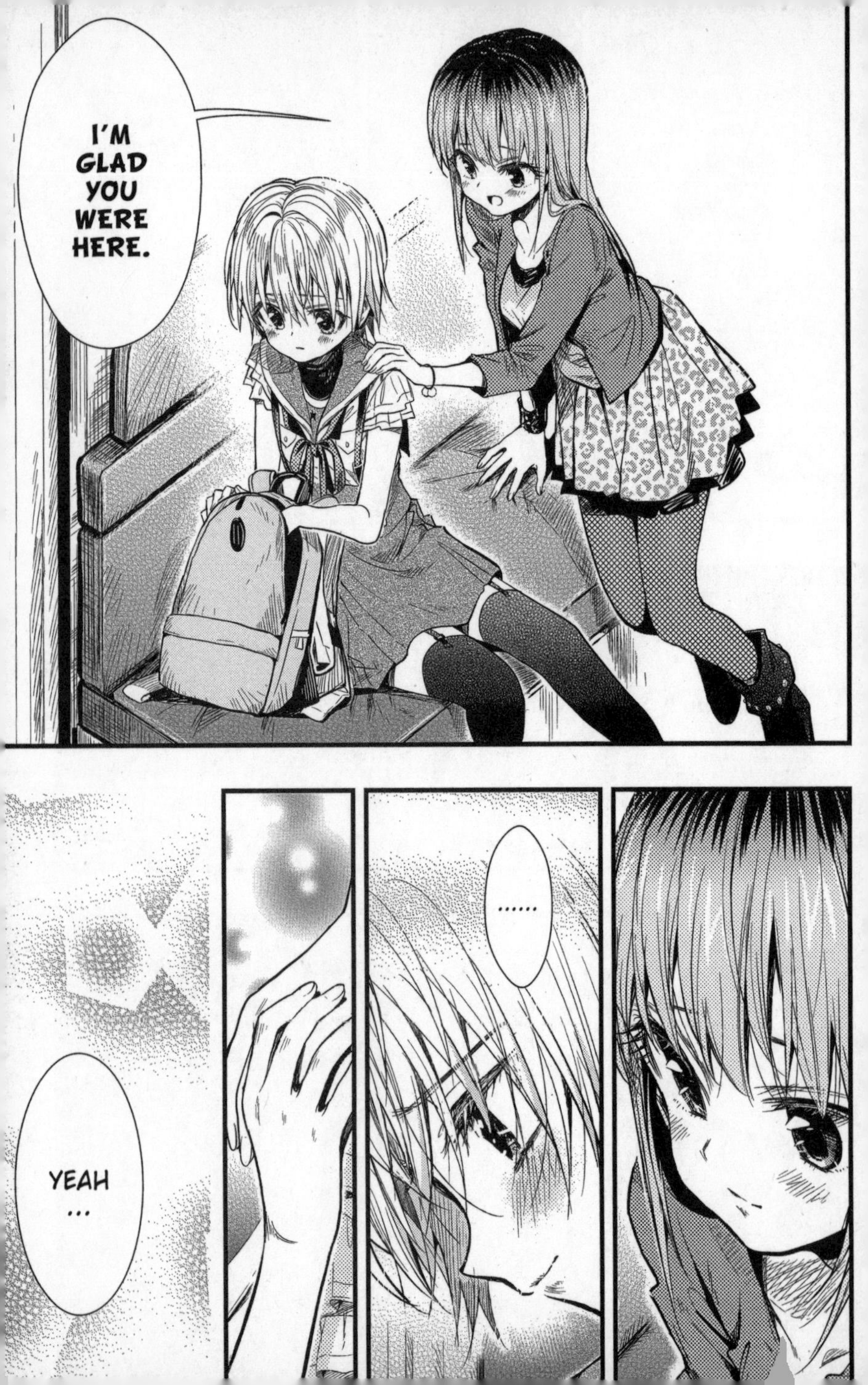
I'M GLAD YOU WERE HERE.
......
YEAH ...

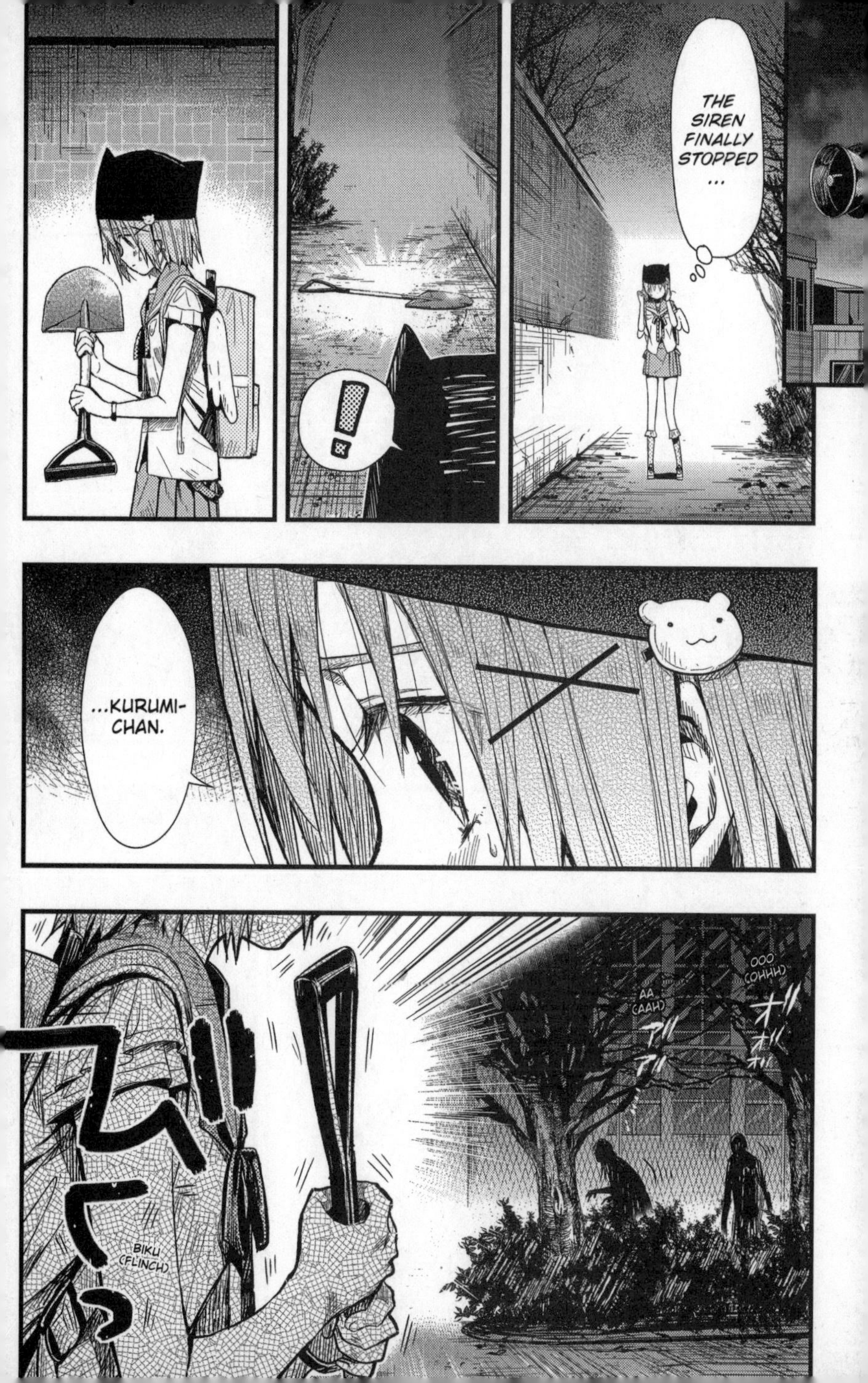
THE SIREN FINALLY STOPPED ...
!
...KURUMI-CHAN.
OOO (OHHH)
AA (AAH)
BIKU (FLINCH)

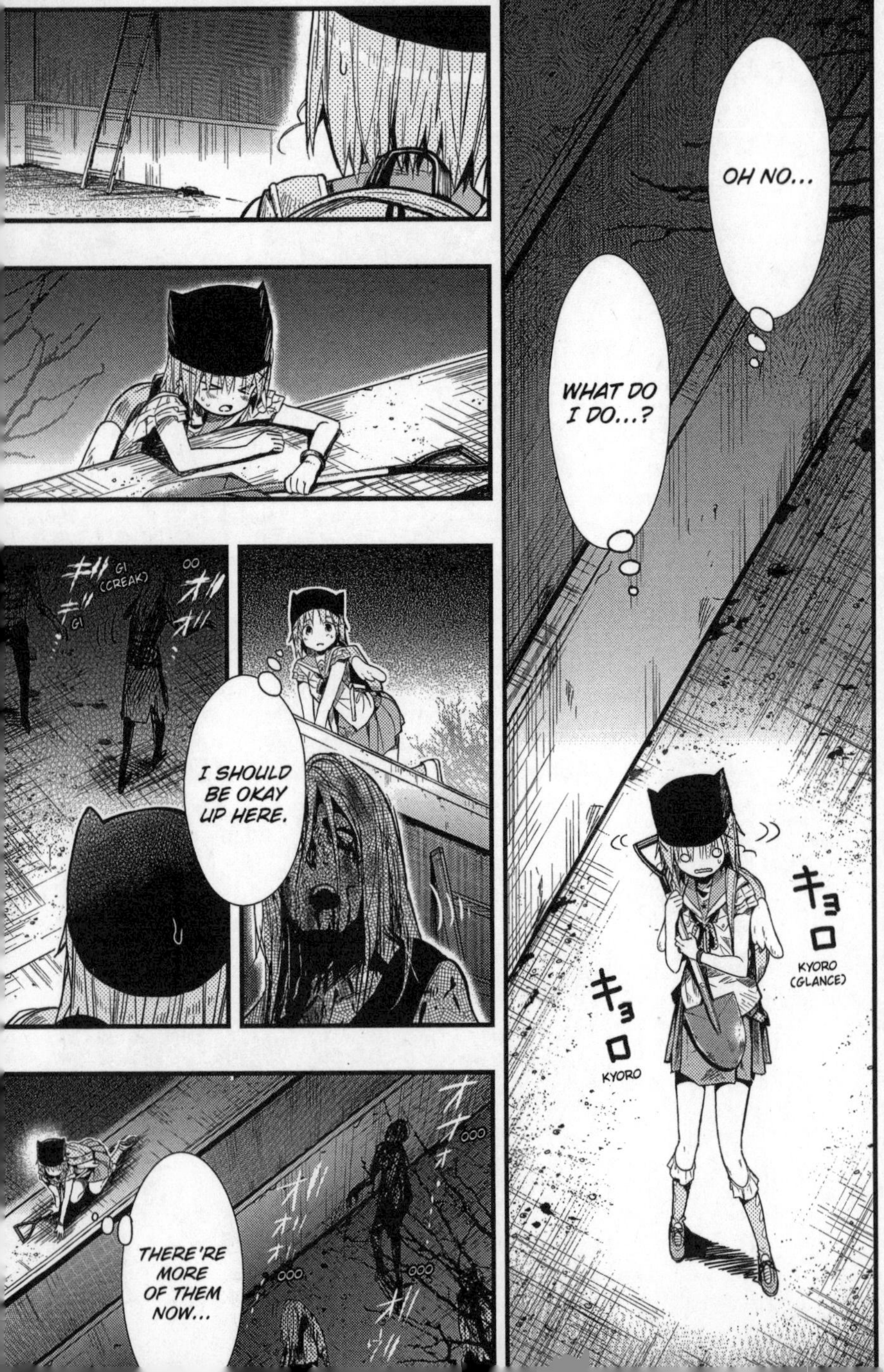
OH NO...
WHAT DO I DO...?
キョロ
KYORO (GLANCE)
キョロ
KYORO
I SHOULD BE OKAY UP HERE.
GI (CREAK)
GI
OO
THERE'RE MORE OF THEM NOW...
OOO
OOO
OOO

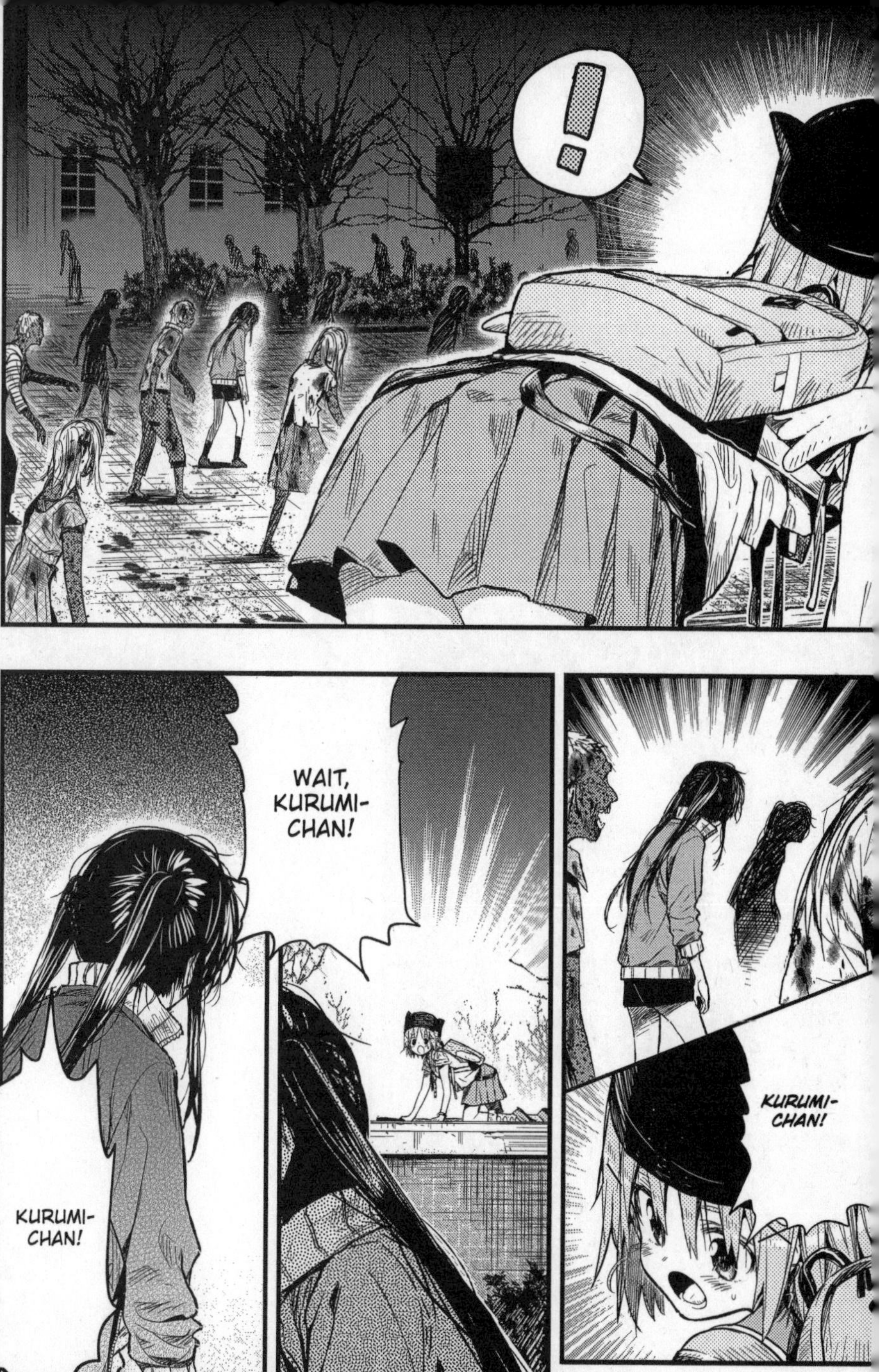
!
KURUMI-CHAN!
WAIT, KURUMI-CHAN!
KURUMI-CHAN!

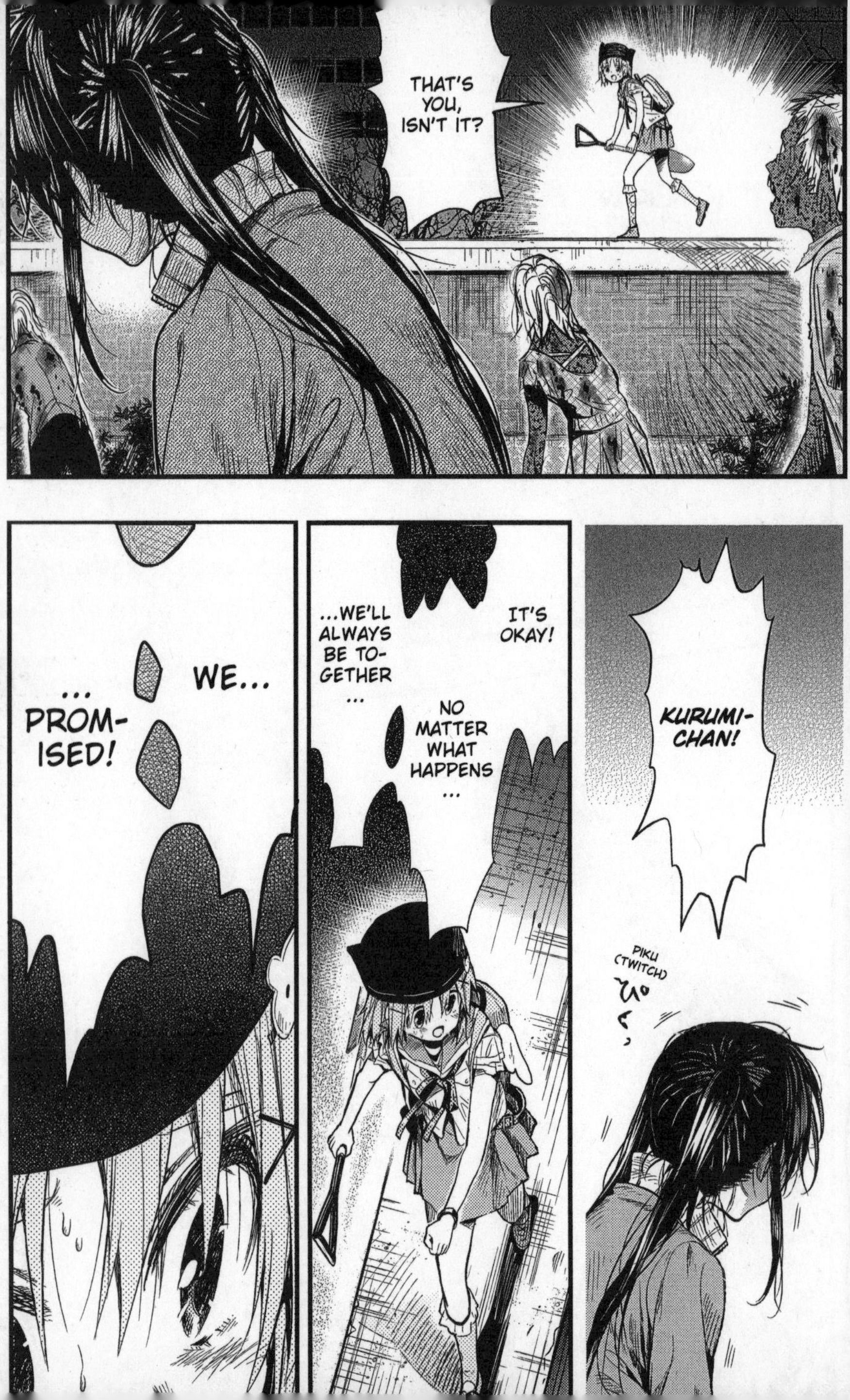

THAT'S YOU, ISN'T IT?
KURUMI-CHAN!
PIKU (TWITCH)
ぴく
IT'S OKAY!
NO MATTER WHAT HAPPENS...
...WE'LL ALWAYS BE TO-GETHER...
WE...
...PROM-ISED!

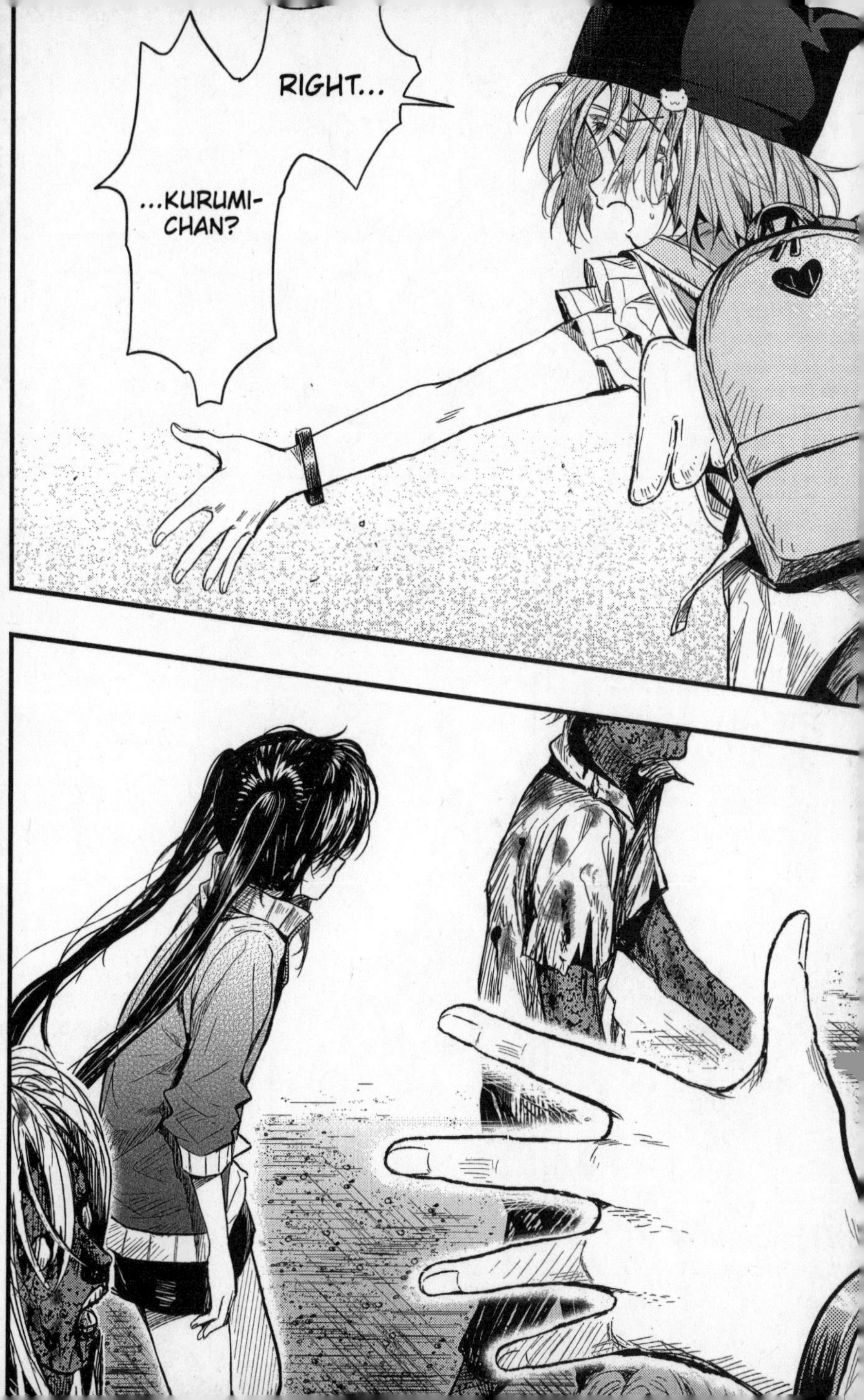
RIGHT...
...KURUMI-CHAN?

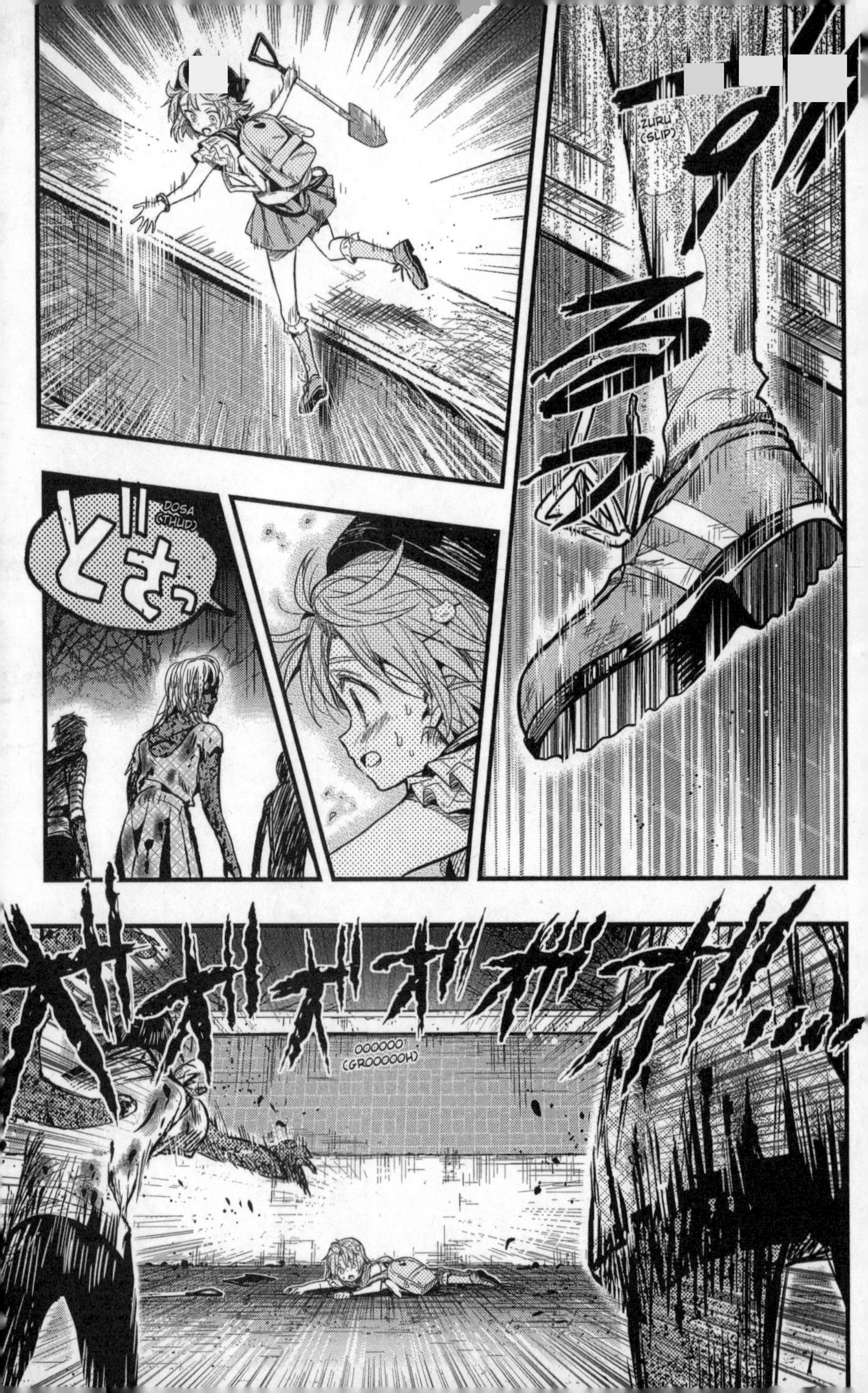
ZURU (SLIP)
どさっ
DOSA (THUD)
OOOOOO (GROOOOOH)

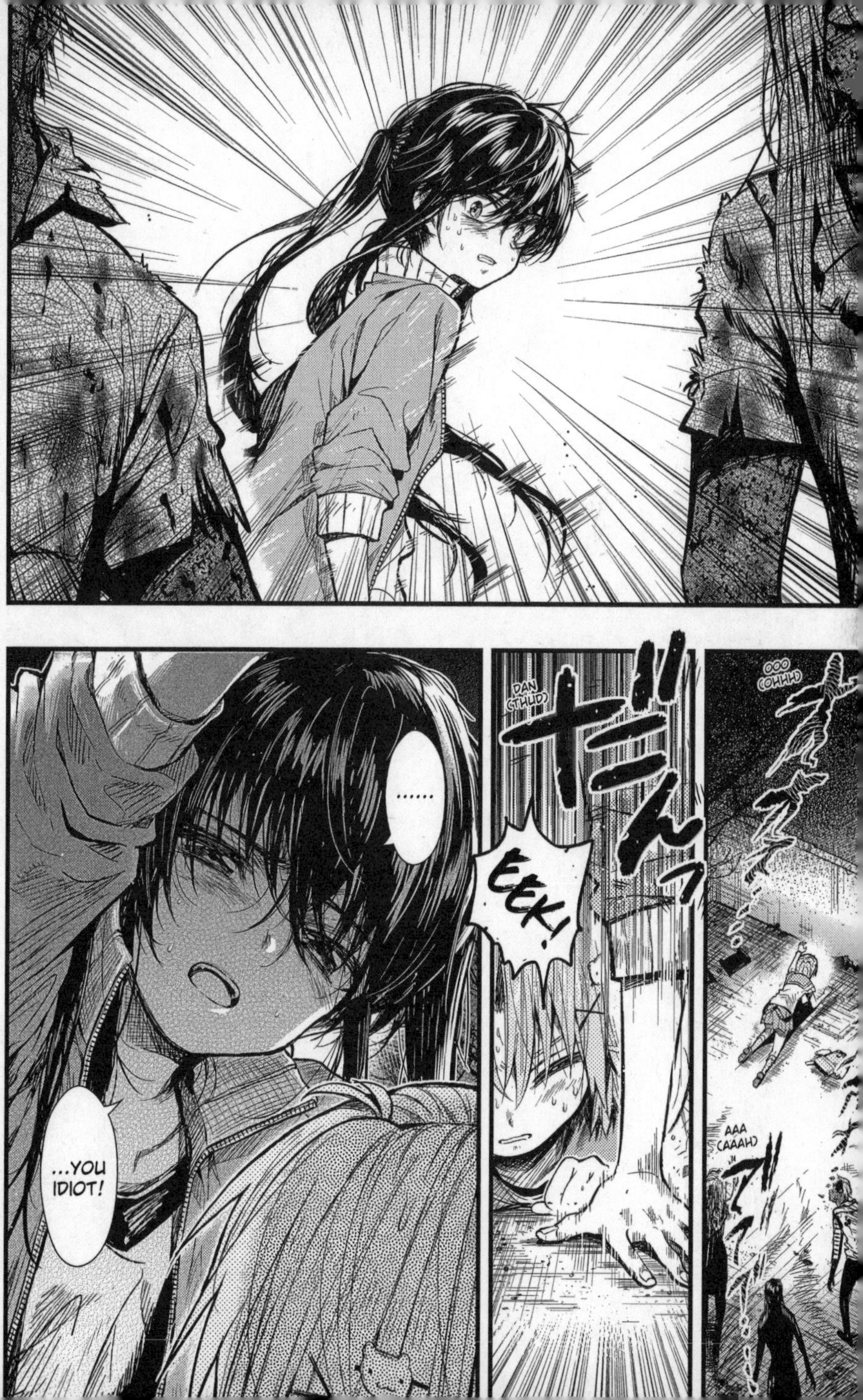
OOO (OHHH)
AAA (AAAH)
DAN (THUD)
EEEK!
......
...YOU IDIOT!

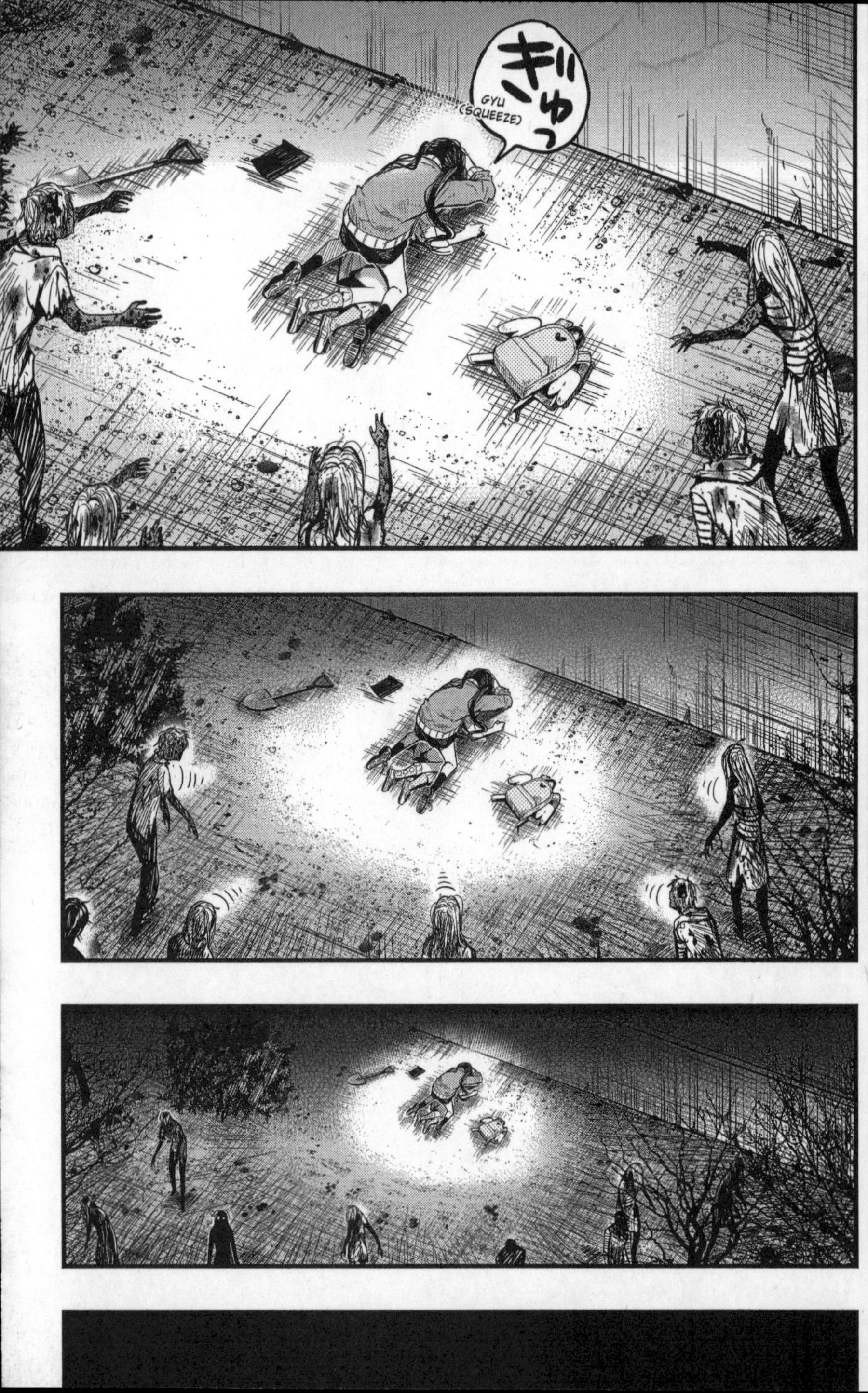
ぎゅっ
GYU (SQUEEZE)

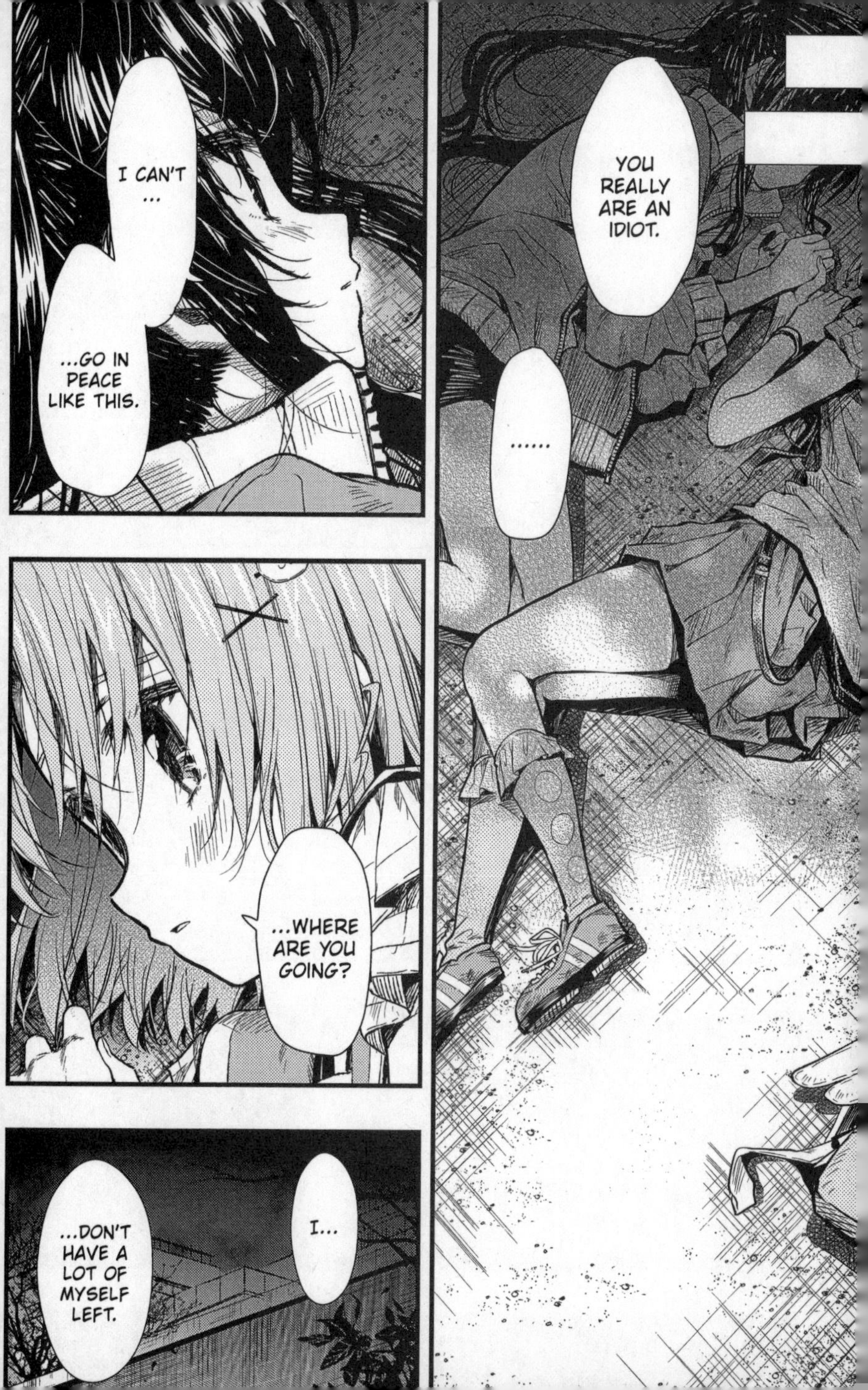
YOU REALLY ARE AN IDIOT.
......
I CAN'T ...
...GO IN PEACE LIKE THIS.
...WHERE ARE YOU GOING?
I...
...DON'T HAVE A LOT OF MYSELF LEFT.

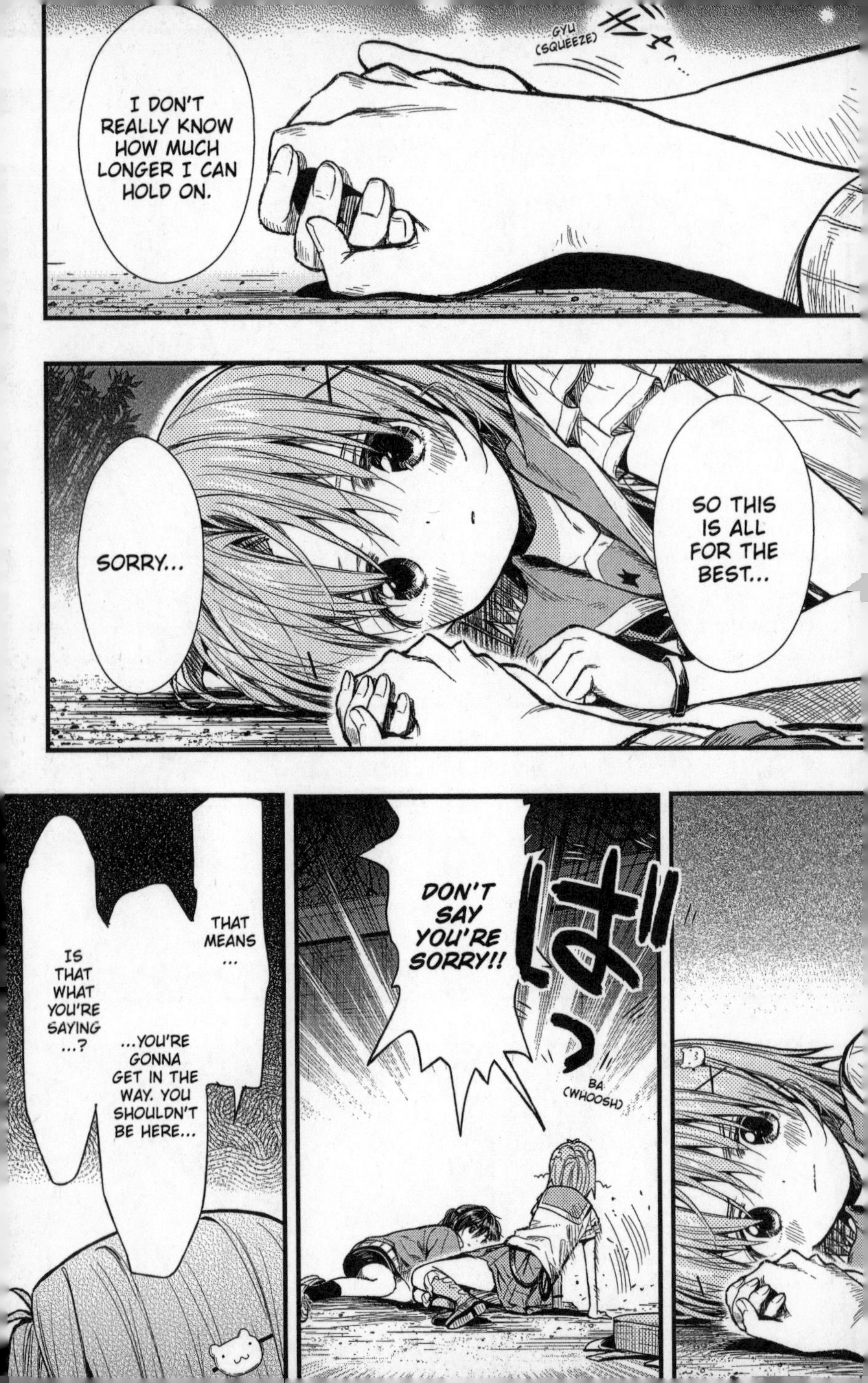
ギュ
GYU (SQUEEZE)
I DON'T REALLY KNOW HOW MUCH LONGER I CAN HOLD ON.
SO THIS IS ALL FOR THE BEST...
SORRY...
ばっ
BA (WHOOSH)
DON'T SAY YOU'RE SORRY!!
THAT MEANS...
...YOU'RE GONNA GET IN THE WAY. YOU SHOULDN'T BE HERE...
IS THAT WHAT YOU'RE SAYING...?

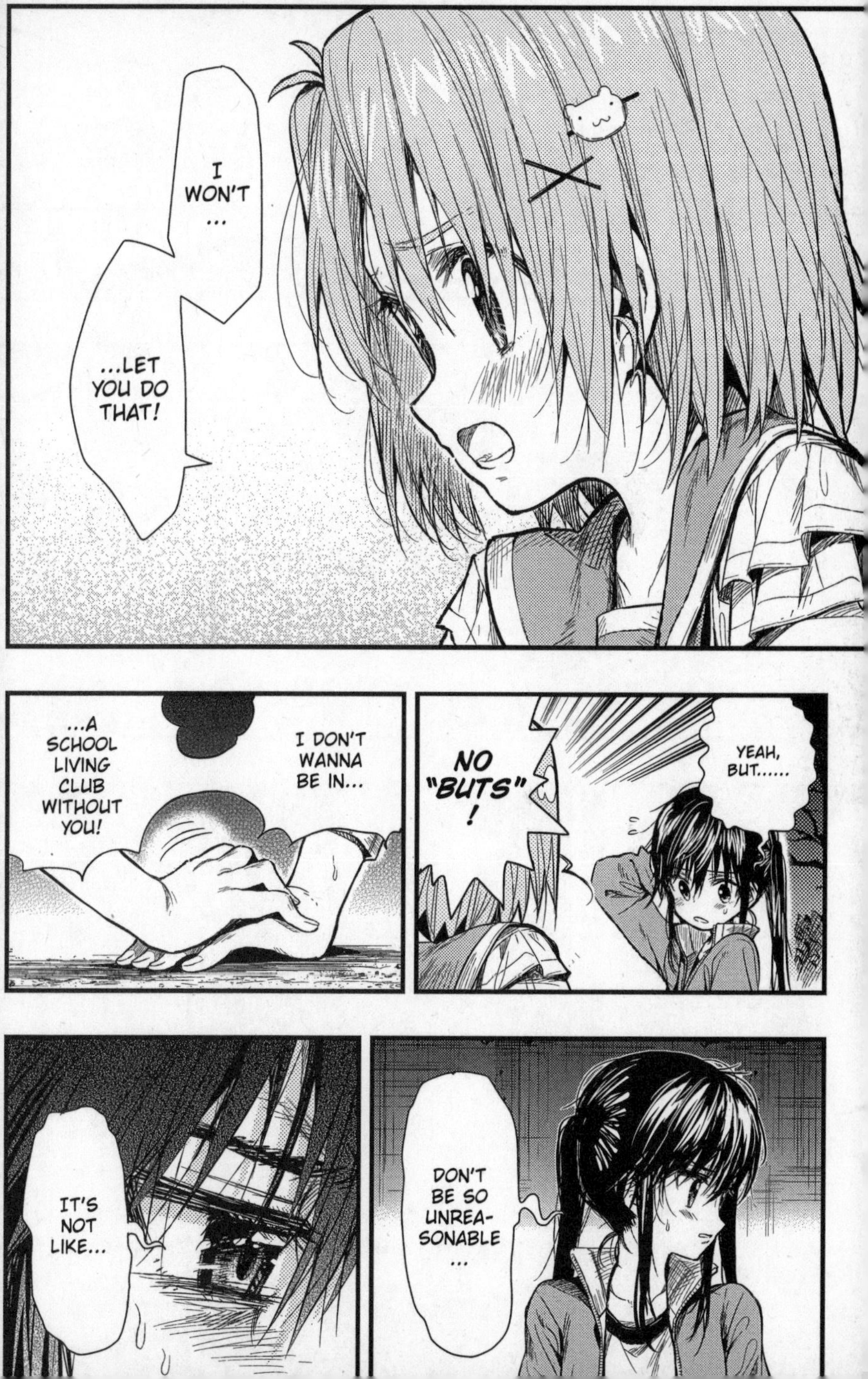
I WON'T ...
...LET YOU DO THAT!
YEAH, BUT......
NO "BUTS"!
I DON'T WANNA BE IN...
...A SCHOOL LIVING CLUB WITHOUT YOU!
DON'T BE SO UNREA-SONABLE ...
IT'S NOT LIKE...

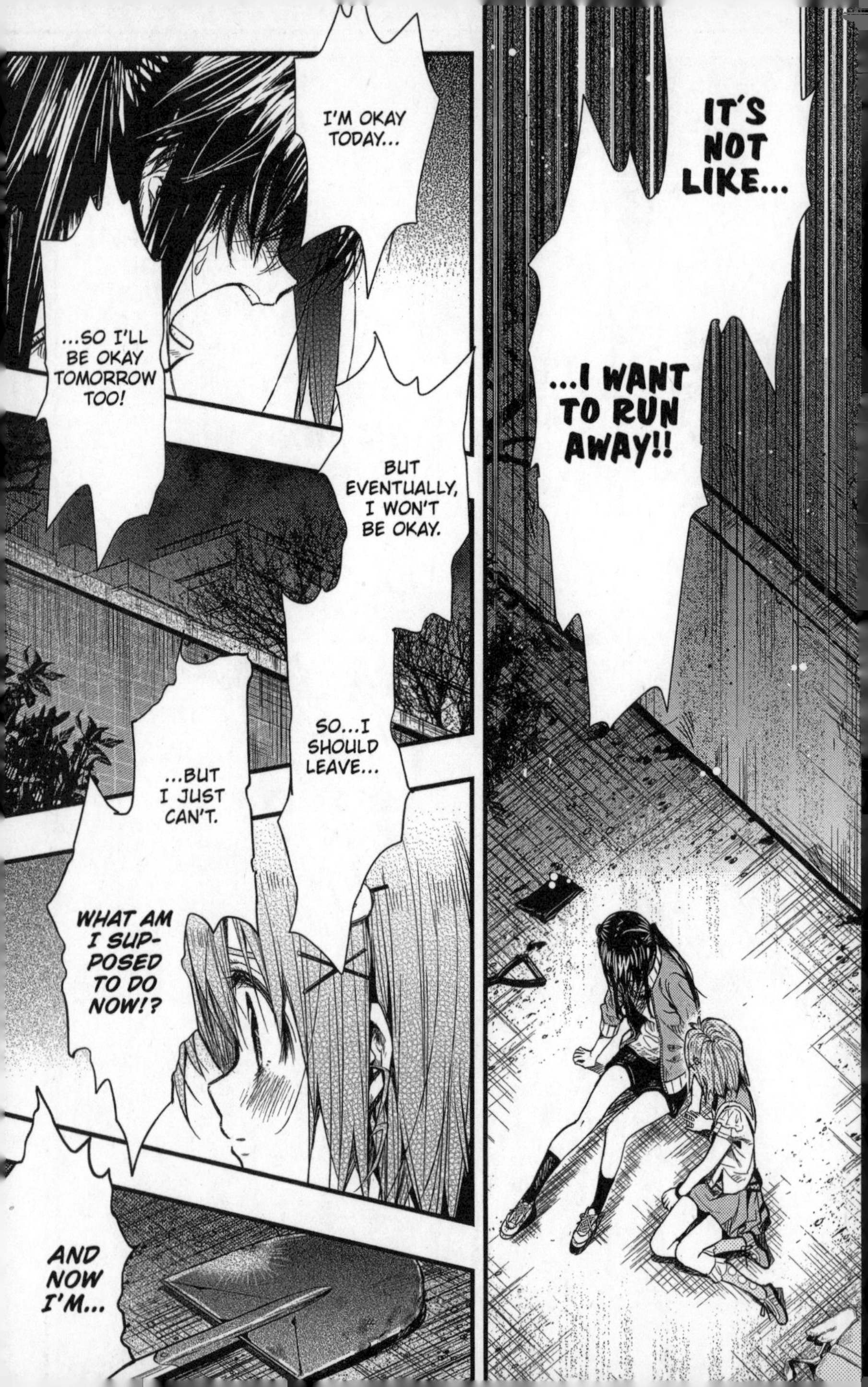
IT'S NOT LIKE...
...I WANT TO RUN AWAY!!
I'M OKAY TODAY...
...SO I'LL BE OKAY TOMORROW TOO!
BUT EVENTUALLY, I WON'T BE OKAY.
SO...I SHOULD LEAVE...
...BUT I JUST CAN'T.
WHAT AM I SUP-POSED TO DO NOW!?
AND NOW I'M...

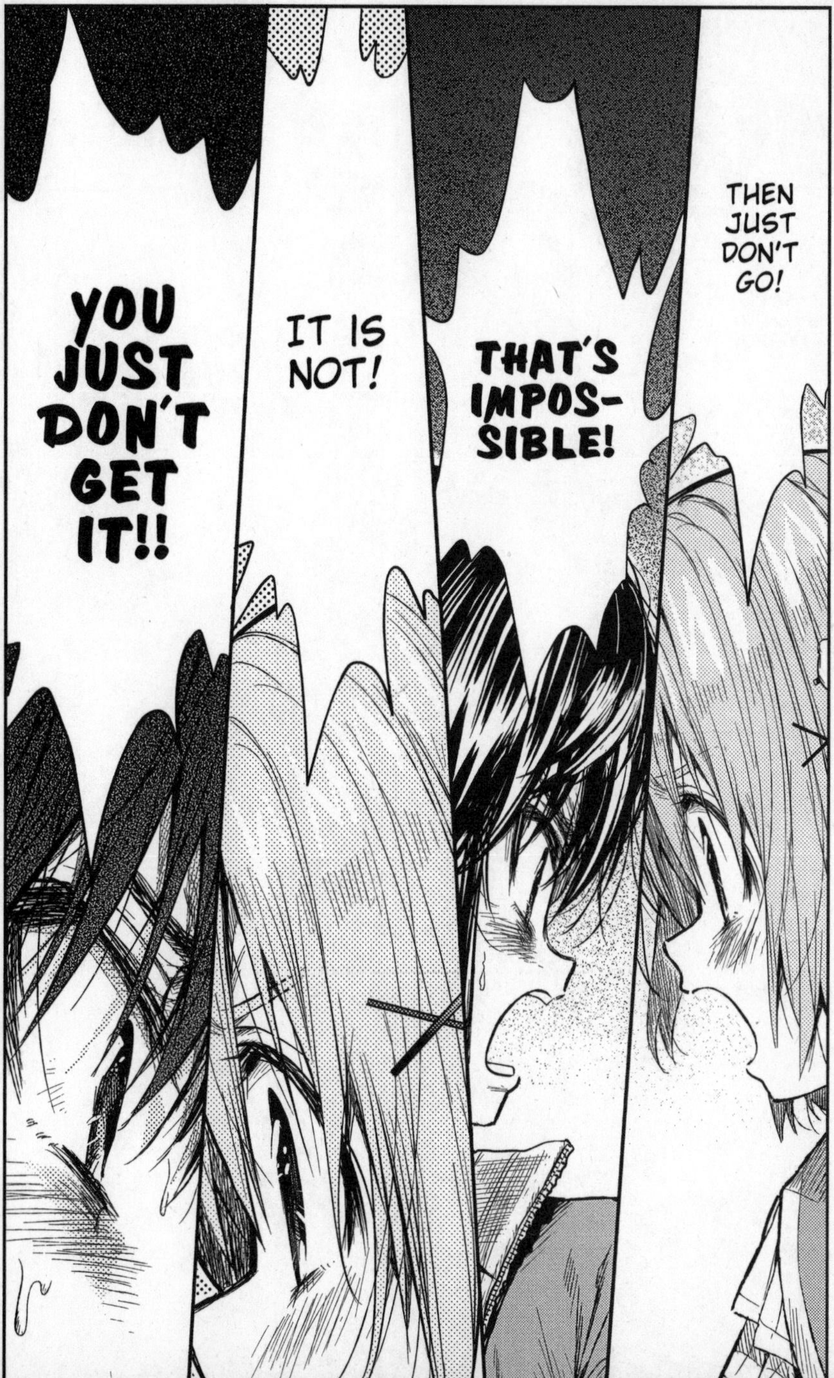
THEN JUST DON'T GO!
THAT'S IMPOS-SIBLE!
IT IS NOT!
YOU JUST DON'T GET IT!!

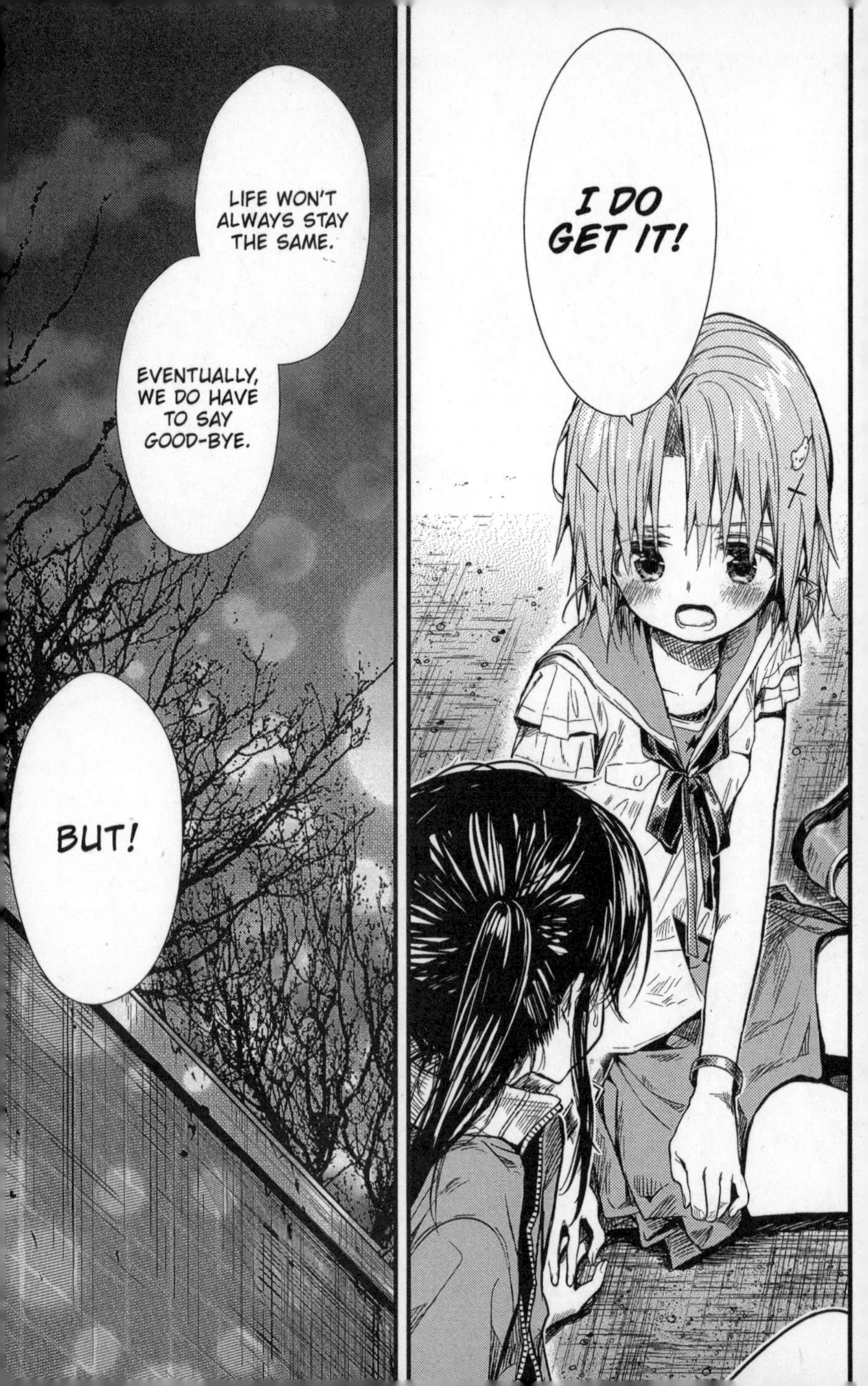
I DO GET IT!
LIFE WON'T ALWAYS STAY THE SAME.
EVENTUALLY, WE DO HAVE TO SAY GOOD-BYE.
BUT!

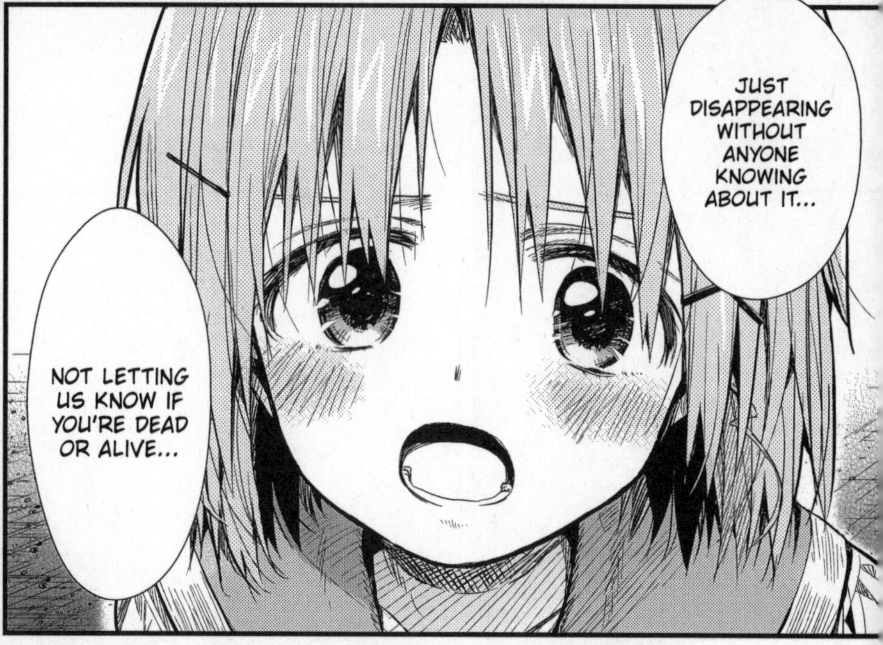
JUST DISAPPEARING WITHOUT ANYONE KNOWING ABOUT IT...
NOT LETTING US KNOW IF YOU'RE DEAD OR ALIVE...

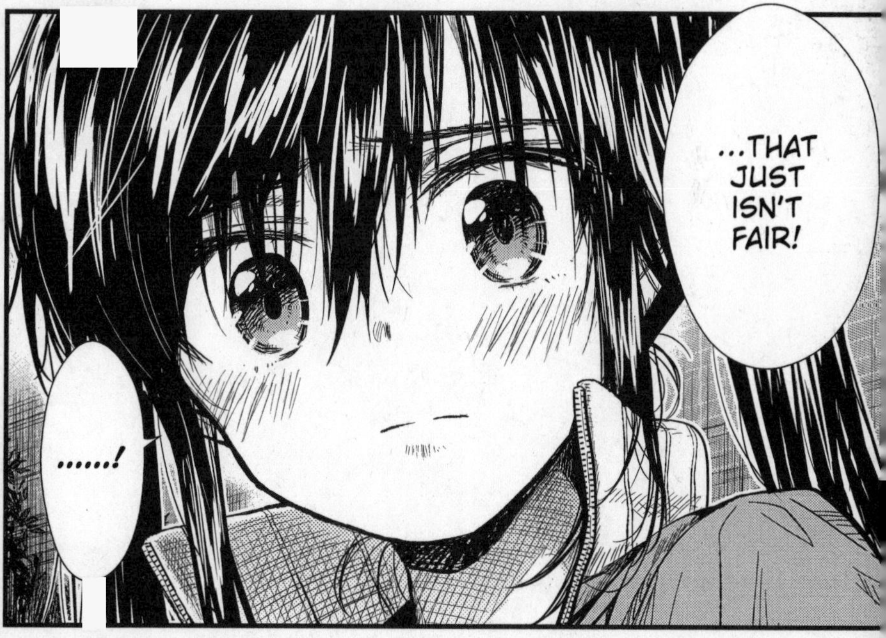
...THAT JUST ISN'T FAIR!
......!

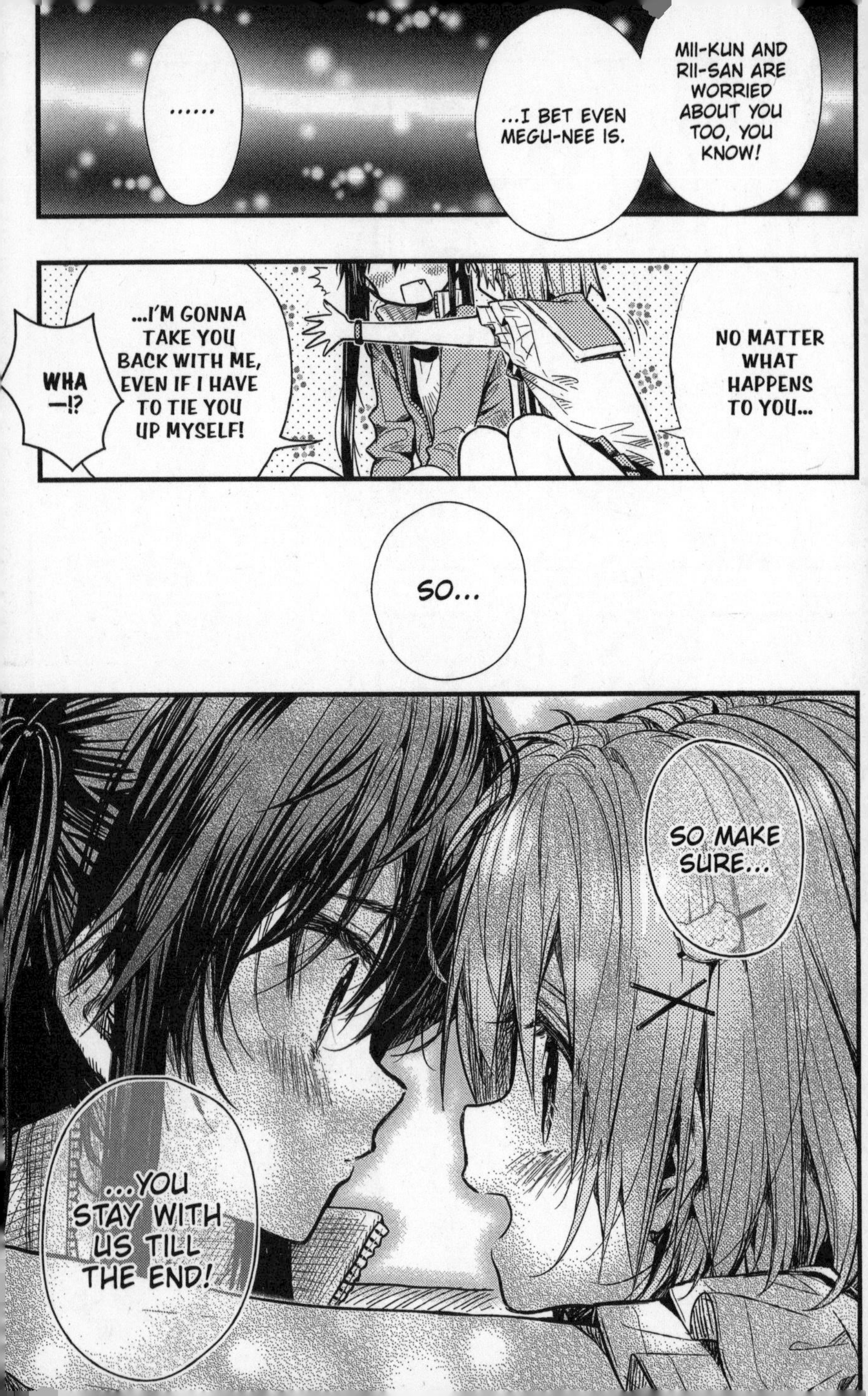
MII-KUN AND RII-SAN ARE WORRIED ABOUT YOU TOO, YOU KNOW!
...I BET EVEN MEGU-NEE IS.
......
NO MATTER WHAT HAPPENS TO YOU...
...I'M GONNA TAKE YOU BACK WITH ME, EVEN IF I HAVE TO TIE YOU UP MYSELF!
WHA—!?
SO...
SO MAKE SURE...
...YOU STAY WITH US TILL THE END!

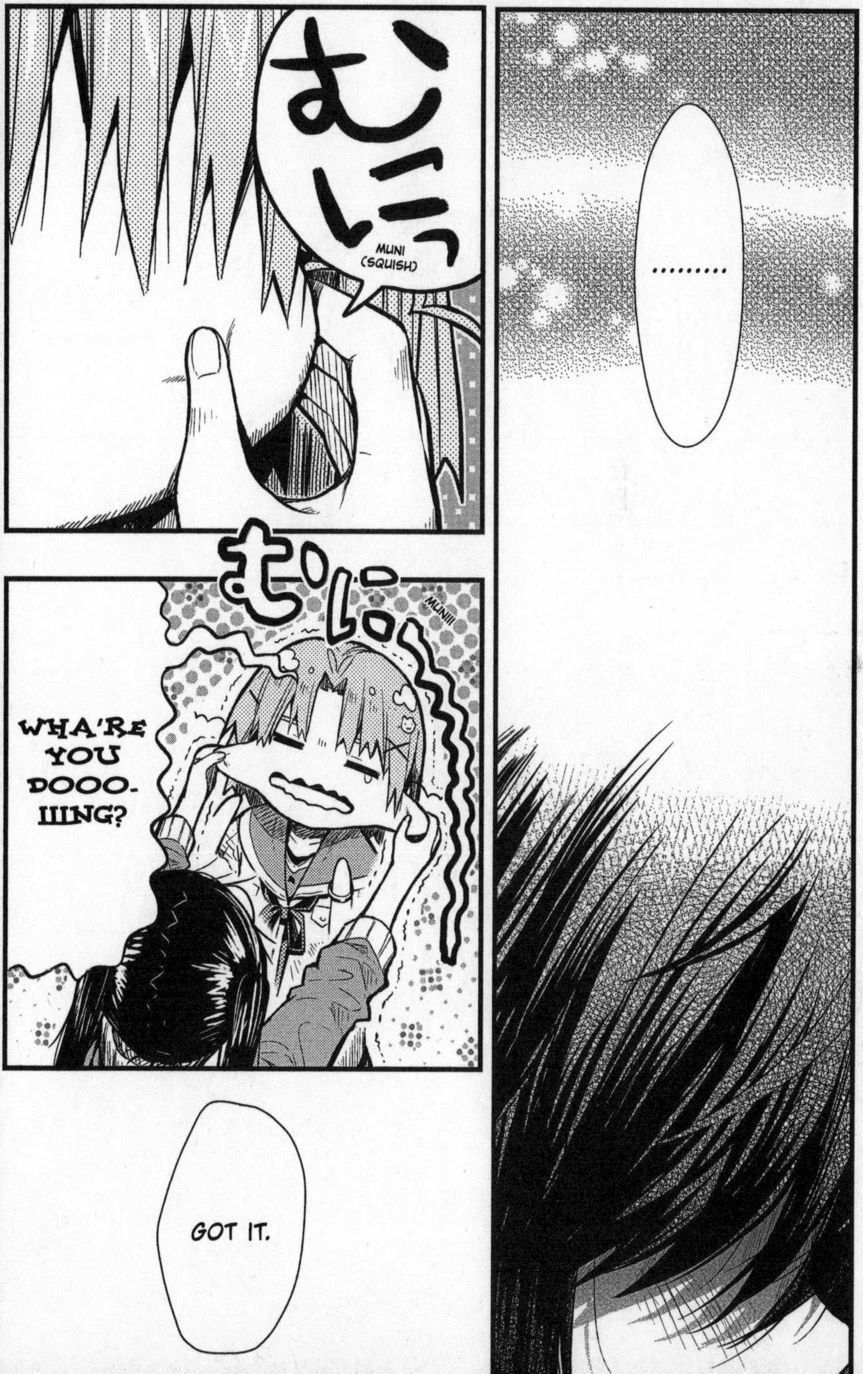
……….
むにっ
MUNI (SQUISH)
むにぃ
MUNIII
WHA'RE YOU DOOOO-IIING?
GOT IT.

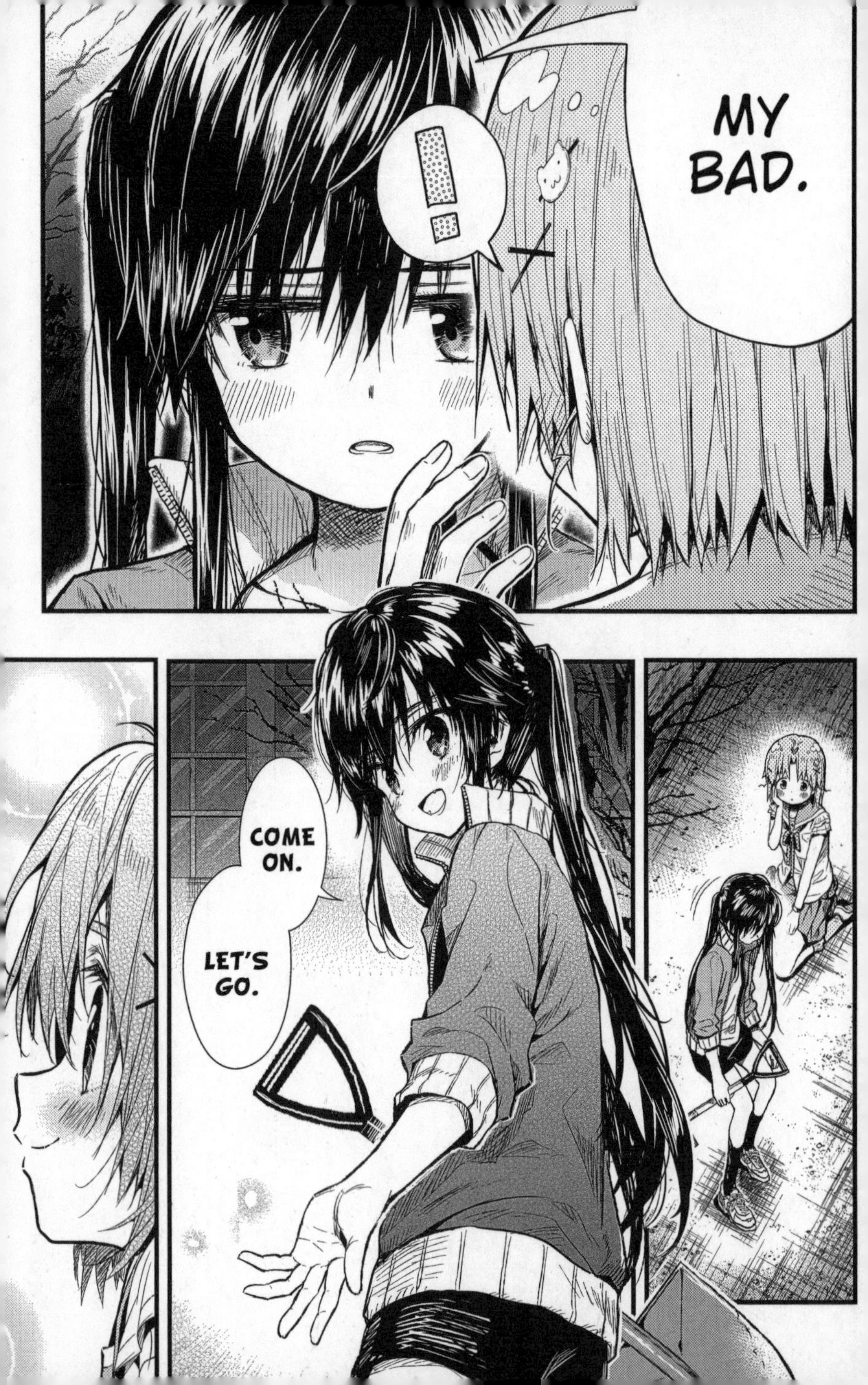
MY BAD.
!
COME ON.
LET'S GO.

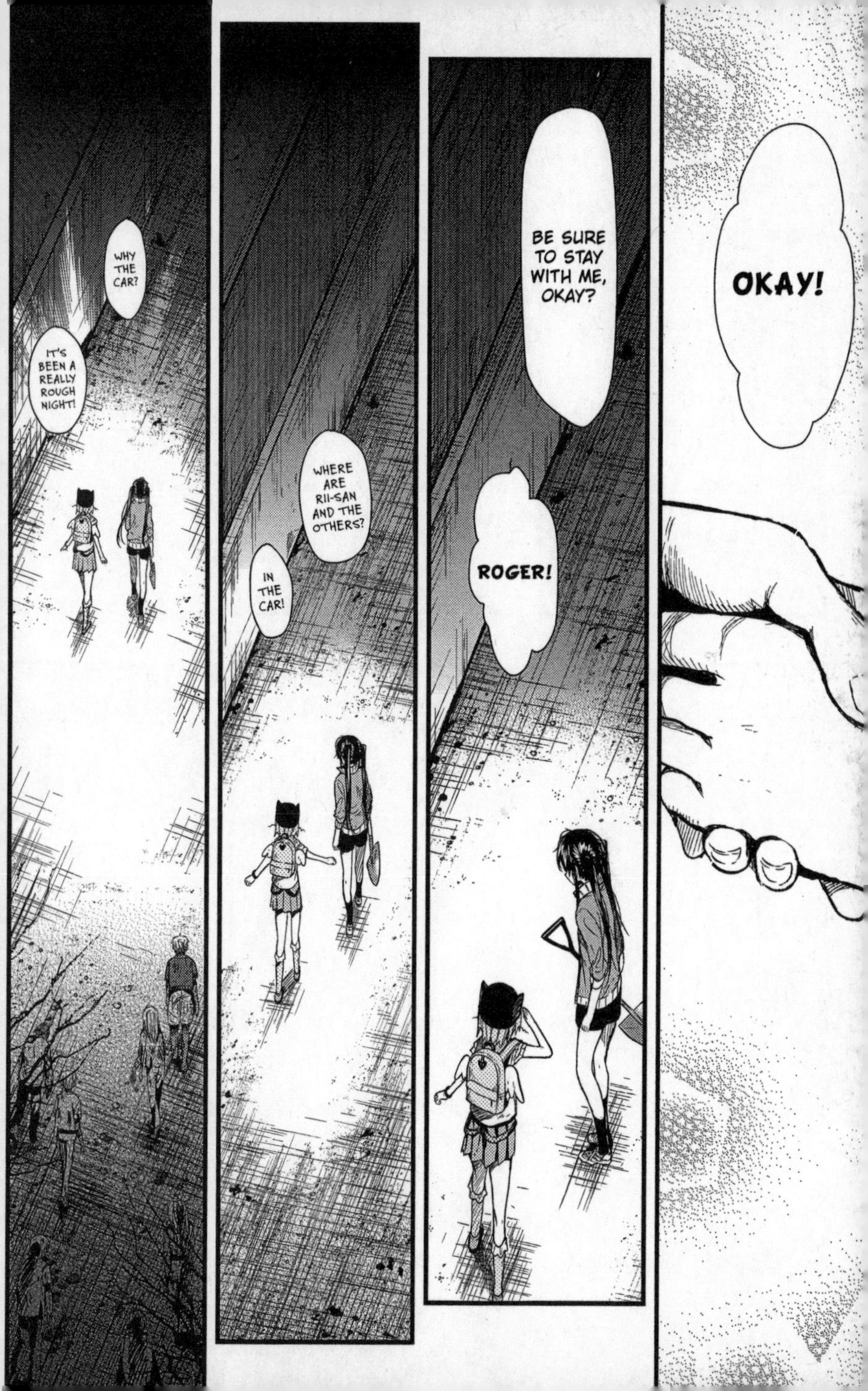
OKAY!
BE SURE TO STAY WITH ME, OKAY?
ROGER!
WHERE ARE RII-SAN AND THE OTHERS?
IN THE CAR!
WHY THE CAR?
IT'S BEEN A REALLY ROUGH NIGHT!

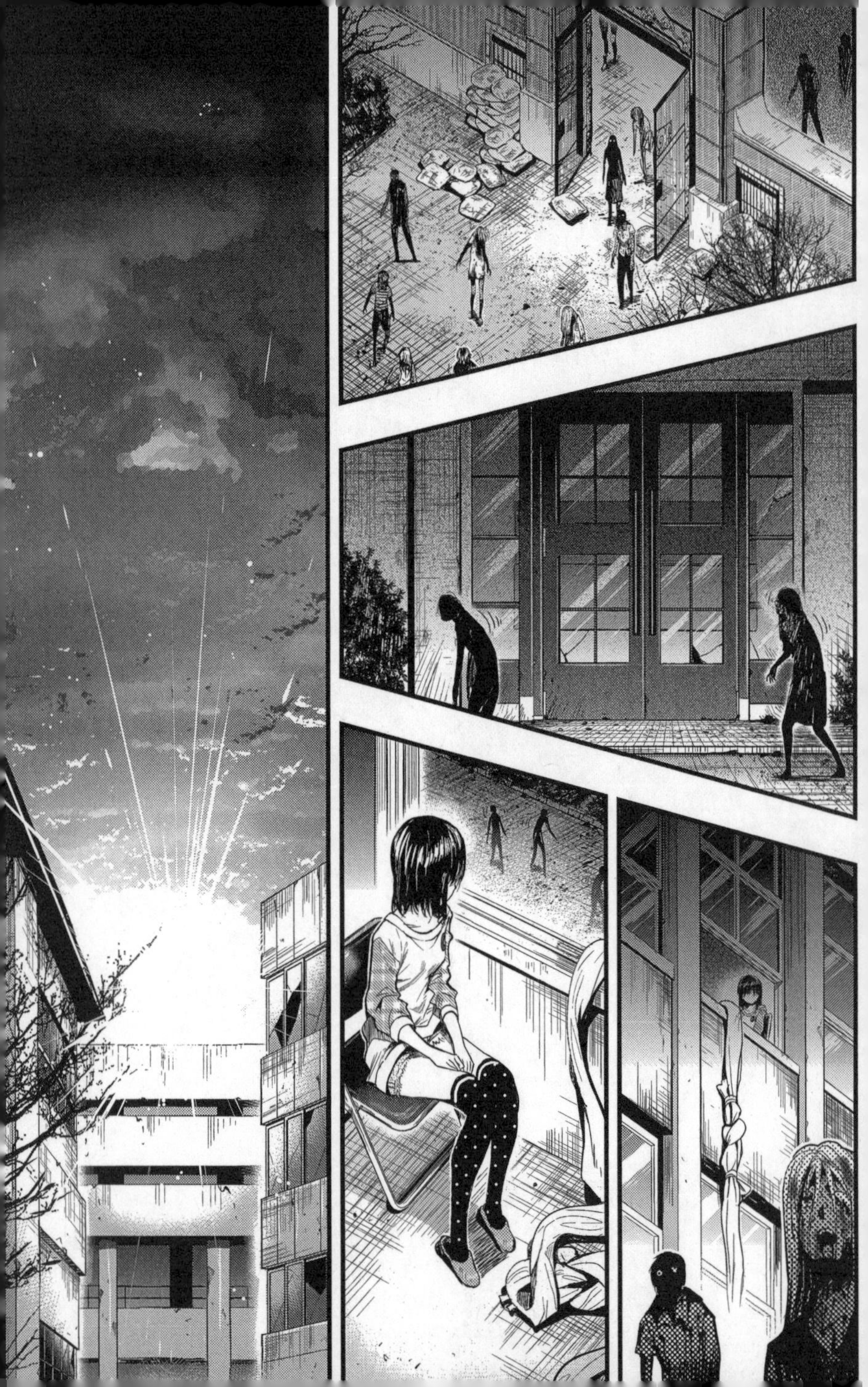

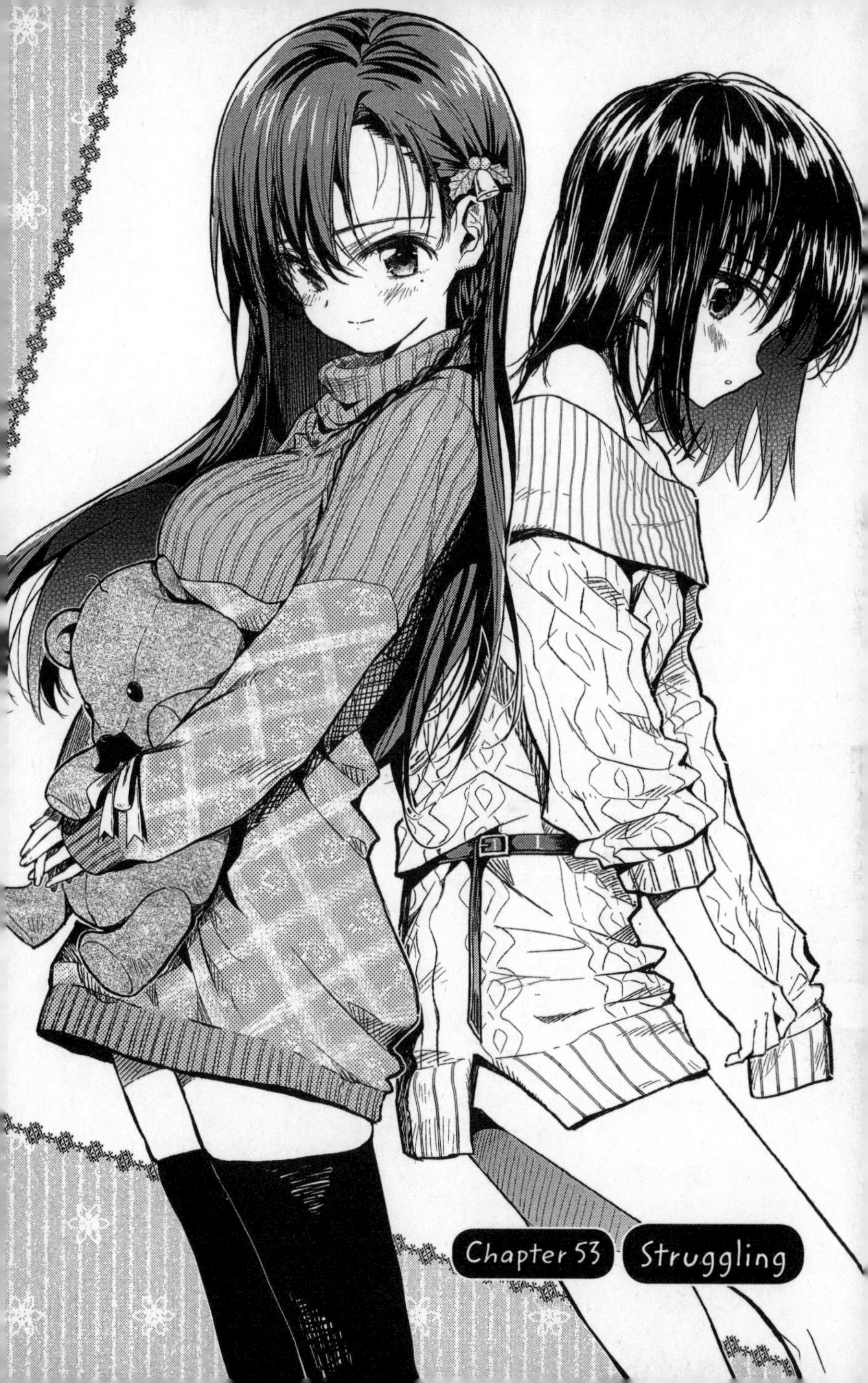
Chapter 53
Struggling

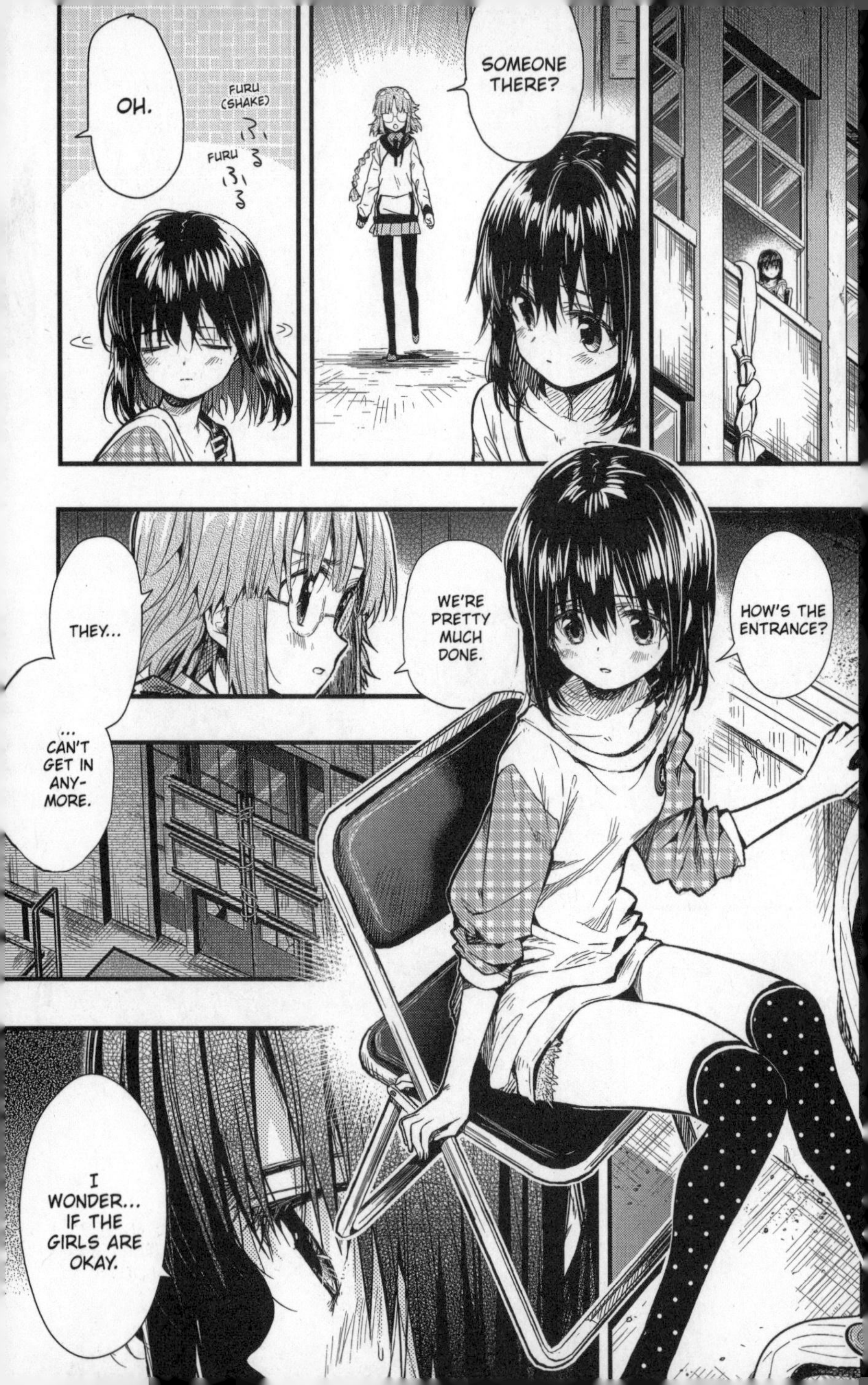
SOMEONE THERE?
OH.
FURU (SHAKE)
ふる
FURU
ふる
HOW'S THE ENTRANCE?
WE'RE PRETTY MUCH DONE.
THEY...
... CAN'T GET IN ANY-MORE.
I WONDER... IF THE GIRLS ARE OKAY.

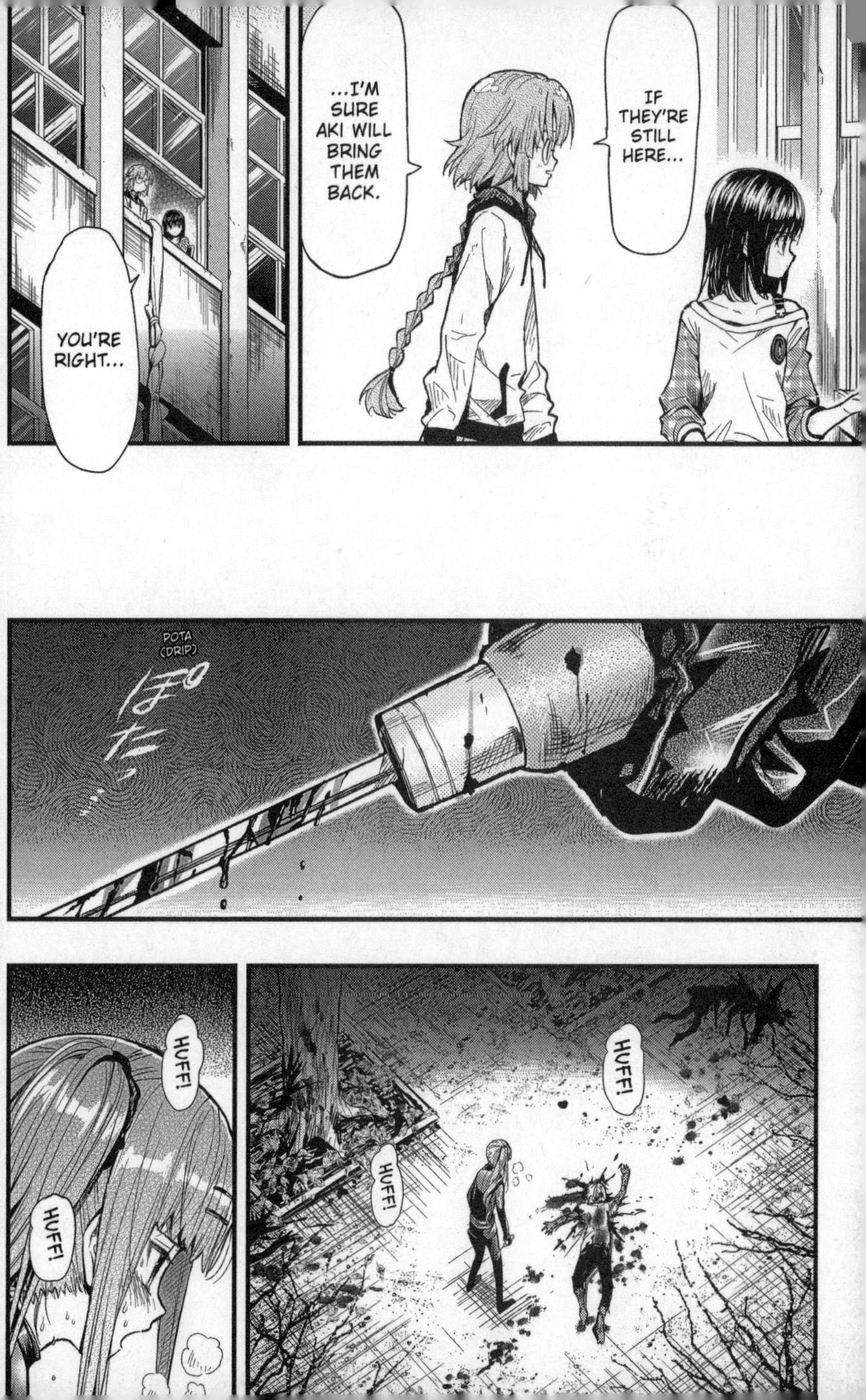
IF THEY'RE STILL HERE...
...I'M SURE AKI WILL BRING THEM BACK.
YOU'RE RIGHT...
POTA (DRIP)
ぽたっ
HUFF!
HUFF!
HUFF!

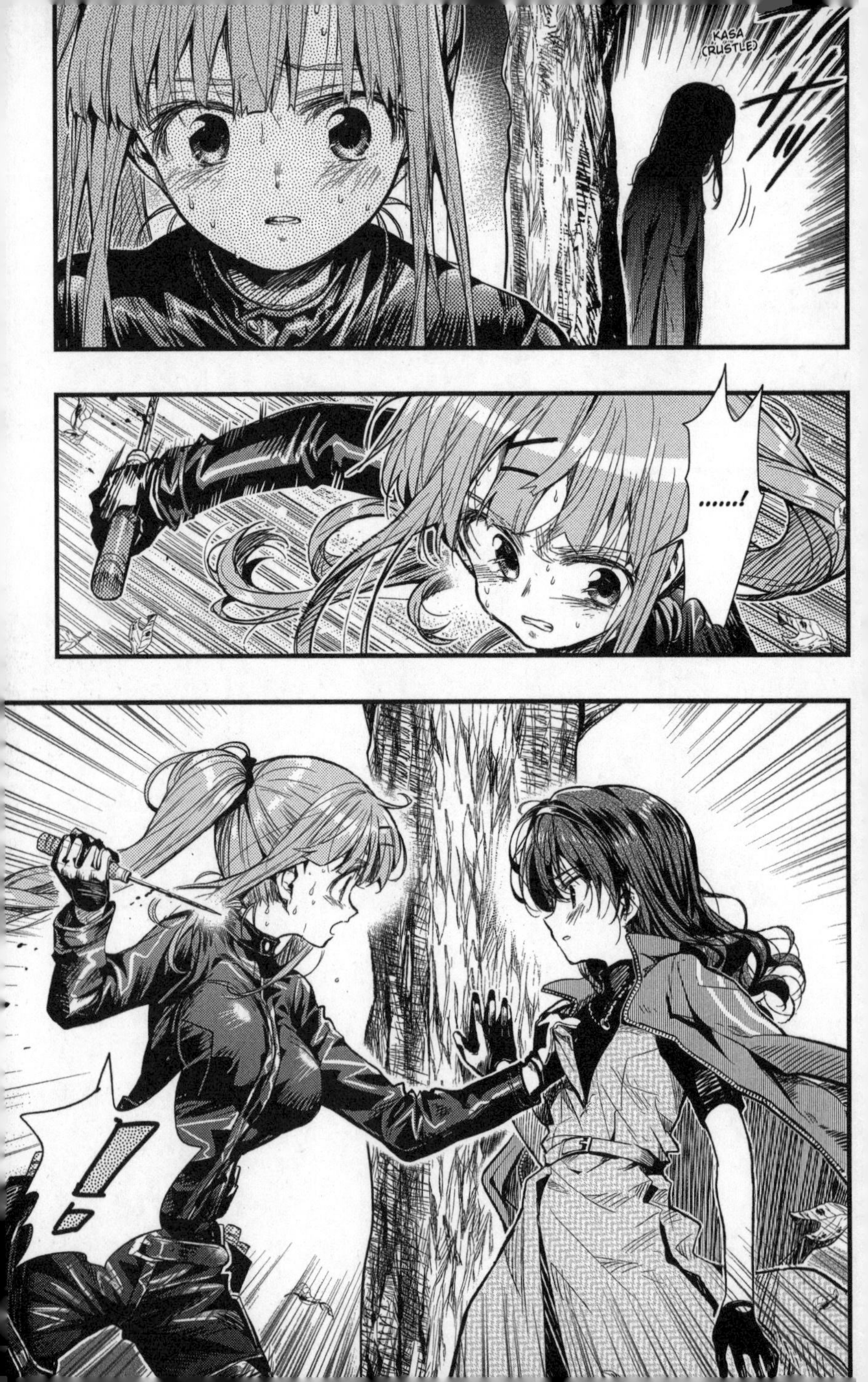
KASA (RUSTLE)
......!
!!

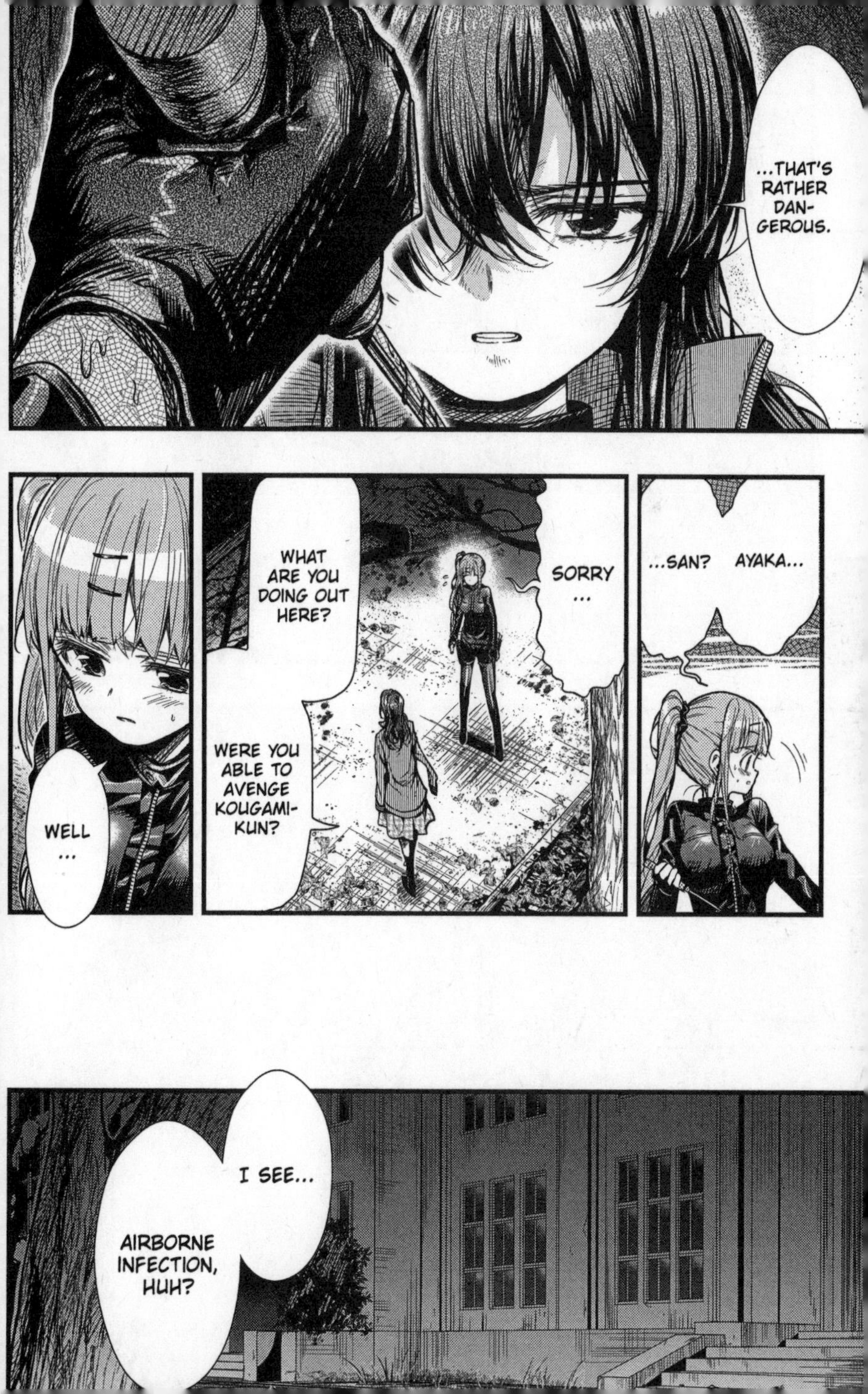
...THAT'S RATHER DAN-GEROUS.
AYAKA...
...SAN?
SORRY ...
WHAT ARE YOU DOING OUT HERE?
WERE YOU ABLE TO AVENGE KOUGAMI-KUN?
WELL ...
I SEE...
AIRBORNE INFECTION, HUH?

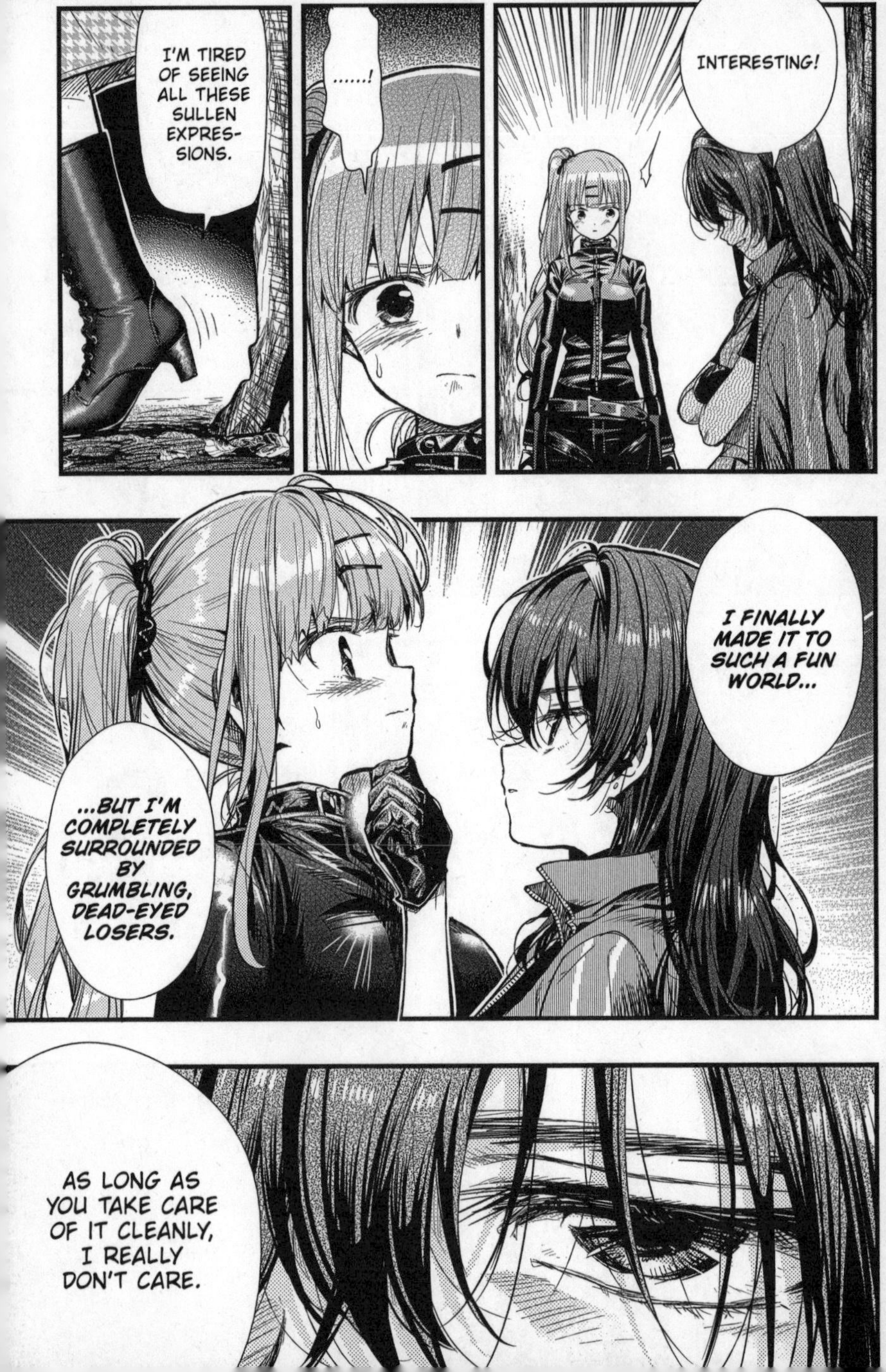
INTERESTING!
......!
I'M TIRED OF SEEING ALL THESE SULLEN EXPRESSIONS.
I FINALLY MADE IT TO SUCH A FUN WORLD...
...BUT I'M COMPLETELY SURROUNDED BY GRUMBLING, DEAD-EYED LOSERS.
AS LONG AS YOU TAKE CARE OF IT CLEANLY, I REALLY DON'T CARE.

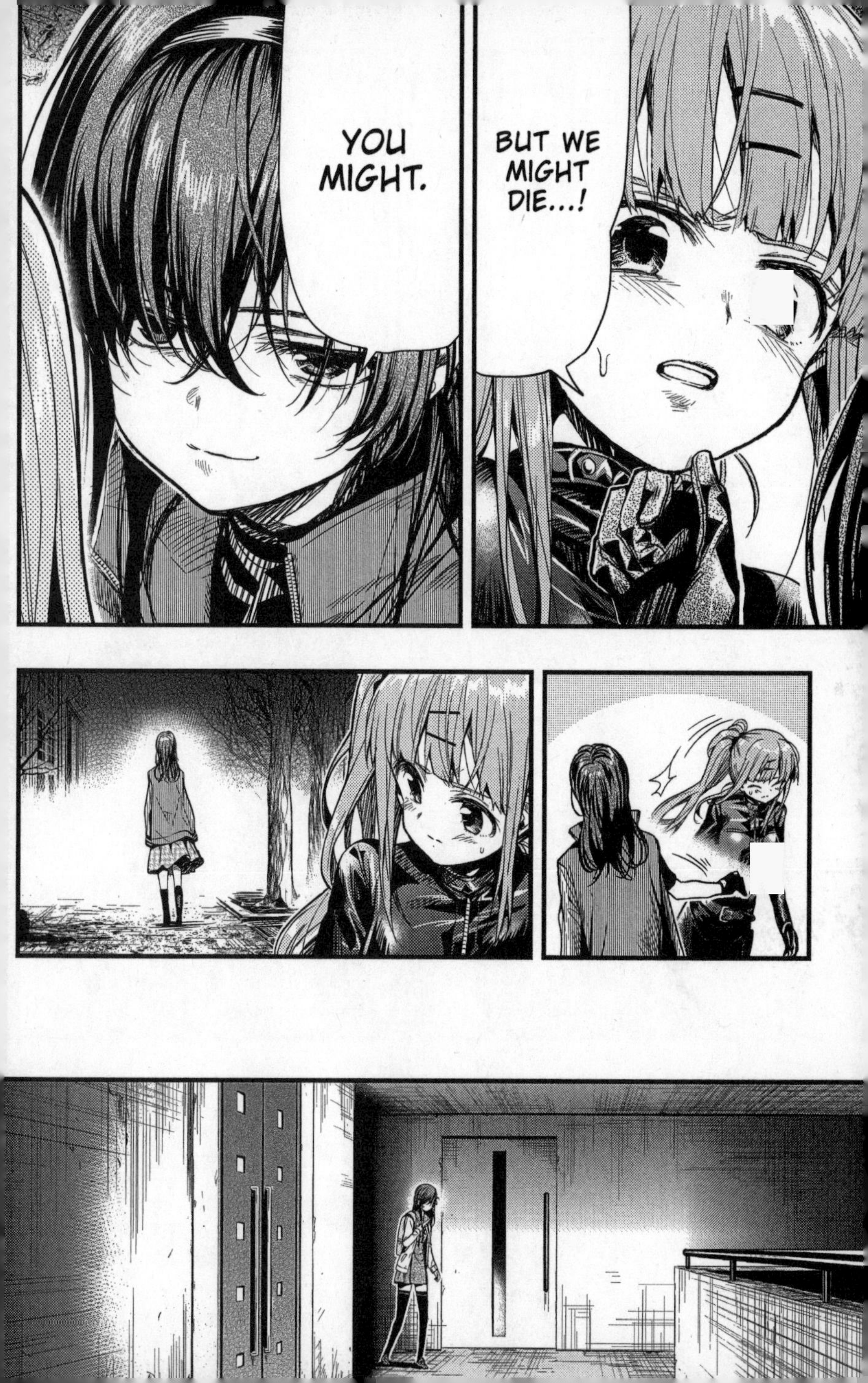
BUT WE MIGHT DIE...!
YOU MIGHT.

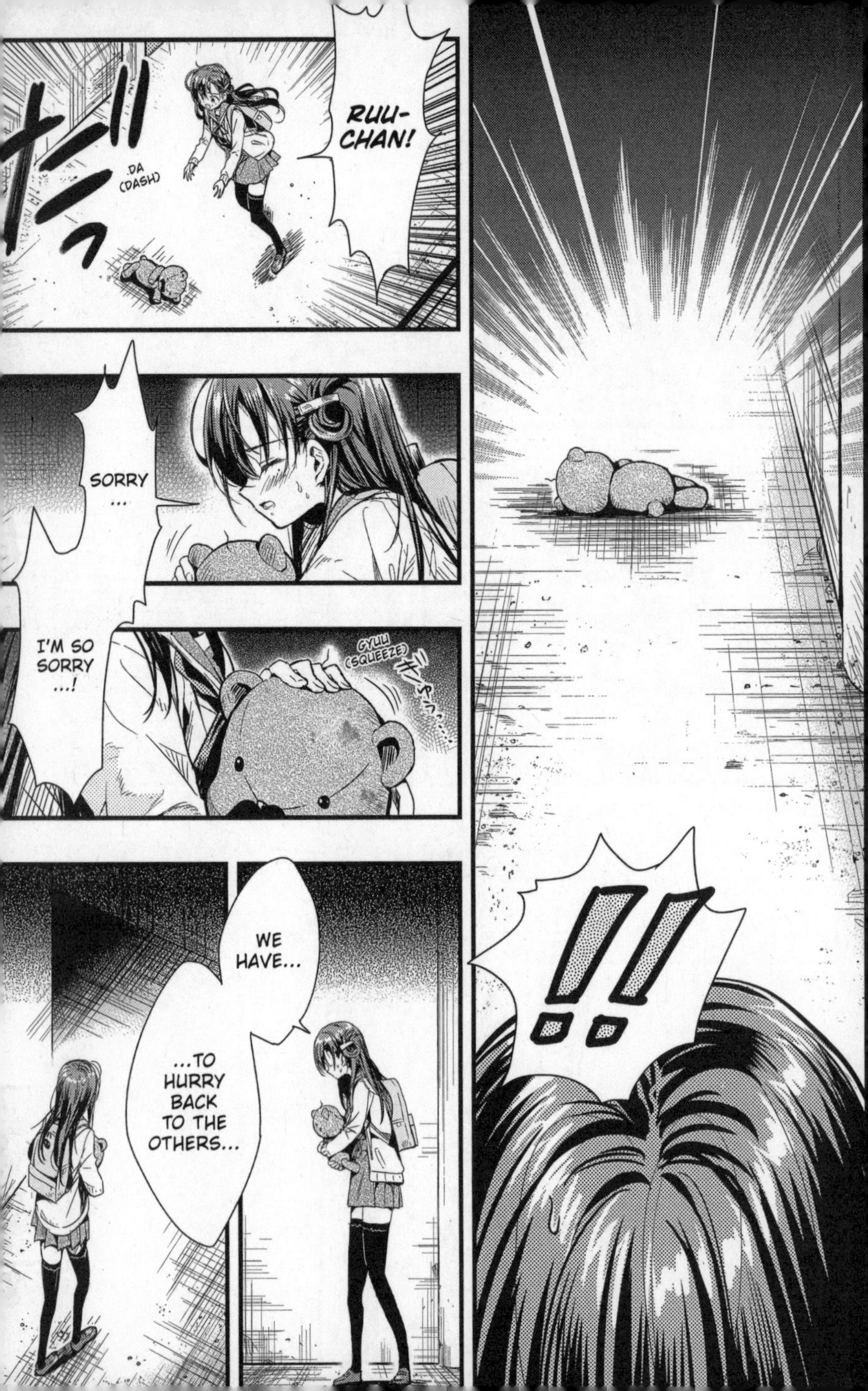
!!
RUU-CHAN!
DA (DASH)
SORRY ...
I'M SO SORRY ...!
GYUU (SQUEEZE)
WE HAVE...
...TO HURRY BACK TO THE OTHERS...

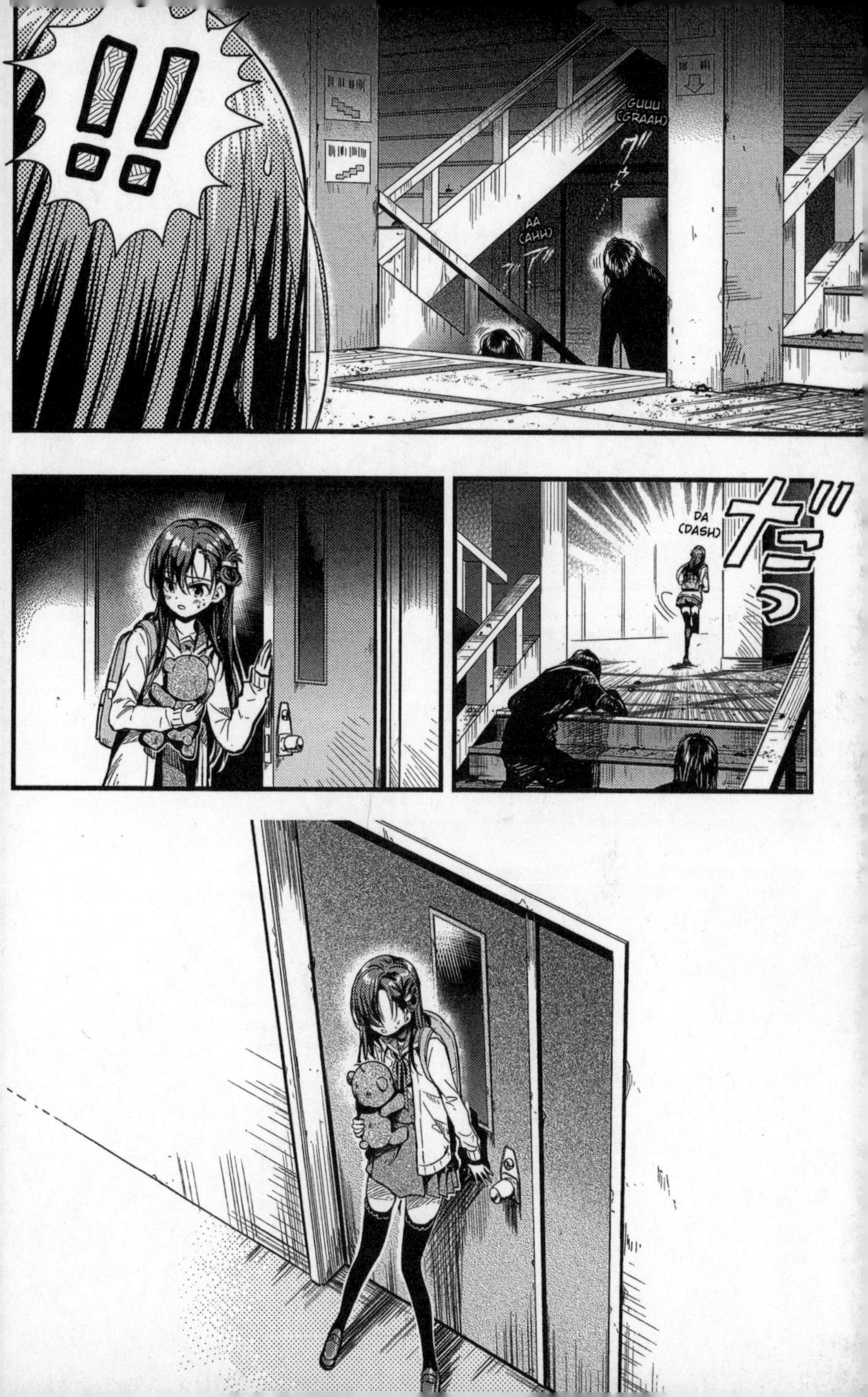
GUUU (GRAAH)
AA (AHH)
!!
DA (DASH)

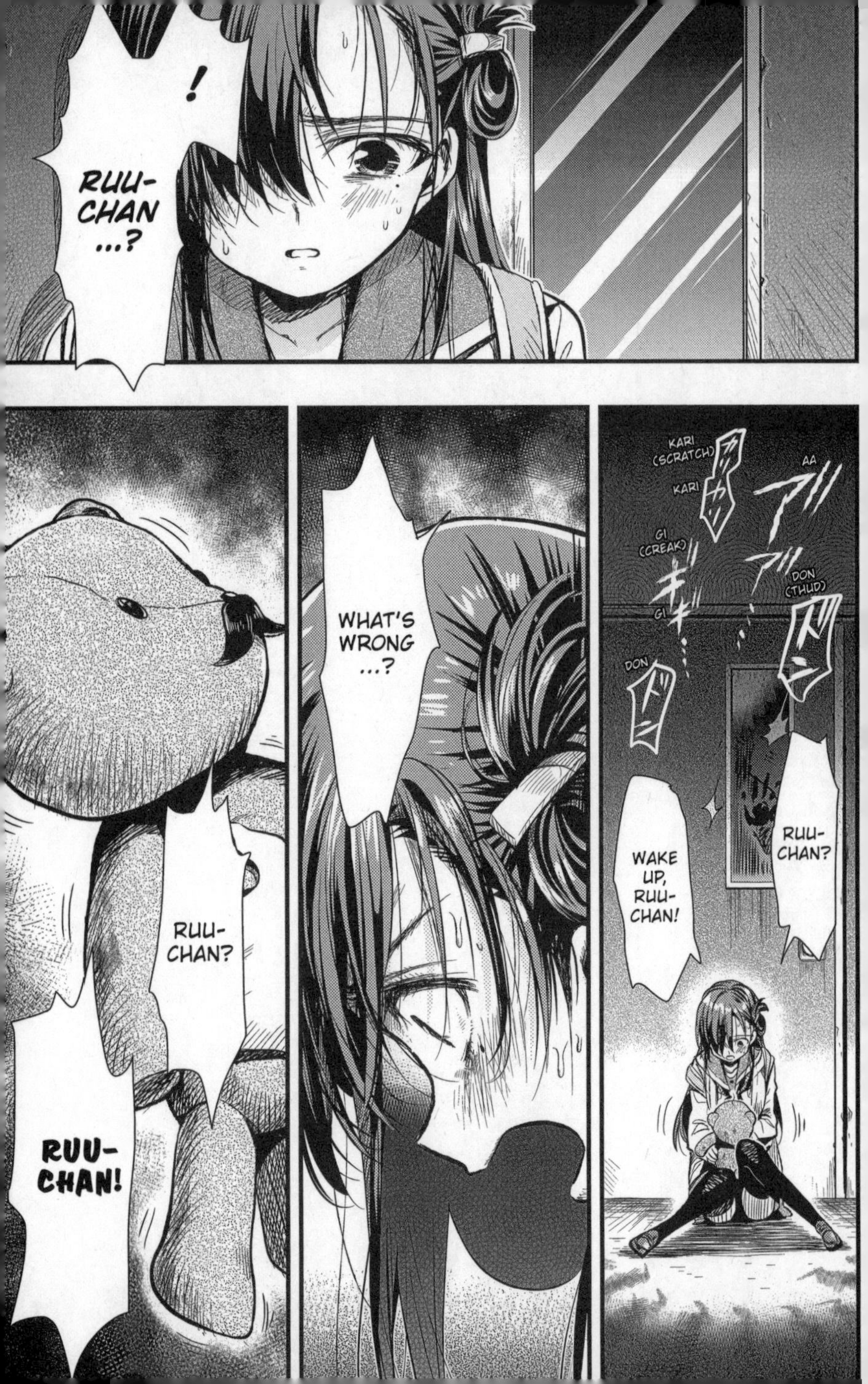
!
RUU-CHAN ...?
AA
KARI (SCRATCH)
KARI
DON (THUD)
GI (CREAK)
GI
DON
RUU-CHAN?
WAKE UP, RUU-CHAN!
WHAT'S WRONG ...?
RUU-CHAN?
RUU-CHAN!

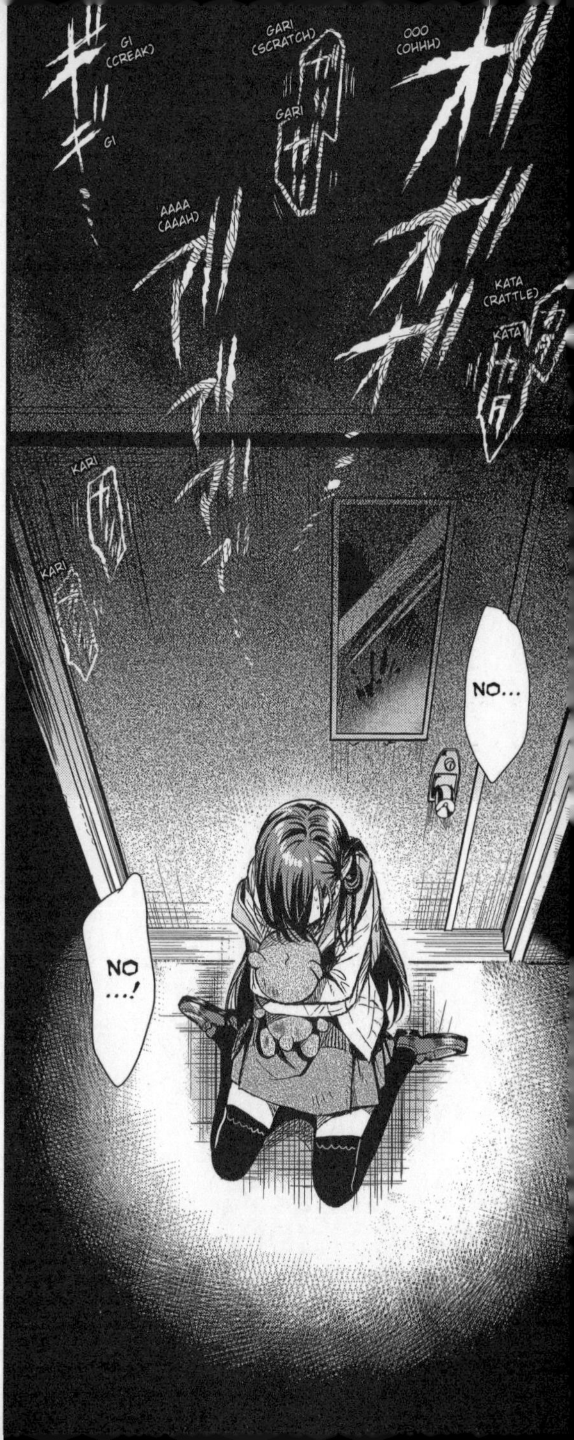
OOO (OHHH)
GARI (SCRATCH)
GARI
GI (CREAK)
GI
AAAA (AAAH)
KATA (RATTLE)
KATA
KARI
KARI
NO...
NO ...!

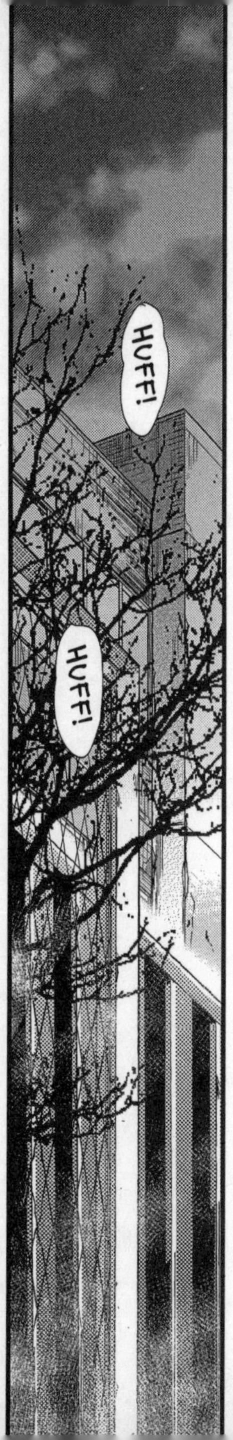
HUFF!
HUFF!

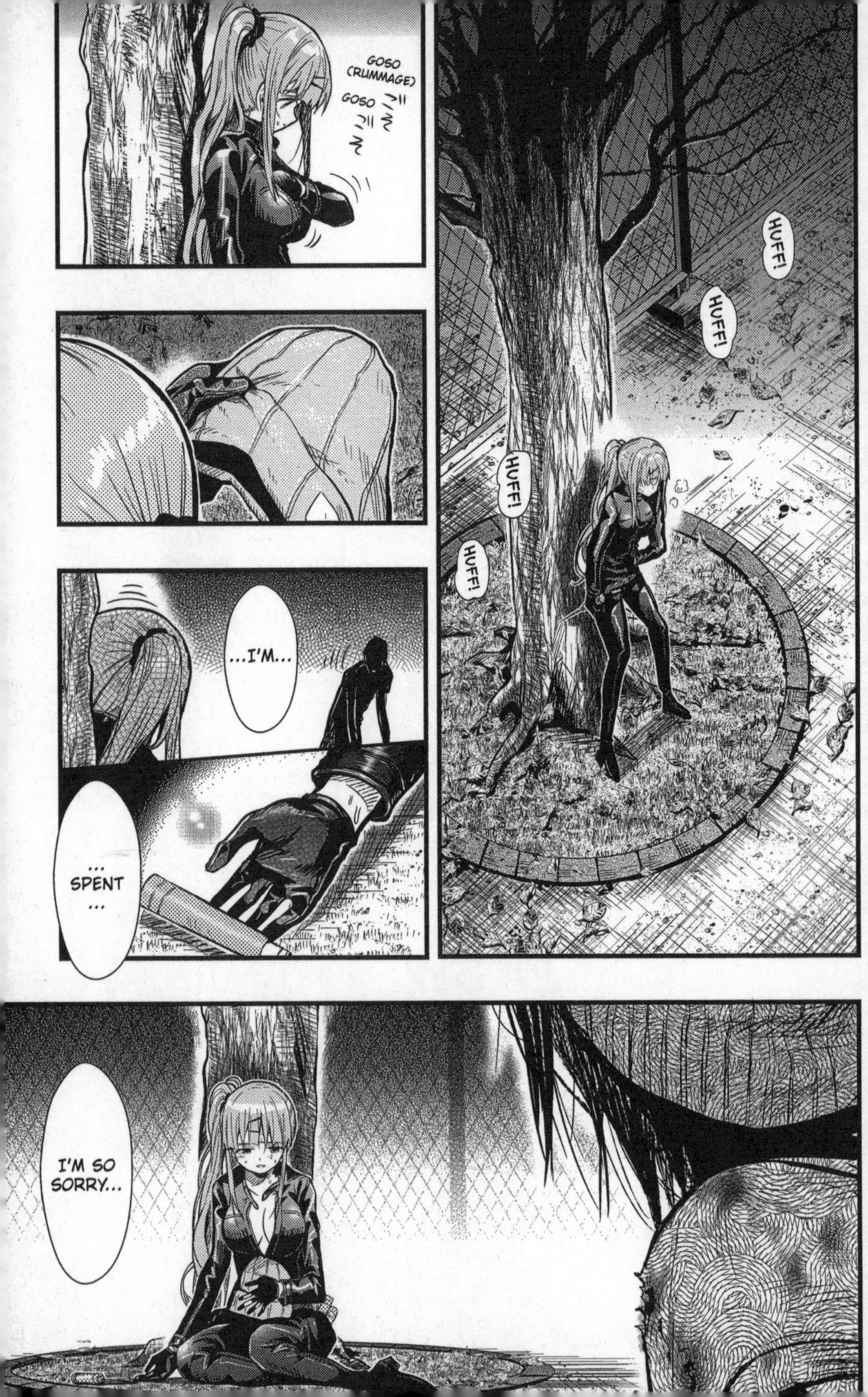
HUFF!
HUFF!
HUFF!
HUFF!
GOSO (RUMMAGE)
GOSO
ごそごそ
...I'M...
...SPENT...
I'M SO SORRY...

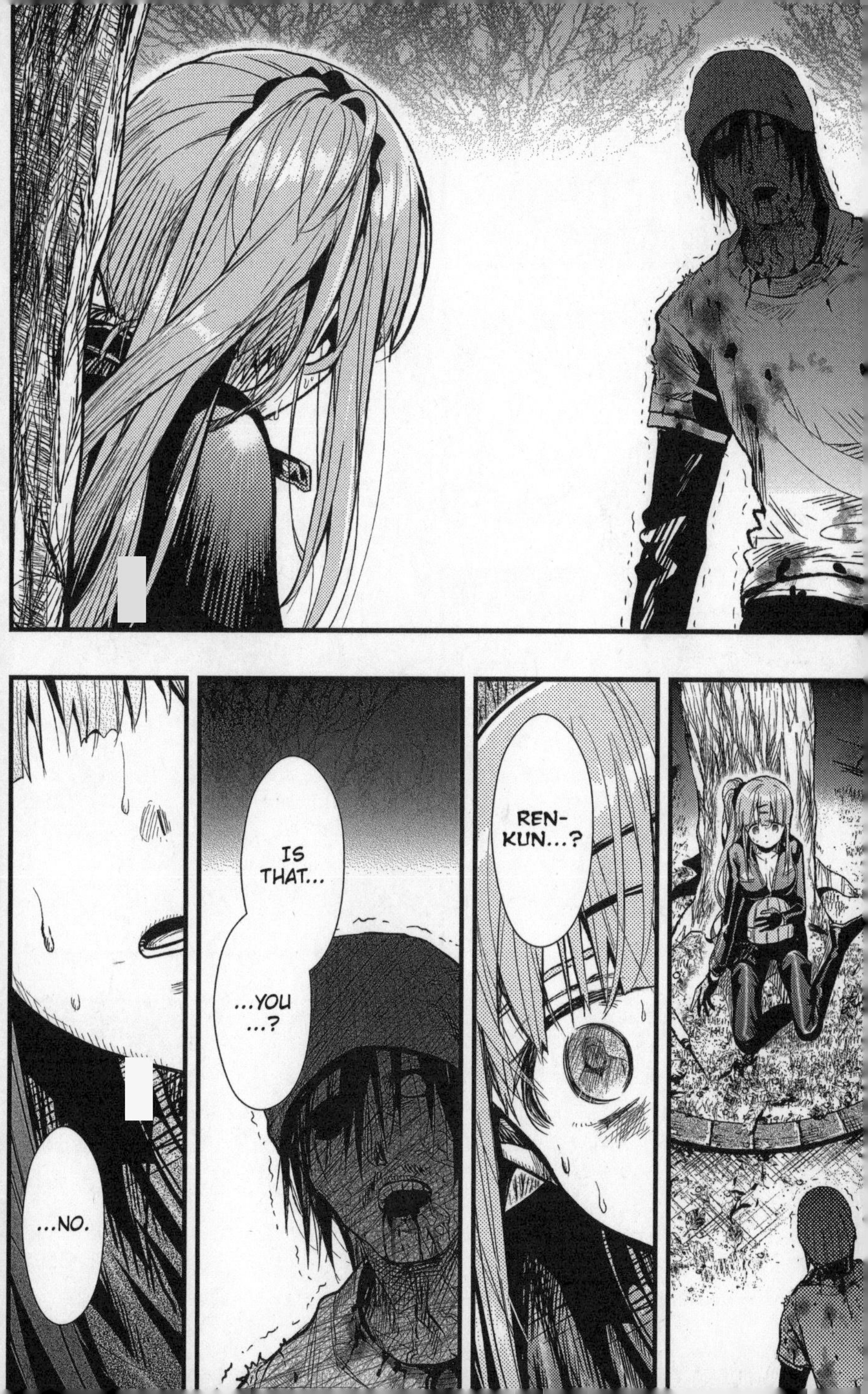
REN-KUN...?
IS THAT...
...YOU ...?
...NO.

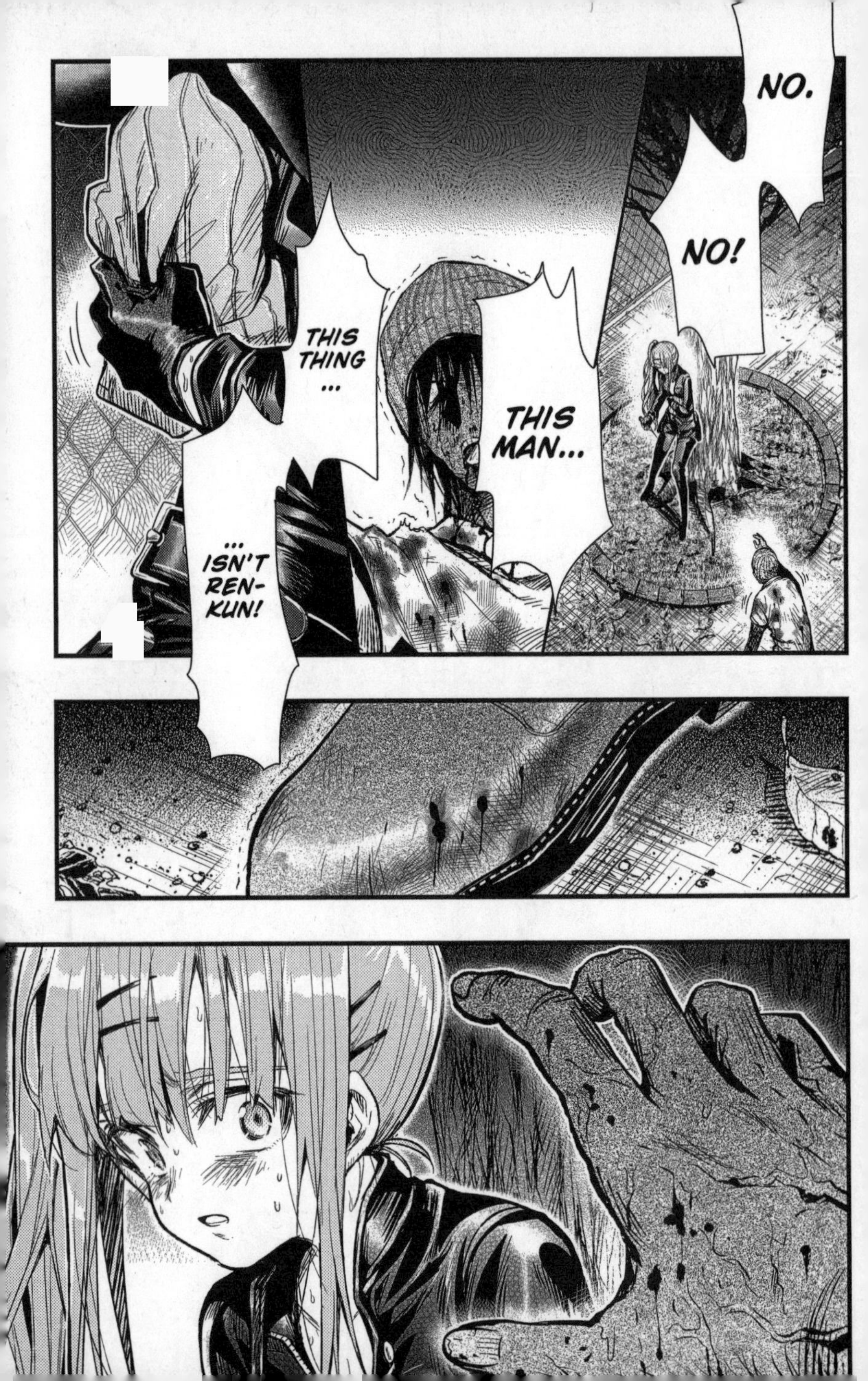
NO.
NO!
THIS THING ...
THIS MAN...
... ISN'T REN-KUN!

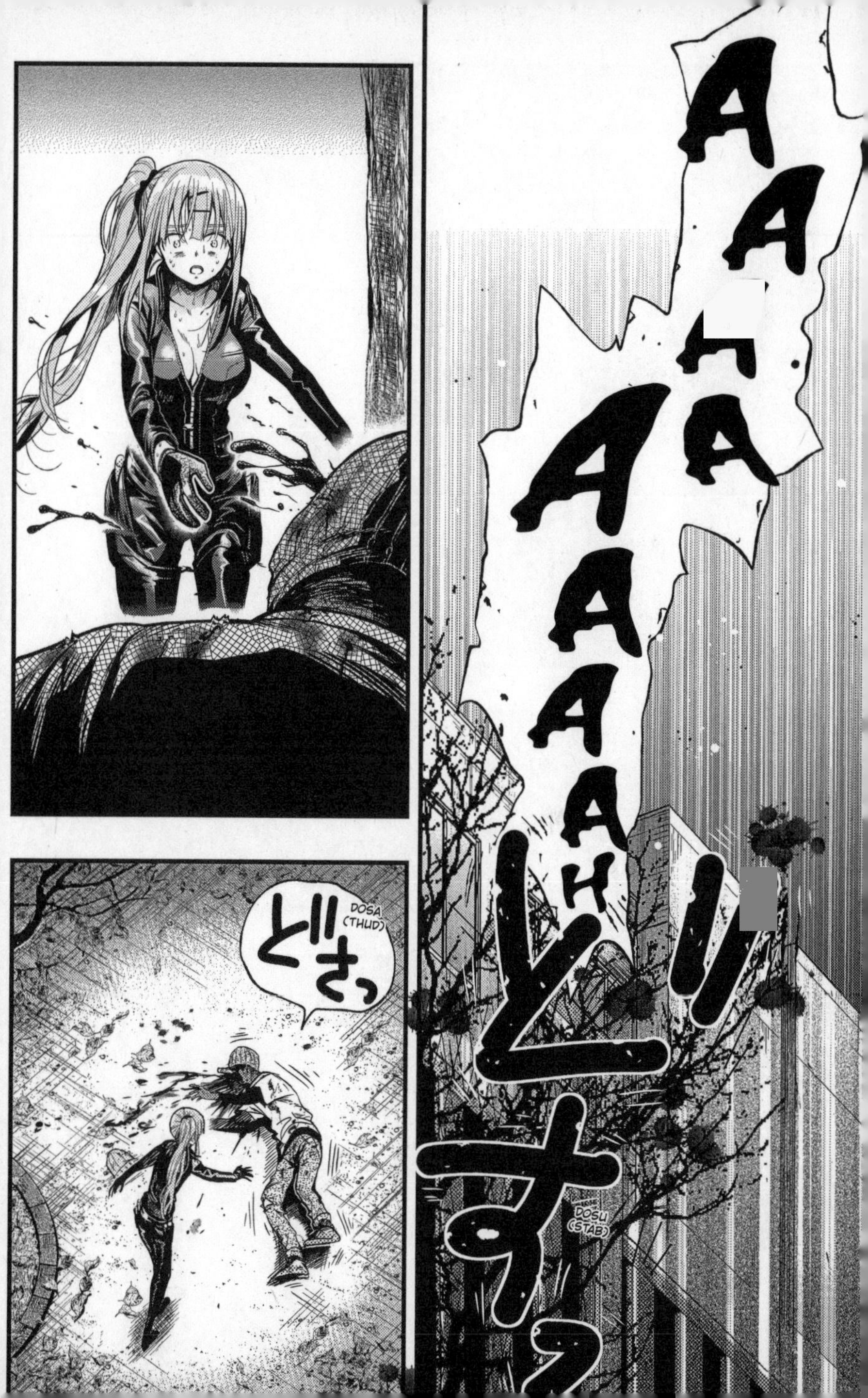
AAAAAAAAAH!!
どすっ
DOSU (STAB)
どさっ
DOSA (THUD)

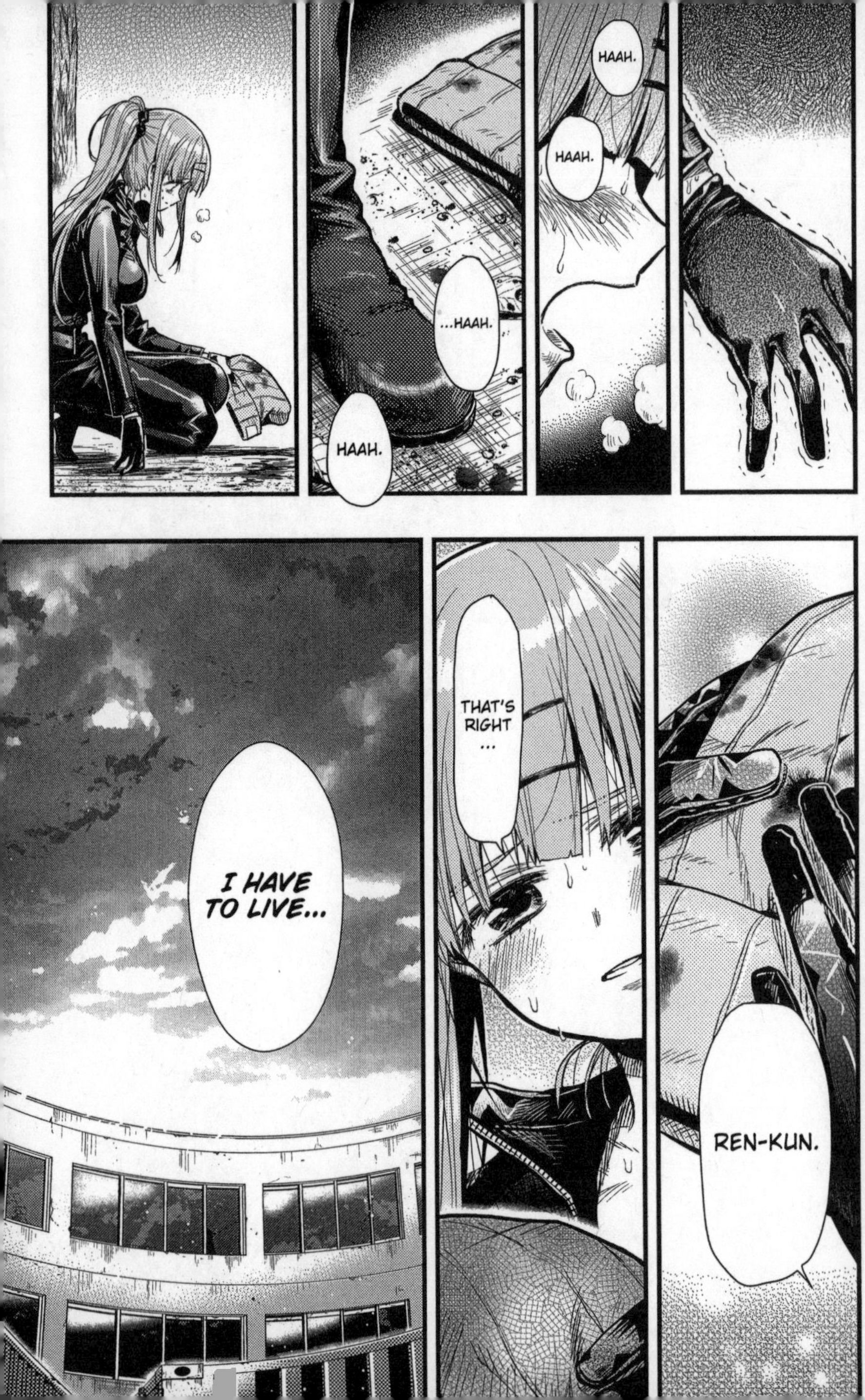
HAAH.
HAAH.
...HAAH.
HAAH.
REN-KUN.
THAT'S RIGHT ...
I HAVE TO LIVE...

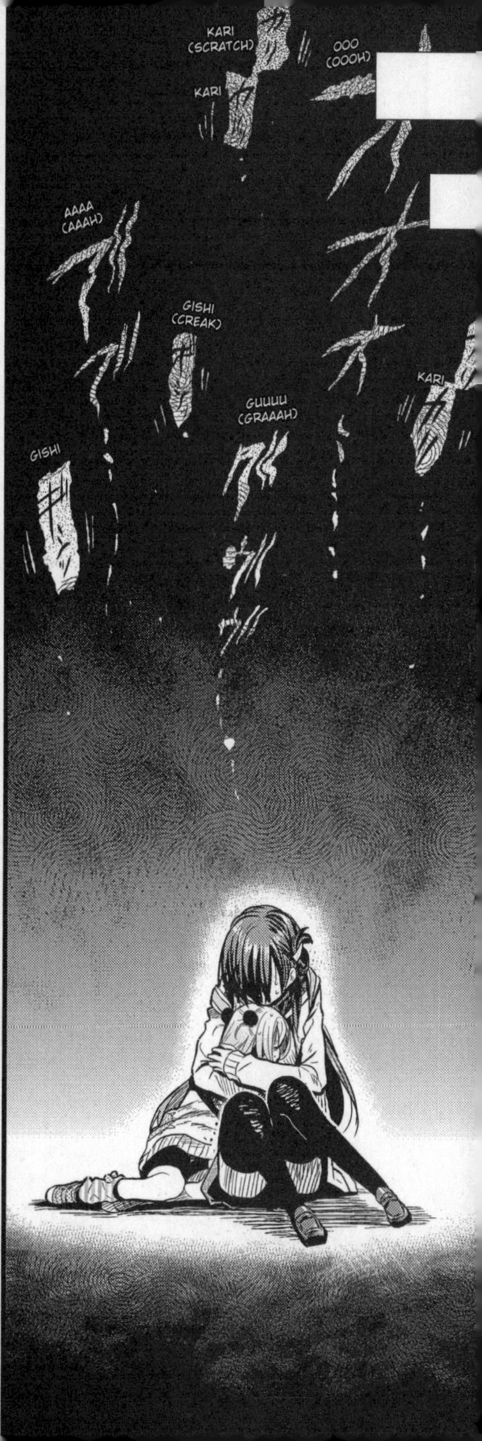
OOO (OOOH)
KARI (SCRATCH)
KARI
AAAA (AAAH)
GISHI (CREAK)
KARI
GUUUU (GRAAAH)
GISHI
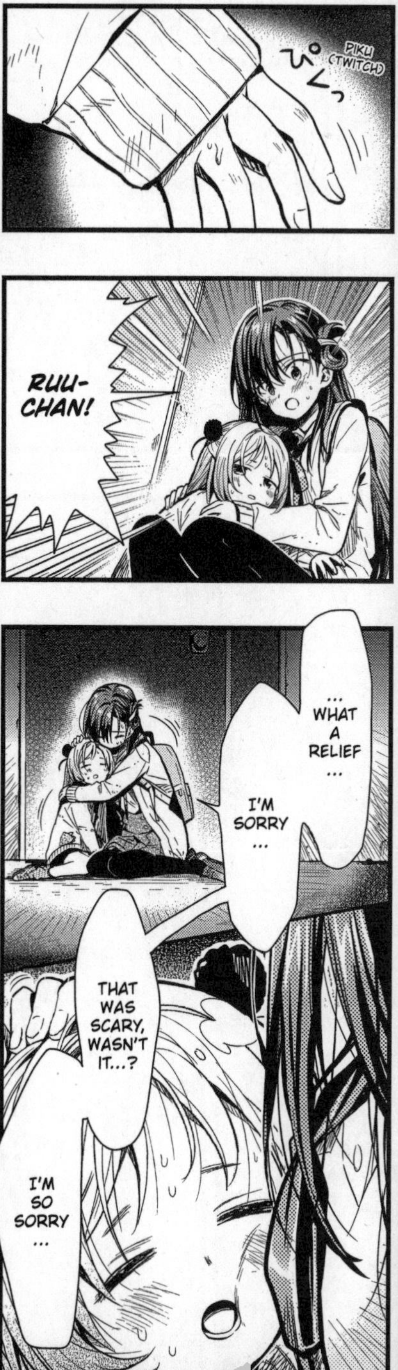
PIKU (TWITCH)
RUU-CHAN!
...WHAT A RELIEF...
I'M SORRY...
THAT WAS SCARY, WASN'T IT...?
I'M SO SORRY...

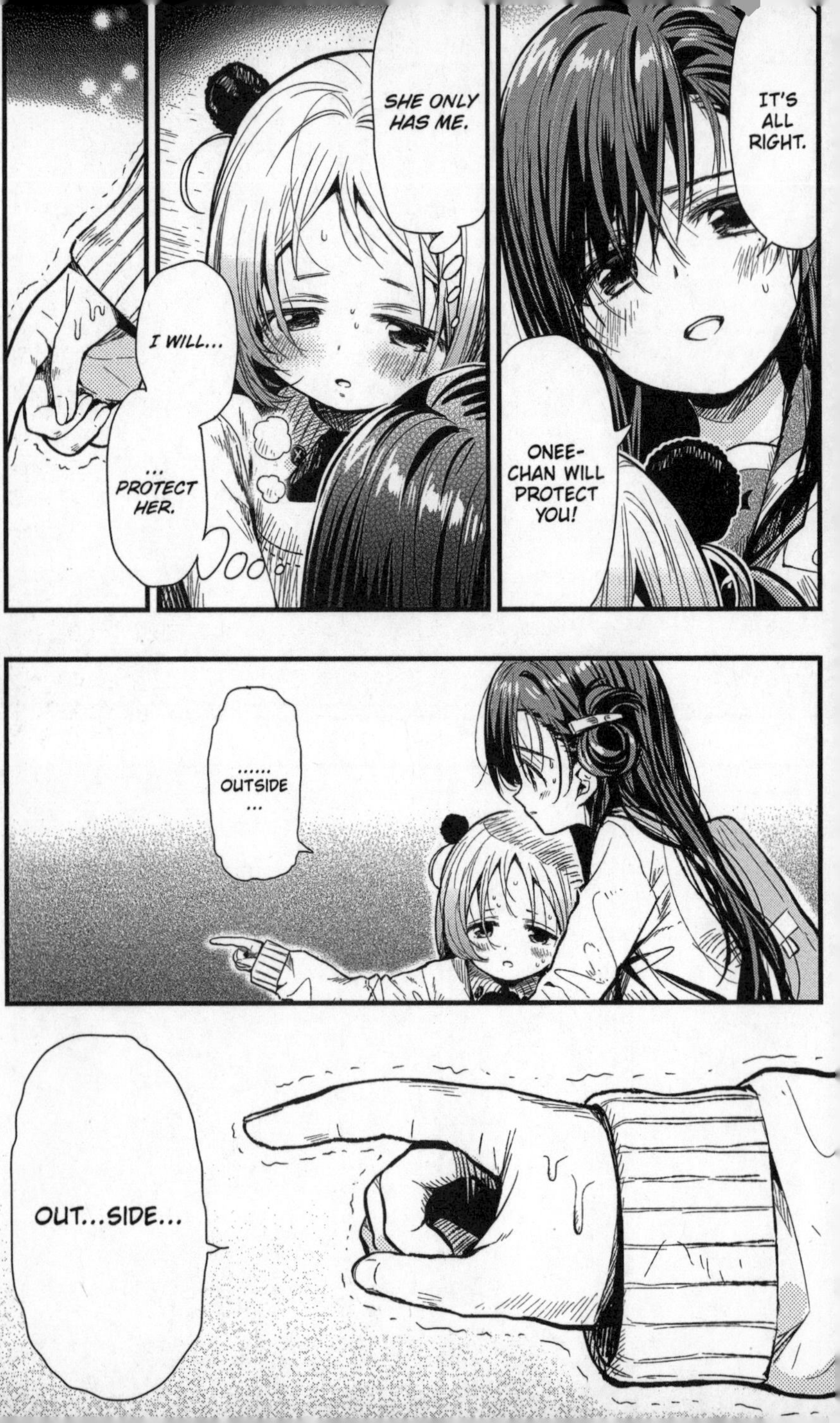
IT'S ALL RIGHT.
ONEE-CHAN WILL PROTECT YOU!
SHE ONLY HAS ME.
I WILL...
...PROTECT HER.
......OUTSIDE...
OUT...SIDE...

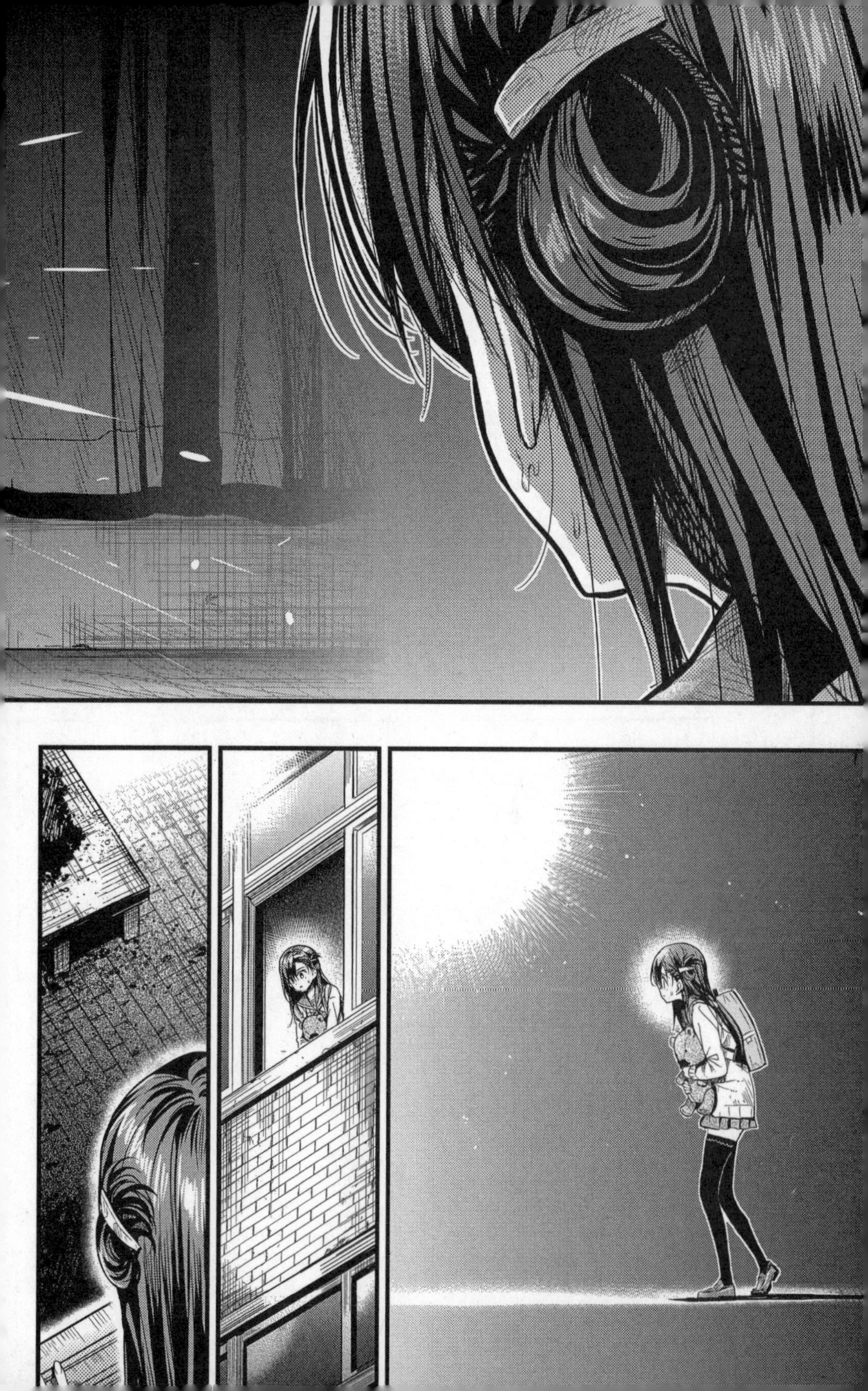

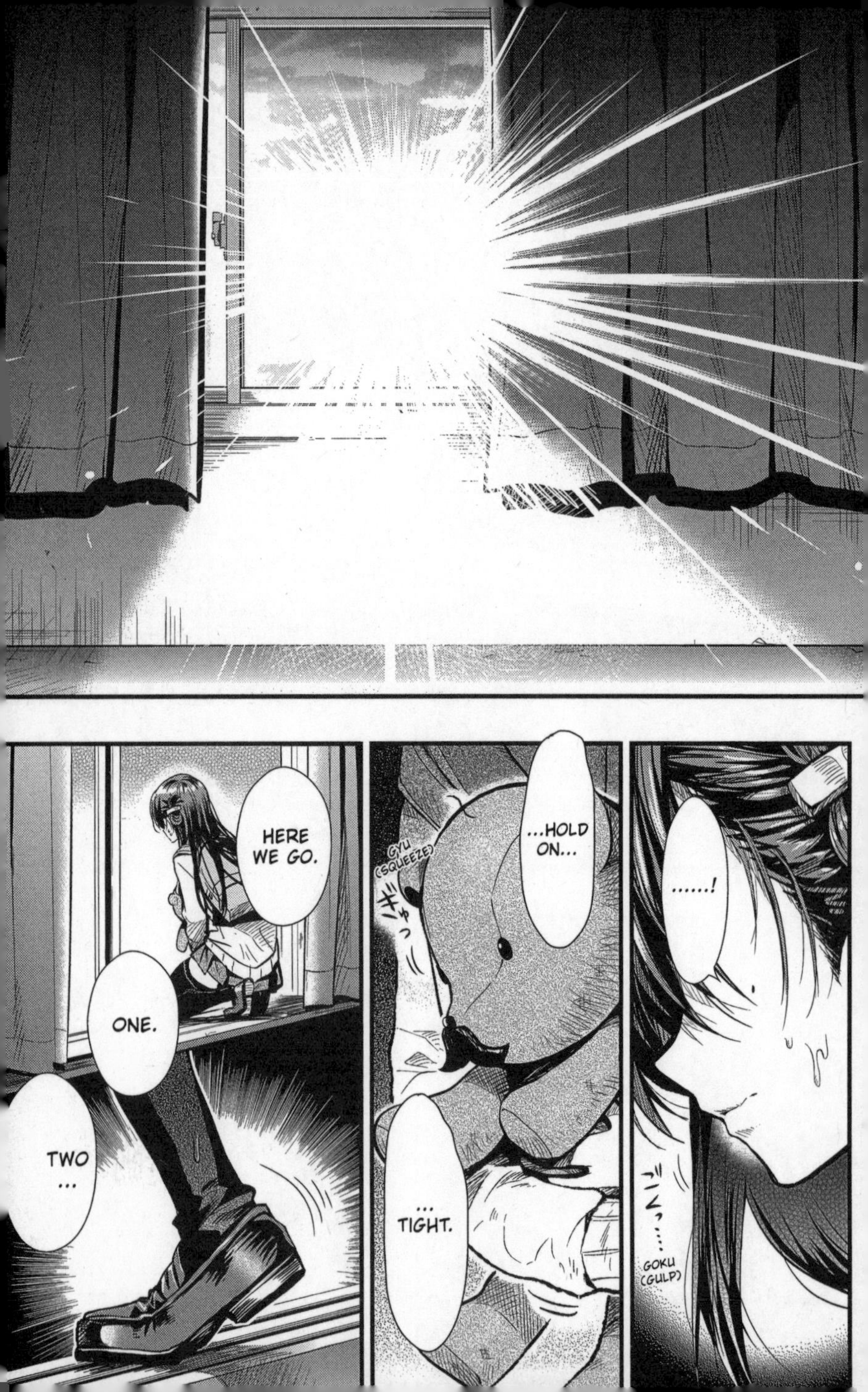
......!
GOKU (GULP)
...HOLD ON...
GYU (SQUEEZE)
... TIGHT.
HERE WE GO.
ONE.
TWO ...

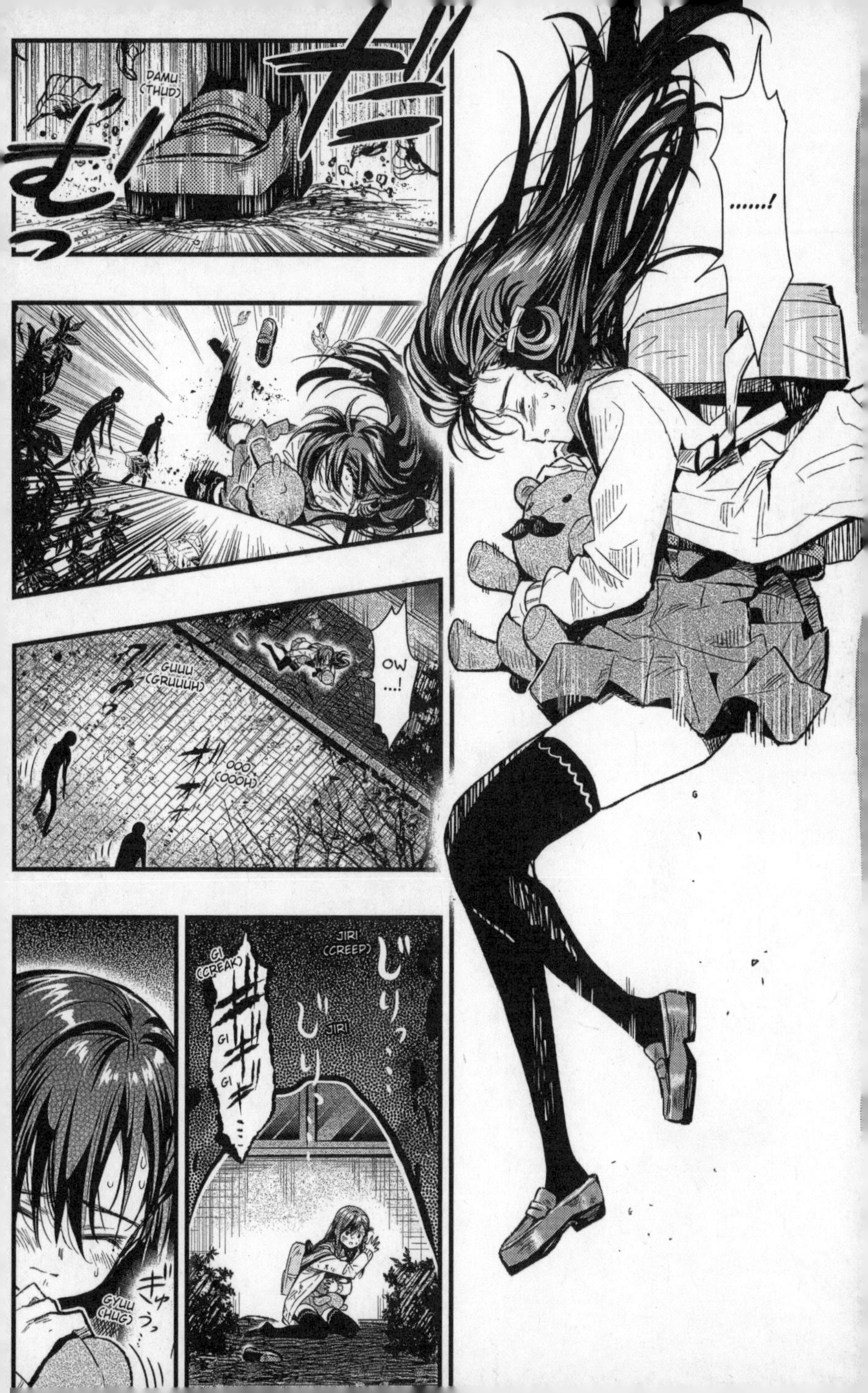
......!
DAMU (THUD)
OW ...!
GUUU (GRUUUH)
OOO (OOOH)
JIRI (CREEP)
JIRI
GI (CREAK)
GI
GI
GYUU (HUG)

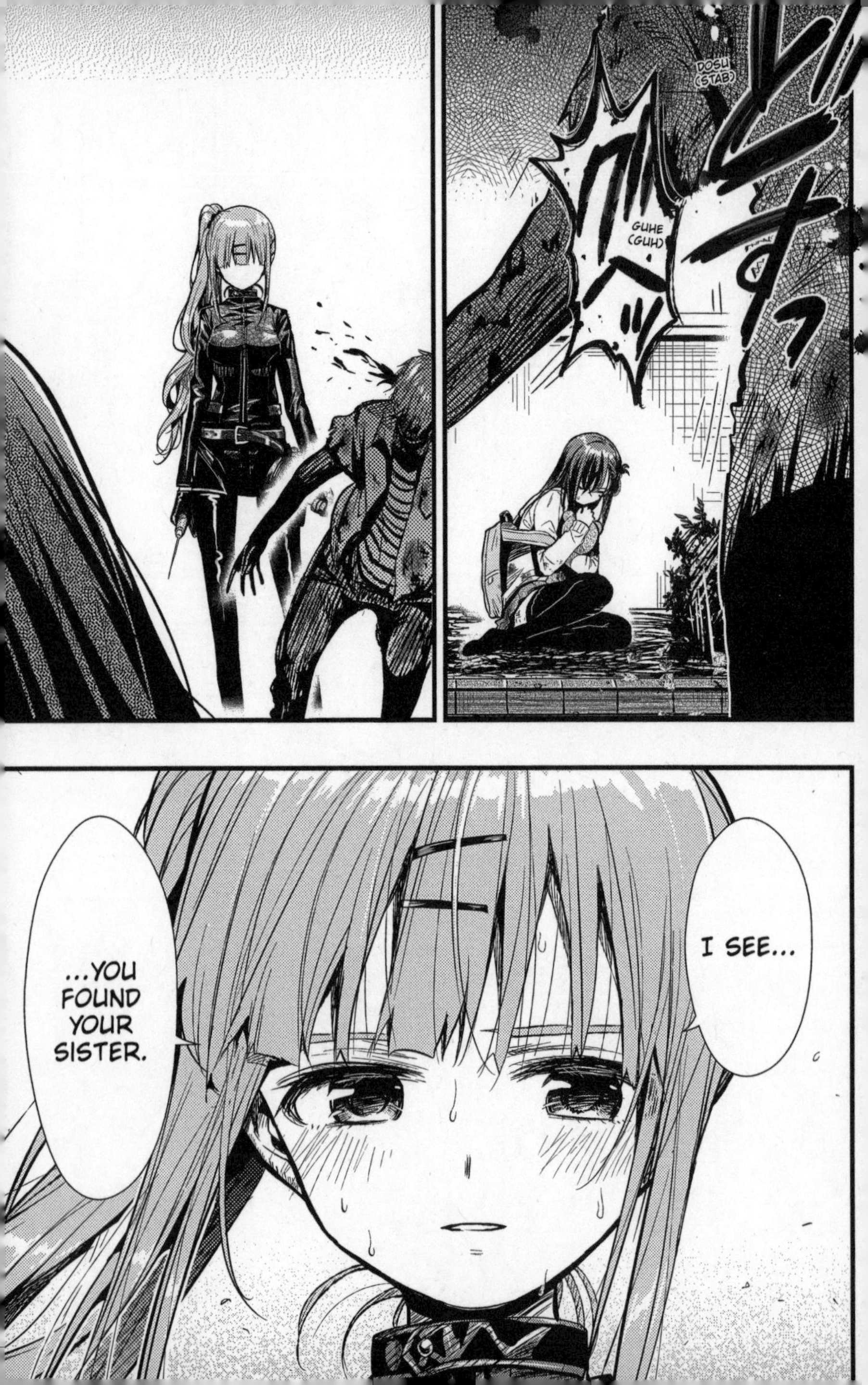
DOSU (STAB)
GUHE (GUH)
I SEE...
...YOU FOUND YOUR SISTER.

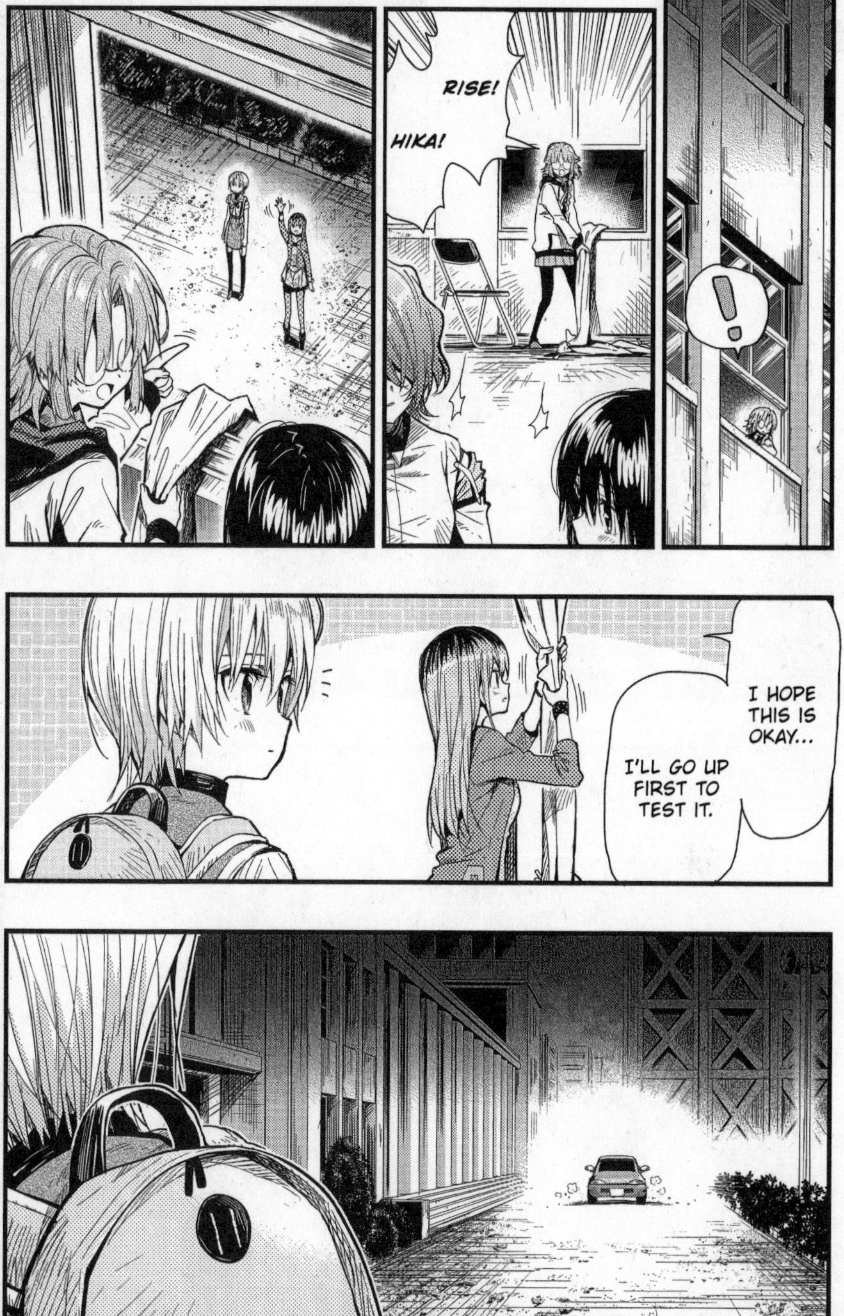
!
RISE!
HIKA!
I HOPE THIS IS OKAY...
I'LL GO UP FIRST TO TEST IT.

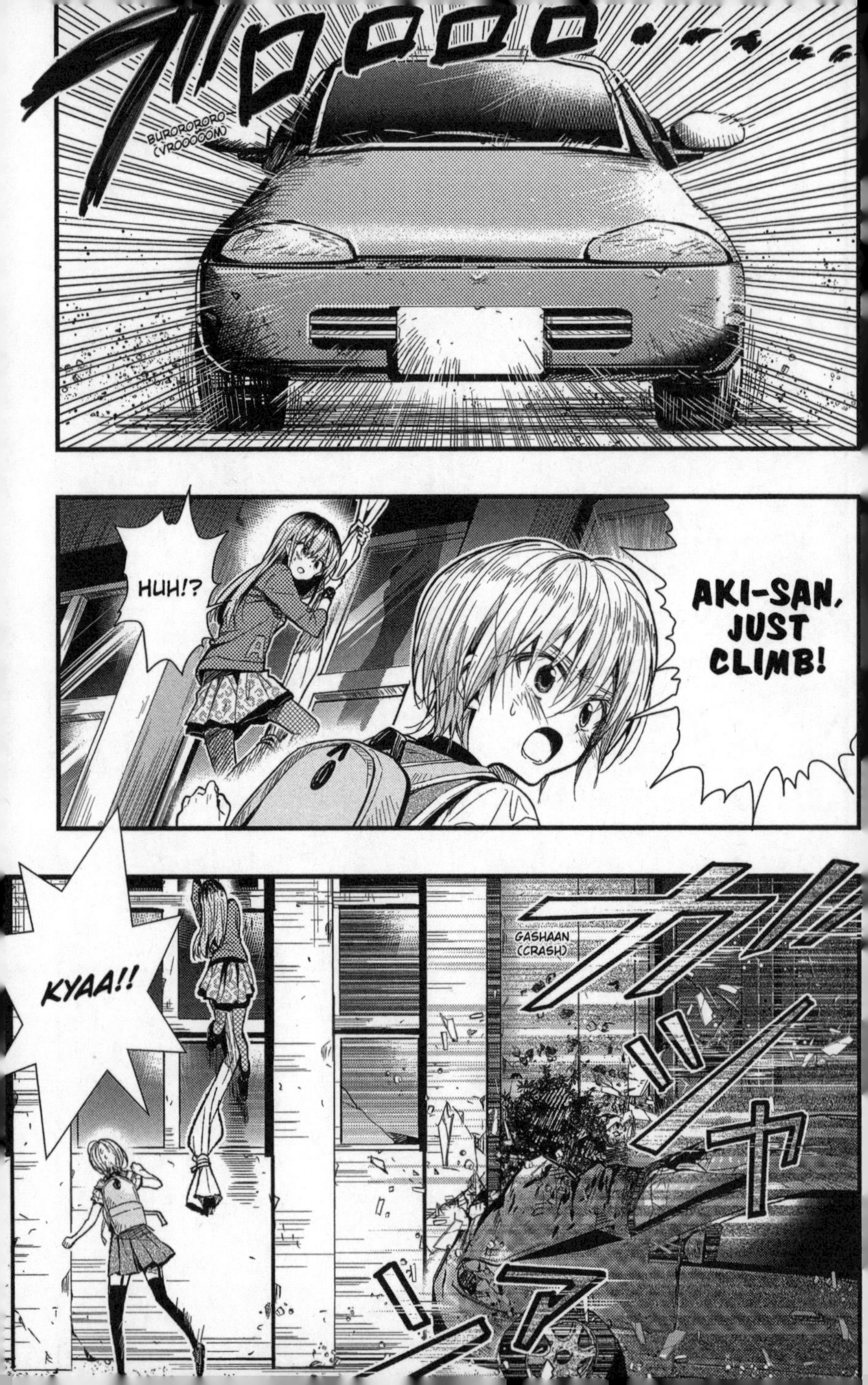
BUROROROROR (VROOOOOM)
AKI-SAN, JUST CLIMB!
HUH!?
GASHAAN (CRASH)
KYAA!!

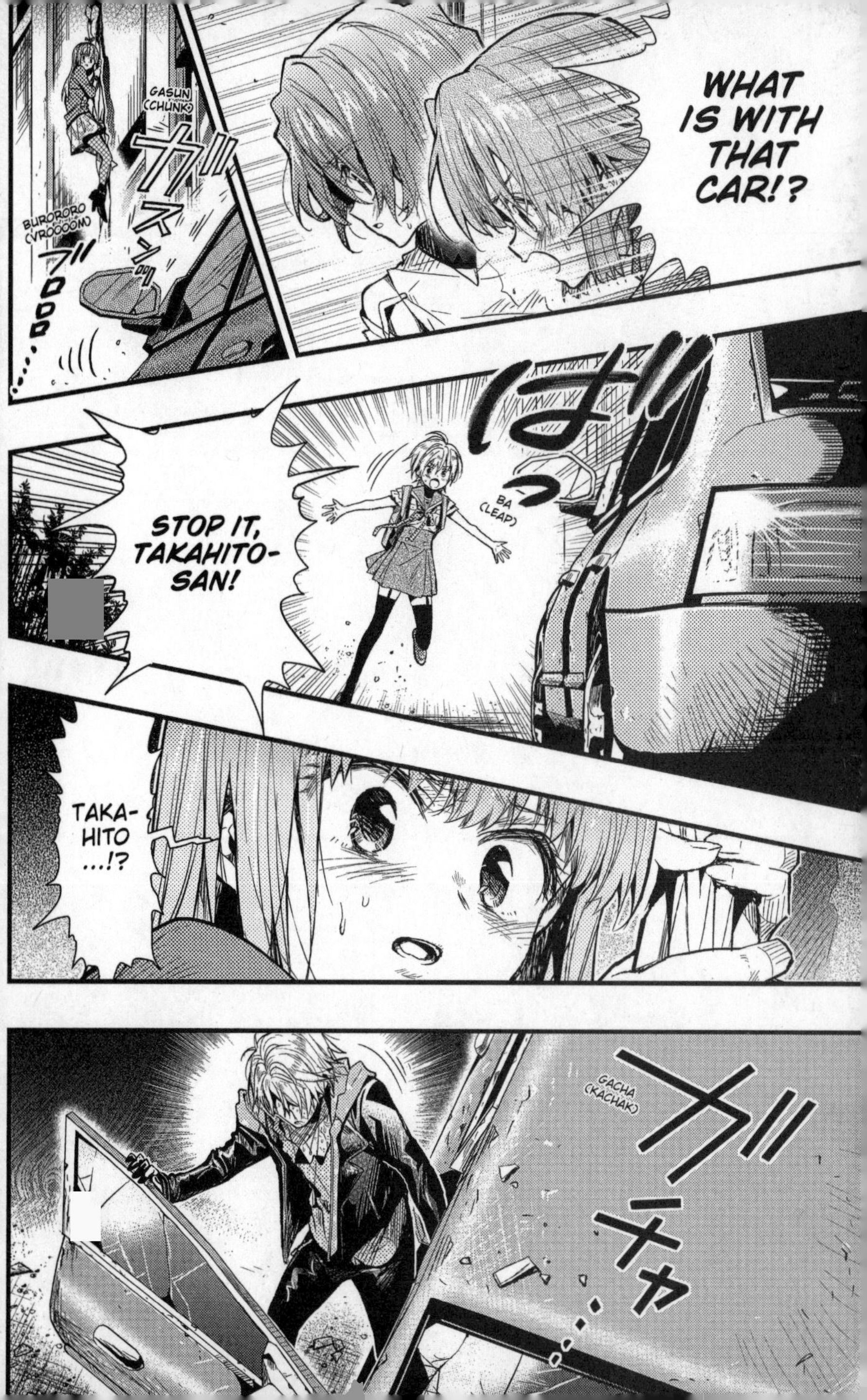
WHAT IS WITH THAT CAR!?
GASUN (CHUNK)
ガスン
BURORORO (VROOOOM)
ブロロロ…
ばっ
BA (LEAP)
STOP IT, TAKAHITO-SAN!
TAKAHITO ...!?
GACHA (KACHAK)
ガチャ…

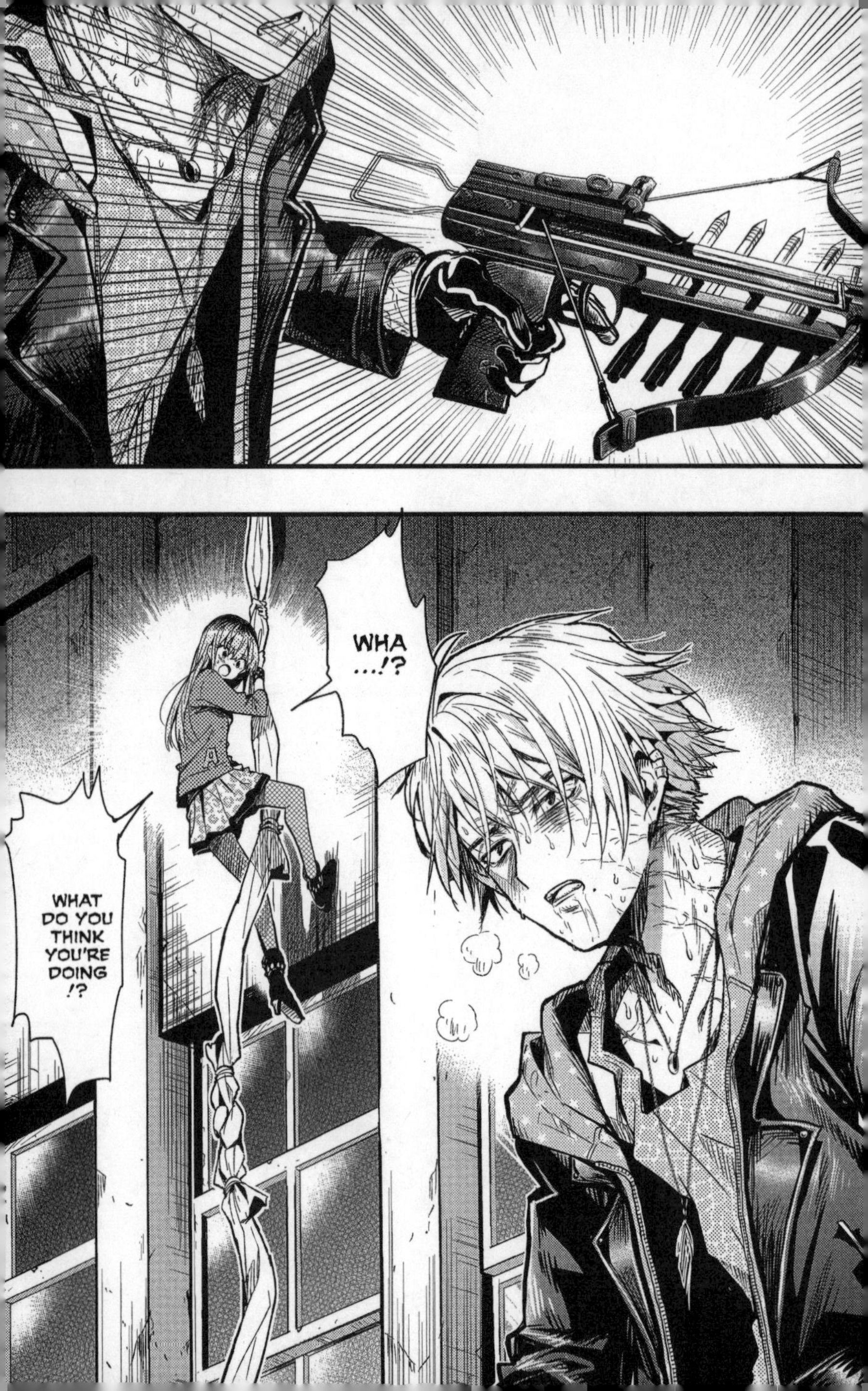
WHA ...!?
WHAT DO YOU THINK YOU'RE DOING !?

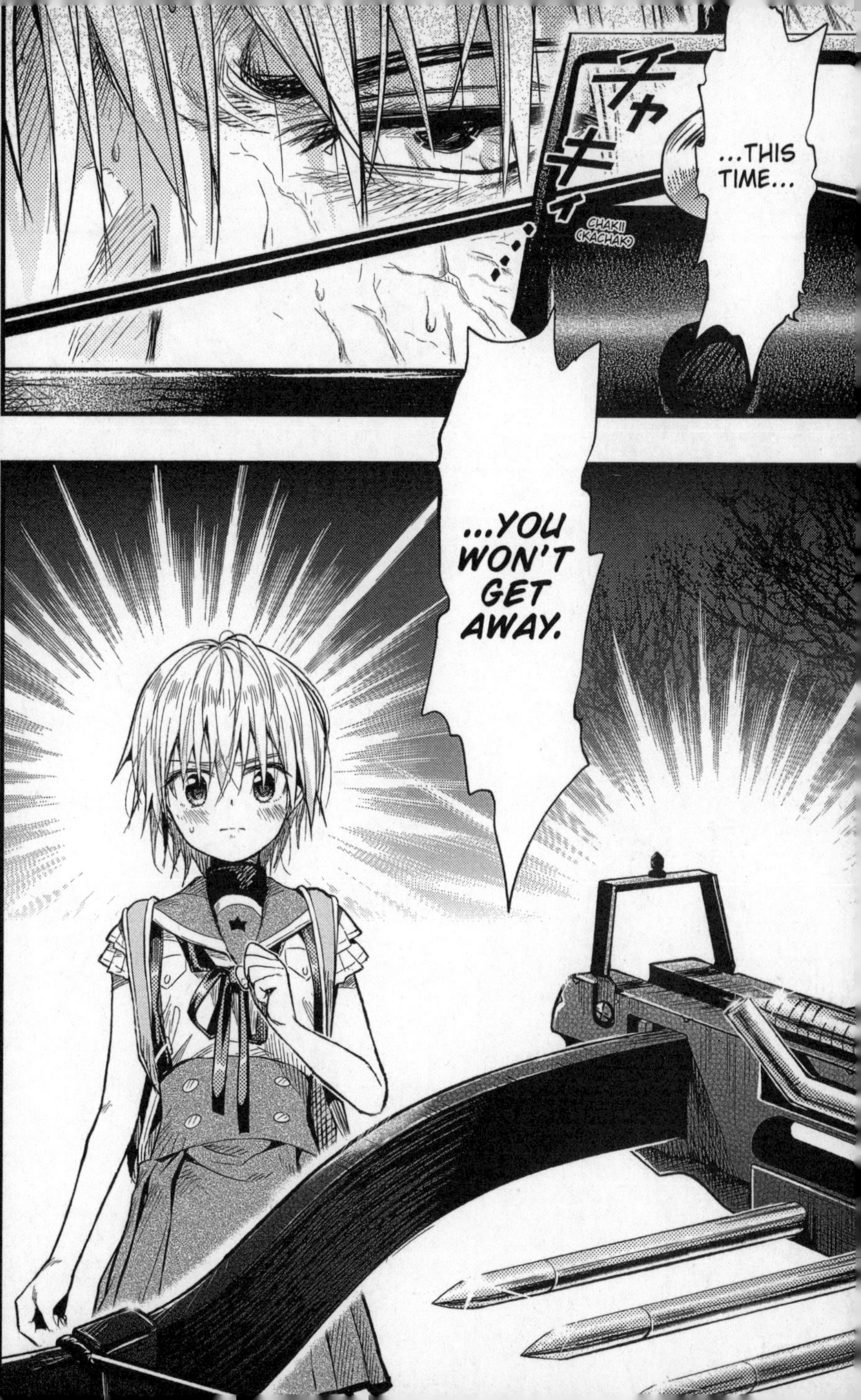
チャキィ
CHAKII (KACHAK)
...THIS TIME...
...YOU WON'T GET AWAY.

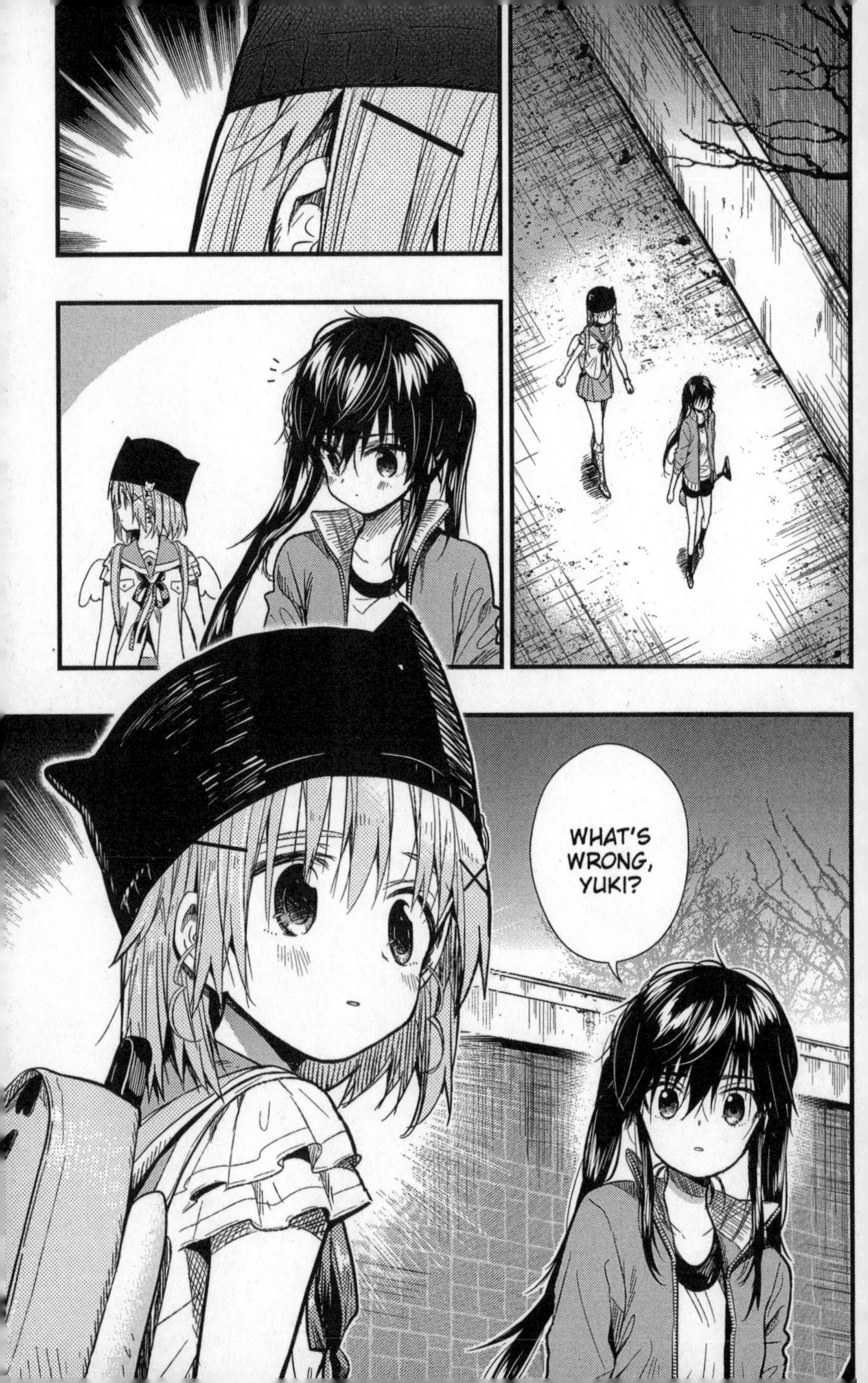
WHAT'S WRONG, YUKI?

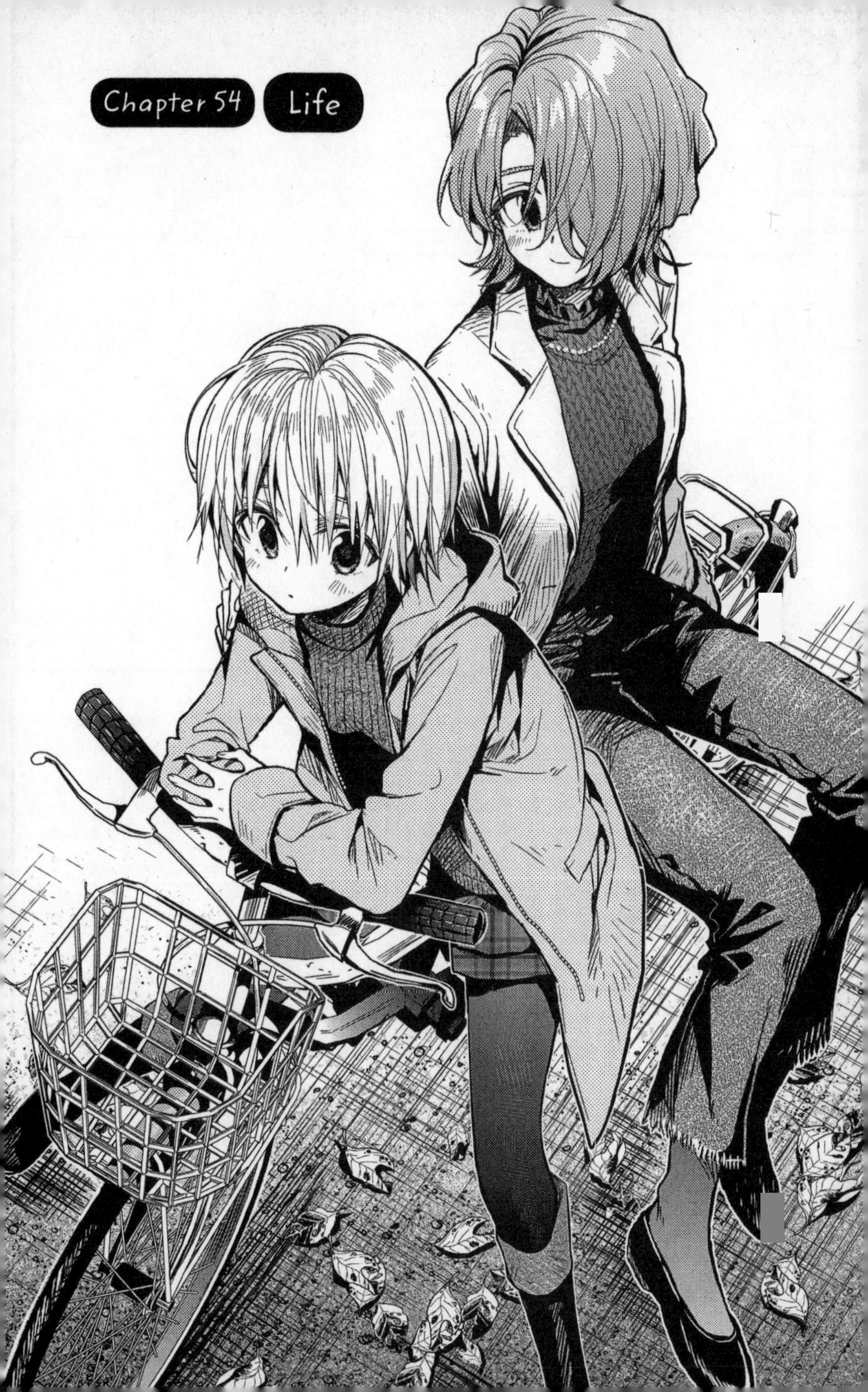
Chapter 54
Life

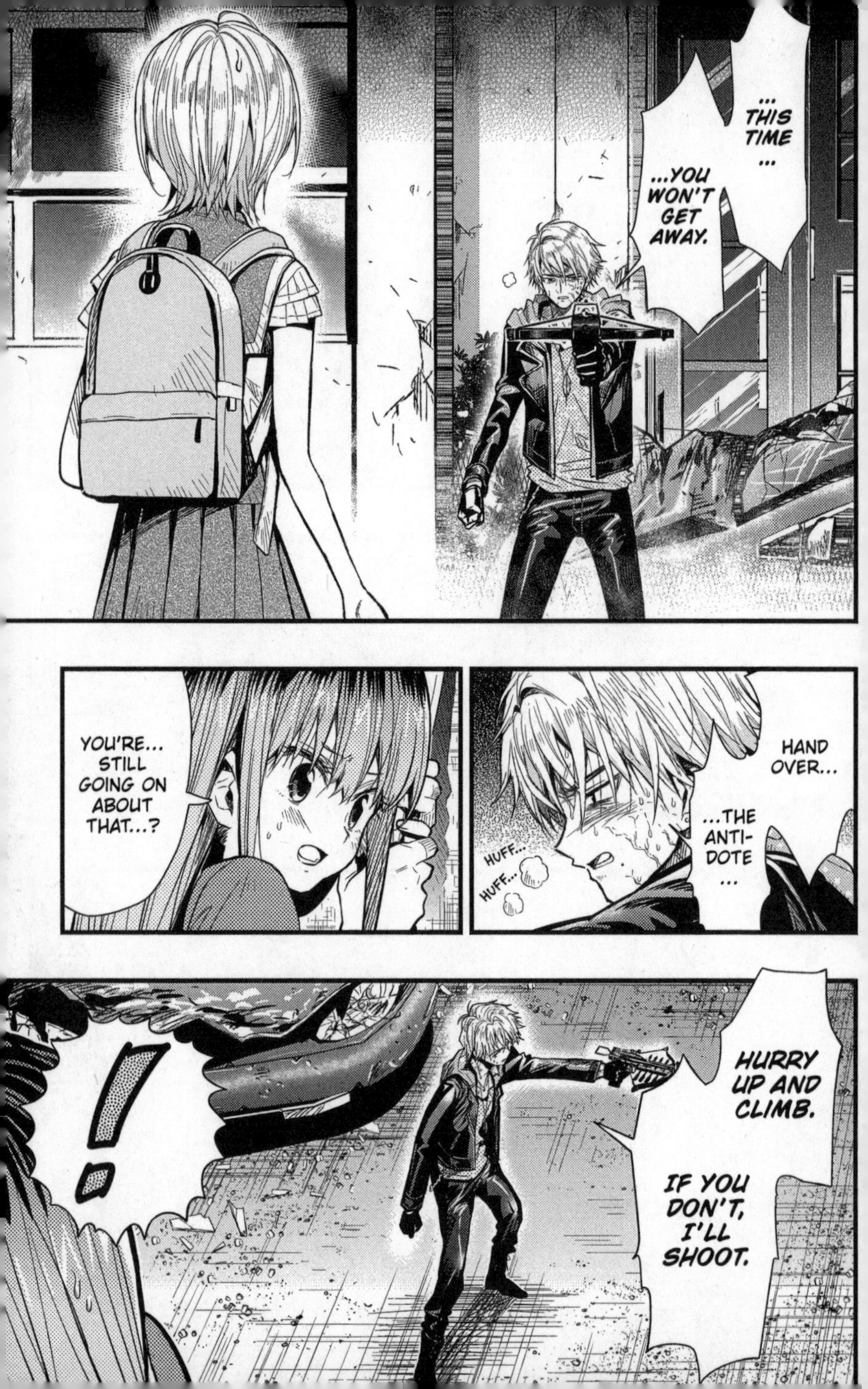
...THIS TIME...
...YOU WON'T GET AWAY.
HAND OVER...
...THE ANTI-DOTE...
HUFF... HUFF...
YOU'RE... STILL GOING ON ABOUT THAT...?
HURRY UP AND CLIMB.
IF YOU DON'T, I'LL SHOOT.
!

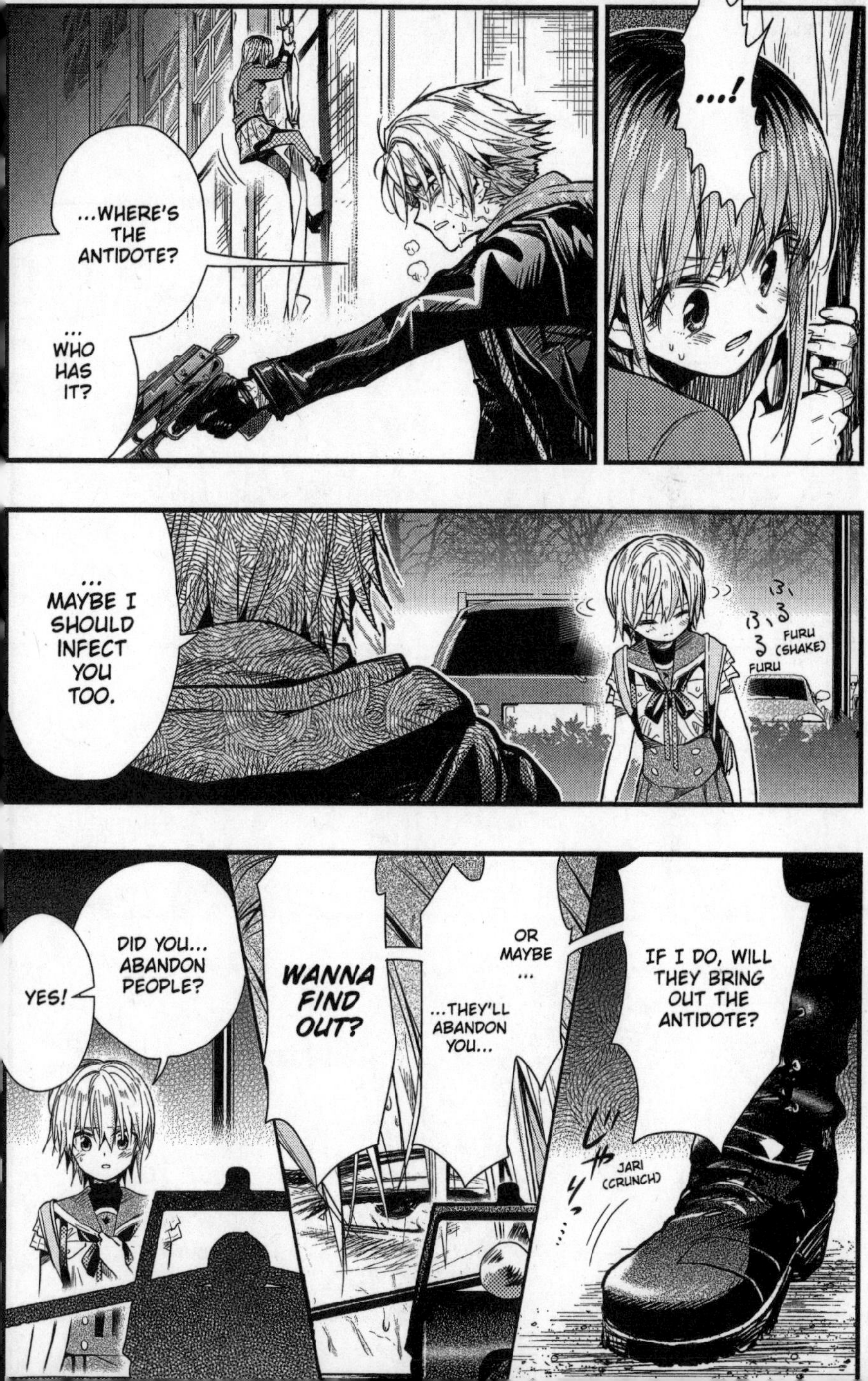
...!
...WHERE'S THE ANTIDOTE?
... WHO HAS IT?
ふるふる
FURU (SHAKE) FURU
... MAYBE I SHOULD INFECT YOU TOO.
IF I DO, WILL THEY BRING OUT THE ANTIDOTE?
JARI (CRUNCH)
OR MAYBE ...
...THEY'LL ABANDON YOU...
WANNA FIND OUT?
DID YOU... ABANDON PEOPLE?
YES!

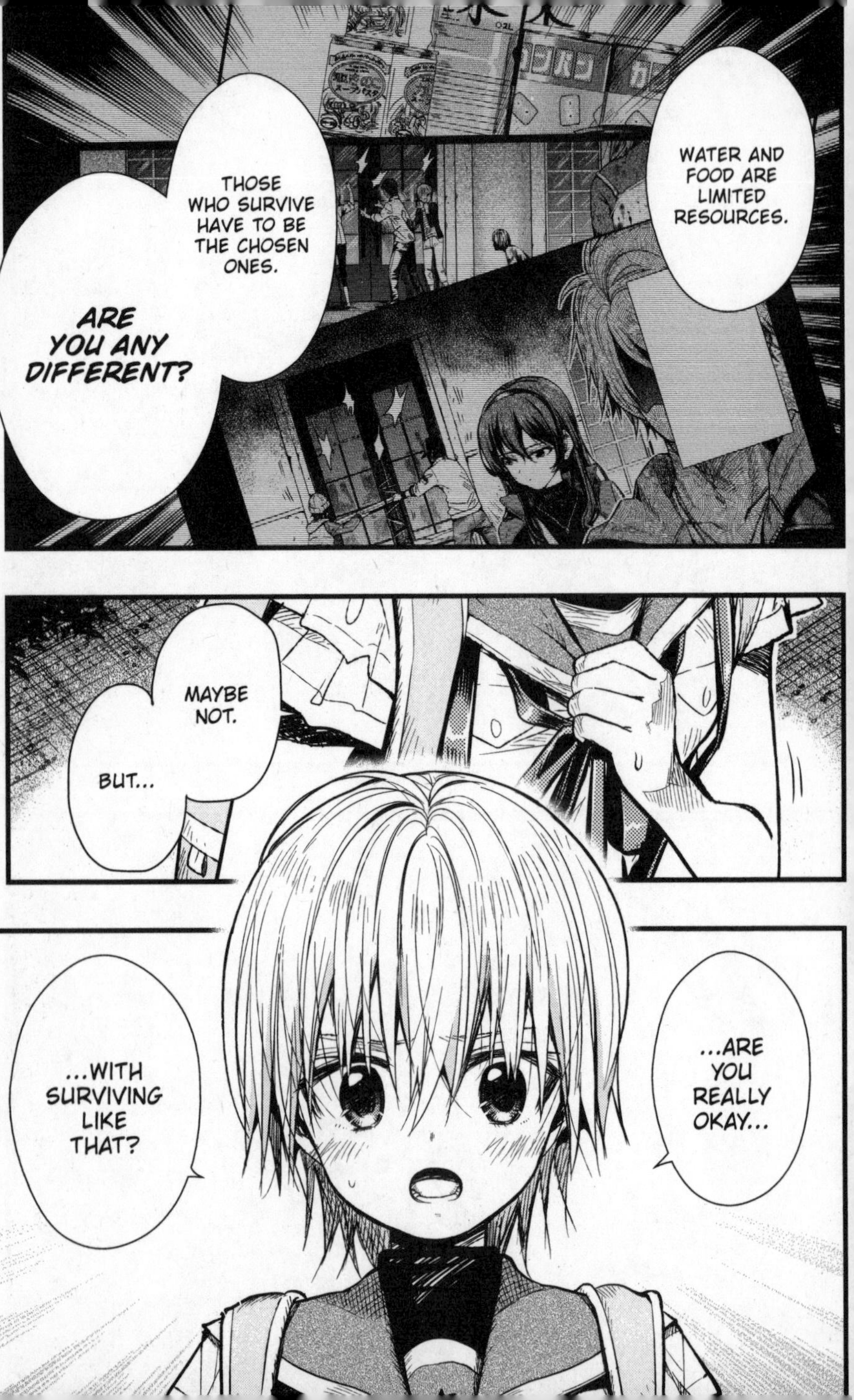
WATER AND FOOD ARE LIMITED RESOURCES.
THOSE WHO SURVIVE HAVE TO BE THE CHOSEN ONES.
ARE YOU ANY DIFFERENT?
MAYBE NOT.
BUT...
...ARE YOU REALLY OKAY...
...WITH SURVIVING LIKE THAT?

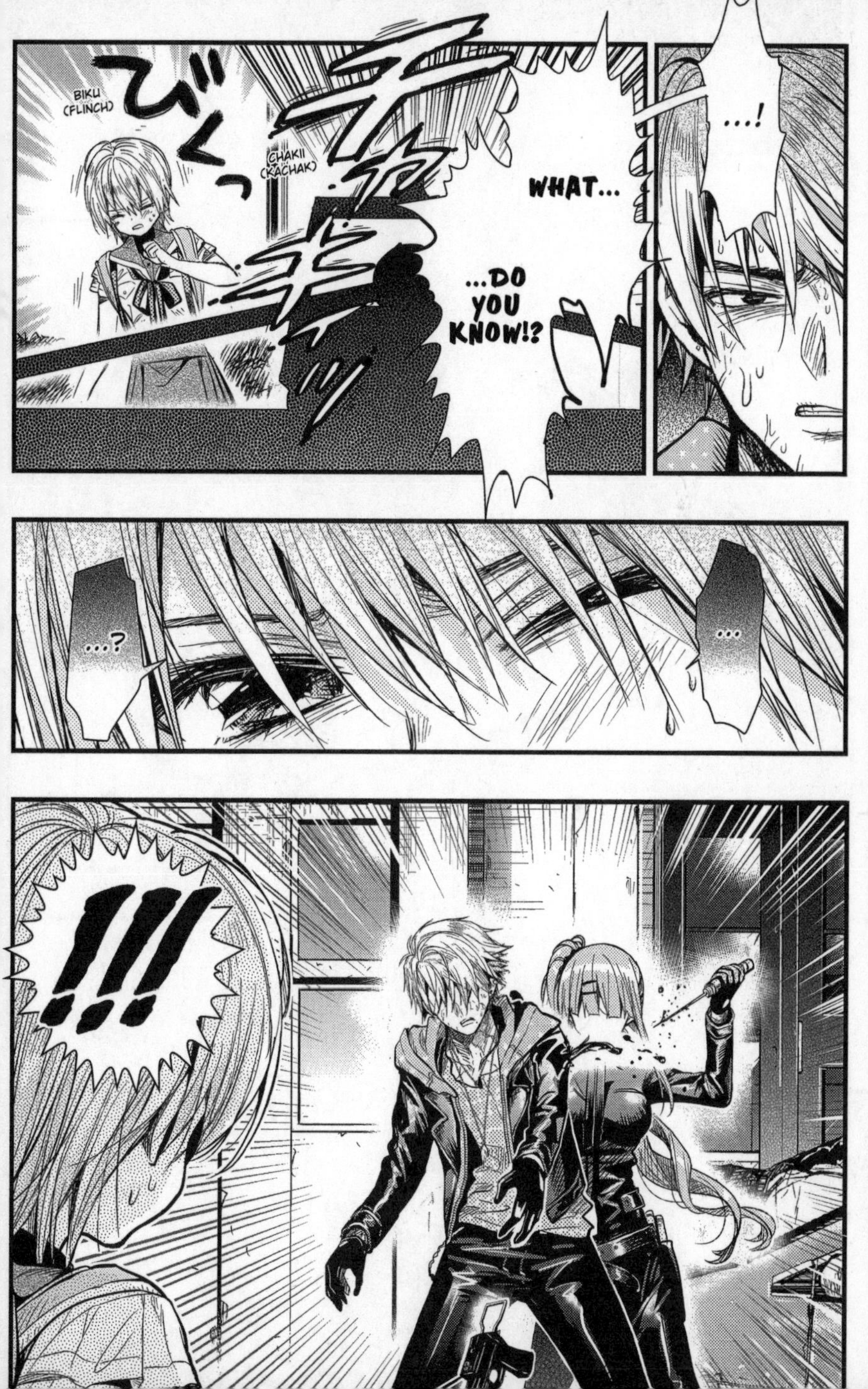
...!
WHAT...
...DO YOU KNOW!?
CHAKII (KACHAK)
BIKU (FLINCH)
...
...?
!!!

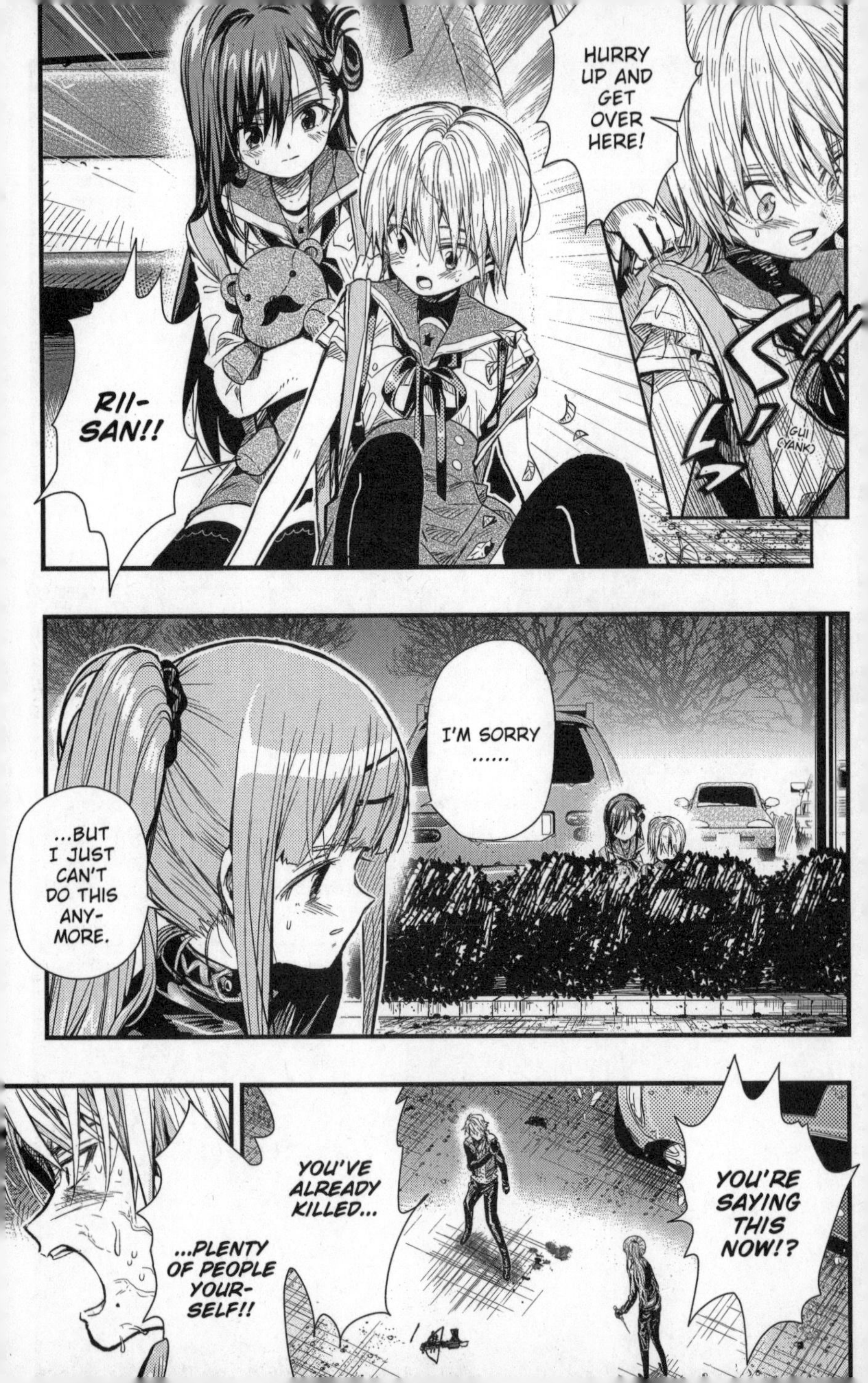
HURRY UP AND GET OVER HERE!
GUI (YANK)
RII-SAN!!
I'M SORRY ......
...BUT I JUST CAN'T DO THIS ANY-MORE.
YOU'RE SAYING THIS NOW!?
YOU'VE ALREADY KILLED...
...PLENTY OF PEOPLE YOUR-SELF!!

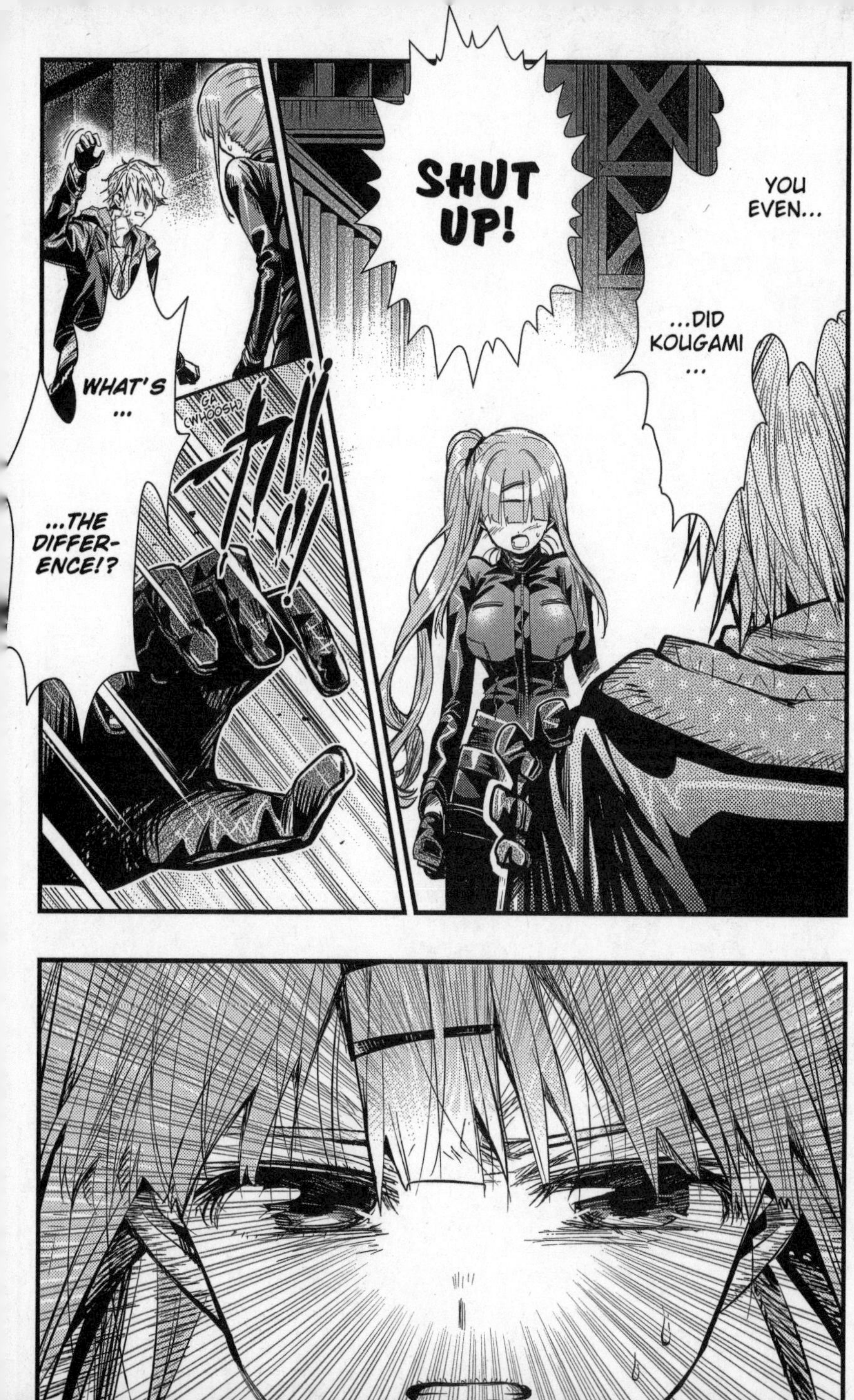
YOU EVEN...
...DID KOUGAMI ...
SHUT UP!
GA (WHOOSH)
WHAT'S ...
...THE DIFFERENCE!?

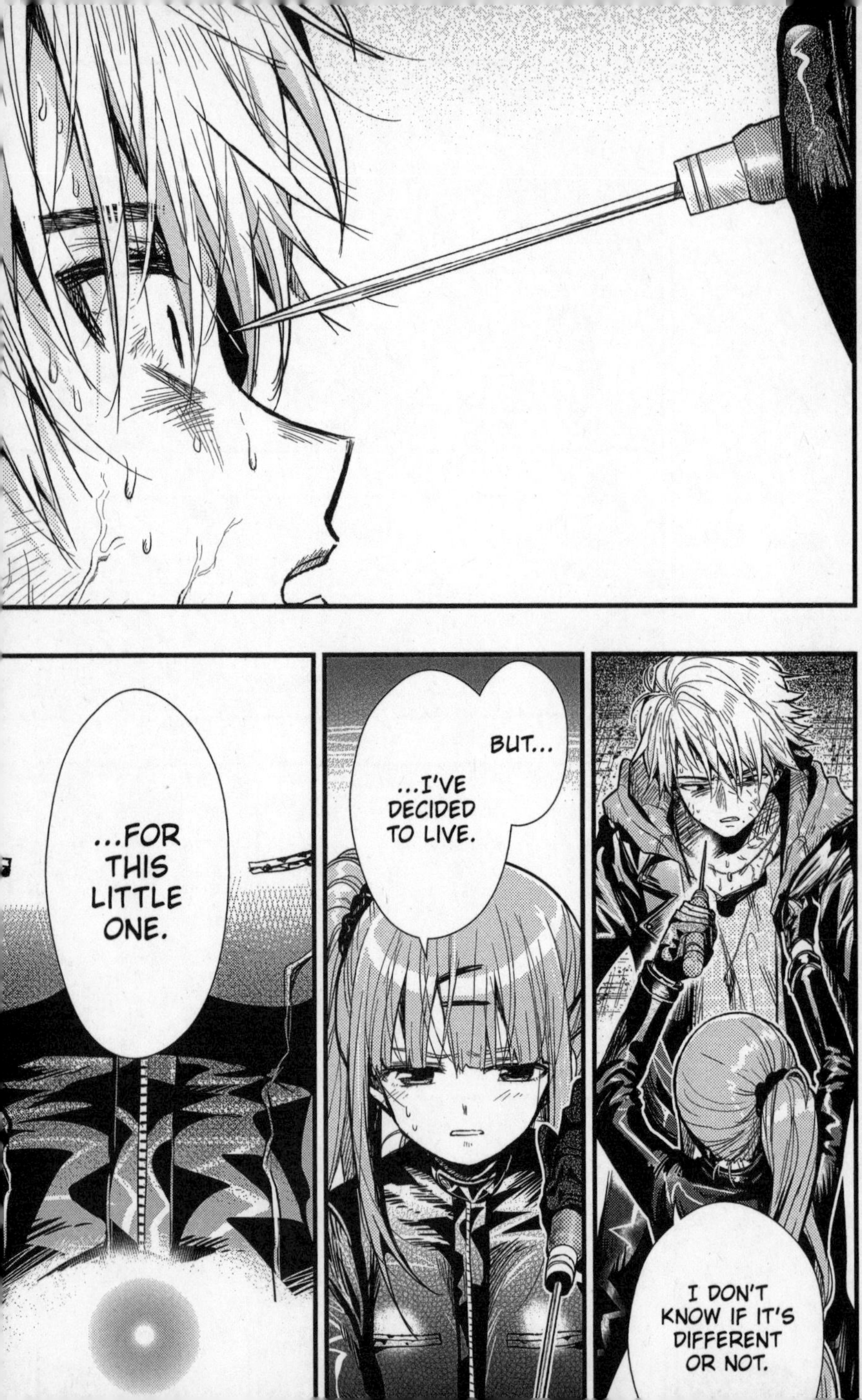
I DON'T KNOW IF IT'S DIFFERENT OR NOT.
BUT...
...I'VE DECIDED TO LIVE.
...FOR THIS LITTLE ONE.

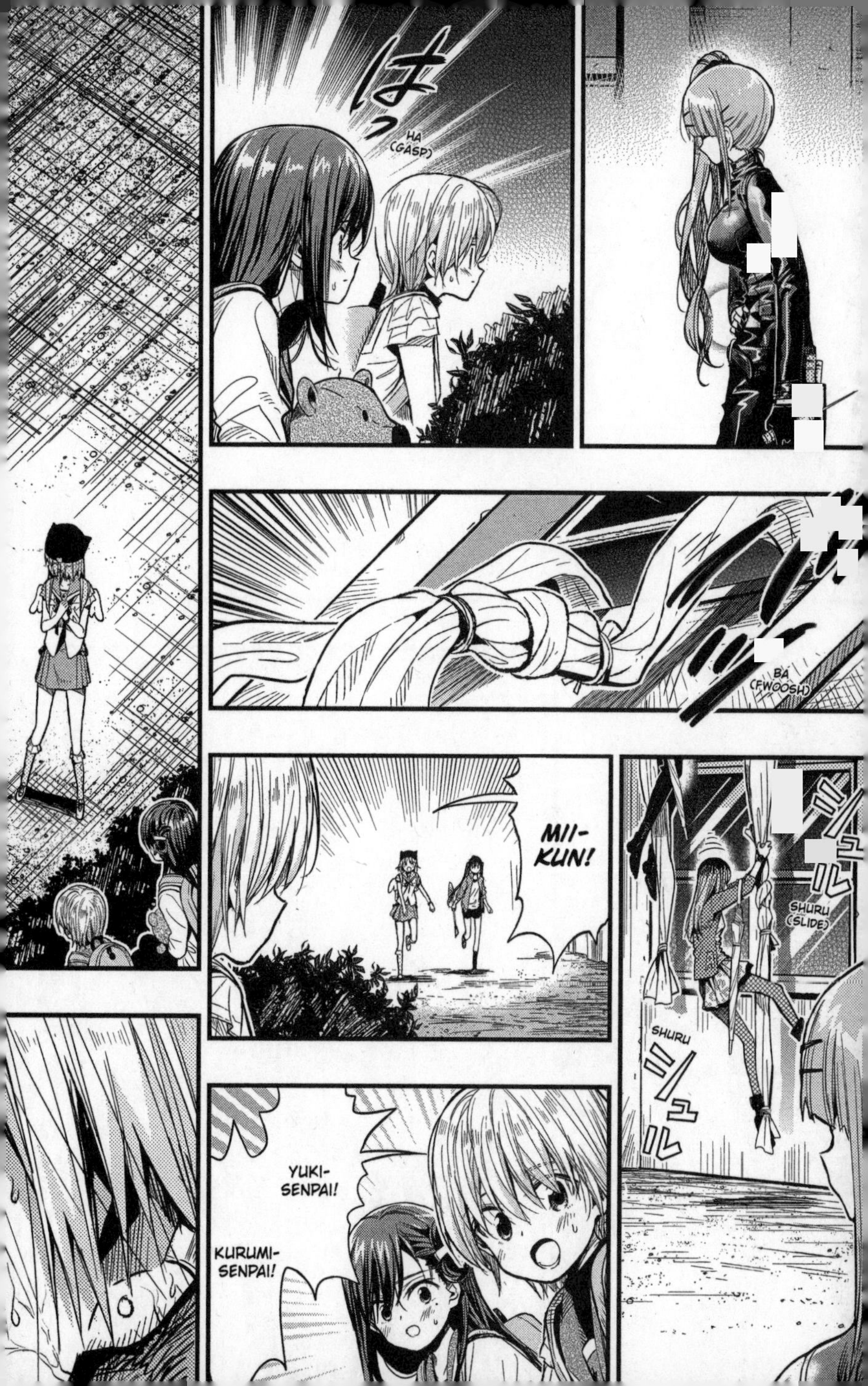
はっ
HA (GASP)
BA (FWOOSH)
シュル
SHURU (SLIDE)
SHURU
シュル
MII-KUN!
YUKI-SENPAI!
KURUMI-SENPAI!

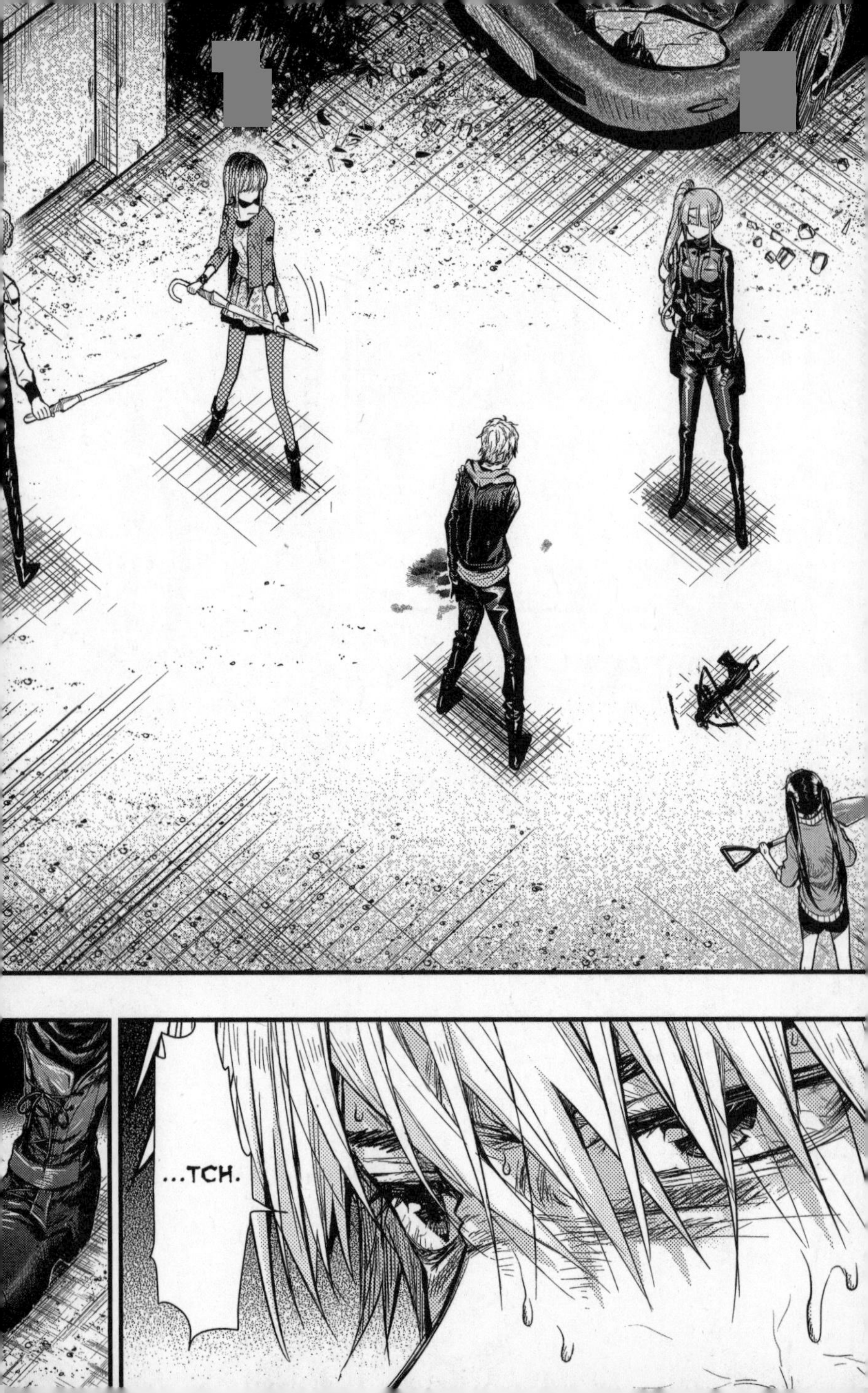
...TCH.

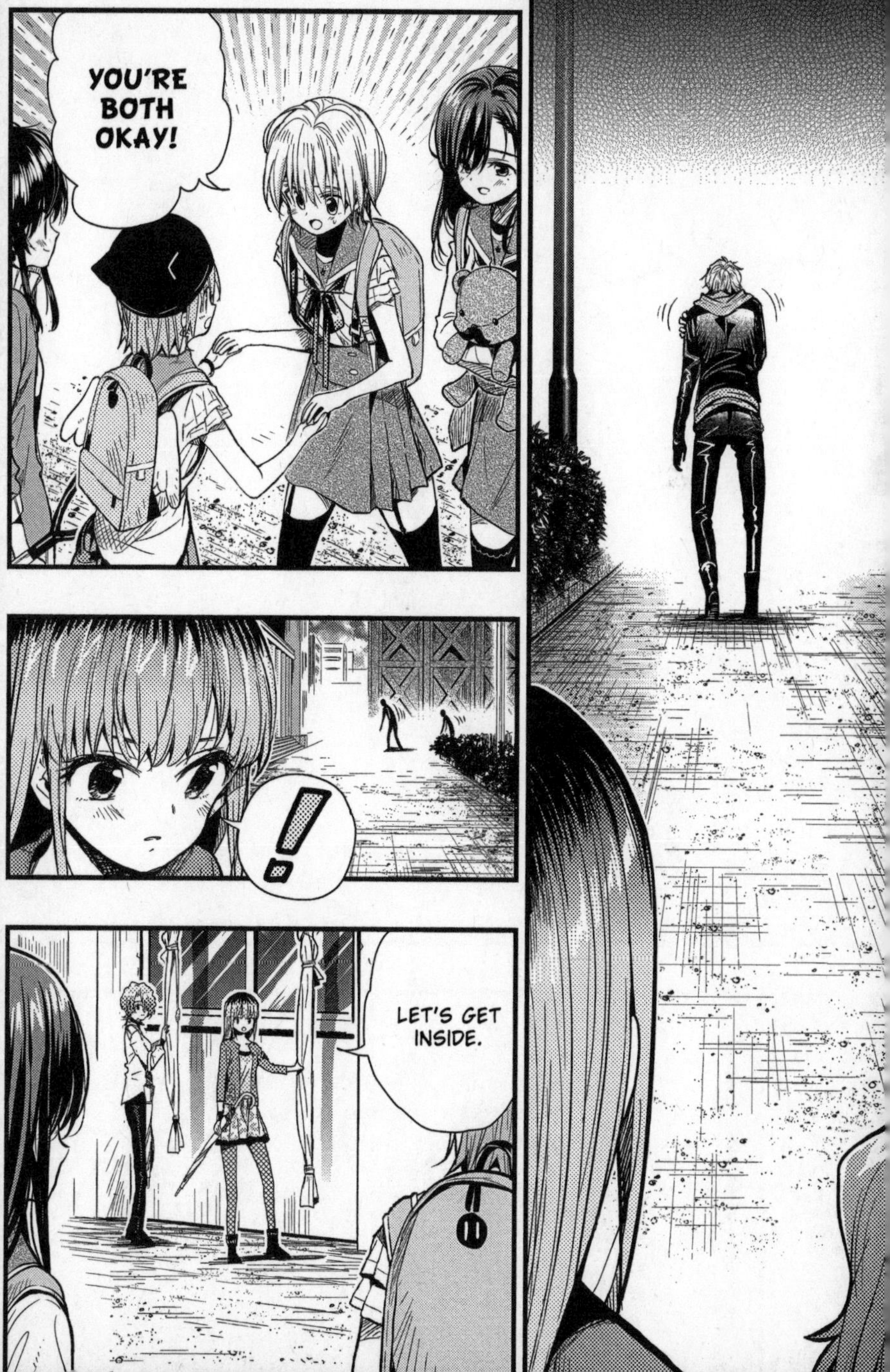
YOU'RE BOTH OKAY!
!
LET'S GET INSIDE.

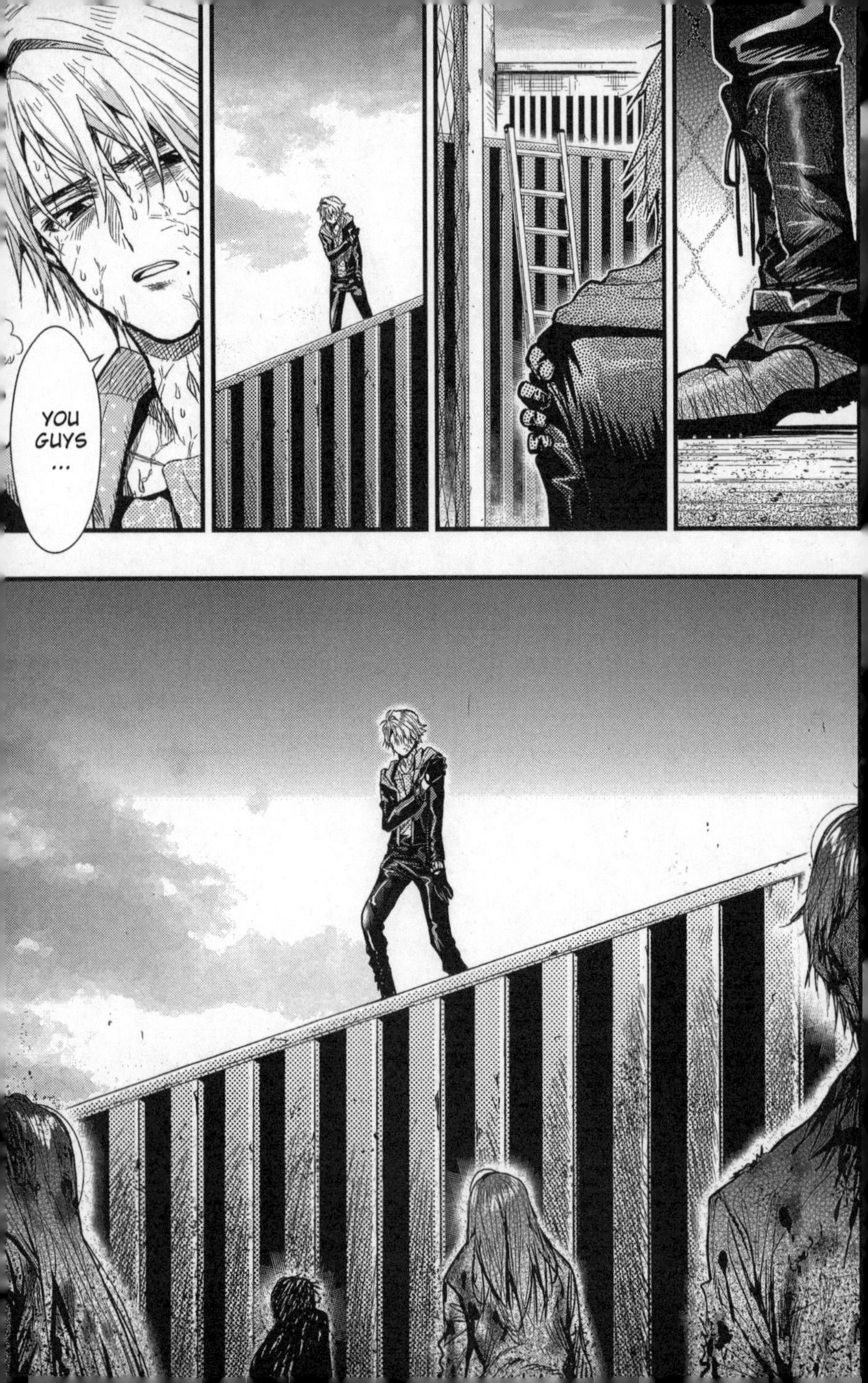
YOU GUYS ...

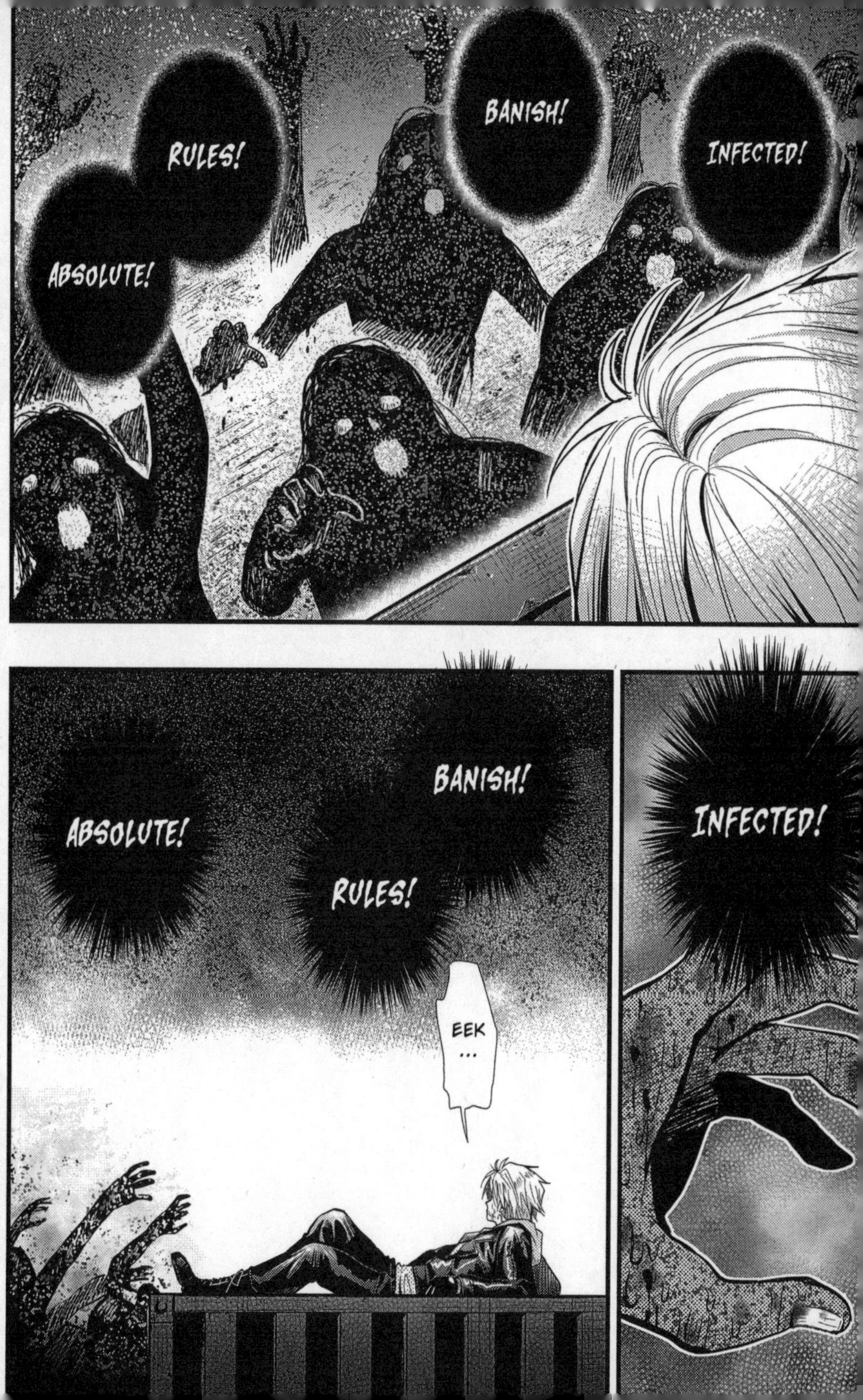
INFECTED!
BANISH!
RULES!
ABSOLUTE!
INFECTED!
BANISH!
ABSOLUTE!
RULES!
EEK
...

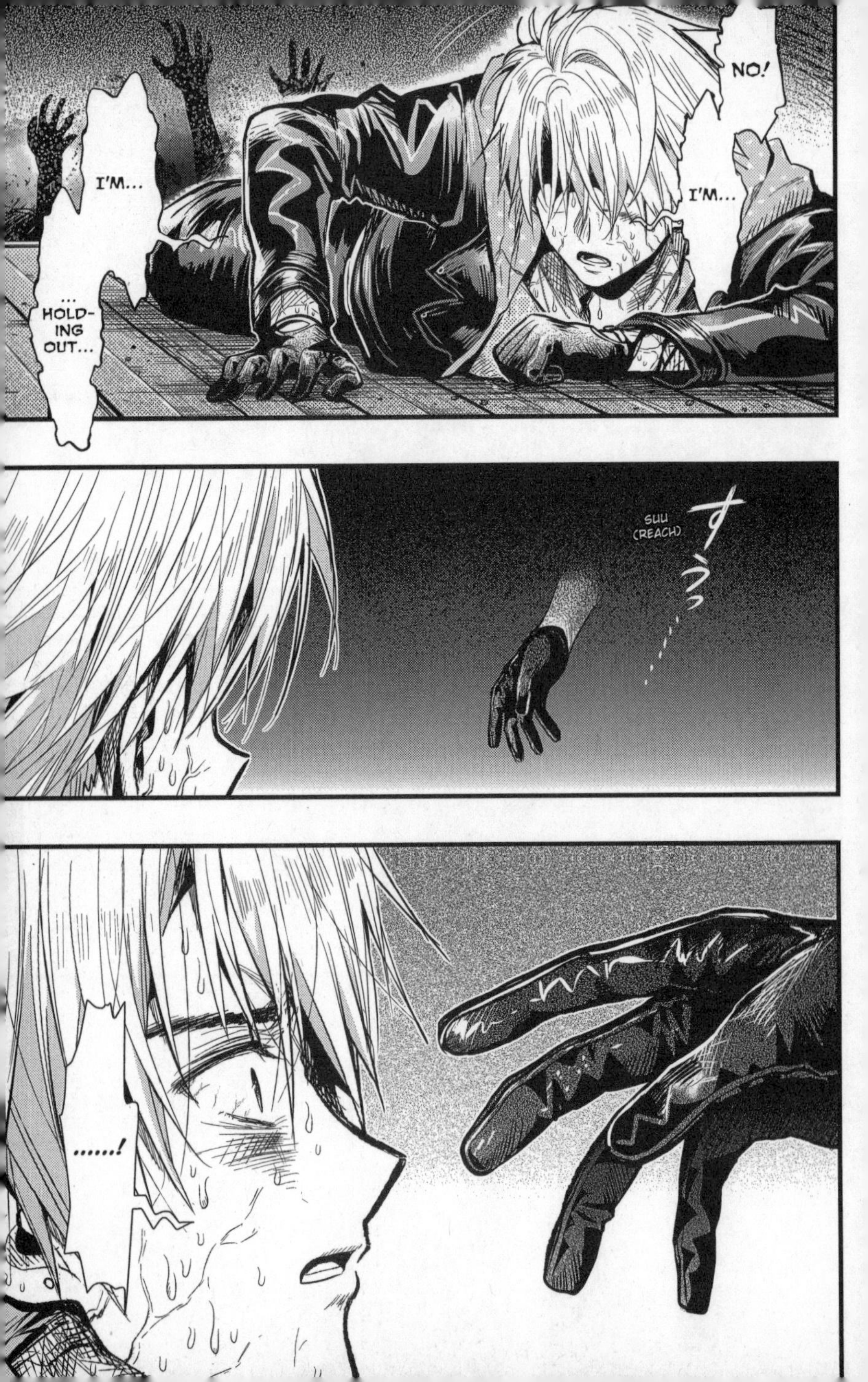
NO!
I'M...
I'M...
...HOLDING-ING OUT...
SUU (REACH)
すぅ......
......!

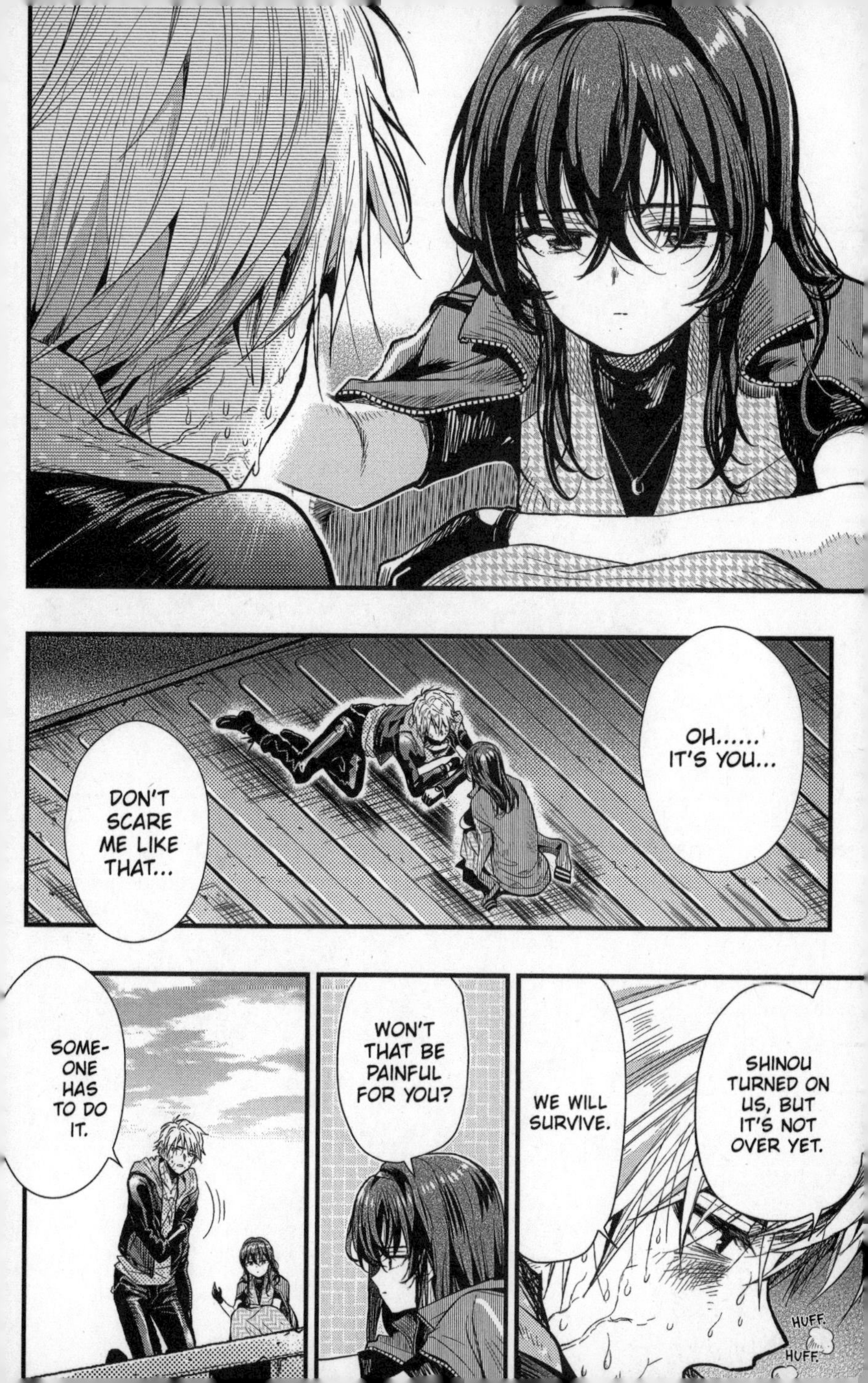
OH...... IT'S YOU...
DON'T SCARE ME LIKE THAT...
SHINOU TURNED ON US, BUT IT'S NOT OVER YET.
WE WILL SURVIVE.
HUFF.
HUFF.
WON'T THAT BE PAINFUL FOR YOU?
SOME-ONE HAS TO DO IT.

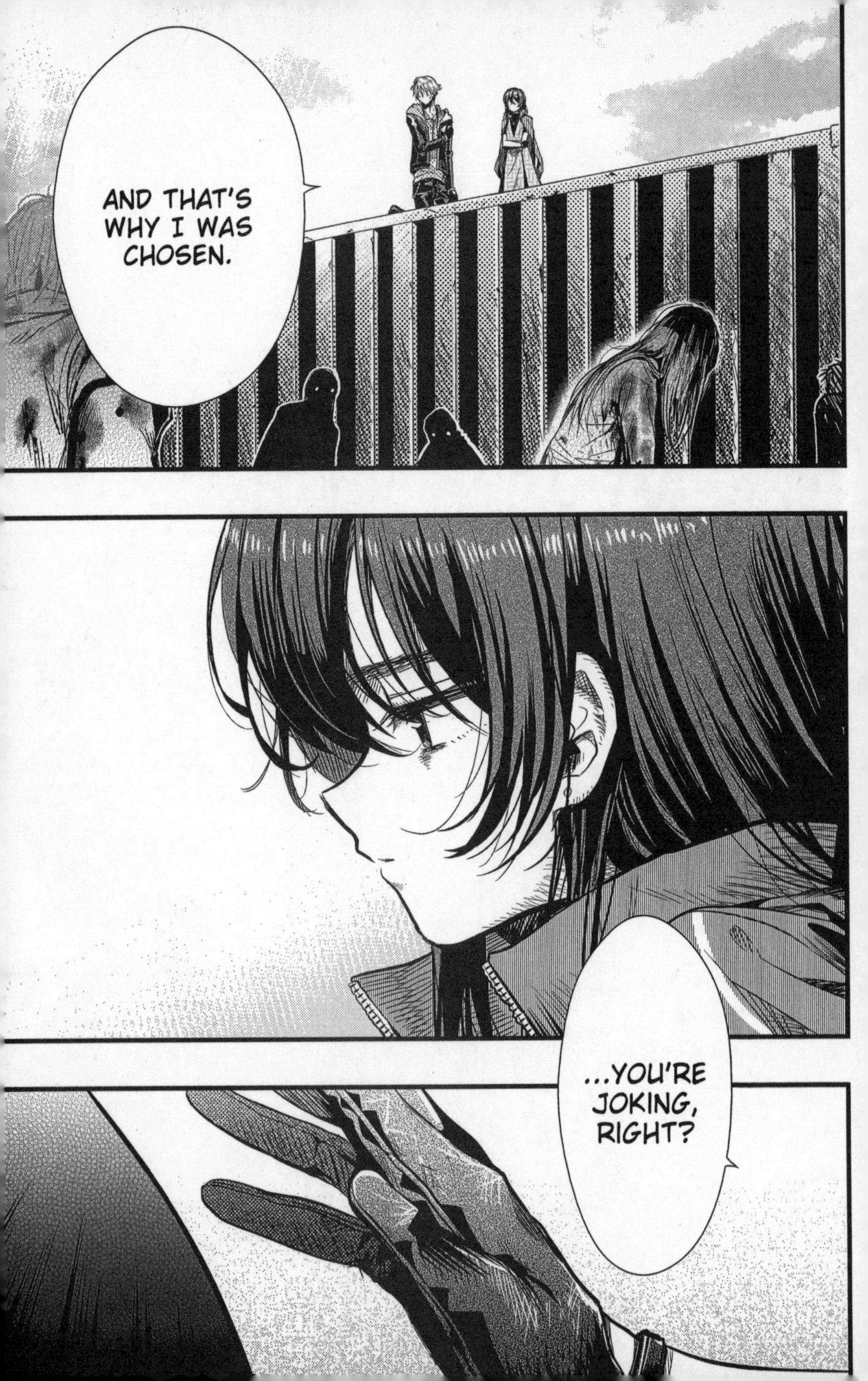
AND THAT'S WHY I WAS CHOSEN.
...YOU'RE JOKING, RIGHT?

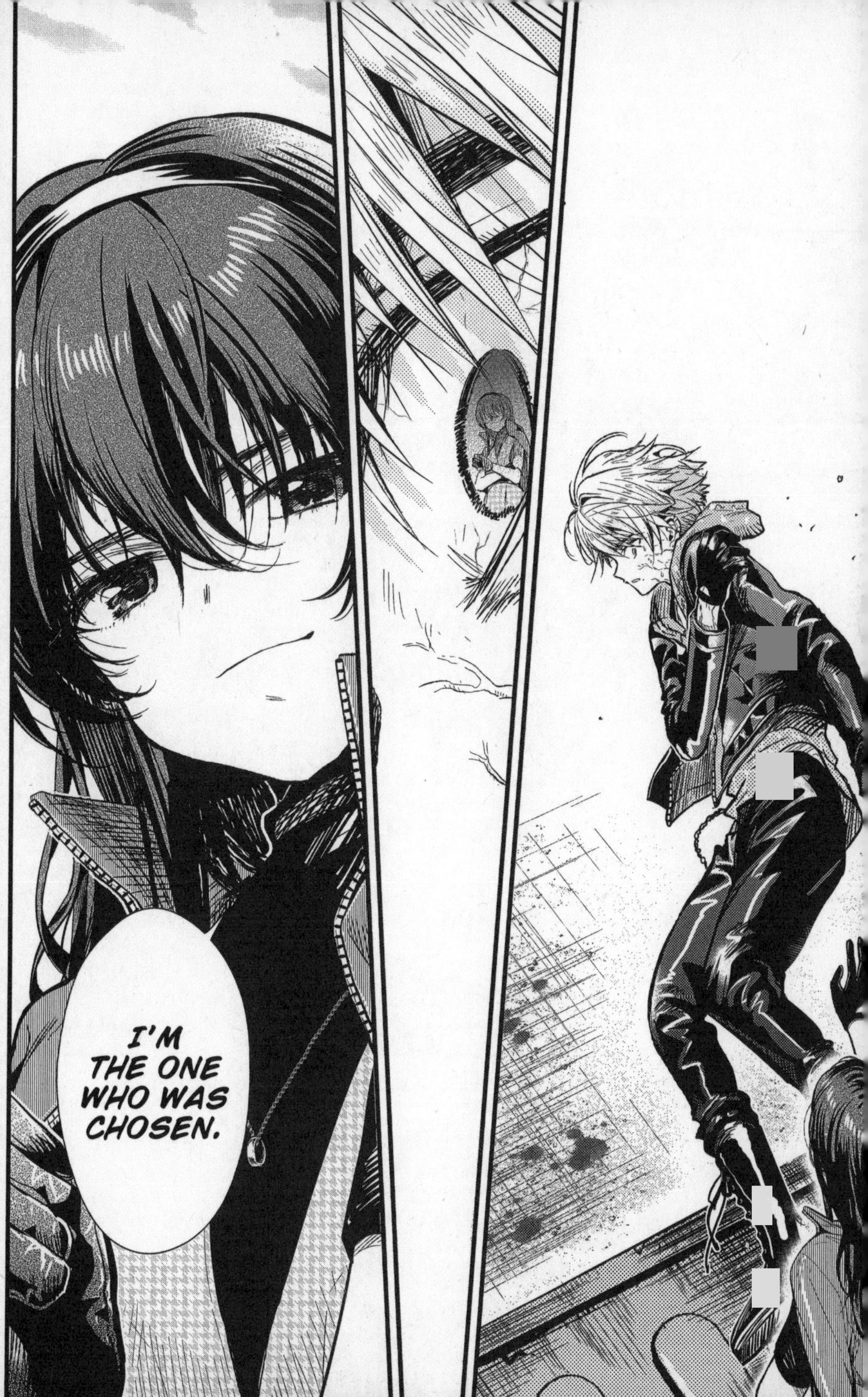
I'M THE ONE WHO WAS CHOSEN.

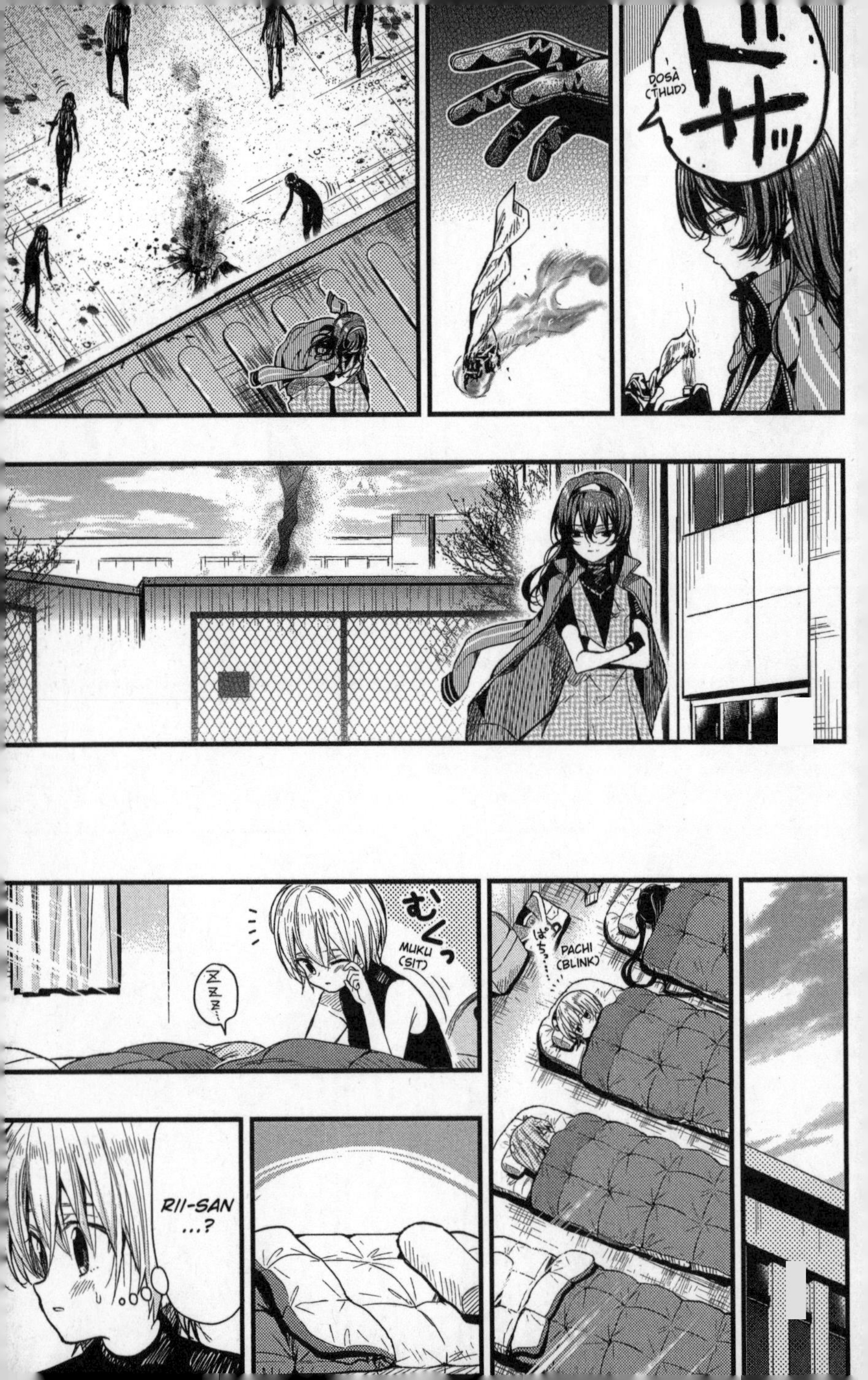
ドサッ
DOSA
(THUD)
ぱち…
PACHI
(BLINK)
むくっ
MUKU
(SIT)
んん…
RII-SAN
...?

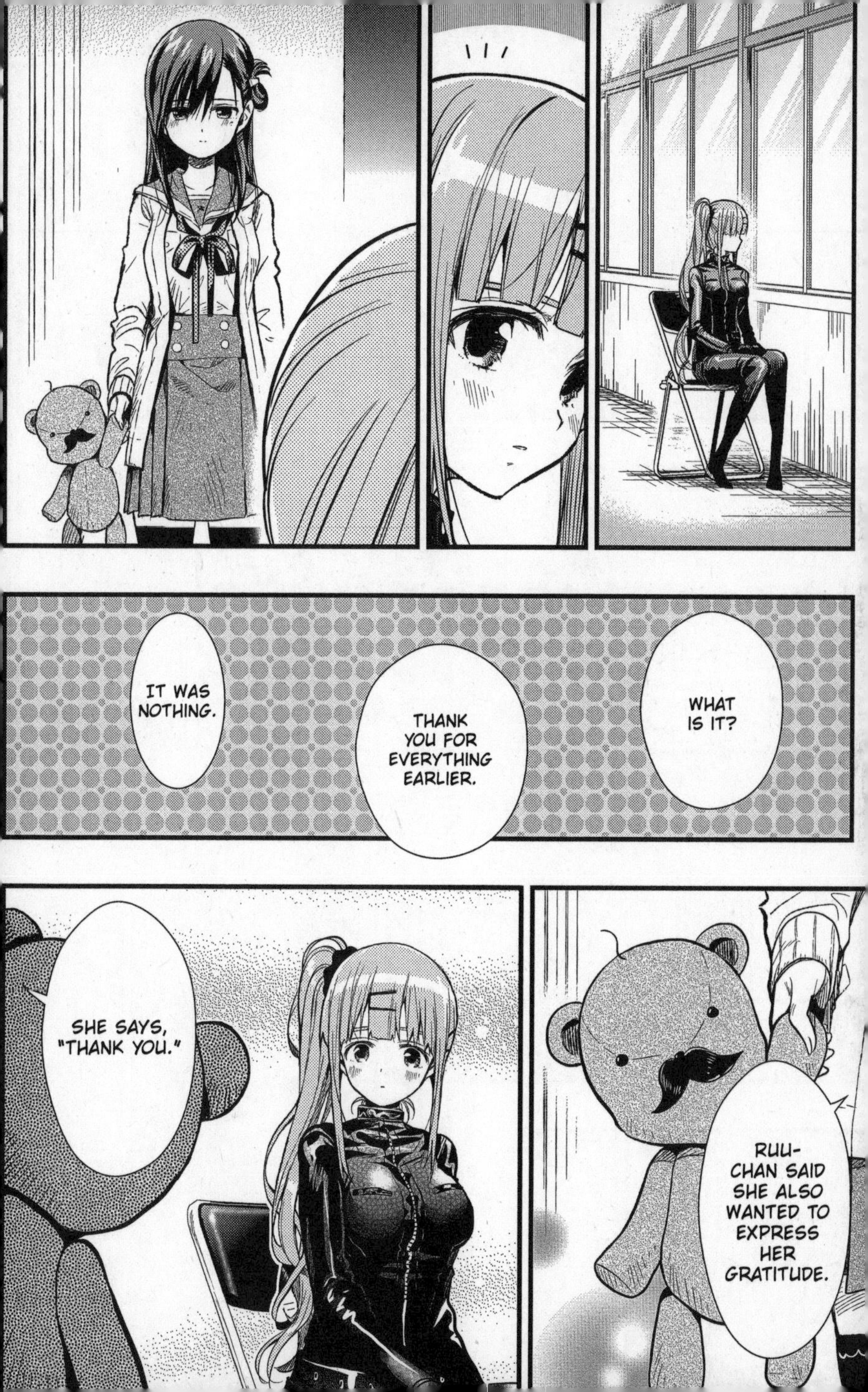
WHAT IS IT?
THANK YOU FOR EVERYTHING EARLIER.
IT WAS NOTHING.
RUU-CHAN SAID SHE ALSO WANTED TO EXPRESS HER GRATITUDE.
SHE SAYS, "THANK YOU."

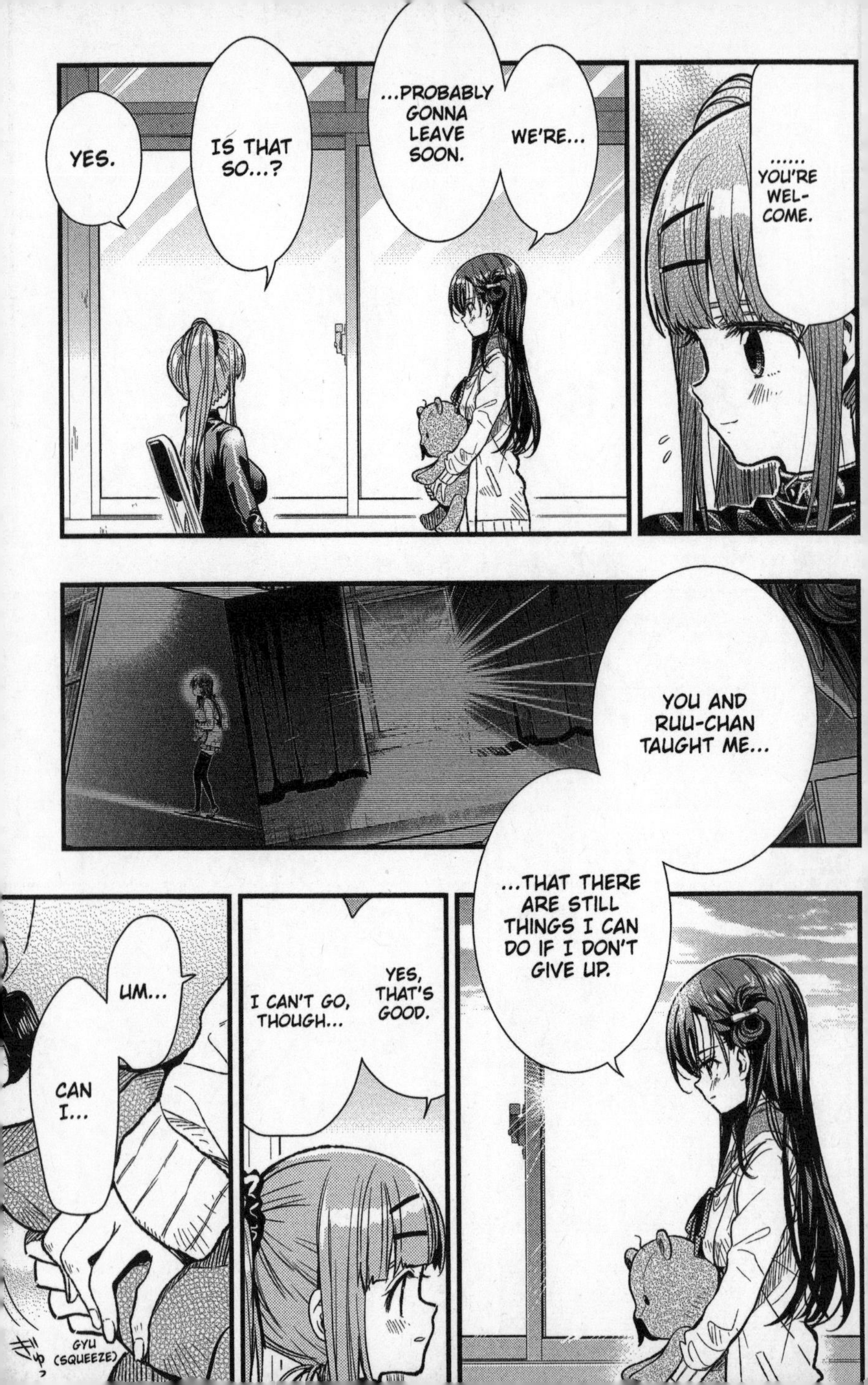
...... YOU'RE WEL-COME.
WE'RE...
...PROBABLY GONNA LEAVE SOON.
IS THAT SO...?
YES.
YOU AND RUU-CHAN TAUGHT ME...
...THAT THERE ARE STILL THINGS I CAN DO IF I DON'T GIVE UP.
YES, THAT'S GOOD.
I CAN'T GO, THOUGH...
UM...
CAN I...
GYU (SQUEEZE)

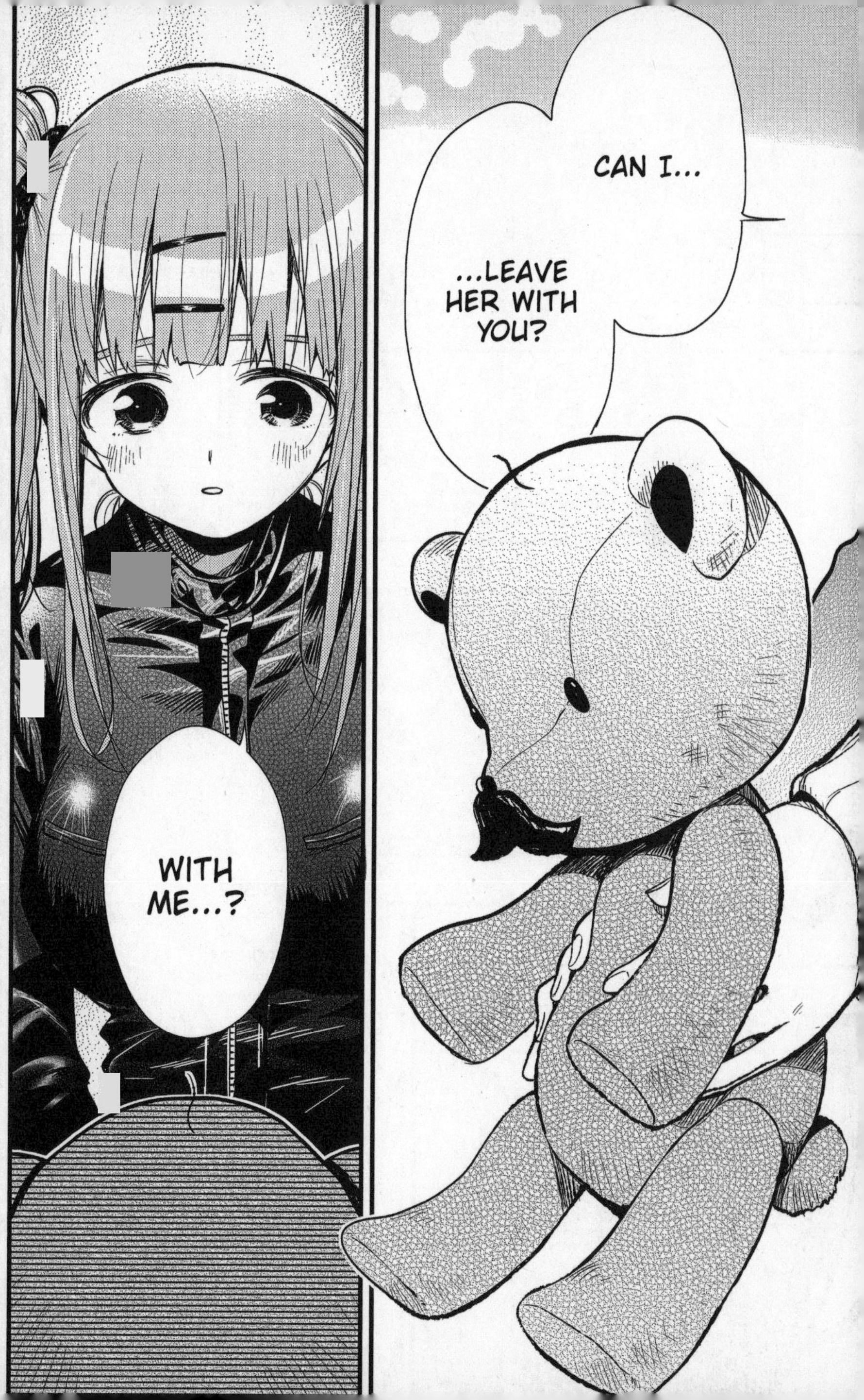
CAN I...
...LEAVE HER WITH YOU?
WITH ME...?

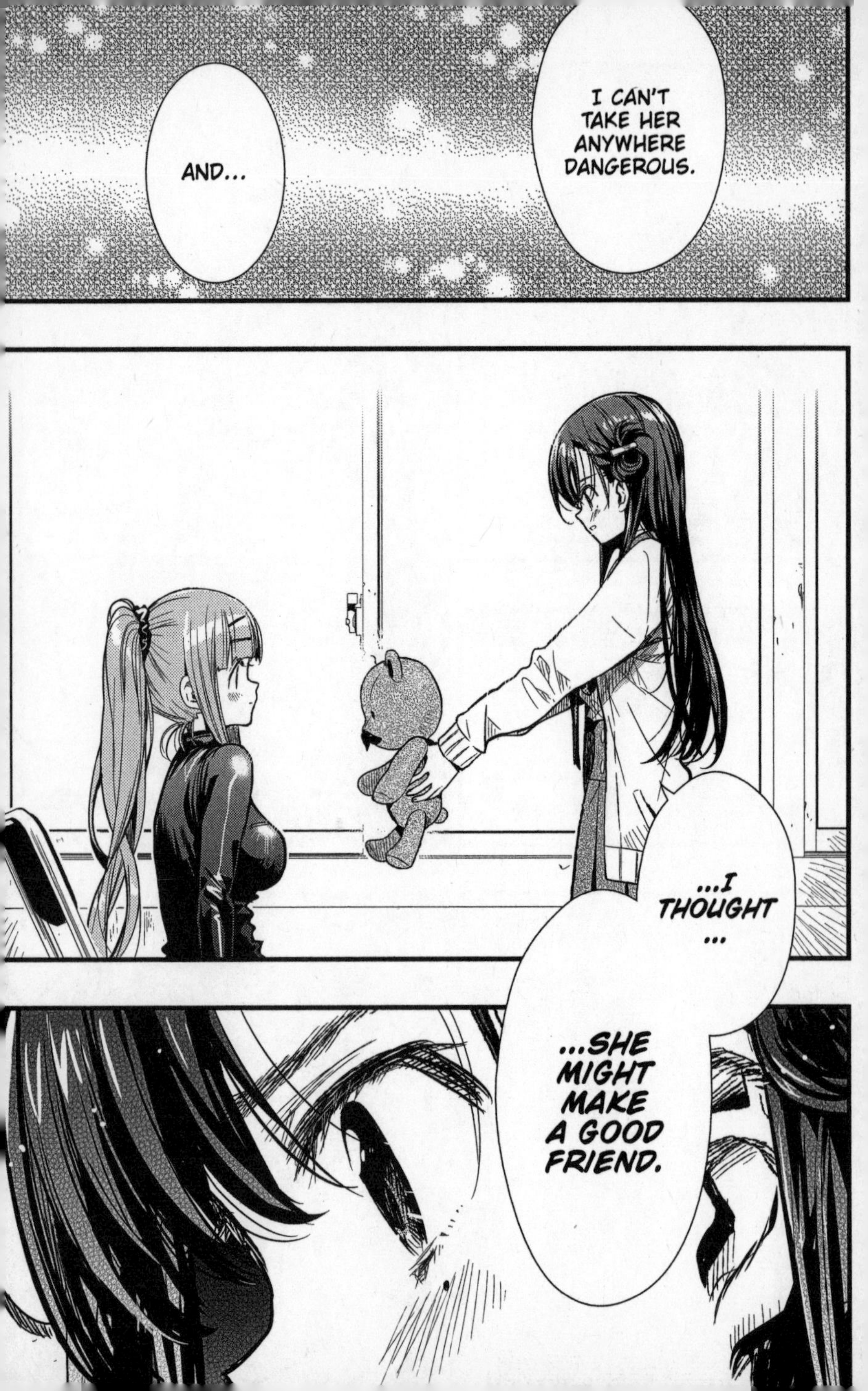
I CAN'T TAKE HER ANYWHERE DANGEROUS.
AND...
...I THOUGHT...
...SHE MIGHT MAKE A GOOD FRIEND.

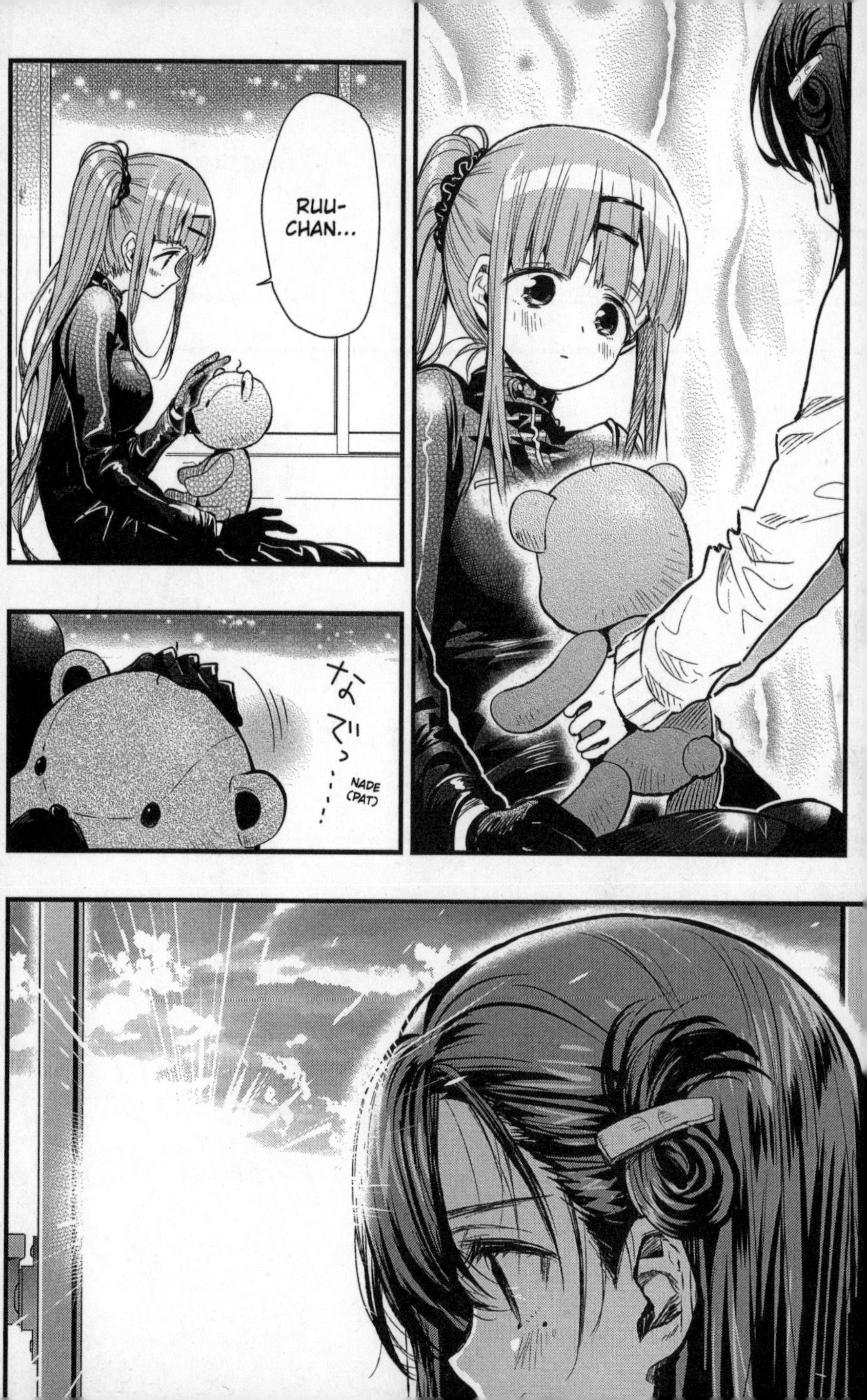
RUU-CHAN...
なでっ・・・
NADE (PAT)

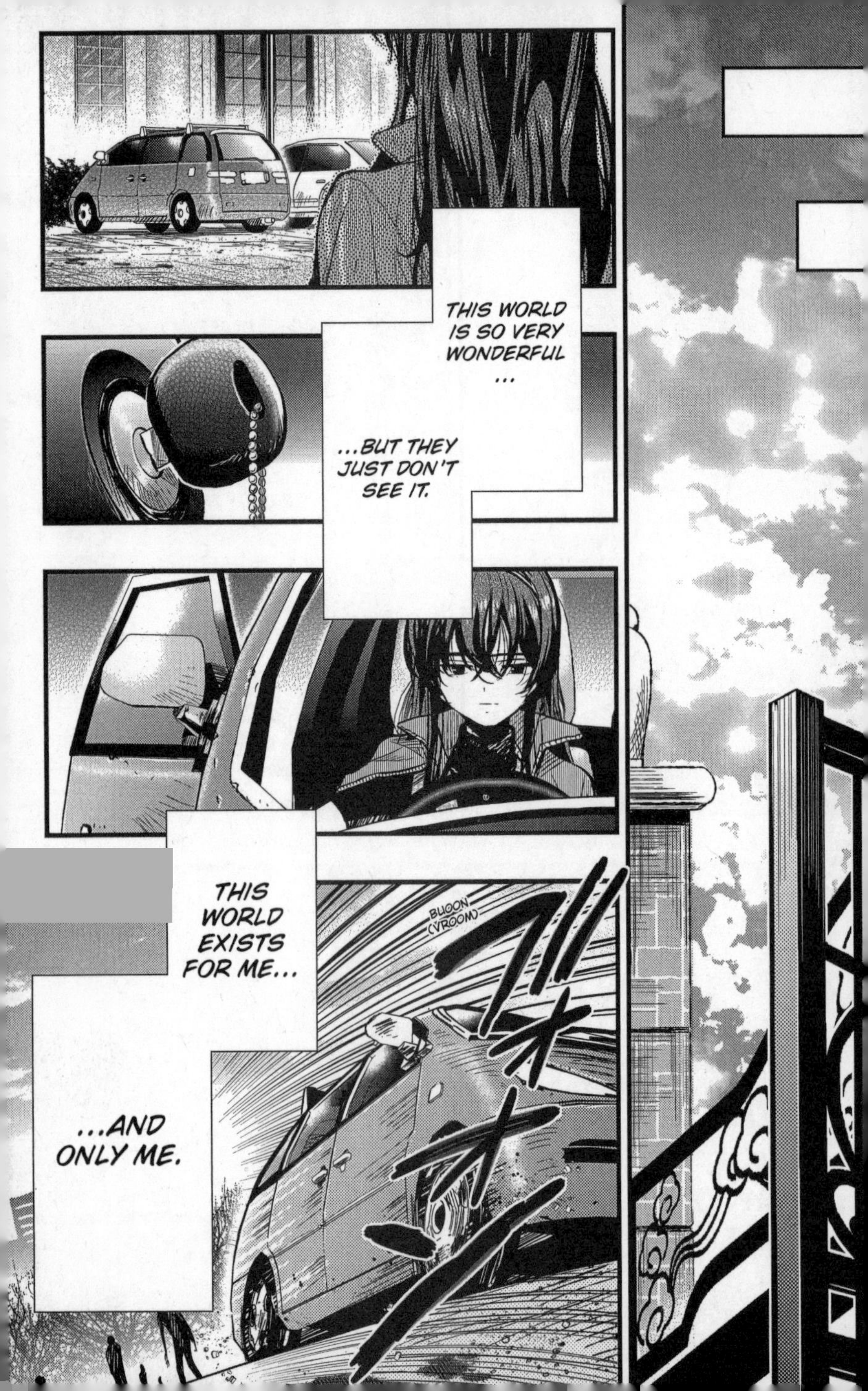
THIS WORLD IS SO VERY WONDERFUL ...
...BUT THEY JUST DON'T SEE IT.
THIS WORLD EXISTS FOR ME...
BUOON (VROOM)
...AND ONLY ME.

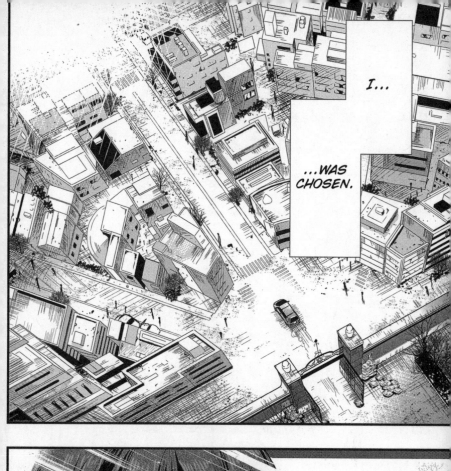

I...

...WAS CHOSEN.

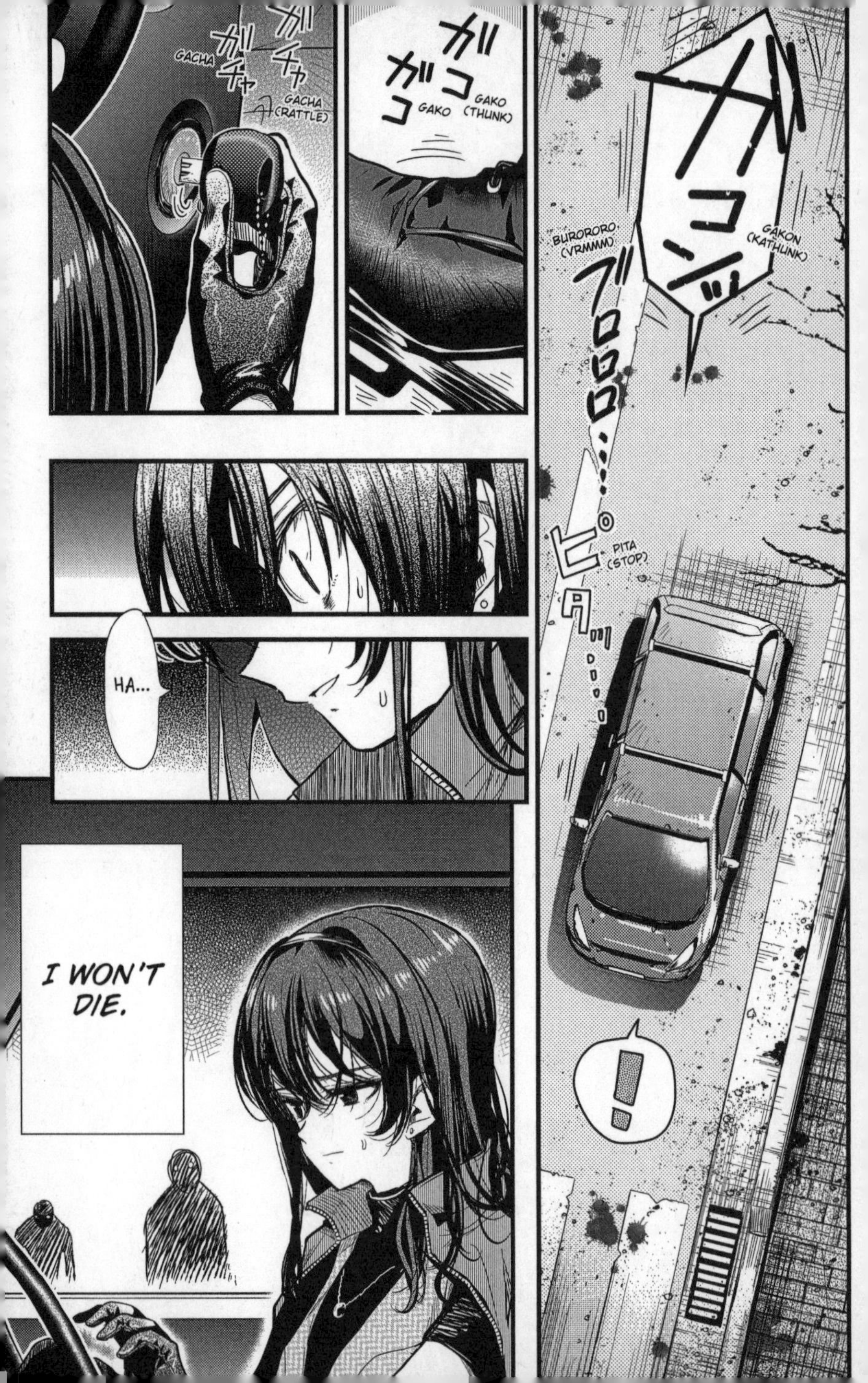
ガコンッ
GAKON (KATHUNK)
ブロロロ…
BURORORO (VRMMM)
ピタッ
PITA (STOP)
!
ガコガコ
GAKO GAKO (THUNK)
ガチャガチャ
GACHA GACHA (RATTLE)
HA...
I WON'T DIE.

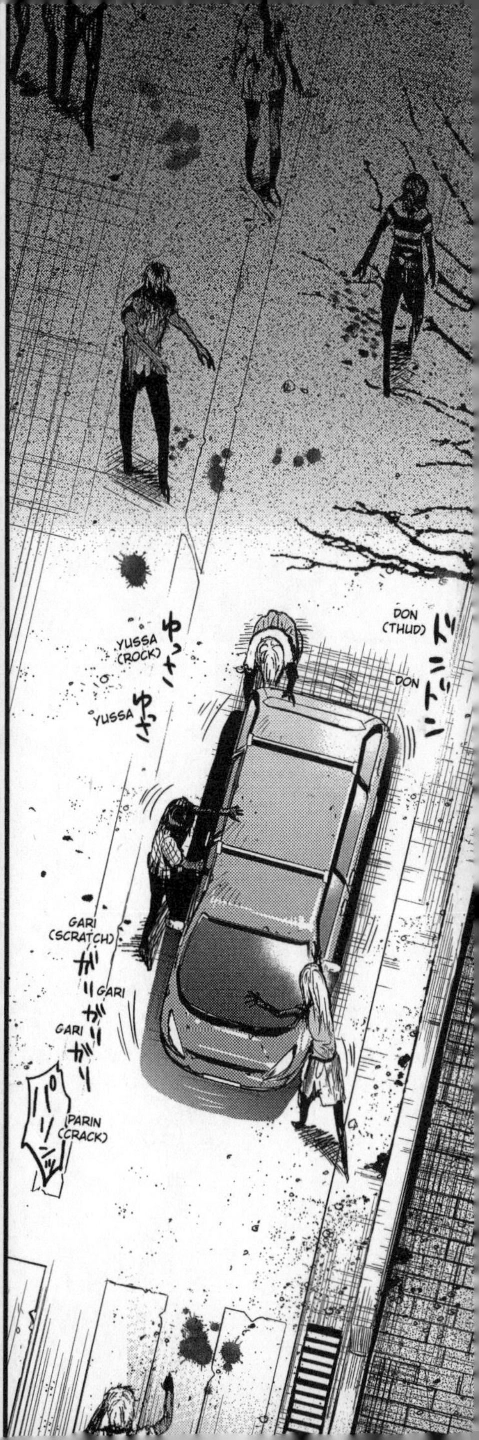
DON (THUD)
ドン
DON
ドン
YUSSA (ROCK)
ゆっさ
YUSSA
ゆっさ
GARI (SCRATCH)
ガリ
GARI
ガリ
GARI
ガリ
PARIN (CRACK)

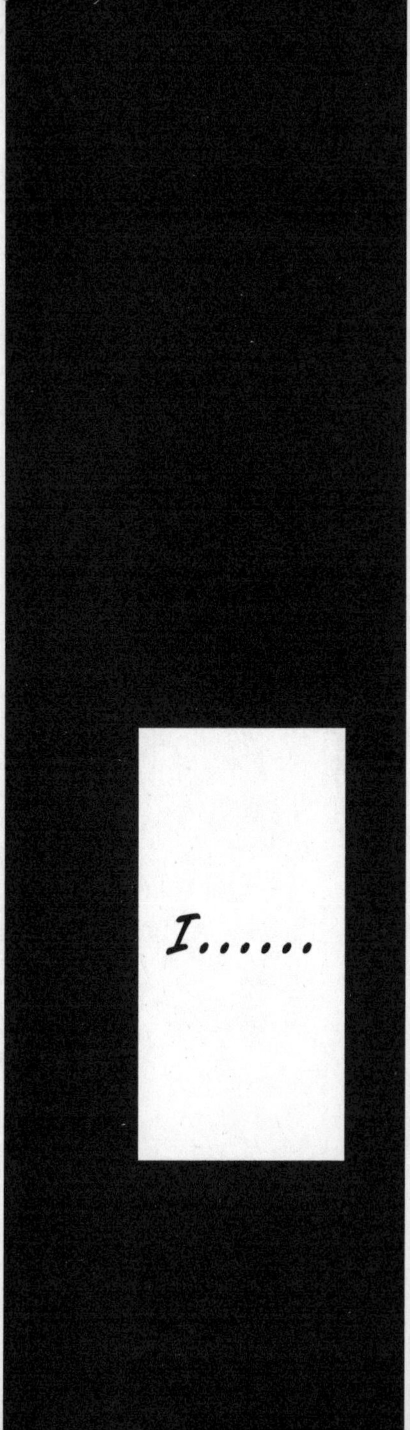
I......